CONTENTS

Simplicity is Sometimes the Hardest Thing
Philip Vernau 1

Editorial Introduction: Aesthetics and the Ends of Art
Gary Banham 5

A Good Enough Hostess
Sharon Kivland 9

To Hans
Nayan Kulkarni 15

Digital Lascaux: The Beginning in the End of the Aesthetic
Howard Caygill 19

Speechless
Ricardo Bloch 27

Toposmia: Art, Scent, and Interrogations of Spatiality
Jim Drobnick 31

Time and Again
Gill Houghton 49

Why Aesthetics Might be Several
Joanna Hodge 53

Bungled Memories
David Bate 69

Clement Greenberg, Radical Painting, and the Logic of Modernism
Henry Staten 73

Two Images
James Thornhill 91

De-Assembling Vision: Conceptual Strategies in Duchamp, Matta-Clark, Wilson
Dalia Judovitz 95

Artificial Life ~ Virtual Worlds
Cheryl Sourkes 115

Mapplethorpe, Duchamp and the Ends of Photography
Gary Banham 119

Anastylosis
Anne Ramsden 129

From Painting's Death to the Death in Painting: Or, What Jasper Johns Found in Marcel Duchamp's *Tu m'*/Tomb
Isabelle Wallace 133

How to Make it Come Back
Pavel Buchler 157

Duchamp and Kant: Together at Last
Robert J. Yanal 161

It is Occupied
Stephen Cornell 169

The Aesthetic of Failure: Net Art Gone Wrong
Michele White 173

A Thousand Moths Reside and Died Here
Maria Fusco 195

Sublime Ascesis: Lyotard, Art and the Event
Simon Malpas 199

Analogue London
Lucy Harrison 213

Towards a Communal Body of Art: The Exquisite Corpse and Augusto Boal's Theatre
Kanta Kochhar-Lindgren 217

Plaies-Images II
Nicole Jolicoeur 227

Variations on the Work of Art: Sound, Space and Some Compositions by Mutlu Çerkez
Lewis Johnson 231

Throughout the issue runs:
Ride
John X. Berger

Notes on the Contributors 252

Angelaki Information 256

volume 7 number 1 april 2002

ANGELAKI
journal of the theoretical humanities

special issue: **aesthetics and the ends of art**

issue editor: **gary banham**

curator: sharon kivland

ANGELAKI
journal of the theoretical humanities

SUBSCRIPTION RATES

Angelaki: journal of the theoretical humanities, Volume 7, 2002, 3 issues, ISSN 0969-725X

Institutional rate (includes free online access):
£150.00   US$246.00

Personal rate (print only):
£35.00   US$57.00

Personal subscriptions are welcomed if prepaid by credit card or personal cheque.

Subscription rates include postage/air speeded delivery

ORDERING INFORMATION

Please complete in full the details on the Order Form and return to:

Routledge Journals, Taylor & Francis Ltd, Customer Services Department, Rankine Road, Basingstoke, Hants RG24 8PR, UK

OR TO

Routledge Journals, Taylor & Francis Ltd, Customer Services Department, 325 Chestnut Street, 8th Floor, Philadelphia, PA 19106, USA

By Fax:

+44 (0)1256 330245 (UK)
+1 215 625 2940 (USA and Canada)

By Telephone:

+44 (0)1256 813002 (UK)
+1 800 354 1420 (USA and Canada)

By WWW:

http://www.tandf.co.uk

By E-mail:

enquiry@tandf.co.uk

For further details on the journal, including contents pages, please visit the Taylor & Francis Website at: http://www.tandf.co.uk/journals

COPYRIGHT

Copyright © 2002 Taylor & Francis Ltd and the Editors of *Angelaki*. All rights reserved. No part of this publication may be reproduced, stored, transmitted, or disseminated, in any form, or by any means, without prior written permission from Taylor & Francis Limited, to whom all requests to reproduce copyright material should be directed, in writing.

Taylor & Francis Limited grants authorization for individuals to photocopy copyright material for private research use, on the sole basis that requests for such use are referred directly to the requestor's local Reproduction Rights Organization (RRO). The copyright fee is $14.00 exclusive of any service charge or fee levied. In order to contact your local RRO, please contact: International Federation of Reproduction Rights Organizations (IFRRO), rue du Prince Royal, 87, B-1050 Brussels, Belgium, e-mail: ifrro@skynet.be; Copyright Clearance Center Inc., 222 Rosewood Drive, Danvers, MA 01923, USA, e-mail: info@copyright.com; Copyright Licensing Agency, 90 Tottenham Court Road, London W1P 0LP, UK, e-mail: cla@cla.co.uk This authorization does not extend to any other kind of copying, by any means, in any form, and for any purpose other than private research use.

Angelaki: journal of the theoretical humanities is available online (ISSN 1469-2899). Please connect to http://tandf.co.uk/journals for further information.

ORDER FORM

Please enter my subscription to *Angelaki: journal of the theoretical humanities*, Volume 7, 2002, 3 issues, ISSN 0969-725X.

Institutional rate (includes free online access)
☐ £150.00
☐ US$246.00

Personal rate (print only)
☐ £35.00
☐ US$57.00

Personal subscriptions are welcomed if prepaid by credit card or personal cheque.

METHODS OF PAYMENT

☐ Payment has been made to:
Girobank plc, Bootle, Merseyside GIR 0AA, UK
Sort Code: 72-00-00. Account No: 551 3057

☐ Payment has been made by bank transfer to one of the following accounts (please indicate):

  ☐ UK (Sort Code—60 02 49)
  National Westminster Bank plc, Old Market Square Branch, 3 London Street, Basingstoke, Hants RG21 7NS, UK
  £ Account No: 01 484400
  US$ Account No: 01 328735

  ☐ USA
  Fleet Bank N.A., 3rd Floor, 1185 Avenue of the Americas, New York, NY 10036, USA
  Account No: 9417201589; ABA No: 021200339; Swift Ref: NBNAUS33

☐ Payment enclosed. Cheques or bank drafts should be made payable to *Taylor & Francis Ltd* and be drawn on a UK or US bank.

Please charge: ☐ American Express   ☐ Eurocard
                ☐ MasterCard   ☐ Visa

Card Number   Expiry Date
☐☐☐☐ ☐☐☐☐ ☐☐☐☐ ☐☐☐☐   ☐☐☐☐

Signature _____ Date _____

Our Value Added Tax Registration number is
_____

☐ We are not registered for Value Added Tax

INSPECTION COPY

☐ Please send me an inspection copy of *Angelaki: journal of the theoretical humanities.*

NAME _____

ADDRESS _____

_____

_____

POST/ZIP CODE _____

COUNTRY _____

TELEPHONE _____ FAX _____

ANGELAKI
journal of the theoretical humanities
volume 7 number 1 april 2002

SIMPLICITY IS SOMETIMES THE HARDEST THING

PHILIP VERNAU

CLOSE SHAVE

~~CHOSE~~
~~THOSE~~
~~CLOVE~~
CLOVE
CLOVE
CLOVE
CRAVE
BRAVE
BRACE
CRACE
CLACK
CLADE
SLADE
SHADE
SHAVE

CLOVE
CLOVE
~~CLOVE~~
CLARE
CLADE

CLOVE
CLOVE
CLOSE
CLOVE
CLOVE
CROVE
CRAVE
CRAVE
CRANE
CRAZE
CRAZE

CRACE
~~CRAVE~~
CRAPE
CROPE

SLANT
~~SCANT~~
PLANT
PLANE

BLANK
PLANK
PLANE
~~PLACE~~
PLANT
SLANT
SLANG

SLUNG
CLUNG
CLING
SLING
FLING
~~AINT~~
FLUNG

CLOVE
CLOVE
CROVE
CRAVE
BRAVE
BRACE
~~CRACE~~
TRACE
TRACK
CRACK
~~CLOCK~~
CRANK
CLANK
PLANK
~~PLONK~~
PLANT
~~SLANT~~
~~PLANE~~
PLANK
DANK
~~DANE~~
DUNK
TRUNK

~~CLOSE~~

CLOSE
CHOSE
CHASE

CLOSE
CHOSE
CHASE
PHASE

CLOSE
CLONE
ALONE
ALONG

CLOSE
CLOVE
CLOVE
CROVE
CRAVE
CRAPE
~~CRAPE~~
CRAVE
BRAVE
BRACE
TRACE
~~TRADE~~
TRACT
TRACK
CRACK
CLOCK
CLOCK
BLOCK
BLACK
SLACK
SMACK
SMOCK

CLONE
~~ALONE~~
CLONK
PLONK

CLOSE
CLOVE
CLAVE
SLAVE
SHAVE

journal of the theoretical humanities
volume 7 number 1 april 2002

Since the advent of modernism at the beginning of the twentieth century there has been a perpetual crisis about the status, definition and meaning of art. This crisis has had a number of components. The shifting characterisation of representation in the traditional arts in the wake of the eruption of new possibilities through photography and film is one large area. The status of these new possibilities themselves and the comprehension of the manner of their relationship to art mark another. In literature the encounter with urban life is productive of interaction with the mediums of newsprint, journalism and a growing awareness of non-Western forms of poetry and prose. The rise of theoretical reflection by artists in the form of manifestoes and self-conscious organisation into movements that represent an "avant-garde" was the most striking effect of these changes. Along with them, however, has arisen an awareness of a separation between art and many sectors of the public, a separation now ritually rehearsed in Britain around the spectacle of the Turner Prize.

The nature of this split between a self-consciously theoretical artistic vanguard and the supposedly "intelligent" public has many characteristics of drama and also many of farce. In thinking today about the fall-out after modernism of this set of events, however, one is immediately struck by the diversity of the responses to artistic history that contemporary art presents. Where once it seemed plausible to set out a progressive story about the development of artistic modernism so that it culminated in a drive towards abstraction, this is no longer claimed by anyone. The nature of this development is what I wish to focus on in this introduction as a way of setting out the rationale for this issue of *Angelaki*.

EDITORIAL INTRODUCTION

gary banham

AESTHETICS AND THE ENDS OF ART

Clement Greenberg was the critic famously responsible for setting out the classic account of artistic modernism as a progressive movement towards increasing abstraction. Greenberg traced a line from the Cubists to the Abstract Expressionists that was based on the notion of an increasing purism of forms, so that the arrival of the blank canvas came to seem the necessary outcome of the development. There were always many problems with this story. It focused primarily on French developments in its account of the period from the beginning of the twentieth century until the Second World War, at which point it conveniently represented post-war American art as a descendant of the French tradition. This account traded on a marginalisation of alternative forms of modernism such as

editorial introduction

German Expressionism, Dada, Surrealism and the Russian avant-gardes' own particular development that threw up such anomalous movements (by Greenbergian standards) as Constructivism. It also was tailored to fit a history of painting much more than a history of the other arts, forcing sculpture into a subsidiary position and paying practically no attention to the new art forms, let alone developments in areas such as dance or music.

Despite these inherent difficulties in Greenberg's story the real challenge to it came from within the development of American art itself. With the onset of the 1960s, Greenberg found himself bewildered. Rather than artists continuing to engage in the abstractionist programme there emerged firstly the arrival of what was perilously close to the blank canvas in the work of many artists classified as producing "minimal art" and subsequently an explosion of interest both in "mixture" of forms and with this an increasing tendency to find subject matter and inspiration outside the realm of art. The works of Andy Warhol made a mockery of the abstractionist story and even more the development of overtly conceptual art forms seemed to divest the artist even of any commitment to formal creation at all (though this was clearly prefigured by Warhol's extensive use of technical reproducibility).

This sets the scene, to take the UK, within which the annual fracas of the Turner Prize around the nature of art and the problems of taste is now set. With the onset of explicitly conceptual accounts of art and justifications of productions that would often involve arrangements being more significant than anything arranged, the shipwreck of Greenberg's account became apparent. As Greenberg's narrative became increasingly clearly unable to explain the nature of contemporary art, so began the turn to theories developed in the rest of the humanities by artists, art historians and art critics. The Conceptual Art movement itself was largely based on appeals to semiotics and forms of structuralist analysis. This had a number of consequences. Firstly, this paradoxically decreased the distance between art and at least a portion of the public. As increasing numbers of gallery visitors arrived with some awareness of the vocabulary of "theory" so did the artist and this part of the public begin to share a language in which they could express their comprehension of the place of the work. This narrowing of the gap between art and part of its public has to be set against a widening of the gap between the art and other parts of the public, the parts, however, not conversant with or interested in such recondite matters as "theory."

Secondly, the use of this vocabulary had itself to be constantly adjusted as the period of "high" theory ended with the proliferation of justificatory and critical resources available. This produced a new form of split as the public who appreciated art became split into subgroups of adherents to different languages and sets of references. Thirdly, a unificatory feature of the new landscape was a widespread abandonment, with regard to the progressive story of modernism articulated by Greenberg, of any reference to aesthetics at all. Towards the close of his life Greenberg's criticism became increasingly explicit in its references to Kant, an explicitness matched by a growing denial by others that aesthetics, particularly of the Kantian type, could tell us anything of any use about art, not least contemporary art.

It is this third pattern that prompted me to think that a special issue of *Angelaki* that tried to address the question of the relationship between aesthetics and art would be worthwhile. In the rise of anti-aesthetic accounts of art there is a name that is most significant in terms of the denial of criteria of taste or any relevant use of the aesthetic in critical purchase on art works. This is the name of Duchamp. The work of Duchamp is appropriated selectively by Conceptual, Neo-Conceptual and Post-Conceptual critics and artists, as what is at issue in the branding of his name as an effective slogan is the readymades, perhaps most importantly *Fountain*. This selective form of relationship to Duchamp is matched by a focusing on statements Duchamp made towards the end of his life about the significance of these works, statements given much greater prominence than the accounts of the works that Duchamp gave at the time he first chose to present them. There is, therefore, a

editorial introduction

considerable story to be told about the nature of Duchamp's own shifting account of these works and the rationale for focusing on only one part of this story by later critics and artists. There is also a story to be told about the forms of use of the readymade in terms of the manner in which the readymades are themselves exhibited and the nature of the relationship between them and other works that they are connected to both within the overall works of Duchamp himself and in connection with artists with whom he was associated.

To begin telling these stories would be a considerable work. Within the scope of consideration opened in this issue, however, what seemed to me of significance was to set the Duchampian and post-Duchampian art works and critics in relationship to the traditions of aesthetics that they had supposedly made redundant. This requires new accounts to be given both of classical theories of aesthetics and the development of responses to the forms of aesthetics that are more distinctive of the twentieth century. The articles in this issue have attempted to do both these things.

Howard Caygill's article "Digital Lascaux: The Beginning in the End of the Aesthetic" sets out a response to the dual situation of the reclamation of the cave paintings of Lascaux within the story of art (albeit as "primitive" art) and the hyper-modern attempt at accounting for these works within a computerised project of modular programmes. The clash between primitive and futural within such an encounter prompts Caygill to revisit the status of "aesthetics" as both the mapping out of the characteristics of sensibility in general and the determination of a relationship to the characteristics of a certain set of experiences that themselves require a transcendental setting to be provided for them. This incisive investigation mobilises a relationship to the work of Georges Bataille to allow an investigation of the relationship between beginnings and "ends."

Jim Drobnick's piece "Toposmia" has the quite different task of addressing the failure of traditional forms of aesthetics to include an account of the olfactory. Focusing on works that force an engagement with strong types of odours, Drobnick provokes a different response to the articulation of fundamental sensibility to that of Caygill. Drobnick does share the conviction that an account of the aesthetic should connect the description of spatio-temporal fundamentals with the vivid and rich nature of the distinctive characteristics of that which classical theory mobilised under the term "taste," but attention to such phenomena as the olfactory teaches us the need for another term.

Joanna Hodge in "Why Aesthetics Might be Several" returns to the status of the aesthetic in a triply determined manner. Learning from and yet also posing critical questions to the work of Jean-Luc Nancy she reminds us of a third level of aesthetic alongside the two that are encountered in such vivid ways by Caygill and Drobnick. Alongside the spatio-temporal form of sensibility in general and the transcendental affectivity that is the subject matter of the critique of taste, Hodge places the aesthetic that is required to account for morality itself. In rescuing this third level of the aesthetic Hodge is enabled to pose anew the problem that Nancy finds so intriguing: why are the arts multiple? If the multiplicity of the arts is placed alongside the several characters of aesthetics a differently inflected question of plurality appears necessary that does not rest merely on empirical variety but on some irreducible "mixture" that characterises experience itself.

Henry Staten's article "Clement Greenberg, Radical Painting, and the Logic of Modernism" returns to addressing the nature of Clement Greenberg's original project through an encounter with both recent critical re-evaluations of it and in terms of an artistic movement that enables a return to thinking painting differently. Focusing on the works of Marioni and the movement of "radical painting" Staten provides a nuanced and faceted response to the fate of Greenberg that enables a retrieval of more of his critical vocabulary than has been conventionally thought possible. In intertwining the aesthetic with a necessary relationship to teleology, Staten returns it to a philosophical problematic of considerable richness and in the process demonstrates its relevance for artistic criticism.

Dalia Judovitz is the first of many in the issue to respond to the challenge of the legacy of Duchamp. In "De-Assembling Vision" Judovitz

editorial introduction

places Duchamp into relationship with the contemporary art practices of Matta-Clark and Wilson and so enables a positioning of Duchamp within a tradition of "post-modern" art that decentres the visual even whilst presenting it. In describing Duchamp in this foundational role she moves away from the conventional concentration on his early work to focus instead on the important and still inadequately theorised *Given*. This enables a location of Duchamp in terms of the questions that have emerged as central in the wake of "high" theory, and in placing him in connection with contemporary artists stakes a claim for a living legacy.

Gary Banham's "Mapplethorpe, Duchamp and the Ends of Photography" puts Duchamp in quite different company in an analysis of the works of Robert Mapplethorpe. Rather than focusing on the issues of direct political import that have surrounded the reception of Mapplethorpe's work, Banham suggests that his practice enables a response to the readymade that is rather more inventive than a simple appropriation. In articulating this connection Banham also undertakes a double displacement of the role Mapplethorpe is argued to have in contemporary art by demonstrating his connection with figures of classical modernism and at the same time rehabilitating a "Kantian" vocabulary for the description of his works. As with the works of Hodge and Caygill, this effects a considerable and surprising rehabilitation of Kantian criticism that proposes an innovative aesthetic ethics.

In "From Painting's Death to the Death in Painting," Isabelle Wallace places Duchamp's work in relation to that of Jasper Johns. In providing an account of Duchamp that enables a connection with an artist of the generation that spanned the acme of abstractionism and its rapid demise, Wallace helps to locate one of the central divergences from the classic narrative of modernism. In doing so she focuses attention on both the forms and narratives of the works of Duchamp and Johns, demonstrating acutely the impossibility of separating them from each other. In also interrupting the notion of the place of "death" in art Wallace implicitly challenges accounts of the death "of" art in a nuanced appropriation of psychoanalysis.

Robert Yanal – "Duchamp and Kant" – proposes a new encounter between the two rather than accepting the critical story that sets them at opposite poles. Reminding us of the role and nature of the work of art in Kant and setting this in connection with his accounts of the ideal, Yanal rescues Kant from the imputations of formalism that have been so influential. In providing this rescue of Kant, Yanal simultaneously allows a new type of critical appreciation of Duchamp's achievement.

Michele White's article "The Aesthetic of Failure" focuses on the status and claims of one of the latest innovations within artistic practice, the notion of "net art." Describing in considerable detail the main proponents of this type of art, White acutely diagnoses a crisis within its terms as she presents a circular structure of repetition. The nature and dangers of this new form of artistic practice are related to a form of aesthetic that it attempts to embody, with White posing critical questions about the limits of its concerns.

Simon Malpas presents a very different description of the "post-modern" from that of Dalia Judovitz. In "Sublime Ascesis" Malpas draws directly on Lyotard's essays on Barnett Newman to present the very different response to classic abstractionism that emerges if we move away from a Greenbergian account of its works. This allows a disruptive account of the nature of temporality within the works of Newman and a new set of thoughts about the nature of claims to be clearly within a "present."

Kanta Kochhar-Lindgren's "Towards a Communal Body of Art" focuses, by contrast, on the theatrical practice of Augusto Boal. In addressing the subject of theatre, Kochhar-Lindgren places Boal within a post-Surrealist concern with chance that is also aligned with an aesthetic not of genius but of collective enterprise. This displacement of the status of the aesthetic within artistic practice and criticism is simultaneously political and innovatively theoretical, suggesting an important alternative to the Brechtian model of radical theatre.

Lewis Johnson, in the concluding piece of the issue, presents a reflection that is inventive in both form and content. Johnson's essay

"Variations on the Work of Art" responds to Mutlu Cerkez, whose work involves multi-media composition. Johnson presents a criticism that is as complex and faceted as its object. Beginning from the reflections on music by Barthes, he utilises the resources of Derrida to present a criticism that is unafraid to embrace its own condition as produced by and requiring a dense placement in the history of modernity. Johnson's fine and open piece provides an important and fitting conclusion to this issue.

acknowledgements

I would like to thank all the following for help with this issue: Susan Best, Charlie Blake, David Boothroyd, Howard Caygill, Jim Drobnick, Diane Elam, Mike Garfield, Moira Gatens, Kyriaki Goudeli, Richard Hamilton, Ullrich Haase, Greg Haine, Joanna Hodge, Lars Iyer, Lewis Johnson, Dalia Judovitz, Barbara Kennedy, Sharon Kivland, Gregg Lambert, Simon Malpas, Diane Morgan, Forbes Morlock, Tim Murphy, Ben Norland, Karin Spirn, Saul Ostrow, Henry Staten, Suzanne Stern-Gillet, Jim Urpeth, Isabelle Wallace, Michele White and Rob White. In addition, thanks should go to my supportive partner Don Milligan and to Gerard Greenway for the opportunity to edit this special issue.

editorial introduction

a good enough hostess
sharon kivland *(curator)*

I have read carefully, and with interest, my colleague's editorial introduction above, and must declare now my own position and introduce a rather different style. Indeed, I will tell you what I will not do. But before that, let me tell you, dear reader, how Gary and I came to meet. Quite a long time ago now, my friend F., who happens to be on the editorial committee of *Angelaki*, took me for a coffee one morning. In the course of the usual gossip sprinkled with theoretical speculation (the foundation of our friendship), F. showed me a proposal for an issue of the journal that was then under consideration. It was rather densely written, and I pretended to read it with attention, then made one or two comments to demonstrate my cleverness. The talk passed on to other subjects, and I forgot about aesthetics and the ends of art for some time, for I had other concerns.

Almost a year passed. One day I received an e-mail message from G., the managing editor of *Angelaki*, asking, in his usual direct way, if I would be interested in working with a guest editor of a forthcoming issue of the journal to provide a number of contributions from artists. In an issue devoted to aesthetics and the ends of art, very little art was going to appear (it was feared), in the form of images at least. This came as no surprise to me, for having collaborated with art historians and philosophers before, as well as having attended many conferences, I knew that it was a rare thing to be given such an encounter. It is true, of course, that slides are frequently shown to illustrate a particular point a speaker is making, or to conveniently locate the audience within the oeuvre of an artist. In these cases, the artist is usually well known (as well known as is possible within such an enclosed field) or dead. Often – I am sorry to tell you – these slides are back to front or upside-down, out of focus, or gently curved and distorted, following the fold of the page from which they have been poorly photographed. Sometimes videos are shown, a brief extract, accompanied by an apology that this is, of course, not the correct way to

editorial introduction

experience the work. Sometimes, in these situations, I despair. I feel all these things *matter*.

I had worked twice before with the journal, both times forming a pleasant relationship, producing something with which I was reasonably pleased, as much at least, as one ever can be. I accepted G.'s proposition at once, for I am not one to turn down an opportunity, despite the constraints of time, and the greater limitations of print quality and budget. I felt that I would be allowed to work as I wished, after discussion to be sure, that I would be given carte blanche if I were convincing enough in my argument. I enjoyed reading each issue of the journal, and welcomed the chance to collaborate once more.

In fact, it was some time before I met with Gary, who had moved to another university and acquired what was to me a glamorous and enviable title. We exchanged e-mails over several months, but as I was living in France, completing the writing of a book (or so I hoped), it was difficult to meet. Even though I returned to London from time to time, Gary lived in Manchester, and it began to seem as though our paths would never cross. Finally we were able to agree a date, and met on a Saturday afternoon in the Royal Festival Hall. As a place of rendezvous, I had first met with G. there, in 1998. He was accompanied by B., the art director of the journal, and its designer, J. – who was actually a former student of mine, last seen in 1984. G. had described his appearance over the telephone, and I had been looking for someone with a briefcase and formally dressed. I had failed to identify him, but did not fail to identify Gary. This was not because his description was particularly accurate, but because he seemed to be so obviously looking for someone, and though he looked at me several times, he did not make any connection between my description of myself and my real appearance (small, very long hair, very red lipstick, dressed in black no doubt – I do not remember exactly, nor do I remember Gary's description of himself). We collected a coffee, sat down at a table, and began our discussion. I was touched that earlier in the day he had bought me a postcard in the National Gallery, that he was offering me an image.

So I have brought you to our encounter. Let me now tell you what I wanted to do but what proved impossible. Gary has described the split between the "artistic vanguard" and the public. There is also the gap between a theory of art and its practice. Like many others, I have worked against this for many futile years, as an artist, a teacher, a writer, and a curator, especially in my connection with the milieu of psychoanalysis. As a teacher in the studio (an abstract concept, for in truth I enter the studios as little as possible unless invited) I tell my students, in the words of Charcot, a favourite dictum that Freud was also to repeat: that theory is good, but it does not stop things from existing. As an artist, I am weary of the demand that a work should speak for itself, and that this thing practitioners or would-be practitioners call theory demonstrates only the failure of a work of art to do its work. I am divided.

But I forget myself. I wanted to introduce each writer in this issue to an artist. I wanted them, once presented, to work together, if not to fall in love. I wondered – and so wanted to see – if theory loves practice more than practice loves theory. I wanted to set up blind dates, brief encounters between an academic and an artist (though certainly, some artists are equally academics, though it is less certain if academics are also artists). I have done this before, first in 1991, and in different ways ever since then. I am, one might say, a matchmaker. However, I am seldom successful in this self-imposed task. Nor was I to succeed this time, for as Gary hastened to tell me, politely acknowledging an interest in my proposal, the articles for inclusion were almost all already written, and some even were accompanied by images, copyright permitting. If I could not make pairs meet or produce happy endings, then I had to find another strategy.

I would then continue with a kind of coupling, if only in selecting the same number of artists to participate as there were already writers. I wanted no wallflowers; no one left on his own in the encounter with aesthetics and the ends of art. If writer and artist could not meet, then I would at least separate writer from writer, placing images in between to disrupt the flow of words. Yet it was quickly clear that some of the contributions would not be images in a conventional sense at

editorial introduction

all. I would not call upon artists to decorate, to illustrate, to make beautiful the pages of *Aesthetics and the Ends of Art*, and in my selection process I went through my guest list. Some were artists with whom I had worked already, often on more than one occasion, the kind of guest upon whom one may rely for intelligent and engaging conversation and good behaviour. Others were more unpredictable, like those people one invites to dinner, sometimes rashly, after a brief introduction by a third party. Many were at first confused, wanting me to clarify my demand – perhaps I had explained badly, but I think it was more that I did not know exactly for what I was looking and so could not describe it. Some seized upon my strategy immediately and re-invented it as their own, which led to some elucidation on my part at least.

I sent each artist abstracts of the articles as soon as they were available, a feat of photocopying. I asked them to read the abstracts and Gary's introductory proposal. I suggested certain possible relationships between a text and their own practice, some of which I felt were evident. I asked them to consider the theme of the issue, particularly the tradition of aesthetics in relation to contemporary art. I now speculate on how many actually read them or paid any attention to my remarks, save in the most cursory way. Artists, like writers, have a way of doing what they want anyway, despite the rules of the game. This is, of course, one of the pleasures of working. The most common question concerned the precise nature of the relationship between the articles to appear in the issue, and the interventions – as I had by now come to think of them – of the artists. Were the interventions to support arguments that might precede or follow, should an article be chosen and interrogated, should there be a specific response to a specific text? If you like, if you like, I replied weakly, insincerely. Sometimes I said no, then at other times yes. It was, I felt, important to trust my dear contributors.

Gary has asked me to provide a readers' guide to the artists' pages herein. He has requested me to write brief paragraphs on each of the works, perhaps saying something about them in relation to the articles. It must be clear by now that I am not going to do that, for indeed there may be no relationship at all. The arrangement may be quite random For example, *A Thousand Moths Reside and Died Here* may have little to do with "Sublime Ascesis: Lyotard, Art and the Event." On the other hand, they may be linked, fitting like hand in glove, and, in fact, the juxtaposition was particularly requested. As reader, you may be tempted to make your own connections, even those that seem banal or reflexive, such as the conjuncture between a communal body, an exquisite corpse, and the *Plaies-Images II* of Nicole Jolicoeur. You may jump to a conclusion in forming a relation between the shattered and restored china of Anne Ramsden and death in painting. The titles may lead to this kind of free association, which might also be a false connection, produced by the hysteric's drive to fill the abyss that opens all too often in reality. The titles, you must understand, are in some cases part of the works themselves, and so will not lend themselves to an easy or efficient explanation. Throughout this issue runs *Ride*, a text work by John Berger that asks both to be read and to be seen. It is this that distinguishes writer from artist in this issue I know that properly I should say just a little something about every contributor, but this would undo my intention.

I have argued elsewhere, and this is not the place, in only our first meeting, to do so in any depth, that the work of art does not give itself up completely to this kind of deciphering (which is not to say that it should be prohibited, or that it is always useless). I cannot tell you what each set of artists' pages *does*, and indeed I am only assuming that it does anything at all. Let me just say the following (forgive me if I go on a bit). The work of art is supposed to mean something, and its meaning is supposed to reveal itself to a viewer through the encounter. Its precise meaning, however, appears elusive and, moreover, seems either wilfully obscure or, in refusing any signification, remains completely unavailable. The work of art appears to have knowledge, and moreover it appears to deny access to this knowledge to the subject who approaches it with his demand. For the dumb work of art, it is only the viewer or reader who is the subject supposed to know, a subject who is inhabited by meaning of

editorial introduction

which he knows either nothing or too much, and will certainly choose to ignore for as long as possible. A viewer may challenge the work of art, demanding it to show its stuff, and if the work of art fails to deliver, it may be accused of duping its observer. The challenge is made in the role of the master, a role that renders its bearer a dupe.

The work of art may be more (or less) than the page that you as viewer or reader encounter, and this does not aid in the clear-cut delivery of the work's supposed meaning. While it may be imagined that there is nothing outside the work, it is precisely in question as to what the work is, for it may involve not only the physical space of the encounter, but indeed everything that precedes, surrounds, or follows the encounter. You will get my drift, I am sure. The plaintive demand is that a work should speak for itself, for if it is assumed to speak, the viewer will not have to give up his illusion.

The work of art will never give up what is demanded of it, for it does not have it. The work of art is often challenged as a cheat; it is no better than a robber, swindling the viewer of his hard-earned cash or more. If you allow me to turn to psychoanalysis for a moment, everyone has stories about its deception, from complaints about the high price of treatment to apocryphal tales of Lacan's variable sessions. In either case, viewer and analysand do not get enough, do not get what they think they are paying for at least. There is not much chance of a mutually satisfying exchange, if one hoped to buy knowledge that is. Lacan acknowledges that psychoanalysis is an *escroquerie*, a swindle. That is also a common perception of contemporary art – the children's story of *The Emperor's New Clothes* is frequently and tediously cited as a metaphor for art practices. The story is understood well enough, but desire is left out of the interpretation. If desire is left out, one is left with nothing, like the Emperor to be sure, but also his people, who have nothing, not even an emperor. I hope that you are not disappointed.

After our meeting in the Royal Festival Hall, Gary and I went to a seminar together, and later that same day he travelled back to where he was staying that evening on the Northern line with me and P., whose leather-clad crotch, against the livery of the train seat, I was photographing for a new work. P.'s own work, *Simplicity is Sometimes the Hardest Thing*, is the first thing, more or less, that you will have encountered in this issue. Gary descended from the train at King's Cross station, I believe, and I have not seen him since, though we correspond by e-mail from time to time.

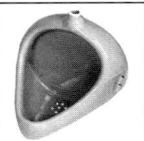

ride

john x. berger

As part of the artists' contribution to this collection, following each article and starting with this editorial introduction there runs a text-piece by John X. Berger entitled "Ride."

cover image

The cover image is designed by Sharon Kivland and is from the series "Mes Fils."

Gary Banham
Manchester Metropolitan University
Department of Politics and Philosophy
Geoffrey Manton Building
Manchester M15 6LL
UK
E-mail: g.banham@mmu.ac.uk

Sharon Kivland
Brizard
22490 Plouer-sur-Rance
France
E-mail: sharonkivland@wanadoo.fr

Each situation in which the chronicler is touched by the breath of lost time is thereby rendered incomparable with and removed from the sequence of the days.

If you want to relive an epoch, forget that you know what has happened since.

ANGELAKI
journal of the theoretical humanities
volume 7   number 1   april 2002

ISSN 0969-725X print/ISSN 1469-2899 online/02/010015-03 © 2002 Nayan Kulkarni

howard caygill

DIGITAL LASCAUX
the beginning in the end of the aesthetic

The project of establishing a "World Archive of Rock Art" (WARA), comprising several hundred thousand figures and images of prehistoric art selected from the twenty million known to have survived, originated in a 1983 UNESCO global report on the state of research in prehistoric art. Many of these figures and images, the most ancient among them over forty thousand years old, will become available on the Internet (www.globalnet.it) and will form one of the most ambitious online digital art archives. This presents the spectacle of a technology set to transform and even transcend the structures of human perception and affect – in short to mark the "end" of the human – being used to archive the geometrical figures and images held to mark the aesthetic "origin" of the human species.[1] What is more, the formation of the archive is supported by an international organisation dedicated to the creation of a global human culture that would transcend ethnic and political differences – the realisation of Schiller's dream of an aesthetic education of mankind.[2] The evocation of an archaic aesthetic origin in order to assert the unity of the human species by means of a technology that is sublimely inhuman in its scale and power provokes a number of questions regarding not only the place of the aesthetic between the beginning and the end of the human but also, and inseparably, the broader set of relations between the human, the pre-human and the post-human.

Perhaps the best way to approach some of the questions concerning the relationship of the aesthetic and the concept of the human is to look more closely at the notion of the aesthetic. An understanding of the ambition of the aesthetic to unite the technology of perception – whether geometrical or digital – with the affects of pleasure and creativity makes it possible to appreciate not only why the human is repeatedly defined aesthetically, but also why this definition is always beset by ambiguity. In the case of the aesthetic origins of the human testified by the survivals of rock art, this ambiguity is registered in the divergent readings of that aesthetic origin provided by Bataille and Leroi-Gourhan. For Bataille, the aesthetic origin of the human to which rock art bears witness consists in the excess of creativity over labour and the technology of perception, while for Leroi-Gourhan it bears witness to the inauguration of the human in the technological mastery of perception. In the case of the aesthetic origins of the human it is the definition of the human and its future that are at issue, an argument whose parameters anticipate the current digital celebration of archaic human creativity.

digital lascaux

The extravagant ambition of the modern aesthetic to unite perception and affect was from the beginning marked by the movement between an archaic creative origin and a technological future. This movement is evident in Kant's canonical *Critique of Judgement* (1790a), which summed up the previous half-century's debate on aesthetics and bequeathed to the future an irresolution around the scope and definition of the aesthetic that has still to be settled. The movement between the past and the future of aesthetics is already evident in the prefatory material to the *Critique of Judgement*, where Kant reflects on the task of uniting the aesthetic of perception, the "transcendental aesthetic," with the aesthetic of affect or pleasure in the beautiful and the sublime. At one point in his reflection Kant summons up an archaic moment when perception was thus united with affect, a time when the experience of the conceptual organisation of nature was attended by pleasure, a time that persists overlooked in nature and works of art. Kant adds that it is "only because the commonest experience would not be possible without [pleasure] has it become mixed with perceptions and is not particularly noticed anymore."[3] While summoning the phantasm of a forgotten archaic unity of affect and perception Kant also intimates that it may be recovered through a "technic" of judgement. The latter serves as a technology for producing a unity of perception and affect, and is linked in complex ways to the modalities of imagination. It is, however, a technology of the future that is in question, since the machine technology with which Kant was familiar could not satisfy the demand for an integrated aesthetic capable of unifying perception and affect. While the *Critique of Judgement* occasionally divines this future unity it remains on the whole as phantasmal as the archaic unity that it would retrieve. What he does make clear, however, is the discovery of the technology of the future – and the human of the future that will shape and be shaped by it – will itself be an aesthetic act, that is, it will unify the technology of perception with an act of creation.[4]

The character of the phantasmal aesthetic of the future differed from that of the past, even though it still depended on the memory of the archaic unity. On some occasions Kant imagines a technology that no longer works on a material but whose process is its material. An important consequence of this imagined technology is the detachment of the aesthetic perception of geometry and the aesthetic affect of art from objects – in his discussion of the *sensus communis* Kant thus imagines the production of pleasure through pure communication without the need of an object. To the phantasm of an "archaic" aesthetic fusion of perception and affect sited in the human body is contrasted a fusion that is not corporeal. Since this incorporeal fusion is barely imaginable, Kant defined it negatively as both non-sensible and non-conceptual. What it involves, however, is not simply a new form of art or technology but a transformation of the human body.

To some degree the non-machinic technology imagined by Kant has been realised by digital technology and the strange phantasmal movements between the archaic and the future set in play across the computer screen. In the case of WARA, the translation into digital signals of what are perceived to be the archaic remains of the aesthetic origins of the human attempts to create a loop between the aesthetic beginning of the human and its end. The physical dispersal of over twenty million archaic geometrical figures and images across the five continents provides the phantasm of an archaic global generic unity of the human – a *sensus communis* – which is then affirmed in the centralisation of their digital analogues in an archive and their dispersal around the world through the Internet. The inhuman technology becomes the stage for the recollection of the aesthetic origins of humanity and through it the creation of an incorporeal *sensus communis*.

The motivation for representing the remains of archaic art is clearly complex, moving from the conviction that the figures and images present the inaugural moment of the human to the desire that their technological representation will somehow reaffirm the aesthetic unity or *sensus communis* of humanity. Yet both the conviction and the desire are open to question. The conviction that the remains represent the aesthetic unity of the human is already compromised by the division within the aesthetic evident in Kant. The remains of archaic inscription have themselves already been interpreted in terms of the tension within the aesthetic itself. The surviving fragments have been assigned to the generic categories of the "figurative" and the "geometrical," imposing the division between an aesthetic of affect and of perception. The division within Kant's aesthetic between the geometrically oriented "Transcendental Aesthetic" of the *Critique of Pure Reason* concerned with the organisation of space and time and the aesthetic of the *Critique of Judgement* concerned with the pleasure provoked by aesthetic representation is here projected onto the archaic remains. The work of classification is not innocent, but represents considerable differences concerning not only the understanding of geometry and art but the nature of the human. The leading philosophical reflections on archaic art and the origins of the human – those of Bataille and Leroi-Gourhan – themselves repeat this division, appealing to a unity while working in terms of a division. Bataille provides what might be described as the "third critique" of archaic art, focusing on images and the affects of pleasure and dread that they evoke, while Leroi-Gourhan's focus on geometrical figures and spatial and temporal dispositions offers a "first critique" or "transcendental aesthetic." Informing these differences in orientation is a fundamental disagreement on the definition of the human, and its relation to the animal and technological inhuman.

Bataille's reading of the images from the grotto of Lascaux in *Lascaux ou la naissance de l'art* (1955) is an unequivocal statement of the claim that origins of art constitute the origins of the human. Lascaux for Bataille has an eminent place "in the history of art and more generally the history of humanity" and this because "the work of art was intimately related to the formation of humanity."[5] Bataille sustains this claim for the aesthetic origins of the human by recourse to the concept of a historical break between the animal and the human that he describes repeatedly and consistently as a "miracle." The "miraculous moment of history," the "decisive moment," was not Ancient Greece, but prehistoric Lascaux, at least twenty thousand years before Greece. The moment of Lascaux or the invention of art also "is the dawn of the human species."[6] This dawn, the transition to the human, necessarily retains traces of a "strange inhumanity" – the origin of the human bears the mark of the inhuman, or, for Bataille, the animal, whose mark on the walls of Lascaux is a witness and "*sensible* sign of *our* presence in the universe."[7] For Bataille, the aesthetic origin of the human lies in the inscription of the image of the animal through which the human marks its distance from inhuman animality.

It is necessary to look more closely at the miraculous moment of emergence in which, for Bataille, we are still suspended and to note a feature that subsequently will shape his understanding of archaic aesthetics. This is the refusal to consider technology as a central feature in the emergence of the human. Early in his text he refers to the tools of pre-humanity, but while conceding that "these tools prove the intelligence of ancient man" he insists that "this intelligence is still crude" governed by the needs of animality. Technology is not the source of the powerful affect that Bataille calls the "inner life" or "inner experience" and which for him is witnessed for the first time in Lascaux.

The concern at the very outset to establish a distance between technology and art is clarified in the course of Bataille's analysis of Lascaux. He sees the origin of the human – *Homo sapiens* – in its passage from human/animal of *Homo faber* that he sometimes identifies with *Homo neanderthal*. The world of *Homo faber*, the world of work, tools and the satisfaction of animal need, is not human but pre-human, between the animal and the human. The human emerges within *Homo faber* through the ability to experience death, testified for the archaeological record in the mortuary rituals of *Homo neanderthal* that preceded the full emergence of the human. For Bataille, the inaugural moment of the human occurs when in the face of death *Homo faber* experiences the difference between themselves and the world of objects, and then crucially the affect of excess in transgressing this difference. The site of this founding transgression of the human is the work of art, thus locating the origin of the human in the aesthetic event.

digital lascaux

In Bataille's account of the aesthetic origins of the human the affect of transgression is far more significant than the magical power of the world provided by technology. In distinguishing the origin of the human from work and technology Bataille interprets archaic art almost exclusively in terms of affect. The affect originates, as arguably it does for Kant in his notion of the sublime, in transgression, in particular the transgression of the laws governing two areas of what emerge from *Homo faber*'s world of work but which also exceed it – death and sexuality. The laws in question regulate areas of experience that cannot be made objects of work. Bataille then argues that the work of art – far from being a form of magical/religious technology serving to control even these areas of experience – instead figures their excessive transgression.

Bataille traces a double movement in the origin of the human, one that contains both the establishment of law and the system of cognition that attends it and also the transgression of these laws – the former establishes the laws of perception while the latter overturns them, provoking the affect of excess: "the movement of transgression is the necessary counterpart of the arrest, of the restraint of the ban [*l'interdit*]. Above all the festival is essentially the sudden time of raising the rules whose weight is normally supported … The festival is a time of relative licence."[8] The archaic work of art testifies to the origin of the human in transgression, in madness and laughter and the affects of pleasure and dread that accompany them. For Bataille "The name of Lascaux is the symbol of epochs that accompany the passage from the beastly human to the mad being that we are."[9] In the case of Lascaux, the representations of animality signify the excessive becoming animal of the human in festive transgression rather than the being animal of *Homo faber* that remains trapped in meeting its animal needs.

It is difficult to avoid the suspicion when reading *Lascaux ou la naissance de l'art* that for Bataille the movement from the industrious animal of *Homo faber* to the festive human of *Homo sapiens* is being reversed in the epoch of industrial modernity and that contemporary humanity in its obsession with work and production is becoming *neanderthal*. Art, and in particular Lascaux, remains a miraculous, excessive moment, inaugurating a human that is as capable of transcending itself in the *Ubermensch* as it is in regressing to the pre-human or *neanderthal*. From this perspective, Lascaux presents not only the past but also the future of humanity, especially to a culture in full regression from *Homo sapiens* to *Homo faber*. The future of the human lies in the aesthetic affect of joyous transgression and not in the continued development of the technology of *Homo faber*.

Leroi-Gourhan's work on archaic art also formed part of a broader project on prehistory and the emergence of the human,[10] but one conducted on quite different terms from those of Bataille. Bataille was fascinated by the figures of the animals in Lascaux, the affect they provoked and the evidence they represented of the transition from animality to the human. Leroi-Gourhan's fascination lay more with the abstract, geometrical marks that are left in the caves and which are probably more widespread than the figurative images exclusively discussed by Bataille. For Leroi-Gourhan, these marks document the aesthetic emergence of the human in the act of perception allied to technological control rather than to the affect of excess. Thus, in his great study of archaic art *The Dawn of European Art: An Introduction to Palaeolithic Cave* Painting,[11] the focus of his enquiry rests on the emergence of human spatio-temporal perception testified to in the archaic marks. The attention paid to the emergence of space and time – each of which is allotted a chapter – relates Leroi-Gourhan's work to Kant's transcendental aesthetic, whose exposition is also organised in terms of space and time. The aesthetic origins of humanity for Leroi-Gourhan lie more in the organisation of human perception than in affect; this organisation, furthermore, is technologically mediated. As distinct from Bataille, Leroi-Gourhan sees technology as crucial for the definition of the human; for him *Homo sapiens* is *Homo faber* and the works of archaic art are called up as evidence for the continuity.

Leroi-Gourhan's emphasis provides a fascinating contrast with that of Bataille, and between them they offer a repetition of the division in the formulation of the modern aesthetic evident in

Kant but now projected onto archaic art. Leroi-Gourhan's transcendental aesthetic of archaic art seeks the origins of the human in geometry and the experience of space and time, and suggests that these experiences are inseparable from the development of technology. From the beginning to the end of *The Dawn of European Art*, technology is the central protagonist. In the "technical gesture" of the archaic artist Leroi-Gourhan finds the affirmation of *Homo sapiens*: "Although, in spite of the surprising degree of efficiency of flint tools, the techniques of manufacture still had 15,000–20,000 years to go before reaching the present efficiency of our machines, the palaeolithic artist himself recognised from the very beginning the possibility of affirming his nature as *Homo sapiens*."[12] The use of technology to create works of art is an affirmation by the artist of the technological achievements of the species. The link between technology and *Homo sapiens* is described even more concretely in the conclusion, where technology is related through art to magic: "among populations at the stage of a hunting economy, the religious side is inseparable from the technological side and that it may have seemed essential to create these underground monuments, the decorated caves, in order to govern the physical world."[13] The technological control of the world is celebrated in the art as the magical power over the world, the ability to give shape and figure to an alien environment.

Crucial to Leroi-Gourhan's argument is the view of technology as a magical means of organising and controlling the world and the parallel between the general use of technology and its specific use in works of art. The latter not only give evidence for the former, but more significantly for Leroi-Gourhan, they also give evidence for the structure of human consciousness. He claims that "research into the meaning of paintings, engravings and sculptures on the walls of caves and rock shelters" will provide an understanding not only for ethnology of "certain fundamental aspects of the mental behaviour of Upper Palaeolithic man" but also of "the facts of technical life."[14] The two aspects are indeed complementary, for the analysis of "Assemblage (for space) and animation (for time)"[15] combines technology and ethnology – the technical organisation of space and time provides the structure for the experience of space and time.

The repetition of the modern division between an aesthetic of affect and perception in the reflections on the aesthetic origins of the human gives some idea of the conceptual difficulties that attend the formation of a global archive of archaic art. The organisers of the archive implicitly agree with both Bataille and Leroi-Gourhan that the origin of the human is an aesthetic phenomenon, intimately connected with the production of art, but on the whole incline to a modified version of Leroi-Gourhan's thesis. Emmanuel Anati follows Leroi-Gourhan in reading the figures and images in terms of an archaeology of perception, but with perhaps the crucial qualification that spatio-temporal perception is shaped by the imagination. The human capacity for "abstraction, synthesis and idealisation" is inseparable from the creative excess of imagination, the "capacity for externalisation of artistic creativity."[16] The attempt to link aesthetic perception and affect through the exercise of imagination itself repeats Kant's attempt in the critiques to unite both through the imagination. Yet the work of Bataille has made it necessary to be more precise about the sources and modalities of excess.

The definition of the human in terms of a balance between affective and perceptual aesthetics that is achieved through the excess of the imagination sets at the centre of the human something that is more than human. The more than human or inhuman is related in some way to the division within the aesthetic – the fact that perception and affect do not add up points to a lacuna or an excess in the aesthetic definition of the human. Kant's return to a primal unity of perception and affect and his projection of a future technically integrated aesthetic may be understood in terms of the figures of excess proposed by Bataille and Leroi-Gourhan. The emergence from animality in the transgressive festival of the former might be taken as an equivalent for the Kantian archaic unity, while the technological birth of the human of the latter provides a perspective in which to think Kant's technical unity of the aesthetic. Each of the two positions remains dependent upon the other –

the affects provoked by the Bataillean festival of transgression require the presence within it of the technological in order for it to be negated, while Leroi-Gourhan's technological organisation of perception requires to be supplemented by the affects generated through power and control over nature, namely that the view that technology is magic.

The conduct of the complicated negotiations between the divided aesthetic and the inhuman in the human on the terrain of archaic art has been complicated by the entry of archaic art into the Internet. In a sense the enquiry into the origins of the aesthetic and human that arrived at the recognition of the inhuman is now to be conducted in inhuman terrain. The digital translation of the archaic images in the name of a global unity of the species seems to vindicate Leroi-Gourhan's view that this art is the technical celebration of technical ability and control. The celebration is raised a power by itself being re-celebrated by means of the most recent technological revolution. But the celebration of the unity of the human species by the digital translation of the figures and images surviving from the origin of the human is no longer the Bataillean festival of a transgression of the limits of *Homo faber*. The digital translation and global dissemination of archaic figures and images may be understood as an inhuman celebration of the human, of the passing of the human into a future of technological animality. The figures and images that marked the aesthetic beginnings of the human are gathered, preserved and presented at a moment and by a technology in and through which the human structures of perception and affect are put radically into question. It is by no means clear whether this is the moment of a Bataillean festive transition from the human to the *Übermensch* or a regression from *Homo sapiens* to the less than human *Homo faber*.

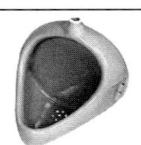

notes

1 The view that this art marks the beginning of the human species was shared, it will be shown below, albeit with important differences, by Georges Bataille and Leroi-Gourhan. It is a view that is echoed by Emmanuel Anati, one of the key figures in WARA: "Because of the implications that artistic creativity has for the functioning of the mechanisms associated with synthesis and abstraction it may be affirmed that, intellectually, *Homo sapiens* was born with the capacity to produce art" (Anati 1998, 57–59).

2 Friedrich Schiller, *On the Aesthetic Education of Man* (1793), trans. E. Wilkinson and L.A. Willoughby (Oxford: Oxford University Press, 1967). It is striking how Schiller's theme of the aesthetic education of humanity reappears in the assumed link between archaic art and the emergence of the human as well as in the late-human project of a cosmopolitan cultural unity that is predicated upon a respect for cultural differences.

3 Second Introduction to *The Critique of Judgement*, sect. VI.

4 In one of its clearest statements in the *First Introduction to the Critique of Judgement*, Kant distinguishes the *Technik* of reflective from the schema of determinate judgement: the former works "not just mechanically like a tool controlled by the understanding and the senses, but artistically according to a universal but at the same time undefined principle of the purposive ordering of nature into a system" (Kant 1790b, no. 5).

5 Georges Bataille (1955, 9).

6 Ibid. 11.

7 Ibid. 12.

8 Ibid. 40.

9 Ibid. 22.

10 See *Les religions de la prehistoire* (Leroi-Gourhan 1964).

11 This provides the theoretical foundation for the collaborative work *Lascaux inconnu* (Leroi-Gourhan 1979).

12 Leroi-Gourhan (1965, 13).

13 Ibid. 73.

14 Ibid. 36.

15 Ibid.

16 See Anati (1998, 59, 1999, 84).

bibliography

Anati, E. "Verso una nuova lettura dell'arte preistorica." *Le Scienze* 354 (1998): 50–59.

Anati, E. "WARA: Archivio mondiale dell'arte rupestre." *Le Scienze* 367 (1999): 82–89.

Bataille, G. *Lascaux ou la naissance de l'art, Ouevres completes* IX. Paris: Gallimard, [1955] 1979.

Kant, I. *The Critique of Judgement.* Trans. James Creed Meredith. Oxford: Oxford UP, [1790a] 1952.

Kant, I. *First Introduction to the Critique of Judgement.* Trans. James Haden. Indianapolis: Bobbs Merrill, [1790b] 1965.

Leroi-Gourhan, A. *Les religions de la prehistoire.* Paris: Presses Universitaires de France, 1964.

Leroi-Gourhan, A. *The Dawn of European Art: An Introduction to Palaeolithic Cave-Painting.* Trans. Sara Champion. Cambridge: Cambridge UP, 1965.

Leroi-Gourhan, A. et al. *Lascaux inconnu.* Paris: CNRS, 1979.

Sanders, N.K. *Prehistoric Art in Europe.* Harmondsworth: Pelican, 1985.

Howard Caygill
Department of Cultural and Historical Studies
Goldsmiths College
New Cross
London SE14 6NW
UK
E-mail: h.caygill@gold.ac.uk

Every cloud has a silver lining, a delightful proverb, predating any of the philosophical relativisms that have been spawned, and which wisely teaches us that it is pointless trying to judge life's events as if we were separating the wheat from the chaff.

ANGELAKI
journal of the theoretical humanities
volume 7 number 1 april 2002

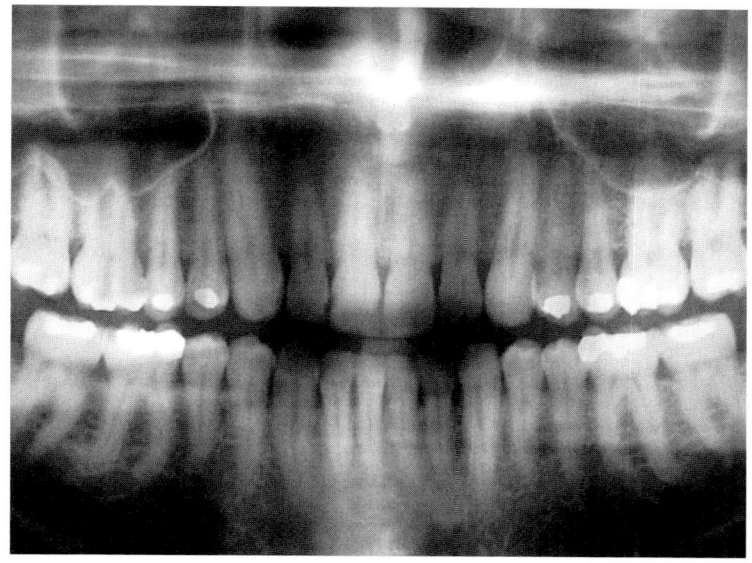

RICARDO BLOCH

ISSN 0969-725X print/ISSN 1469-2899 online/02/010027-03 © 2002 Ricardo B och

One tongue

gently strokes

my clitoris

once

then once more

and once again

The tongue

gently strokes

my glans

once

then once more

and once again

jim drobnick

TOPOSMIA
art, scent, and interrogations of spatiality

In the waning of Greenbergian opticality as the reigning theory of late modernism, artists explored a number of strategies which re-engaged with precisely those social and corporeal aspects that had been excluded by ocularcentric and formalist aesthetic theories: everyday life, popular culture, political activism, technology, audience engagement and the complexities of identity and difference.[1] The hierarchical position of Greenberg's autonomous eye, or what Pierre Bourdieu (1996) calls "the pure gaze," became irreparably vitiated by these artistic forays, literally so when the non-visual experiences of taste, touch, or smell intruded upon the sensory apparatuses of spectators. The reintegration of corporeal sense experiences, especially the modalities of the so-called "lower senses," not only de-privileged the eye, it also reinvested olfaction, gustation and tactility with the potential for epistemological and aesthetic significance.

The sense of smell serves as a particularly interesting case study, partly because of the obstacles to its acceptance as a legitimate vehicle for artistic expression. Scents undoubtedly exist on the fringe of aesthetics, despite the logical argument of J.-K. Huysmans, who wrote in *Against Nature* that "it was no more abnormal to have an art that consisted of picking out odorous fluids than it was to have other arts based on a selection of sound waves or the impact of variously coloured rays on the retina of the eye" (1959, 119). The impassioned pleas for a more sensorially diverse art contained in manifestos by the Futurists, Surrealists and other avant-gardists in the first half of the twentieth century often mentioned smells, yet manifestations of olfactory art appeared only intermittently. On the other side of the high–low divide, perfumes have been compared to art (Piesse 1891; Roudnitska 1977), but the credibility of this position is compromised by perfume's link to the fashion world, its craft-like status and overt commercialism, as well as by the latent moralistic reluctance to indulging in olfactory pleasures for their own sake.

Despite the recent surge in scented products and therapies, the stigmatization of smell over the past two centuries and the resultant odorphobia still persists, as olfaction is often considered to be the most animalistic of the senses (Freud 1961) or the least essential of the five for survival and quality of life (Synnott 1993), thus rendering it unsuitable or unnecessary to the pursuits of civilization, especially in regard to the fine arts. In surveying the history of aesthetics, it is of no surprise to find little support for an olfactory art. While some philosophers acknowledge an implicit, theoretical potential for fragrance as an artistic medium – Croce, for instance, remarks expansively that "all sense impressions can enter into expressions and aesthetic formulations" (1992, 20) – in most theories smell serves as the test case by which the limits of the aesthetic are set, or as the negative example which foregrounds the virtues and justifies the hierarchy of the visual and sonic arts. Arguments mobilized against smell as an aesthetically viable sensory mode range from the arbitrary (since some odours are repugnant, none can be aesthetic), to the biological (smell is a primal and functional sense, too immediate and sensuous for elevated pursuits), to the semantic and physical (smells lack a clearly defined language and intrinsic structure of order and measurement). The ideological bias in assessing the potential for smell in art by aestheticians is evidenced by the comparisons often utilized, e.g., the aroma of coffee or the fragrance of a flower versus a symphony or narrative painting. The absence of any mention of an existing olfactory artwork underscores the stakes in this debate. To acknowledge such an entity undermines two central aesthetic tenets: disinterestedness (smells are highly subjective and directly implicate the beholder's body) and autonomy (olfactory artworks most often utilize evaporating objects, ethereal atmospheres, and performative experiences).[2] The qualities of scent which denied it conventional aesthetic viability – evocativeness, intimacy, variability, primality, and so on – in fact turn out to be the very qualities most attractive to artists seeking to redefine aesthetic experience.

While aestheticians have attempted to establish inherent properties and objective criteria by which to articulate limits of art and to separate it from non-art, many artists, especially avant-garde and contemporary ones, have made it their mission to extend notions of the aesthetic into new domains. Artists have not waited for theoretical justification in order to utilize the presence of smells in artworks. They have utilized perfumes, fragrant substances, atomizers and malodorous atmospheres regardless of the so-called impossibility of scents and the sense of smell to participate in aesthetic experience. One can understand the reluctance of philosophers writing before 1950 to admit a place for smell in art. While artistic engagement with scent extends back to the 1890s (and even to the Renaissance), these experiments were intermittent and often overlooked. In the aesthetic pluralism unleashed in the post-war era, scents have found surprising currency. Aromatic artworks strategically counteract the increasing virtualization of experience and the hegemony of visual media, as well as concentrate on everyday experiences and the actuality of materials. With the invention and development of accessible fragrance technologies, smells are easier to synthesize, diffuse and thus control. In the 1980s and 1990s the prominence of the body in artistic practice (and with it an intensified focus on the senses), as well as the entrance of non-Western artists into the mainstream artworld (exhibiting different cultural perspectives towards smell), have contributed to scent being more than just an anomaly or novelty. Fragrant artworks, in fact, have appeared in such numbers that it is now possible to conduct investigations into their unique characteristics (see Drobnick 1998, 1999, 2000). My goal in this text is not to analyse the literature on the aesthetics of smell, but to examine olfaction in art as it is actually practised, to start from a select group of odorous artworks and let them direct the discussion.

Organized into four parts, this article focuses on a specific "olfactory turn" in the visual arts – artistic engagement with issues of spatiality, e.g., in terms of landscape, architecture, or public space. The first section surveys aspects of the phenomenology and cultural politics infusing the intersection of spatiality and odours. The other three parts will elaborate genres of olfactory artworks that interrogate space in specific manners: "pungent loci" that mark and define locations by virtue of their exudations; works that foreground "olfactory affects," i.e., the emotional and psychological aspects of scent; and, finally, "dialectical odours" that disrupt and challenge the habitual functioning of spatial experience.

smellscapes

Many theorists of spatial experience gesture toward the necessity of understanding places via all of the senses, noting that something like synaesthesia or "simultaneous perception" is required (e.g., Hiss 1990; Abram 1996). Yet these theorists neglect to follow through and explore the ramifications of such statements, only to reiterate, ultimately, a methodology centred on visualist and discursive modes. A few examples of smells in certain locations – such as at a farm, bakery or paper mill – may demonstrate the point but leave the more challenging questions of what exactly these sensory experiences mean and how they factor into individuals' cultural and emotional lives unasked and unanswered.[3] What is required is a new field of inquiry, what I designate as *toposmia* (place+smell), which describes the spatial location of odours and their relation to particular notions of place. Contemporary artists are at the forefront of exploring the dynamics of toposmia, which implicate a number of disciplines, namely geography, cultural history, sociology, and urban studies, as well as aesthetics.

A first step in the toposmic understanding of place will be to define how olfaction alters or concurs with visualist studies of the landscape. J. Douglas Porteous, in coining the word "smellscape," initiates such an endeavour (1985, 362). Smells, he argues, unlike the information present in vision, yield experiences that are inherently discontinuous, fragmentary and episodic (i.e., time based). Intensity, complexity and affect replace considerations of perspective, scale or distance. And in contrast to being able to stand outside of a landscape and frame a view, smells are environmental and immersive: they are inhaled and thus become intimately bound with the body; they permeate the atmosphere and thus are inescapable; they are directly linked to the brain's limbic system and thus tend to evoke associations more emotional than rational (Porteous 1985, 359–60).

The causes giving rise to a particular smellscape are manifold: its position on the urban–rural–wilderness spectrum, distinctive flora or fauna, climatic conditions, level of industrialization, forms of habitation, sanitation practices, cooking customs, seasonal cycles, among others. As well, smellscapes may exist at varying levels of scale, i.e., continents, countries, regions, cities, neighbourhoods, houses, rooms, drawers.

Given the right climatic conditions, odours can easily travel over the physical barriers and visual markers that conventionally divide the landscape. The origin of a smell and the location of its ultimate perception may be separated by dozens of miles. Vision, then, is not the only "distance" sense, as smoke-spewing polluters may discover. Because of the "habituation effect," whereby the intensity of odours continually experienced in one's everyday environment decreases to the point of imperceptibility, most smells are noticed by visitors, outsiders, newcomers (Porteous 1985, 358). Odour is thus a key constituent (and marker) of encountering difference, a sensory fact often remarked upon in tourism promotions and travel literature. One need only scan travel sections in newspapers to verify the connections between odours and colonialism – in either creating fragrant, paradisiacal "eau-topias" or condemning non-Western locales as foul, uncivilized places.

In one sense, then, smellscapes are an aromatic variant of the picturesque – what I would call the *odoresque*. The odoresque could be defined as affective responses to place-specific smells that extend beyond the mere fact of noticing its identification with a certain location. Whether it is the mixture of incense, dust and the smoke from dung fires characterizing rural India, the composition of brine and seaweed prominent at a Nova Scotian seascape, or the stale, musty, rotted wood odours of an abandoned house, the odoresque engages with the spectrum of emotional–aesthetic experiences much like what is encountered when the term picturesque is invoked: experiences which range from the beautiful and memorable to the inspiring and sublime.

This is not to say, however, that this concept of the odoresque is a transparent one. As much as the genre of the picturesque has been deconstructed in recent critical art history, so too can the odoresque be subject to problematization. Implicit in the conceptualization of both the odoresque and smellscapes are notions that align, contradictorily, with humanist and radical perspectives. On the one hand, Porteous, along with Bachelard (1969), provides many examples of smell-saturated place descriptions, nostalgic reminiscences of pre-industrialized life, and poetic musings about childhood that might be said to portray a humanist orientation: in which smell is a neglected but rich dimension of experience that one should be aware of and sensitized to, which should be savoured and cherished. Odours, Bachelard writes, are "the first evidence of our fusion with the world" and "rare sublimators of the essence of memory" (1969, 136, 140). O.W. Milosz underscores the power of a re-experienced smell to encompass a multitude of childhood feelings:

> The foamy and somnolent odor of old lodgings is the same in all countries, and very often, in the course of my solitary pilgrimages to the holy places of memory and nostalgia, it was enough for me to close my eyes in some old dwelling to carry me back immediately to the somber house of my Danish ancestors and thus relive, in the space of an instant, all the joys and all the sadnesses of a childhood accustomed to the tender odor which was so full of rain and of the sunset in antique houses. (Quoted in Bachelard 1969, 137)

Like James Clifford's articulation of "the salvage paradigm" in relation to the cultures of indigenous peoples, the fragrant environment is often positioned as one in danger of being lost for ever. That the smells deemed imperilled are for the most part rural, natural and organic may strike a conservative (or Luddite) note to some, for along with the mourning of their passing into history a kind of "golden age" of environmental aromas is also imagined. Whether or not this prelapsarian time – the time before the processes of industrialization drastically altered the sensescape of cities and countrysides – was predominantly fragrant and pleasing is a matter for debate. Nostalgia all too easily creeps in, especially that form of "tender yearning" which mythifies some moment in the past as a stable, innocent, coherent or pure refuge in comparison to the present, a "domain of authenticity" (Rosaldo 1989; Frow 1991). Problems also arise because of the ease to which the humanist cherishing of smellscapes can be taken to another, more blatantly ideological, level, such as when Tuan (1995) attempts to make explicit links between sensory appreciation, beauty, morality and nationalism. The point is that the ephemerality of smellscapes demands an acknowledgment of their semiotic polyvalence – that because of their volatility, signification can never be objective, closed or definitive. As Doreen Massey (1995) points out, in many discourses on place, only "the past" is believed to embody its "real" character. Places, she argues, are conjunctions of multiple histories; they are essentially hybrid and continually in process. In regards to smellscapes, then, the radical flux of their existence forces acknowledgment of how they perpetually change and evolve according to natural, social and political forces.

To say this, however, is not to dispute the fact that an extreme diminution of smellscapes, and a desensitization of experience, has occurred because of the machinations of progress. An interest in smellscapes may be due to the increase in "blandscapes": those aseptic places, created by the modernist drive towards deodorization, that are so empty of stimuli that they lead to an alienating sense of placelessness (Porteous 1985, 368). The sanitizing imperative, in which all traces of the organic, not just waste, are eliminated from everyday life, leads to what Porteous calls *sensuous death*: "Because all environmental smells cannot be pleasant, we will have none at all" (ibid.). Homogenization and globalization also take their toll on the erasure of difference. Economic and market factors lead multinational corporations to instil a standardized sensory order at the expense of local cultures, whether it be in terms of what fruits and vegetables get grown and distributed, what flavours and fragrances are synthesized and packaged into foods and commodities, or what architectural styles and working conditions are favoured for the most efficient form of production (Seremetakis 1994). One cannot ignore the degradation of the natural habitats of the world via mining, deforestation and desertification, in which the ecological niches that support rare plants and flowers are rapidly diminishing. As well, smogification, whereby the diversity and subtlety of smellscapes, mostly in urban centres, are overwhelmed by odours of metal, oil and exhaust fumes, must also be addressed (Porteous 1985, 367).

On the other hand, when linked to a critique of some of the abuses of industrialization, a concern for smellscapes can embody a radical agenda. It is here that the reordering of the hierarchy of the senses overlaps with a programme to reorient the means and pursuits of the modern, Western society. Smellscapes cannot be isolated from social constructions of space which produce them, or from the practices of the body and the senses that create awareness of them. Marcuse argues that the proximity senses of smell and taste are subjected to a greater degree of repression since they offer pleasures that are too intense and bodily:

> Smell and taste, give, as it were, unsublimated pleasure *per se* (and unrepressed disgust). They relate (and separate) individuals immediately, without the generalized and conventionalized forms of consciousness, morality, aesthetics. Such immediacy is incompatible with the effectiveness of organized *domination* ... (Marcuse 1962, 36; emphasis in original)

Smells, in other words, are threatening because they easily subvert the regulation of emotions and behaviour supposedly necessary to societal organization. An appreciation of smellscapes, then, implicitly transgresses a number of social conventions in regard to enjoyment, discipline, functionalism, corporeal deportment. Oliver Sacks, for instance, in "The Dog Beneath the Skin," records the details of a man experiencing hyperosmia, a temporary intensification of the sense of smell, who could recognize every street, corner and store by its scent, and could unerringly navigate New York City solely by his nose. Despite the vividness of such a sensory skill – each smell was "unique, evocative, a whole world" – he hints at the potential for embarrassment and consternation it caused because he had to be careful not to indulge in his ability with others present lest it be judged "inappropriate" behaviour (Sacks 1987, 156–60). Psychiatrists in the nineteenth and early twentieth century labelled individuals expressing such an olfactory predilection with an obtuse, Latinate, and hence predeterminedly demonized, nomenclature: stercoraires, coprolagniacs, and so on (Krafft-Ebing 1965 [1886]). Even the police had a category of crimes attributable to "sniffers" – handkerchief thieves and personal space infringers who swooped down on customers (i.e., women) in department stores in order to smell their perfumed napes (Corbin 1986, 208–09). As deviant as these public acts have been made out to be, I would suggest that there is an untold, untheorized figure to be adumbrated who is the olfactory equivalent to the *flâneur*, namely that of the *flaireur*, or "smeller." It is none other than Baudelaire himself, arch exponent and definer of *flânerie*, who is a precursor, if not initiator, of *flairerie*, as hinted at in a line from his poem "Le Soleil" (Baudelaire 1936): "Flairant dans tous les coins les hasards de la rime," translating roughly as "Sniffing at every risk-filled corner for a rhyme" (Buck-Morss 1989, 185). Perhaps *flairerie* is merely a subset of *flânerie*, subject to the same origins within modernity, class structure, gender privilege and metropolitan spatial dynamics; yet it is entirely possible that *flaireurs*, despite their "inappropriate" and antisocial behaviour, could be considered pioneers in toposmia.

Mapping by smell may seem to be a task solely for the temporarily canine (like Sacks' patient) or for the marginal and suspicious *flaireur*, but for the Situationists exploring alternative pleasures of the city landscape, "urban ambiances" were central elements of their radical aesthetic. Although smell is not explicitly stated in Guy Debord and the Situationists' delineations of psychogeography and the *dérive*, hints of the olfactory and smellscapes are unmistakable: the usage of terms such as "distinct psychic atmospheres," "microclimates," "zones of influence" and "direct emotional effects" (Knabb 1981, 5–13) all point to a conception of the city as a complex sensory matrix that includes the presence of smell. Critical of the obsessively utilitarian and rationally designed city, the Situationists proposed, instead, an architecture fostering ecstatic, adventurous, disorienting experiences rather than ones that were conditioning, alienating, oppressive. The liberation of everyday life would be achieved in part by a "free architecture," one based on "the atmospheric effects of rooms, hallways, streets, atmospheres linked to the gestures they contain" (Knabb 1981, 23). One Situationist architect, Constant, imagined the possibilities of a participatory and ludic architecture, in which variations in temperature, lighting, humidity – and smells – could be experimented with and artistically orchestrated:

> The future cities we envisage will offer an original variety of sensations ..., and unforeseen games will become possible through the inventive use of material conditions, like the conditioning of air, sound and light. [Air conditioning] will offer the possibility of creating an infinite variety of ambience, facilitating the dérive of the inhabitants and their frequent chance encounters. The ambiences will be regularly and consciously changed, with the aid of every technical means, by teams of specialized creators who, hence, will be professional situationists. (Andreotti and Costa 1996, 94–95)

The Situationist ambition to map the ambiances of the city and revolutionize everyday life in the mid-twentieth century alludes, inversely, to the ambition enacted just prior to another revolution. In the late eighteenth century, Alain Corbin (1986, 27) notes, Paris stood out not only as the "center of science, arts, fashion, and taste," but also as "the center of stench." Whereas the Situationists desired to revel in the city's atmospheres, the reformers of the Parisian smellscape constructed maps of foul and putrid emanations in order to eradicate their ill effects. Thus began the period of "olfactory vigilance": an intolerance towards odours that initiated a massive reorganization of the urban environment and persists till the present day. While some aspects of this intolerance were justified by legitimate health concerns, it was also based on a mistaken theory of disease – in which doctors of the day blamed noxious airs and stinking miasmas as the causes of illness – which persisted in the public imaginary and still constitutes a driving impetus in the politics of space. Even in contemporary urban centres, the wealthy do not only typically live in the western ends of towns, upwind from factories and the poor, but also on higher ground, with better drainage and sanitation facilities; the poor, meanwhile, reside in lowlands and former swamps. Dyos and Reeder describe the characteristic olfactory outcome of this topographical schism:

> [T]he undrained clay beneath the slums oozed with cesspits and sweated with fever; the gravelly heights of the suburbs were dotted with springs and bloomed with health. (Quoted in Sibley 1995, 55)

If the recollections compiled by Porteous and Bachelard above reveal the profound extent to which odours are fundamental to topophilia, a love or extraordinary affection for places, the reverse could also be argued: topophobia can be a result of offensive smells. The contrast between stinking "ooze" and fragrant "bloom," and concomitant judgments about the people who live in each locale, hint at how the sense of smell can be harnessed for ideological ends. The material origins of odours have, at times, been employed to naturalize what is at root a socially manufactured division of space. The evidential immediacy of smells tends to justify not only essentialist views of inferior or superior places, but also desirable and undesirable people.

Because of such intertwinings of ideology and perception, using smell to define a place carries with it a number of problematic aspects. Distinguishing the differences between "place" and "space" has preoccupied geography theorists for several decades, partly because of the social sciences' bias for temporal paradigms over spatial ones, and because of the contestability of the terms' semantic connotations and conceptual overlappings. It is not possible to summarize the complexity of the place/space discussions in this text (see, for example, Bird et al. 1993; Duncan and Ley 1993; or Keith and Pile 1993), but I will make some brief comments on the relationship of smell to both terms of this binary. Unfortunately, there is no simple or clear influence of smell on this ongoing debate, since smell can be deployed discursively in a number of manners. Keith and Pile, for instance, describe the common meanings of the two terms (without, it must be added, arguing for their validity):

> [A] term like "place" triggers a chain of associations with parochialism, difference and ultimately reaction for some, and for others the term "space" may set off a more approbatory chain tied to transcendence, universality and enlightenment. (1993, 23)

Two pitfalls emerge from this normative description. The first relates to "place" being the repository for problematic ideas of fixity, authenticity, the true, the real – in other words, essentialism. Like the examples from Bachelard (1969), smells may indeed be a considerable support for essentialist understandings of place. That a mere whiff of a certain fragrance could bring one to re-enter a past world attests to the power of smell to be a key indicator of place, offering a kind of olfactory anchor for being-in-the-world. By contrast, an attention to smell and the complexity of smellscapes may also oppose such essentialist leanings. Attention to the temporal shifts in a smellscape, by hour, day, season or year, or to the diversity of odours present at any single moment, may be brought to bear to disrupt singular, static notions of place, and instead articulate a model that is heterogeneous, dialectical, impossible to fully or finally characterize.

The second pitfall relates to "space" being problematically conceptualized as rational, intangible, pure, transparent – in other words, abstract. As above, smell can be argued either to affirm or contest such a definition. Emanating from discrete objects and situations, smells can confirm the materiality of space. The immediacy of smellscapes and their implication of the body can be strategically utilized to reveal the repression of corporeality in Western thought and reverse geographers' trend towards denying how space is a mediated concept (see Rose 1993). On the other hand, smells may be synthesized and artificially disseminated in places they would never have been experienced. If smell is a means of simulated transport (remembering or evoking other times and places), technological expertise is already on the way to exploiting this capability, i.e., making space even more abstract by rendering it internal and virtual. Synthetic odours which replicate the ambience of specific locations, then, continue the trajectory of increasingly imaginary travel in which the traveller is immobilized and place is unimportant, with the end result that space is even further dematerialized.

It is perhaps to be expected that smellscapes would not resolve theoretical debates about such terminology, but rather provide room for extending and complexifying their scope. This variability of smell in relation to the problematics of place/space is not an impediment to toposmia, but an impetus for further research. Artworks operating at the conjunction of smell and location offer intriguing case studies in the variabilities of toposmia, especially since smell is utilized in self-conscious, strategic manners. Whether subtle or confrontational, these artworks demonstrate the ways in which smells influence how place can be perceived, fetishized and problematized. Below I will discuss three groups of artists' work: those in which smell serves as a "pungent locus," that is, employs odours to mark specific physical locations; those which work with "olfactory affect," or how aromas induce subjective, emotive identifications with place; and those that introduce "dialectical odours," fragrances which critically intervene into public situations and oppose overdetermining ideologies of space.

pungent loci

Defining places by physical, visual, kinaesthetic or discursive means – fences, lookout stations, paths, signs – are commonplace practices, ones that have been profitably appropriated by artists questioning the politics of looking and institutional appropriations of the landscape, among other issues. This tradition of "marked sites," as Rosalind Krauss (1985) has described as one of the "expanded" sculptural genres of earthworks, involves drawing attention to specific sites and contexts, pointing to certain features of the built or natural environment. In the non-invasive forms of the genre, it is a way of saying "Look here," "Notice this"; otherwise, it is an opportunity for the artist to occupy, transform, mark a location with a signifier of authorial presence – by digging holes, drawing lines, piling rocks, etc. The artistic markings I will be concerned with here, however, define physical parameters or concentrate upon a certain spatial specificity by the means of "pungent loci," an olfactory parallel to *genius loci* or "spirit of the place." Contrary to the egoism so often associated with monumental earthworks, artworks engaging with pungent loci could be hardly less self-effacing or subtle. Pungent loci, despite their sometimes dramatic locations, exist on the edge of abstraction and sensory awareness even as they mark or define the physicality of a place.

Odorous places, both foul and fragrant, have long been associated with spirits of various kinds, benign as well as malevolent. Temples have been built upon just such sites so as to honour or appease them. The artists below – James Lee Byars, Katharina Fritsch and Thomas Zitzwitz – work with pungent loci not to rejuvenate any particular kind of spiritual system but to utilize smell as an active, animating presence to mark a certain place, e.g., Byars' *The Drop of Black Perfume* (1983), a performance sited at Furka Pass, Switzerland, a gap in the mountains near the Rhône Glacier frozen for most of the year. Byars timed the event to occur on the first day of the Pass's opening for travel. Garbed in a gold suit and black top hat, the artist climbed "to the precipitous edge of a grassy slope, place[d] a drop of black perfume in a small depression of a large boulder," and exited (Elliott 1990, 131). Influenced by the Japanese tradition of monastic retreats in remote mountain landscapes for meditation, penance and purification, the artist's alpine act (an offering?) resonated with commemorative, ritualistic overtones. Despite the simplicity, even absurdity, of the gesture, it reverberated, in Byars' inimitable style, with shamanistic mystery. Mountaintops, subject to extremes of weather and unpredictable winds, are places that hardly require or are conducive to the civilizing intervention of a perfume, so Byars' esoteric performance operated on a more conceptual level rather than embodying a genuine effort to alter the olfactory character of the site. It referenced the mania once held for "the vivifying air of the mountains" in the eighteenth and nineteenth centuries when "the air cure" and mountain spas were popular for elites seeking to escape the urban congestion of the masses (Corbin 1986, 78, 256). Aerotherapy's "ascensional" aspirations evoked spiritual as well as physical benefits – namely rejuvenation and, by extension, resurrection – associations congruent with Byars' own mystical leanings.

Sited in an urban location, Katharina Fritsch's *Perfume in Hallway* (1984) transformed a liminal and unremarkable architectural feature into one haunted with significance. Located in the stairway leading up to the gallery, the fragrance greeted visitors in an anticipatory frame of mind – on their way to view art (or just after) but not quite in the conventional place of its display. The transitional nature of the space – between two floors, meant to be passed through not inhabited – was matched by an equally transitional artwork, one with varying intensities and dispersions, one ambiently present but with the potential to catalyse attention. The perfume thus performed something of an olfactory ambush, enveloping unsuspecting passers-by with a fleeting vapour existing on the edge of conscious awareness. Whether or not gallery-goers realized that the trace of a scent on the steps was intentionally art, the sensation that an individual had left invisible, aromatic evidence of their passing charged the stairway with an uncanny, even epiphanic, encounter. Like the stirring of a long-forgotten memory by the chance whiff of a particular fragrance, or the scented visitations recorded in ghost stories and after-death communications, Fritsch's rendezvous with an odour recast the steps and curving balustrade into a stage for confronting an ethereal otherness. With the simple addition of a perfume, Fritsch created a pungent locus that metamorphosed a functional aspect of institutional architecture into one resonating with allusions to passing strangers, absent bodies and mythical states of being.

Teresa from Madrid with Yellow Dress (1997), a domestic intervention by Thomas Zitzwitz, involved the application of seven smells to various portions of a New York City apartment, marking it into a series of distinct olfactory zones. Some smells, like "lipstick" at the bathroom sink or "brioche-cafe" in the kitchen, confirmed the smell one might expect at those locations. Other scents, such as "Arabian market," alluded to the geographical origins of objects (a rug) or to a prominent decorative motif ("narcissus" for flower-patterned bedsheets). Still others contradicted their locales, creating a kind of associational dissonance: "street after rain" near a bookshelf, "cedar wood" at a vanity table. These scents are unlike the instrumental aromas suggested by interior design doyens, such as Martha Stewart and her potpourris and wreaths that inundate a room with a uniform ambiance, instil ersatz feelings of "freshness" or "festivity," and testify to the ability of the resident to be a paragon of "gracious living." Instead, Zitzwitz's multiple aromas, spread amidst everyday, lived-in clutter, mark, divide up, and concentrate visitors' attention upon details and nooks of the apartment, rather than impose a spectacular effect. In fact, without prompting, it might be difficult to know for certain which smells the artist applied and which ones were already ambient in the space; in other words, all smells in the apartment are heightened. As a series of pungent loci, Zitzwitz's aromatized apartment frustrates any kind of one-to-one relationship between smell and place, and instead offers up a provocative chain of olfactory clues that cause one to contemplate the poetic and narrative logics (or illogics) of their placement (Zitzwitz 1999).

For artworks that feature pungent loci, even as the place is marked and defined, there is a challenging dynamic in operation: the figure–ground relationship so conventional for the privileging and experiencing of art is hopelessly problematized. In the next series of smellscape works, scents (or fragrant substances) are extracted from their environment, synthesized and/or commodified, so that the primary goal is an interrogative focus on the subject–object relationship of artist/viewer and smellscape.

olfactory affect

The contestation over definitions of "place," while emerging in spatial analyses in the middle of the century, have gained special emphasis in the postmodern era of global capitalism, tumultuous real-estate speculation, enhanced mobility and "schizophrenic" spatialities. David Harvey, for instance, attributes the significance of place to the fact that it is a radically threatened entity which can no longer be taken for granted:

> [W]hile the collapse of spatial barriers has undermined older material and territorial definitions of place, the very fact of that collapse ... has put renewed emphasis upon the interrogating of metaphorical and psychological meanings ... (1993, 4)

Places, then, without the conventional markers or stability for a Lynchean or Jamesonian "cognitive mapping," figure more prominently as an imaginary ideal to strive for, one in which, if created, is done so self-consciously. If no longer precise physical entities, places, as Harvey writes, are still "constructed in our memories and affections through repeated encounters and complex associations" (1993, 4).

For my understanding of "place," I would like to draw upon John Agnew's tripartite definition of it as an integration of location, sense of being, and locale – that is, one embodying objective, subjective, and social features. Places, in other words, are situated in physical settings that can be geographically distinguished from other locations, exhibit some recognizable sense of identification or "structure of feeling," and connect its residents in some way by forms of everyday practices and activities that relate them socially (Agnew 1993, 263). Smells, undoubtedly, can feature prominently in each of these three categories, but the one I'd like to discuss in this section is the second: structure of feeling and its extension into the realm of smell, or what I designate as "olfactory affect."

Raymond Williams' provocative but polysemic concept, "structure of feeling," has been useful to discussions of "place," and further confirms the significance of smell in topographical studies. As the description of the "inalienably physical" and "effective presence," structure of feeling relates to those qualitative aspects of lived experience that resist representation, which exist "at the very edge of semantic availability," and reflect emergent sensibilities, as opposed to the solidity of a worldview or ideology (Williams 1977, 128–35). By combining the contradictory terms "structure" and "feeling," a productive tension is created between the analytical and the amorphous world of the everyday, thought and emotion, the concrete and the intangible. While Williams illustrates structure of feeling with examples from drama and literature, I would propose that smell, too, even without an established artistic tradition, can serve likewise. Numerous examples, such as the "somnolent odors" of old houses in Bachelard (1969) and the fragrant farms in Porteous (1985), attest to how smell, as much as a script or novel, can evoke and encode the feelings of not only a certain place but also a specific time.

My construction of the term "olfactory affect" is indebted to Williams, but also Lawrence Grossberg's (1997) rethinking of structure of feeling as it is embodied in his elaboration of "affect." Affect overlaps to some degree with Williams' term – by referring to the everyday, the unrepresentable, the emotional – but it also differs in that its application is broader; not having to define an entire period, affect can be employed on a smaller, more idiosyncratic, scale to explain particular attitudes and moods. My notion of olfactory affect draws from both theorists to try to express how the artistic engagement of smellscapes operates at that contradictory intersection of lived experience, states of feeling, and non-signifying sensations that nevertheless communicate something important about a place or period.

For Williams, art played an important role in defining new structures of feeling. Progressive and challenging art carried with it a "generative immediacy" in which "experience, immediate feeling, and then subjectivity and personality are newly generalized and assembled" (1977, 129–33). Artworks described by the term olfactory affect use smell as an "effective presence" and try to articulate what Williams would call "emergent" sensibilities – articulations of private consciousnesses that have yet to be conventionalized or systematized in the social imagination (ibid.). The artists below – Oswaldo Maciá, Kate Ericson and Mel Ziegler, and Rebecca Belmore – convey the "scent of a place" as a particular configuration of private interpretation and communal meaning. Each sets out to explore the aromatic means by which identification occurs and what consequences it may have. By isolating certain odours, creating a selective blend that mimics a specific mise-en-scent, or by physically removing and transporting aromatic sections of a place, these artists address not only the experience of olfactory affect but also its social and political dimensions.

Oswaldo Maciá's *1 Woodchurch Road, London NW6 3PL* (1994–95) is a sculptural installation that selects and highlights the odours of a small apartment complex in north-west London. A home for the artist, it was also the residence for singles and families, harbouring a mix of generations and cultural backgrounds. The neighbours included people of Irish, Lebanese and English ancestry (the artist himself was born in Colombia), and so offered a range of cuisine preferences, consumer practices, grooming habits and domestic situations. The five garbage cans of the piece present a cross-section of the smells Maciá found most provocative and characteristic of the building and its occupants: naftalin (mothballs), olive oil, Listerine, eucalyptus, baby powder. Visitors to the installation lifted the top of the cans (akin to the artist's own method of research) to inhale the vaporous substances. In a kind of sociological shorthand, Maciá's olfactory clues hint at the personalities and lifestyles of his neighbours, whether it be that olive oil connotes a Mediterranean sensibility or that mouthwash evidences an excessive concern with personal hygiene (Maciá 1999). If smellscapes bear a tendency towards essentialism, the polyodorous *tranche-de-vie* of the dwelling at 1 Woodchurch Road reveals the degree to which "place" is necessarily composed of a plurality of identities. While the smells are incommensurable, a fact underlined by the condition that they must be sampled individually, Maciá's construction of olfactory affect is one in which odours coexist in a unique, heterogeneous mix. The community represented here may not abide by all of the utopian psycho-emotional presumptions of place – such as rootedness, wholeness, purpose, security, for there are hints of irreconcilable differences – but it is a sniff of a certain location, a sense of a specific conjunction of people at a particular time and engaging in the everyday practices of living, that nevertheless transpires to form a small-scale, if diversely constituted, community.

Olfactory affect takes on a fetishistic twist in two works by Kate Ericson and Mel Ziegler that synthesize and bottle the distinctive scents of the National Archives in Paris and Washington, DC. *Etes-Vous Servi?* (1992) appears in an edition evoking a sense of indulgent luxury – an etched glass bottle on a silver platter, with a spate of bookmarks conveniently provided for diffusing the scent. The identifying odour of the French

National Archives – a mixture of decaying leather and paper, mustiness and sweat, created in collaboration with a scent expert, a "nose," from Nina Ricci – captures the essence of the building by virtue of its distinctive olfactory affect. Conjuring up the aristocratic world of Proust or Huysmans' Des Esseintes, the Archive's "odour *sui generis*"4 is distilled and refined, seemingly to be given out like olfactory hors d'oeuvres, liqueurs or snuff at an upscale salon event or exclusive cocktail party. In contrast to these allusions of privilege, the odour of the Washington archives of *The Smell and Taste of Things Remain* (1992) is presented in a manner which underscores a democratic, even folksy, demeanour. Its scent, created with perfumer Felix Buccellato and bearing a more musky character, is contained within eighty jars and secured in a late nineteenth-century pie safe. The bottles bear the sandblasted names of four hundred pies garnered from recipes representing geographic and cultural regions across the country – evoking the tastes as well as smells of daily life that are impossible to archive.

Both pieces demonstrate the lapses in preserving historical artefacts and the politics evident in collecting certain forms of cultural heritage over others (Weintraub 1996, 212–17; Ziegler 1998). As the archetypal representative of the everyday, the sensual and the ephemeral, smells are the unarchivable other to the official, preservable, commodity realm of material culture. Yet the odours of disintegration foregrounded in these works intimate that not only are smells subject to dissipation and forgetting, but every culturally produced object is ultimately destined to decompose. As much as the archives intend to instil a sense of stability to the ideology of the nation, the "smell of history" is an insistent reminder of mortality and impermanence. Ericson and Ziegler's olfactory affect demonstrates that despite the state's concerted efforts to produce a cumulative and lasting inheritance, the overpowering result is the "perfume of decay" redolent in these archives' reading rooms and bookshelves.

The olfactory affect of Rebecca Belmore's work is not due to the synthesis and blending of scents, but the physical relocating of a place's fragrant materiality. *Wana-na-wang-ong* (1993)

drobnick

is an installation that surrounds visitors with the natural aromas of woodland flora from Sioux Lookout, Ontario, home to the artist and traditional territory of the Anishinabe people. The fragrance of cedar envelops the exhibition, in the form of a bowl of finely ground powder at the entrance and hot tea served on a cedar plank table at the exit. A crescent of sand makes literal the Anishinabe title, translated as "a dip or curve in the land" (Martin 1993). The centrepiece of the installation is a set of suspended panels composed of spruce roots, lichen, peat moss and club moss that work like a pair of parentheses to create an intimate space full of the fragrance of soil, woods, and plant life. The floor of the forest is here pivoted ninety degrees into a vertical position, placing our faces in direct contact. The sylvan aroma, the silence, and veritable palpability of this chamber evokes, as Martin (1993) and other commentators have noted, the sensation of being underground. If Freud is taken at his word and civilization depended on the assumption of an upright posture and the lifting of the nose from the ground – thereby diminishing the role and importance of smell (1961, 46n) – then Belmore's upended slice of earthiness is a decivilizing act, one that overturns the objectification of the Western eye for the connectivity of smell. *Wana-na-wang-ong* exemplifies a relation to land based on principles other than real-estate development, resource extraction or touristic consumption. As much as the affinity between "native" and "land" can be romanticized (Townsend-Gault 1994), Belmore's installation invokes the political struggles over land claims as well as the cultural struggles of First Nations' peoples for a sense of identity. It is the immersion into a place's smell, and its primal olfactory affect, that provides *Wana-na-wang-ong* with an expressive power to convey an inarticulable knowledge of place, one that is the basis for both sacred and secular attachments to the land.

dialectical odours

Places, besides having physical and subjective dimensions, are also defined ideologically. Theorists of public space, especially as it is embodied in cityscapes, unavoidably have to address space in its mythical discursive form – neutral, universal, transcendent – because that is the predominant method by which power constitutes, reproduces and legitimates its own self-interested uses of space. Advocates of "uneven development," privatization, gentrification, or just a "well-managed city," prefer to construct space as an entity beyond mere contingency and the particulars of special interest groups. Permeating such discourse is the language of objectivity, functionality, coherence and rationality – all terms which tend to essentialize space and elide the social, conflictual processes by which space is manipulated. In her deconstruction of the rhetoric arguing for "intrinsic uses" and transparent practicality of urban spaces, Rosalyn Deutsche insists that "the notion that the city speaks for itself conceals the identity of those who speak through the city" (1986, 109). The ideology of space thus consistently denies its historical and exclusionary nature, making architecture and urban planning an ambient but effective means for social control.

My term "dialectical odours" describes the strategic use of smell as an intervention into and means to critique such abstract or essentialist political conceptions of space. It draws from Walter Benjamin's concept of the "dialectical image" – an image which, in his words, "interrupts the context into which it is inserted" and so "counteracts illusion" (cited in Buck-Morss 1989, 67). The dialectical image exists at the intersection between the poles of dream and wakefulness, the wish for utopian fulfilment of desire and the consciousness of socio-historical and political reality. The dialectical image is one that "crystallizes antithetical elements" and refuses to cohere into a unified presence (ibid. 67, 210). For Benjamin, "where thought comes to a standstill in a constellation saturated with tensions, there appears the dialectical image. It is the caesura in the movement of thought" (ibid. 219). This caesura is not a passive moment, but one which involves a shock of recognition, one which startles its viewer into a politicized "awakening" (ibid.). Dialectical odours, then, contest the "dream odours" (or non-odours) of a sanitized and neutral space. They contradict the conventional assumptions of place and space, render

them more openly schizophrenic, introduce complexes of competing meanings, draw out the implicit political dynamics which construct spatiality. Dialectical odours remain unreconciled to their location, unharmonized to the ambiance of the architectural environment. Notions of place are problematized and estranged. At their best, they create a perceptual and cognitive dissonance not unlike the Brechtian method of defamiliarization.

Because of the success that architecture has had in instilling what Rodolphe el-Khoury (1997) terms an "olfactory silence" in urban and domestic domains, it may be said that any smell inserted into the built environment could work against the grain of deodorization and function dialectically. Odours do not even have to be extraordinary; banal or pleasant scents may cause as much consternation and disapproval as unusual or putrid ones. The work I will focus on here will concentrate on one genre of architectural space – the bathroom. The utilization of odours by Judy Chicago, Janet Murray and Mark Lewis – odours which are either strategically out of context or being returned to where they have been repressed – interrupt the habitual and smooth functioning of the spatial ideology of domestic and institutional lavatories and problematize their status as hygienic, desensualized, and sexually differentiated. The dialectical odours in these artists' works corrupt the neutrality and functionality that conditions the experience of the bathroom.

The figure of the woman in her boudoir or toilette has been a common pictorial genre catering to the male voyeuristic gaze. Whether it is Hogarth's "fallen woman" vainly trying to cover syphilitic sores with make-up, Degas' soapy bather intimately and unsuspectingly observed kneeling in a tub or Wesselman's fully frontal but faceless nude towelling dry in the shower, the female in the bathroom has been continually subject to pornographic or misogynist representations – all signifying, none too subtly, that the feminine condition is inherently "unclean." Women's bodies, strategically, are thus absent in Judy Chicago's *Menstruation Bathroom* (1972), and so frustrate the co-opting male gaze. The installation avoids the problematics of representing women's bodies or a single portion of the body (i.e., vagina) that were to trouble the reception (by both conservative and feminist critics) of Chicago's later central-core imagery and *The Dinner Party*. But what is present, smells and abject materials, graphically conveys the battle women are ideologically forced to wage with their bodies – between cleanliness and disgust, purity and filth (see, for example, McHugh 1997). Odours are literally set against one another, blood vs. disinfectant, with neither being able to overcome the other: a wastebasket, brimming with used tampons, stands in a sterilized bathroom beneath a shelf glutted with commercial feminine hygiene products. As much as menstruation was a hidden and shameful activity, one that must be dealt with behind closed doors (Raven 1994, 55), Chicago unflinchingly addressed its taboo status in a public forum:

> [*Menstruation Bathroom* was] very, very white and clean and deodorized – deodorized except for the blood, the only thing that cannot be covered up. However we feel about our own menstruation is how we feel about seeing its image in front of us. (Quoted in Broude and Garrard 1994, 57)

The smell and traces of blood, what Chicago called the "unmistakable marks of ... animality" (1977, 106–07), bring menstruation out from obscurity and denigration and into the realm of unprejudiced fact. If Germaine Greer suggested tasting menstrual blood to overcome feelings of disgust (1971, 51), smelling it can also strike at internalized repulsion and somatophobia. The dialectical odour of the tampons confronts the ideologically charged space of the bathroom and its role in sustaining women's self-policing and shame. By asserting its presence, occupying space, refusing to be summarily eliminated, the smell of menstrual blood can serve in the process of reclaiming and reaffirming the body's corporeality.

Janet Murray's pair of bathroom installations also addresses the experience of shame and attempts a kind of reconciliation with that which has been banished or repressed. *Expulsion from Paradise* (1998) intervenes into the antiseptic utopia of the restrooms at Toronto's Metro Hall.

Eden is partially re-created in a women's stall featuring bulrushes, water lettuce, wild ginger, lilies and birds of paradise, permeating the air with a floral bouquet. The men's lavatory likewise teems with an eclectic plenitude of nature – club moss, cacti, spider plants and Spanish moss – which exudes a refreshing, verdant challenge to the acrid smell of urinal disinfectant. These miniature oases, nestled in deserts of sanitization, seek a reconciliation of sorts between the indoor and the outdoor, deodorized culture and the aromatic bounty of nature, the germ-free and the life-sustaining. Reconsidering the abject status of waste, *Expulsion*'s porcelain plantings revive a prelapsarian view of human integration with the surrounding environment: where excretion, rather than signifying pollution, sin and debasement, is an inherent (even nourishing) feature of the cycle of life. Murray's ersatz ecosystems mix vegetation from diverse temperate zones, giving the arrangements an outlandish heterogeneity. This sense of transgression also applied to the other "result" of the Biblical expulsion, the reinforcement and hierarchization of sexual difference. The temptation to visit both bathroom installations apparently was too great for many viewers, and men and women often surreptitiously ventured into the other's loo for a peek and a sniff of greenery (Murray 1999). Dialectically, the conflicting odours redolent in Murray's restroom ikebana draw attention to and confound the socio-religious judgments dividing the damned and sterile from the innocent and fertile, blocking the process of elimination and turning it into one of cultivation.

Architecture's role in regulating gender is the focus of Mark Lewis' *Une Odeur de luxe* (1989), installed at Montreal's Mirabel Airport. Bathrooms are the classic places for training and disciplining the body, for composing one's self and appearance for social engagements, and for demanding abidance to the law of gender. Lewis' dialectical odours work contrary to those that merely mask untoward odours; they attempt to expose and corrupt the ideology of sexual difference and what Lacan terms "urinary segregation" (1977, 151). By atomizing women's perfume in the men's bathroom and men's cologne in the women's, Lewis interrogates the politics of identity construction and its performative maintenance. Texts affixed to mirrors and stalls such as "Your scent was blocked by the exudations of the crowd, fragmented and crushed by the thousands of other city odours" and "The rank stench of your excitement is clearly visible" makes visitors self-conscious of the scents present in the environment and exuding from their own bodies (Lewis 1994, 67). The exchange of fragrances sets up an encounter between visual and olfactory forms of self-surveillance, opposing what one sees in the bathroom mirror to what one sniffs as one's smell-persona. This scent-tainted revisitation of the "mirror stage" – or what Johanne Lamoureux (1994, 17) calls *"le stade de la rose"* (after Condillac's famous statue that confused itself with the smell of the flower) – rather than providing a coherent, stable sense of self, seeks to overpower and disrupt the logic by which gender is rehearsed, monitored and reproduced. *Une Odeur de luxe*'s transgendered diffusions of odour, rendering each space (and each person within it) olfactorily hermaphroditic, forces a confrontation with architecture's role in naturalizing sexual difference as a universal and inevitable binary opposition. With a few odoriferous puffs, Lewis' cross-scented interventions not only question the architectural segregation of gender, but also gender itself as an immutable categorization of individuals. Striking at the most concrete signifier undergirding the stability of gender, *Une Odeur de luxe* creates an atmosphere of ambiguity that erases the certainty of a singular gender identity, and instead posits ones that are fluid, multiple, layered, volatile.

conclusion

Directly contrasting the assumptions that smells are passive elements of sites, residual presences without significance or mere decorative embellishments, artists working in a toposmic mode recognize the active, expressive and conceptual roles that scents can command. Through pungent, affective and dialectical means, olfactory artworks extend and reconceive visualist approaches to landscape, architecture and public space. Despite a multitude of deodorizing campaigns over the past two centuries, the artis-

tic engagements described above demonstrate that volatile effects persist and are an inevitability in both natural and built environments. Spaces and buildings remain redolent with characteristic and identifiable auras, and these olfactory traces harbour a potential for a variety of aesthetic and critical strategies.

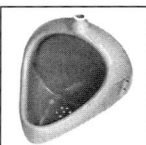

notes

1 I would like to thank *Angelaki*'s anonymous reviewers for their constructive and supportive criticism.

2 See, for example, Hegel (1988, 622, 729), Korsmeyer (1975), Kovach (1974), Osborne (1979), Prall (1967), and Rindisbacher (1992).

3 Besides Porteous, below, exceptions to this state of theorization can be found in Classen et al. (1994, 97–99) who discuss the importance of smell in several indigenous societies' conception of space and place, and Tuan (1995).

4 This phrase is borrowed from Corbin (1986, 26).

bibliography

Abram, D. *The Spell of the Sensuous*. New York: Vintage, 1996.

Agnew, J. "Representing Space: Space, Scale and Culture in Social Science." *Place/Culture/Representation*. Ed. J. Duncan and D. Ley. New York and London: Routledge, 1993.

Andreotti, L. and X. Costa (eds.). *Situationists*. Barcelona: Museu d'Art Contemporani, 1996.

Bachelard, G. *The Poetics of Reverie*. Trans. D. Russell. Boston: Beacon, 1969.

Baudelaire, C. *Flowers of Evil*. Trans. G. Dillon and E. St. Vincent Millay. New York and London: Harper, 1936.

Bird, J. et al. (eds.). *Mapping the Futures*. New York and London: Routledge, 1993.

Bourdieu, P. *The Rules of Art*. Trans. S. Emanuel. Stanford: Stanford UP, 1995.

Broude, N. and M.D. Garrard (eds.). *The Power of Feminist Art*. New York: Abrams, 1994.

Buck-Morss, S. *The Dialectics of Seeing*. Cambridge and London: MIT P, 1989.

Chicago, J. *Through the Flower*. Garden City: Anchor, 1977.

Classen, C., D. Howes and A. Synnott. *Aroma*. London and New York: Routledge, 1994.

Corbin, A. *The Foul and the Fragrant*. Cambridge: Harvard UP, 1986.

Croce, B. *The Aesthetic as the Science of Expression and of the Linguistic in General*. Trans. C. Lyas. Cambridge: Cambridge UP, 1992.

Deutsche, R. "Uneven Development: Public Art in New York City." *Out There*. Ed. Russell Ferguson et al. New York, Cambridge and London: New Museum of Contemporary Art and MIT P, 1986.

Drobnick, J. "Reveries, Assaults and Evaporating Presences: Olfactory Dimensions in Contemporary Art." *Parachute* no. 89 (1998): 10–19.

Drobnick, J. "Recipes for the Cube: Aromatic and Edible Practices in Contemporary Art." *Foodculture*. Ed. Barbara Fischer. Toronto: YYZ, 1999.

Drobnick, J. "Inhaling Passions: Art, Sex and Scent." *Sexuality and Culture* 4.3 (2000): 37–56.

Duncan, J. and D. Ley (eds.). *Place/Culture/Representation*. New York and London: Routledge, 1993.

el-Khoury, R. "Polish and Deodorize: Paving the City in Late Eighteenth-Century France." *Assemblage* no. 31 (1997): 6–15.

Elliott, J. *The Perfect Thought*. Berkeley: University Art Museum, 1990.

Freud, S. *Civilization and Its Discontents*. Ed. and trans. J. Strachey. New York: Norton, 1961.

Frow, J. "Tourism and the Semiotics of Nostalgia." *October* no. 57 (Summer 1991): 123–51.

Greer, G. *The Female Eunuch*. London: Paladin, 1971.

Grossberg, L. "Postmodernity and Affect: All Dressed Up with No Place to Go." *Dancing in Spite of Myself*. Durham and London: Duke UP, 1997.

Harvey, D. "From Space to Place and Back Again: Reflections on the Condition of Postmodernity." *Mapping the Futures*. Ed. J. Bird et al. New York and London: Routledge, 1993.

Hegel, G.W. F. *Æsthetics*. Vol. II. Trans. T.M. Knox. Oxford: Clarendon, 1988.

Hiss, T. *The Experience of Place*. New York: Vintage, 1990.

Huysmans, J.-K. *Against Nature*. Middlesex: Penguin, 1959.

Keith, M. and S. Pile (eds.). *Place and the Politics of Identity*. New York and London: Routledge, 1993.

Knabb, K. (ed. and trans.). *Situationist International Anthology*. Berkeley: Bureau of Public Secrets, 1981.

Korsmeyer, C.W. "On the 'Aesthetic Senses' and the Development of the Fine Arts." *Journal of Aesthetics and Art Criticism* (Fall 1975): 67–71.

Kovach, F.J. *Philosophy of Beauty*. Norman: U of Oklahoma P, 1974.

Krafft-Ebing, R. von. *Psychopathia Sexualis*. Trans. F.S. Klaf. New York: Bell, 1965 [1886].

Krauss, R. "Sculpture in the Expanded Field." *The Originality of the Avant-Garde and Other Modernist Myths*. Cambridge and London: MIT P, 1985.

Lacan, J. "The Agency of the Letter in the Unconscious or Reason Since Freud." *Écrits*. Trans. A. Sheridan. New York: Norton, 1977.

Lamoureux, J. "Mark Lewis and the Pollution of Monuments." *Mark Lewis*. Vancouver: UBC Fine Arts Gallery, 1994.

Lewis, M. "Une Odeur de luxe." *Mark Lewis*. Vancouver: UBC Fine Arts Gallery, 1994.

Maciá, O. Interview with the author (April 1999).

Marcuse, H. *Eros and Civilization*. New York: Vintage, 1962.

Martin, L. "The Language of Place." *Wana-na-wang-ong: Rebecca Belmore*. Vancouver: Contemporary Art Gallery, 1993.

Massey, D. "Places and their Pasts." *History Workshop Journal* no. 39 (1995): 182–92.

McHugh, K. "One Cleans, the Other Doesn't." *Cultural Studies* 11.1 (1997): 17–39.

Murray, J. Interview with the author (June 1999).

Osborne, H. "Odours and Appreciation." *British Journal of Æsthetics* 17.1 (1977): 37–48.

Piesse, C.H. *Piesse's Art of Perfumery*. London: Piesse and Lubin, 1891.

Porteous, J.D. "Smellscape." *Progress in Human Geography* 9.3 (1985): 356–78.

Prall, D.W. *Aesthetic Judgment*. New York: Crowell, 1967.

Raven, A. "Womanhouse." *The Power of Feminist Art*. Ed. N. Broude and M. D. Garrard. New York: Abrams, 1994.

Rindisbacher, H. *The Smell of Books*. Ann Arbor: U of Michigan P, 1992.

Rosaldo, R. "Imperialist Nostalgia." *Representations* no. 26 (Spring 1989): 107–22.

Rose, G. "Some Notes Towards Thinking about the Spaces of the Future." *Mapping the Futures*. Ed. J. Bird et al. New York and London: Routledge, 1993.

Roudnitska, E. *L'esthétique en question*. Paris: Presses Universitaires de France, 1977.

Sacks, O. "The Dog Beneath the Skin." *The Man Who Mistook His Wife for a Hat and Other Clinical Tales*. New York: Harper, 1987.

Seremetakis, C.N. *The Senses Still*. Chicago: U of Chicago P, 1994.

Sibley, D. *Geographies of Exclusion*. New York and London: Routledge, 1995.

Synnott, A. *The Body Social*. New York and London: Routledge, 1993.

Townsend-Gault, C. "Rebecca Belmore." *Parachute* no. 74 (1994): 41–42.

Tuan, Y.-F. *Passing Strange and Wonderful*. New York, Tokyo and London: Kodansha International, 1995.

Weintraub, L. *Art on the Edge and Over*. Litchfield: Art Insights, 1996.

Williams, R. *Marxism and Literature*. Oxford: Oxford UP, 1977.

Ziegler, M. Interview with the author (September 1998).

Zitzwitz, T. Interview with the author (June 1999).

Jim Drobnick
2208 Marcil
Montreal, QC
H4A 2Z1
Canada
E-mail: j_drobnick@compuserve.com

The utmost care has to be taken in the use of words, never using them before the epoch in which they came into the general circulation of ideas, otherwise we shall immediately be accused of an anachronism, which, amongst the reprehensible acts in the terrain of writing, is second only to plagiarism.

Plagiarism is necessary. Progress implies it.

ANGELAKI
journal of the theoretical humanities
volume 7 number 1 april 2002

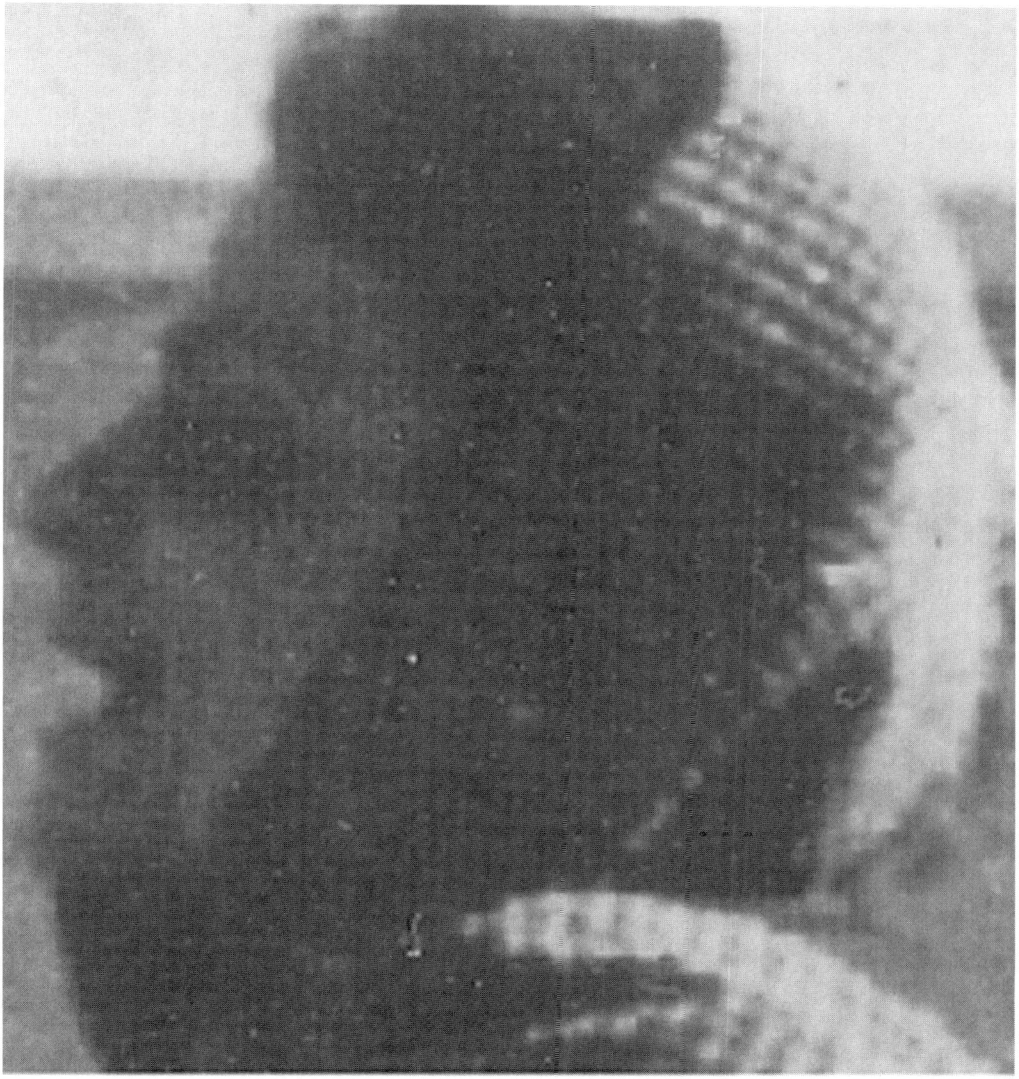

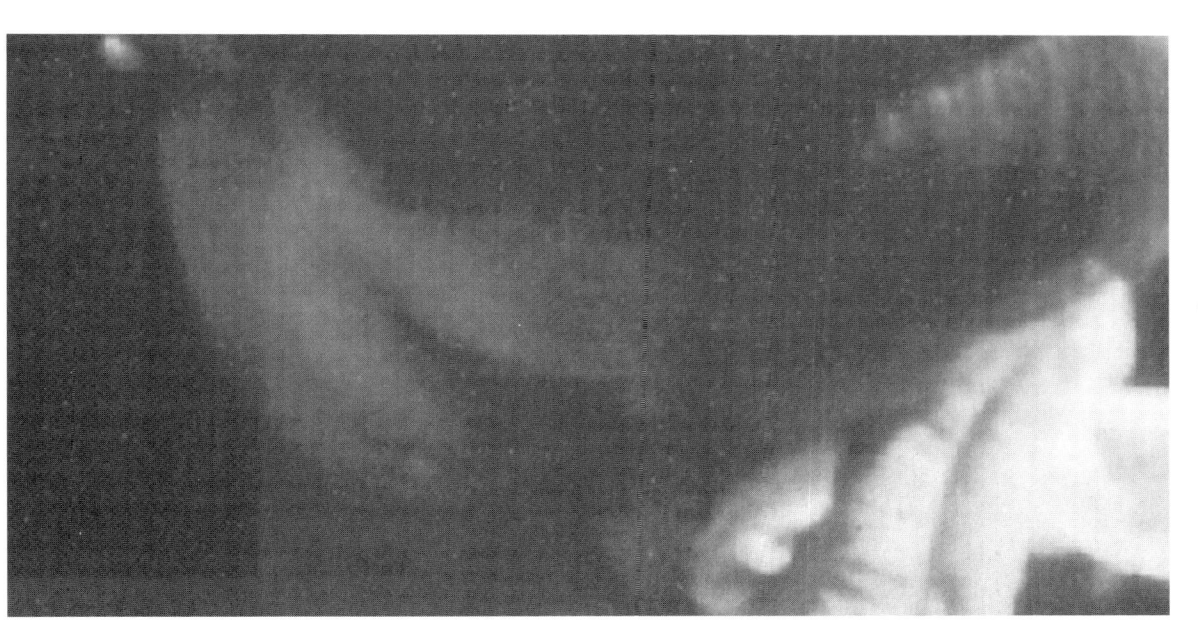

joanna hodge

WHY AESTHETICS MIGHT BE SEVERAL

> A French politician once said it was a special characteristic of the French language that in French sentences words occurred in the sequence in which one thinks them.
> *Wittgenstein*, Philosophical Grammar, sect. VI, 66, 107[1]

I

> Art disengages the senses from signification, or rather, it disengages the world from signification, and that is what we call "the senses" when we give to the (sensible, sensuous) senses the sense of being external to signification. But it is what one might just as correctly name the "sense of the world". The sense of the world as suspension of signification – but we now understand that such a "suspension" is touch itself.
> *Nancy*, The Muses 22[2]

These remarks proceed in four artificially demarcated stages, which then unsurprisingly recoil on their own starting points, throwing their order, individuation and any gesture of cumulative reasoning into disarray. This then reveals a tension in the thought of teleology, which is to be set out in this first section or stage: that it is both presupposed and disrupted in the very practices of argumentation and exposition of argument. This disruption is marked up here by a juxtaposition of citations, a translation of a remark of Jean-Luc Nancy (1994) about an ambivalence in the meaning of the word "sense" and one from Ludwig Wittgenstein, again in translation, on a supposed distinctiveness of the French language. The relation between language and sense, and between language as such and language as translatable will turn out to be instructive towards the end of these remarks.[3] Teleology has in any case, and in standard dictionary definitions,[4] an inbuilt oscillation between designating a system of ideas, a science of ends or completions, and being that system of ends itself: those ends and completions as exhibited in natural objects and in the phenomena themselves. This dictionary ambiguity then resonates with the danger looming within the account of teleology as set out in Kant's *Third Critique*,[5] that the critical distinction between a knowledge of things as they appear and a knowledge of things in themselves may be eroded or may be thought to have been eroded. This ambiguity then revolves on not marking a distinction between a critical and a dogmatic deployment of the notion of teleology.[6]

There is for these remarks a further tension within the notion of teleology to be displayed,

ISSN 0969-725X print/ISSN 1469-2899 online/02/010053-14 © 2002 Taylor & Francis Ltd and the Editors of *Angelaki*
DOI: 10.1080/0969725022014056

concerning the scope of the movement of completion. For there is both a thought of teleology as concerned with a unitary finality, providing a conception of a unity of a world of thought and experiences with the domains of action; and a thought of teleologies as a dispersal of infinitesimally differentiating finalities, achieved and achievable in any fulfilment of meaning intentions, but not in themselves providing access to a unified and ontologically grounded account of what there is, as unified and ontologically grounded. This is the distinction between the idea of teleology as deployed in the Kantian system, concerned with thinking the relations between nature and reason, and the teleologies of Husserl's phenomenology,[7] and its analyses of the conditions under which there are fulfilments of meaning intentions.[8] Out of this second tension or ambiguity in the logic or grammar of teleology there arises the question of the availability of a theory of knowledge, and indeed of what Kant explores through the notion of critique, a knowledge of the scope and limits of what can be known, for if the domain within which knowable relations occur is neither delimited nor delimitable, then while there may be knowledge of those relations, the lack of knowledge of their place within the domain in which they occur might destabilise that local knowledge, rendering it subject to radical revision. Thus there are two levels to any problem of knowledge: a problem about the knowability of discrete states of affairs and a problem about the status of these states of affairs.

The account of teleology generated out of the tradition of aesthetic writing, from Baumgarten to Kant, and from Nietzsche to Adorno, then, makes aesthetic enquiry a competitor with logic and theories of meaning as a site at which to respond to this second-order problem in the traditional philosophical questioning of the possibility of knowledge, about the nature of reality and the availability of a conception of truth. Thus the question about the plurality or severality of aesthetics masks a question about the difference between a theory of aesthetics which concerns itself only with art and one which concerns itself also with providing such a challenge to the right of logic to prevail as the discipline in which the question of the possibility of knowledge, an account of the nature of reality and a thinking of truth might be developed.[9] Teleology provides Kant with an answer to this second-order problem about knowledge, a problem to which Husserl responds through his account of the projection, in retention and protention, of horizons of understanding. It is the concept of teleology, for Kant, and the concept of horizons for Husserl which guarantees that medium-sized dry goods can be reliably expected to stay where they were last seen to be and guarantees that the worlds synthesised by each bearer of a transcendentality of apperception, and the worlds constituted by the bearers of intentionality, are common to those engaged in the synthesising constituting activities in question.

In the *Critique of Judgement*, in his observations "On the Various Systems Concerning Purposiveness in Nature" (sect. 72, 270–73), Kant introduces the notion of a technics of nature, which provides the critical system with an idea, but not a concept, of the productivity and uniformity of nature. This technics, which shows how the whole is to be thought of as a whole, will be contrasted in the second stage of these remarks to "another thinking of technique" proposed by Jean-Luc Nancy in his essay "Why Are there Several Arts and Not Just One," from which the epigraph to this section of the paper is taken. The identification of such a technics of nature is an important result for the Kant of the account of aesthetics and of teleology in the *Third Critique*. The account of aesthetics shows how there can be a deployment of the faculties, with no hierarchical organisation subordinating their interplay to one of their number. This non-hierarchical deployment of the faculties permits the emergence for thought of the idea of purposiveness in artworks and in the natural world, and its thinkability as a unity. This then provides Kant with a response to questions about the shared or intersubjective nature of the world and justifies the transition from hypothesising knowledge of objects of experience to hypothesising knowledge of objects. The account of the faculties then becomes demonstrably one where the faculties do not simply legislate to experience, but are also capable of responsiveness to what is given. The analysis of the faculties as both legislative and as responsive to and in harmony with an objectively given order of things leads Gilles Deleuze (1963)[10] to hypothesise that for Kant the notion of faculty must have two quite distinct senses. Beatrice Longuenesse (1993)[11] responds by distinguishing between a faculty, as a capacity for judgement, which has the status of an unactualised potentiality (*Vermoegen zu urteilen*), and a power of judgement, *Urteilskraft*, which enacts what it proposes, and for which a gap between the intention and the fulfilment does not arise. This is a difference between the power analysed at rest, as a static system of endowment, and these powers understood to be always in some series of dynamic interconnections one with another. This power to judge, which enacts what is proposes, takes the form of constitutive judgement in the *First Critique*. As will emerge in the third stage of these remarks, the performative of reflective judgement has a different formation.

A capacity for judgement as unactualised potentiality can be thought only if a system of the faculties can be brought to a standstill for the duration of the analysis, sufficient to render it simply an object of thought, no longer interacting with the processes of thinking, or of meaning constitution. This, then, is the remarkable achievement of Kant's exposition in the *First Critique*, which holds the faculties up for inspection while all the same deploying them in the thinking which it performs. This is the rationale for the careful distinction between the mathematical and the dynamical categories and principles, a move replicated in Kant's *Prolegomena* between analytical and synthetic modes of exposition;[12] and, indeed, in the *Third Critique* in terms of the mathematical and the dynamical sublime. Synthesis is a dynamic process in which the faculties interconnect; whereas analysis views these processes from the outside as though they were not in play in the very process of thinking the relations under discussion. The difference between the two groups of categories, then, is that the articulations of the latter, relation and modality, assume a system in process, whereas the former, quantity and quality, can be analysed only when abstracted from their contexts of actual deployment, and only in relation to an artificially stabilised context of analysis.[13]

The third section of this analysis will consider some of the implications of different performative structures for the "faculties" in their different deployments, in relation to the forgoing discussion of teleology and technique. The fourth section of these remarks will then be taken up with discriminating between the scopes of various different notions of aesthetics, and coming to some conclusion about whether aesthetics are indeed plural, or whether some underlying unity may be discovered. It will turn out that the main line of contention falls between Hegel and Heidegger on one side who appear to suppose, if for different reasons, that there is such a unity underlying any appearance of plurality, between which some kind of decision might have to be made; and, on the other, Kant, Wittgenstein and as it would seem Jean-Luc Nancy who appear to be committed to the thought that there are distinct deployments of the term "aesthetics." There is then also a decision to be marked between Kant and Nancy: where the writings of Nancy recoil back on those of Kant and displace them.[14] This recoil may be of the order of throwing into question the division basic to the *Third Critique* between the techniques of art and the technics of nature. For once the sensory organs are rethought as transcendental condition, as transcendental touch and, as we shall see, voice as condition for language, the distinction between nature and artifice is suspended along with the sense of the world.

The possibility will be canvassed that an understanding of the distinctnesses of natural languages may assist in thinking the status of these distinct deployments, in line with the suggestion made in the epigraph to this essay, taken from Ludwig Wittgenstein's *Philosophical Grammar*, published posthumously from notebooks dated 1932 and 1933. The spectacle of French philosophers required to learn English in order to a discuss Wittgenstein with his English-reading advocates is of course one of the more comical diversions of the day. More seriously, there is a question about the distinct philosophical potentials of the grammars of the distinct natural languages, which awaits arbitration. This, then, would link in to current discussions about the multiple or single origination of the human species and the potential for resistance to racial hierarchisation to be found in the thought of such mulitiplicity.[15] There is the old question about whether the multiplicity of languages poses a problem for knowledge which only a theorising of knowledge arising from the tradition of aesthetics, by contrast to the logical tradition, can begin to address. For this thinking of aesthetics offers a transcendental ground for meaning, which cannot be appropriated by any one language group, by contrast to the equivocations about the possibility of ascribing meaning to logical formalisation, and the scope of the supposed universal languages of symbolisation already in play from the time of Leibniz. The order of discussion here then is teleology, technique, faculty, aesthetics and then briefly, and by way of a concluding remark, language.

II

> Technicity itself is also the "unworking" of the work, what puts it outside itself, touching the infinite. Their technical unworking incessantly forces the fine arts, dislodges them endlessly from aestheticising repose. This is also why art is always coming to its end. The "end of art" is always the beginning of its plurality. It could be the beginning of another sense of and for "technics" in general.
> "Technique" is a rule for an end. When the end is in-finite the rule must conform. In a sense, this is a summary of thinking about art since romanticism – since the infinitisation of the ends of man.
> Nancy, The Muses 37

These four stages of rumination then begin with these considerations of the notion of teleology and now the focus for attention transfers to the notion of technique. The notion of "unworking" here in the citation invokes the discussion between Nancy and Blanchot on the withdrawal, retrait, of community, as the hidden ground of possibility of meaning and politics. For it is because we do not agree in judgements that we have language and meanings, in which the differences can become emergent. Nancy's essay "*La Communité desoeuvrée*," translated as "The Inoperative Community"[16] in the book of that name, deploys the term in its title, to the effect of marking up a notion of community which does not and cannot work to unify, but rather marks the withdrawal of such unity. It would also perhaps be helpful at this juncture to interleave a remark on the thinking of ends in Heidegger's thinking of the emergence in the twentieth century of the possibility of a new beginning for philosophy, or rather "another beginning," in which a return to the Greek origins of philosophy might make it possible to take up again the task of thinking set out at its inception among the Greeks. In the history of the transmission of this inception, according to Heidegger, the task of thinking has become obscured by the reification of responses and attunements to that task into supposedly definitive answers to questions. This "other beginning" is offered but not delivered by Heidegger in the incomplete enquiry begun in his *Being and Time* (1927) and is reiterated in various different registers, both before and after that publication, and perhaps most emphatically in the posthumously published texts from 1936 to 1938, *On Enowning: Contributions to Philosophy* (1989).[17]

The notion of "another beginning" thought in this way has a double implication tying it back into the question of teleology: that finalities and fulfilments presuppose inceptions and intentions; and that the question of finality for Heidegger is inseparable from a question about the fate of philosophy, in which the destiny of being and the erring of human beings are caught up in recurring relations of misrecognition. For Heidegger, there is an organic process of generation and decay to systems of thinking such that they have their moment and then fall back into a loss of lucidity, demanding a rethinking and retrieval by those who seek to receive the tradition. It would then be possible to interleave here a reading of Heidegger's later essay "The End of Philosophy and the Task of Thinking" (1964)[18] as a description of how philosophy accomplishes itself, how philosophising achieves philosophical status and a capacity to advance theses, by losing contact with its origins in specific occasions for registering an inexhaustible perplexity. Conversely, the task of thinking imposes itself ever anew and the results of philosophy have to be rethought on each occasion. Thus the notion of finalities is to be supplemented not so much with a notion either of inception or of intention but of in-finite undertaking, taking up again and again the task of accounting for knowledge and making sense. This is the Derridean indeed the Husserlian interruption of the processes of articulating philosophical theses by the claim to attention of the event or moment of their being thought, through which and only through which they have meaning.[19]

For Heidegger the arrival of the epoch of technology in the age of the world picture erases this claim for attention for the moment of meaning: as Jean-Luc Nancy puts it, sense goes missing.[20] Heidegger's papers on technology, most notably "The Question of Technology" (*Die Frage nach der Technik*),[21] develop this account by identifying the danger of supposing there to be one privileged technique for articulating all relations between knowing and what is known, in place of a multiplicity of such techniques, each refined in relation to the requirements and scope of a variety of distinct, indeed unique, activities. There is then a transition to be marked up from Kant's invocation of a technics or technique of nature from which human beings can learn about the nature of what there is, to this notion of technology, which for Heidegger blocks understanding, to a redeployment of the notion of technique in the thinking of Jean-Luc Nancy, as marked up in the epigraph at the beginning of this section. This then provides the backdrop for the second stage of these remarks, which consists of an attempt to release some of the implications for aesthetics of Jean-Luc Nancy's essay, "Why Are there Several Arts and Not Just One (Conversation on the Plurality of Worlds)" (1994). Since this essay proceeds by explicitly invoking a three-step move from Kant, to Schelling, to Hegel, on the thinking of the plurality of the arts, and frames this by a juxtaposition, on one side, of the names of Heidegger and Adorno and, on the other, of the names of Wittgenstein and Deleuze, any such attempt must be more than usually mortgaged in advance to its own inevitable inadequacy.

The essay is located, furthermore, between Nancy's interactions with the aesthetics of Kant and with the writings of Blanchot, and is closely aligned to his own concurrent work, published in *The Gravity of Thought* (1993), *The Sense of the World* (1993) and, more recently, *Being Singular Plural* (1996). The subtitle of this essay would also deserve a long exposition, with its joint invocation of Heidegger's use of the notion of "conversation," *Gespraech*, to break up any sense that language is a monological formation, and of Blanchovian "entretien infini," each of which is in turn quite distinct from the notion of dialogue in Plato's writings. The location of Nancy's writings in the register of non-finite dialogue, close to those of both Blanchot and Wittgenstein, is worthy of more detailed consideration than is suitable here. However, it is important to remark the difference between plural voices in conversation where that plurality does not presuppose determinate and fixed identities for empirically given speakers, by contrast to a dialogue as a discussion between actually existing speakers. The former draws attention to a feature of language as shared and as a site for the articulation and constitution of subjective differences and identities; whereas the latter reports on an exchange of views held presupposing a notion of subjectivity as the site for the articulation of such opinions. Nancy, Wittgenstein, Blanchot, and Heidegger are clearly thus far in agreement that understanding language cannot presuppose but must rather show the emergence both of concepts of subjectivity and of subjectivity itself. The remarks in this paper propose that the same must be true for understanding artworks; that a theory of subjectivity and of individuation cannot be presumed to be set out in advance of aesthetic theorising and activity.

To foreclose the dimensions of commentary, then, it is worth stating this single aim: to discover a contribution in Nancy's questioning of the several status of the arts to a questioning of the several status of aesthetics. Nancy moves from Hegel's rejection of a mapping of the plural status of the arts on to the plurality of the human sensory faculties,[22] to a reflection on the multiplicity of technique, which then prompts Nancy to hypothesise "another sense of technique," by contrast to both the Kantian notion of technics and to the Heideggerian "another beginning." There is here, then, a threefold series of levels concerning plurality and severality: the natural endowment of human sensation in the sense organs as plural; the dissemination and stabilisation of techniques into distinctive artistic practices and genres of art, and the question for this essay, the status of aesthetics as one, more than one, less than one, or, as Nancy would have it, as an irreducibly plural unity: the singular plurality, which he takes to be distinctive of twentieth-century thinkings of being.23

In this marvellous essay, which could generate a series of footnotes as long as the history of aesthetics, Nancy arrives at the following reflection: "Therefore the world is dislocated into plural worlds, or more precisely into the irreducible plurality of the unity 'world': this is the a priori and the transcendental of art" (18). A question to be posed here is whether there is a tension between the grammar of the several, introduced in the title, as invoking a logic of multiplicity, and the grammar of the plural, which permits a reintroduction of a non-multiple unity, in place of a unity as a play of differences. The latter, a play of differences, guarantees a displacement of the unities of Hegel's aesthetics by the singularities of their advent. Nancy quotes Wittgenstein from *Remarks on Colour* (1977), to draw this contrast: "Imagine someone pointing to a spot in the iris in a face by Rembrandt and saying "the wall in my room should be painted this colour" (50–51 E), and he then proceeds to consider the operation of the plurality of the arts, in four moments.24

The first is introduced thus: "This plurality," Nancy writes, "breaks down the living unity of perception or action" (21). The second: "While so doing, art dislocates 'common sense' or ordinary synaesthesia, or it causes itself to touch itself at an infinity of points or zones" (22). The third: "But while so doing, this dis-located synaesthesia, properly and technically analysed, sets off as well, not another synthesis, but a reference, or, in Baudelaire's terms, a response from one touch to another" (23), or indeed a correspondence, as this movement has become known in English. And fourth, "Thus," Nancy continues, "the arts are first of all technical …" (24). It should be noted that these four remarks proceed in the order of the Kantian categories of quantity, quality, relation, modality: but with a difference. For this discussion is concerned with questions of ontology, and not simply with an analysis of the nature of judgement, and technique takes the place of a discussion of necessity.

He continues: "Technique is the obsolescence of the origin and the end: the exposition of the lack of ground and foundation, or that which ends up presenting itself as its only 'sufficient reason', experiencing itself as radically insufficient and a devastation of the ground, of the 'natural', and of the origin" (26). "This is why here is not 'technique' but 'techniques' and why the plural here bears the 'essence' itself" (26). So this is certainly not Heidegger speaking and for fear of there seeming to be an unmarked return here behind Heidegger to Husserl, Nancy is then careful to indicate a limit to phenomenology. For the notion that the grammar of the plural here bears the "essence" itself suggests such a return. These, then, are the four moments in the distribution of the operation of the plural of the arts, and the role of the remark from Wittgenstein in permitting this catalogue to be presented while holding off the threat of a reification, not foreclosing the scope of the enquiry is worthy of attention.

Nancy sets out a contrast between the teleologies of good and bad infinities, where the teleology of the bad infinity promises a completion, but not for us. The resolution of the antinomy between good and bad infinity permits a thinking of completion where the distinction between the bad and the good infinite is subverted into the thinking proposed by Nancy, in company with Lacoue-Labarthe, of the in-finite: the non-finite, which arrives in finitude. This is the Husserlian hope, to be contrasted to that of Kafka: the hope which does arrive. The paragraph which begins with the epigraph at the beginning of this section ends:

> To overcome romanticism is to think rigorously the in-finite which is to say its finite, plural, heterogeneous constitution. Finitude is not the deprivation but the in-finite affirmation of what incessantly touches on its end:

another sense of existence and by the same token, another sense of technique. (*Muses* 37)

The disaggregation of technology into this other sense of technique is then to be paralleled by an enquiry about the status of the faculties: whether at one extreme they too similarly disaggregate into a plurality in unity, for which the named faculties are only approximations, or whether at another extreme, and contra Kant, they can be tied back into a single originating power, as a strong interpretation of the role of the transcendental imagination as ground for the transcendental unity of apperception would imply. For another sense of technique still in liege to such a transcendental unity of apperception in which the faculties are organised in a single given hierarchy would still be the subordination of art and judgement to knowledge and the workings of the understanding. This subversion of Kant's pluralising intent may paradoxically be the upshot of Heidegger's reading of the *First Critique*.[25]

III

> Art disengages the senses from signification, or rather, it disengages the world from signification, and that is what we call "the senses" when we give to the (sensible, sensuous) senses the sense of being external to signification. But it is what one might just as correctly name the "sense of the world". The sense of the world as suspension of signification – but we now understand that such a "suspension" is touch itself.
>
> Nancy, The Muses 22[26]

It is now perhaps possible to reread this epigraph with a greater sense for what is in play in terms of an invocation and suspension of transcendental philosophy, both that of Kant and that of Husserl, and in terms of an invocation and suspension of the thoughts and mobilisations of teleology and technique. In this section, I return to the relation between the senses, in the plural, as the five human sensory faculties, sight, hearing, touch, smell, taste, and sense as intelligibility, as marked out in this epigraph. That the distinction between empirical faculties and powers of the mind appears to rest on a body–mind distinction may turn out to be a cause of some of the emergent confusions. Nancy asks: "what is the aisthesis of significance? what is the receiving organ? and What is its sensation, what taste does sense have and what tongue?" (28). Here it would be possible to interleave a reading of Derrida on "Economimesis" and the exemplorality of the Kantian text.[27] Nancy adds in an appended footnote, number fifty-three:

> This question gets multiplied right away: what aspect for which eye, what smell for which nose, what sound for which ear, what consistency for which touch, what movement for which kinoreceptor, and so forth. The philosophical and poetic tradition will have exhausted all these possibilities. (111)

The tense here, of course, is important: it is the mark of the incompleteness of the traditions of philosophy and poetry that poetry and philosophy have not as yet explored, let alone exhausted, all these relations and possibilities. And the move from the plural to the multiple is also worthy of remark.

The empirical faculties listed here appear familiar, and are certainly fivefold, but there is a puzzle. Those that are listed are sight, smell, hearing, and then there is the puzzle, for instead of the expected taste and touch, there are instead two place holders for touch, one for consistency and one for movement, with no place holder for taste. This marks up the further puzzle that for Kantian aesthetics, as remarked by Derrida, one of the five, taste, gets selected out, *pars pro toto*, and judgement in matters of aesthetics is supposed to be a matter of good taste, as opposed to good hearing, or good smell, or sight, or indeed touch. So one of the moves Nancy is making here is to question the privilege to taste over the other four empirical faculties, by installing instead touch, "le toucher" of Jean-Luc Nancy. Before continuing an exposition of Nancy's disruption of Kant, however, a further clarification of the relation for Kant between the empirical and the transcendental faculties is in order.

In the First Introduction to the *Third Critique*, Kant introduces the powers, or faculties, or indeed abilities and habits, of the mind in the following way: "We can reduce all the power of the human mind, without exception to these three: the cognitive power, the feeling of pleasure and displeasure and the power of desire. It is true that philosophers who otherwise deserve unlimited praise for the thoroughness in their way of thinking have asserted that this distinction is only illusory, and have tried to bring all powers under nothing but the cognitive power. Yet it is quite easy to establish, and has in fact been realised for some time, that this attempt to bring unity into that diversity of powers, though otherwise undertaken in the genuine philosophical spirit, is futile" (sect. 3, "On the System of All the Powers of the Human Mind," CJ 394), and indeed for Kant as futile if the privileged power is supposed with Heidegger to be imagination as if it is taken to be understanding. Kant thus insists on a certain plurality, and sets out the differences thus:

> For there is always a great difference between presentations insofar as, on the one hand, they belong to theoretical cognition, when they are referred merely to the object and to the unity of consciousness these presentations contain – or similarly, insofar as they have objective reference, when they are considered at the same time as cause of the actuality of this object and are included with the power of desire (a power which can give rise to practical cognition) – and, on the other hand, presentations in so far as they are referred merely to the subject, for here the presentations themselves are bases merely for preserving their own existence in the subject, and in so far are considered merely in relation to the feeling of pleasure; but this feeling neither is nor provides any cognition at all, though it may presuppose cognition as a basis that determines it. (395)

This, then, is the source of the distinctions drawn by Deleuze in his book, *Kant's Critical Philosophy*, between the three faculties of cognition, of desire, and of pleasure and displeasure. Deleuze then seeks to move this affirmation of plurality into the transformed mode of multiplicity.

In that study, Deleuze cites this differentiation almost verbatim (3–4) and then continues:

> It is a matter of knowing whether each of these faculties – on the basis of the principle in terms of which it is defined – is capable of a higher form. We may say that a faculty has a higher form when it finds in itself the law of its own exercise (even if this law gives rise to a necessary relationship to one of the other faculties). In its highest form, a faculty is autonomous. The *Critique of Pure Reason* begins by asking: "Is there a higher faculty of knowledge?", the *Critique of Practical Reason*: "Is there a higher faculty of desire?", and the *Critique of Judgement* "Is there a higher faculty of pleasure and pain?"

As a consequence of this enquiry there emerges a number of higher interests: that of a speculative interest in phenomena; that of a practical interest in the determination of the will and a third interest in thinking a systematic plurality as indicating a system of ends: "The idea of a systematic plurality and hierarchy of interests – in accordance with the first sense of the word 'faculty' – dominates the Kantian method. The idea is true principle, principle of a system of ends" (7).

Deleuze then draws the contrast between the first and the second sense of faculty: "In the first sense 'faculty' refers to the different relationships of a representation in general. But in a second sense 'faculty' denotes a specific source of representations. Thus there are as many faculties as there are kinds of representation." He then distinguishes between one passive faculty of reception, intuitive sensibility, and three active faculties as sources of real representations. "There are thus three active faculties which participate in synthesis, but which are also source of specific representations when any one of them is considered in relation to any other: imagination, understanding, reason." Deleuze then gives brief chapters on the deployment of the faculties in each of the three critiques and concludes his bravura account of Kant's system by considering Kant's claim that humanity is the final end of divine creation. Deleuze is fairly evidently in disagreement both with the notion of creation and with the notion that humanity might be its end; thus the book is an exercise in exposition of a system supposed by the expositor to be misguided, for reasons presented by Deleuze in other texts and which cannot be explored here.

Kant goes on to remark that while the power of cognition has its a priori principles in pure understanding, and the power of desire has its a priori principles in pure reason, "What is more natural than to suspect that judgment will also contain a priori principles for the feeling of pleasure and displeasure?" (396). He continues:

> while in the general division of all the mental powers both the cognitive power and the power of desire have an objective reference in the presentations, the feeling of pleasure and displeasure is only the subject's receptivity to a certain state (*Bestimmung*). Therefore, if the power of judgment is indeed to determine (*bestimmen*) anything on its own, then presumably this can only be the feeling of pleasure; and conversely, if the feeling of pleasure is indeed to have an a priori principle, then presumably we can find it only in the power of judgment. (396)

This *Bestimmung*, too, would deserve close attention since here the voice (*Stimme*), another technique of orality, to be contrasted to taste, makes itself heard. It is in the next section of this introduction that Kant moots the suggestion that the technics of nature as "nature's causality regarding the form that its products have as purposes" is to be discovered by grasping the significance of the technics of judgement, "So it is usually the power of judgment that is technical; nature is presented as technical only insofar as it harmonises with and so necessitates that technical procedure of judgment" (408). And he goes on to clarify:

> A judgment about the objective purposiveness of nature is called teleological. It is a cognitive judgment, yet it belongs only to reflective not to determinative judgment. For nature's technic as such, whether it is really formal or real, is only a relation of thinking to our power of judgment. In this power only can we find the idea of a purposiveness of nature and only in relation to this power do we attribute this purposiveness to nature. (409)

Thus the technics of nature is referred back to a technique of judgement.

The three relations between faculty and its objects are deduced from the table of categories from the *First Critique*, of inherence and subsistence; of causality and dependence, and of community and reciprocity. The relation relevant for the *Third Critique* is that of community and reciprocity in the harmonisation of the faculties so important for the determination of aesthetic judgement. This should provide a clue for the manner in which this account, while allowing a democracy among the higher faculties, all the same subordinates the empirical faculties to these higher mental faculties without further explanation of how the mental powers are related or not related to the empirical powers. The crucial move is made in the amalgamation of the five senses into the neutral-sounding *Empfindung*, sensation, of the *First Critique*, which provides Kant with the basis for setting up the passive faculty of sensible intuition.

Since this is a move common to empiricist and rationalist philosophers alike, it is not perhaps surprising that Kant should also make it, but the upshot of Nancy's readings here is to put it in question: can the five empirical senses be taken for granted and aggregated in this way, and then subordinated to the supposedly philosophically more significant workings of the so-called higher faculties? Perhaps here is the place to raise a question to the distinction between the two senses of faculty as drawn by Deleuze. For both presuppose the stability of the distinction between legislation and reception; and between higher and empirical powers of faculties. Perhaps there is here a third sense of faculty: one for which the two functions distinguished by Deleuze, and indeed by Kant, are not distinct: one for which there can be no distinction between the intent and the fulfilment. And such a third meaning would both affirm and unravel the distinction between the first two meanings: a sense, which undoes sense.

With this question Kant's critical philosophy is both thrown into crisis and shown to be precisely the horizon of possibility within which that question can be raised: providing the horizon of possibility within which Nancy's remarks, and indeed these responses to them, can take place. For the upshot of the analysis of the supersensible of the *Third Critique* may well be, as Nancy suggests, to install a return of the specificity of the so-called lower empirical senses. The supersensible, the *uebersinnlich*, is that which is in excess of the empirical senses: it is an intensification of the empirical sense, and gives the empirical senses the capacity to reveal meaning, or sense, in the second sense of intelligibility. It is not supernatural, it is transcendental. The fulfilment of the intent of the empirical senses is then intelligible sense. But the invention of new sense must have some new configuration of sensibility at its origin. Thus it is the deployment of the empirical senses, in innovative configurations, which are the conditions for the emergence of the artworks and of new genres, which inaugurate the rule for future activity, the cause of which Kant calls genius.

This genius, however, may simply be a special case of a play of the empirical faculties which continually comes up with new combinations, only some of which emerge for attention and valorisation but all of which are continually expanding and varying the human repertoire of experience. In so doing they actually change the configuration of the empirical faculties. Thus more remarkable than the artistic invention is the resulting reordering of the empirical faculties and of what they suggest the order of things to be like. This remarkable feedback of reordering may also take place in the reorganisation of ordinary language in its continual everyday reconfigurations and this lesson of a feedback from a reordering of language, to a reordering of sensibility, to a reordering of how the world is supposed to be, may be what an understanding of meaning or sense in natural languages might teach us. This, then, would suggest that artistic activity is best understood as a special case of understanding meaning in language, where both language and artistic activity is understood as irreducibly plural, indeed with art as plural, aesthetics several and languages as multiple.

IV

Anything can be a picture of anything, if we extend the concept of picture sufficiently. If not, we have to explain what we call a picture of something, and what we want to call the agreement of the pictorial character, the agreement of forms.

For what I said really boils down to this: that every projection must have something in common with what is projected no matter what is the method of projection. But that only means that I am here expanding the concept of "having in common" and am making it equivalent to the general concept of projection. So I am only drawing attention to a possibility of generalisation (which of course can be very important).

Wittgenstein, Philosophical Grammar, sect. IX, 113, 163

Kant's transcendental philosophy provides the horizon for Nancy's thinking and for these remarks; this then raises a question to the status of the transcendental aesthetic of the *First Critique* as the place within which the Kantian critical system takes place. The forms of intuition as the inner sense of time and the outer sense of space introduce a third notion of sense, alongside the two already identified. They are distinct, for this inner sense is developed by Kant into the form of the transcendental unity of apperception, and subsequently by Heidegger into the site of articulation of auto-affection, the self-touching of temporalisation; whereas the form of outer sense presumably articulates into the five familiar empirical senses, namely touch, hearing, sight, smell, taste. At this point the splitting of touch into two, introduced by Nancy, becomes less puzzling: what he has done is to mark up the difference between the empirical touch, responsive to empirical consistencies and a transcendental touch concerned with a movement, in general and at its purest, as the movement of the syntheses out of which the transcendental unity of apperception emerges. And a third touch makes itself felt, one which is concerned with that other kind of consistency: the possibility of coherence and of orderly thought at all.

This separation of empirical and transcendental touch, of the five outer senses from the one inner sense, is disturbed by the articulations of the power of desire, and perhaps by Heidegger's insistence on reading inner sense as the multiple strands of temporalisation. This separation cannot be taken as given for the analysis of the *Third Critique*. It is for this reason that the role of the aesthetic of the *Second Critique* is crucial in bringing together the aesthetics of perception of the *First Critique*, for which there is a distinction between empirical and transcendental sensation, and the aesthetics of taste and judgement of the *Third Critique* in which precisely the questions of the condition for thinking, movement and sensation are brought back together again. The binding of the drives of the *Second Critique* permits a transition from the incipient disorder of the *Third Critique*, to the affirmation of ordered knowledge of the *First Critique*. In the three critiques the drives, or abilities, or habits, or modes of movement of the soul are bound in different ways, but the possibility of that binding is demonstrated, if at all, in the *Second Critique*.

For Kant there are three instances of the aesthetic, one in each critique, which align to his thinking of the distinctions between the faculties, and of the distinctive functional relations between the faculties in the distinct critiques, and at this point for the word critique, the word technique might be substituted. For these remarks, too, there are three meanings of aesthetics in play, but they are not grounded in this play of the faculties, the status of which remains open to question. There is aesthetics as a theory of fine art; there is aesthetics as a competitor with logic and theories of meaning for a thinking of the possibility of knowledge and of meaningfulness; and here is aesthetics as a topological theory, that is a theory of the morphology and structural movements of thought, about the limits or horizons within which thinking finds its orientation. In the discussion of technique, the first meaning of aesthetics comes to the fore; in the discussion of faculties, the second meaning of aesthetics came to the fore, but in this section, it is this third meaning of aesthetics which is dominant, in a formulation of an aesthetic imperative, which gives the rule for future existence and by so doing brings it into existence.

V

If voice says nothing, that doesn't mean that it doesn't name. Or at least, it doesn't mean that it doesn't clear the path for naming. The voice which calls, that is to say the voice which is a call, without articulating any language, opens the name of the other, opens the other to their name, which is my voice thrown in their direction.
Nancy, Birth to Presence 245

In this earlier paper cited here, "Vox Clamans in Deserto,"[28] Jean-Luc Nancy constructs a multivoiced survey of contributions to a thinking of voice and retrieves a notion of voice as a transcendental condition given in advance of actual speech and of actual languages. A dialogue is staged in which a series of announcements declare an interest for each of a series of named authors in the question of the relation between voice and speech and meaning, but each time without references. This perverse ventriloquism assigns words to names and taunts the reader to undertake the task of first finding and then checking the references. Of course, such finding and checking would be to miss the point, which is rather that each of these citations, each lacking references, is either distinctive of the bearer of the name in question, or not; that the thought bears the signature of its thinker whether a name is cited or not and irrespective of whether or not the lines are to be found in some text, authorised or unauthorised.

The names Saussure, Valery and Rousseau are allowed to set the scene, the names Mozart, Verdi and Schubert interrupt any privilege to the discursivities of literature and theorising. Rousseau, famously a theorist of distinctive musical styles, is quoted to the effect that there are three kinds of voice, the discursive, the melodic and "*la voix pathetique ou accentuée*" (BP 236). From this melee, Nancy takes a step back and derives the observation: "Voice is always shared, it is in a sense sharing itself. Voice begins where the retrenchment of the singular being begins. Later, with speech he will recreate his ties to the world and he will give meaning to his own retrenchment. But to begin with, with his voice, he cries out in pure disparity, which has no distinct meaning" (BP 237). This, then, is the voice of the prophet crying in the wilderness, *vox clamans in deserto*, unheard or not understood. Which makes it all the stranger that those two great writers of the desert, Nietzsche and Heidegger, each wandering solitary, if with different vectors and investments, should not be cited here in this dialogue, Nietzsche not named at all and Heidegger only as writer of dialogue (BP 240). *Die Wuste waechst:* the wastelands grow.

Nancy, the dramaturg of this scene, asks of the bearer of this voice: "then he isn't called by anything, not even his name. It is the voice alone, which says nothing but which calls out?" and then comments:

> the voice calls the other nomad, or else calls him to become a nomad. It throws out the name of a nomad, which is a precession of his proper name. Which prompts him to leave himself, to give his voice in turn. Voice calls the other to come out in his own voice. Listen. (BP 245)

The call of a silent voice, articulating in advance of speech and language, resonates with Heidegger's diagnoses of the call of conscience (SZ, sects. 55–58), which calls silently from nowhere other than the self, to the self to affirm its becoming self: "*der Ruf kommt aus mir und doch ueber mich*" (SZ 275). But the name of the nomad, left unnamed since it is the name of a displacement of philosophy itself, might more likely be thought to be "Nietzsche" than "Heidegger," with the name "Heidegger" here carefully circumscribed by those of the other writers of dialogue: "Plato, Aristotle, Galileo, Descartes, Heidegger" (BP 240), an at first sight surprising list.

However, the unnamed voice of Nietzsche might well be thought to call Heidegger to a greater nomadism than allowed for in the register of the affirmations of a gathering together of beings, in the logos as *Sammlung* (gathering),[29] invoked in *Introduction to Metaphysics* (GA 40).[30] May this voice, still unnamed in *The Muses*, also be thought to call Nancy, too, to a greater nomadism? Derrida, in an aside in 1980, returns the question to Nancy in advance: "The question concerns also the distinction between the voice of reason and the voice of the oracle. (Perhaps here I shall echo without being sure I am responding to, the questioning, the injunction, or the request Jean-Luc Nancy addressed to me the other day.)."[31] The example of Nietzsche, as indeed the example of Wittgenstein (*Muses* 20): "is not chosen at random: it is art and art precisely in the detail of its technique (but 'detail of technique' is a pleonasm) or art as technique of the detail, that is of difference and discreteness, that makes visible local colour, or makes visible that colour is only local."

For Derrida, the silent speech of inner soliloquy brings together the ruminations of Nietzsche's Oedipus, and the pure expression of Husserl's *Investigations*. Derrida in "Of an apocalyptic tone," his second meditation on voice, cites Nietzsche, but not the Husserl so extensively discussed in *La Voix et le phenomene* (1967):

> I call myself the last philosopher, because I am the last man. No one speaks with me but myself, and my voice comes to me like the voice of a dying man! Let me associate for but one hour more with you, dear voice, with you, the last trace of memory of all human happiness. With you I escape loneliness through self-delusion and lie myself into multiplicity and love. For my heart resists the belief that love is dead. It cannot bear the shudder of the loneliest loneliness, and so it forces me to speak as if I were two. (DNT 49–50)

For Derrida, at this time, the question concerns the following:

> whoever would come to refine, to say the finally final (*le fin du fin*) namely the end of the end (*la fin de la fin*), the end of ends, that the end has always already begun, that we must still distinguish between closure and end, that person would, whether wanting to or not, participate in the concert. For it is also the end of meta-language on the subject of eschatological language. With the result that we can wonder if eschatology is a tone, or even the voice itself. (DNT 48–49)

And then adds: "Isn't the voice always that of the last man?" (DNT 49).

The dialogues spoken and unspoken between Heidegger and Nietzsche, between Derrida and Nancy, must be left here in suspense. And it would be the task for another occasion to consider whether, when Nancy and indeed Husserl invoke the voice, they may not rather be attuned to the voices of the higher man, than to one resonating from beyond the human, of an *Uebermensch*, understood as transcendental non-human condition for the human. For Nancy, voices are each distinctly themselves. He writes of voice as the precession of language and then adds:

> you have to listen to each voice. No two are the same. Each of us explains it differently, in his own voice. Don't you know that our vocal impressions are the most unique of all, even more impossible to confuse with one another than finger prints, which are after all particular to each of us. (BP 236)

Beyond the human would be the singularity of each, which makes the generality "human" inadequate to describe the attestations of each as each. To this "beyond" there might be given the name "transcendental voice." Thus arts, aesthetics, voices and, in addition, to return to the subtitle of the first of the essays of Nancy cited here, worlds too are plural or indeed several. Better perhaps; the arts are plural, aesthetics several, languages multiple, voices singular and worlds heterogeneous. "But the multiplicity of the world does not remain even the multiplicity of a world: it qualifies the world as heterogeneity of worlds in which consists the unity of the world" (*Muses* 17). And the puzzles which arise in aesthetics, which are puzzles arising from the effects the arts have, are not puzzles about how things are caused.

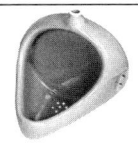

notes

1 Ludwig Wittgenstein, *Philosophical Grammar*, trans. Anthony Kenny (Oxford: Blackwell, 1974).

2 Jean-Luc Nancy, "Why Are there Several Arts and Not Just One" in *The Muses*, trans. Peggy Kamuf (Stanford: Stanford UP, 1996) 1–39, cited as *Muses*.

3 I should like to thank Gary Banham and two anonymous peer reviewers for *Angelaki* for their responses and criticisms of this paper, and an audience at the conference of the Society for European Philosophy, Manchester, 2001, especially Tony O'Connor, Simon Malpas and Ewa Plonowska Ziarek, for listening to a part of these remarks and identifying problems with them.

4 The Compact Edition of the *Oxford English Dictionary* (Oxford: Oxford UP, 1971) has "The doctrine or study of ends or final causes esp. as related to the evidences of design or purpose; also transf. such design as exhibited in natural objects or phenomena" (3251).

5 See Immanuel Kant, *Critique of Judgement* (1790), trans. Werner S. Puhar (Indianapolis: Hackett, 1987), part II: "Critique of Teleological Judgement" 233–381, sects. 61–91. See especially the "General Comment on Teleology" 369–81 for the importance to Kant of differences between physico-teleology, moral teleology and any notion of divine purpose.

6 For an extended discussion of the multiple roles of teleology in the Kantian critical system, and his account of the ends of critique and the purposes of reason, see Gary Banham, *Kant and the Ends of Aesthetics* (London: Macmillan, 2000), especially chapters 1, 6 and 10.

7 See Edmund Husserl, *Logical Investigations* (1900, 1901), trans. J.N. Findlay (London: Routledge and Kegan Paul, 1970), part 2: "Investigations" 1–6. The Husserl cited by Nancy is the Husserl of *Ideas: A General Introduction to Pure Phenomenology* (1911), trans W. Boyce Gibson (New York: Macmillan, 1931) see fn. 60 in Nancy's text (*Muses* 112).

8 Whether the Husserlian account of intentionality and meaning requires the Kantian idea of ends, as suggested by Jacques Derrida in his *Introduction to Husserl's Origin of Geometry* (1962), trans. John P. Leavey (Brighton: Harvester, 1980), fortunately need not be decided here.

9 For a consideration of the emergence of this distinction with respect to the writings of Martin Heidegger see Joanna Hodge, "Against Aesthetics; Heidegger on Art," *Journal of the British Society for Phenomenology* 23.3 (1992): 263–79. In this paper I insist on the importance for Kant of a twofold inscription of aesthetics in the *First* and *Third Critiques*. Gary Banham pointed out to me the importance of the inscription of aesthetics in the *Second Critique*. He rehearses the outlines of the argument in the first chapter of his book; Banham, *Kant and the Ends of Aesthetics*.

10 See Gilles Deleuze, *Kant's Critical Philosophy: The Doctrine of the Faculties* (1963), trans. Hugh Tomlinson and Barbara Habberjam (London: Athlone, 1984), "The originality of the doctrine of the faculties in Kant is as follows: their higher form never abstracts them from their human finitude any more than it suppresses their difference in kind. It is in so far as they are specific and finite that the faculties – in the first sense of the

word – take on a higher form and that the faculties – in the second sense – take on the legislative role" (68–69). See also Gilles Deleuze, "The Idea of Genesis in Kant's Aesthetics," trans. Daniel W. Smith, *Angelaki: Journal of the Theoretical Humanities* 5.3 (2000): 57–70.

11 See Beatrice Longuenesse, *Kant and the Capacity to Judge: Sensibility and Discursivity in the Transcendental Analytic of the "Critique of Pure Reason,"* trans. Charles T. Wolfe (Princeton: Princeton UP, 1998).

12 See Immanuel Kant, *Prolegomena to any Future Metaphysics which Might Lay Claim to Being a Science* (1784), trans. Paul Carus (Indianapolis: Hackett, 1977).

13 This might be thought to be the basis for the difference between the A and the B deduction, that the first demonstrates a system of thinking in process and the second analytically declares its results. This would then further explain the preference of phenomenological readers for the former and of neo-Kantian readers for the latter.

14 The operation of this recoil and displacement is discussed by me under the name "epistemotopology" in a paper entitled "Epistemotopology of the Demon" in *Evil Spirits: Nihilism and the Fate of Modernity*, eds. Gary Banham and Charlie Blake (Manchester: Manchester UP, 2000).

15 For this aspect of the argument I am especially indebted to Ewa Plonowska Ziarek.

16 Jean-Luc Nancy, *The Inoperative Community* (Minneapolis: U of Minnesota P, 1993).

17 See Martin Heidegger, *On Enowning: Contributions to Philosophy* (GA 65, 1989), trans. Parvis Emad (Bloomington: Indiana UP, 1999). "Enowning" is their ingenious translation for "Ereignis," more usually translated as "event."

18 See David Farrell Krell (ed.), *Basic Writings: Martin Heidegger*, revised and expanded ed. (London: Routledge, 1993) 427–49.

19 This is discussed by Derrida in his essay on Husserl cited in n. 7.

20 See Jean-Luc Nancy, *The Sense of the World* (1993), trans. Jeffrey Librett (Minneapolis: U of Minnesota P, 1997).

21 See Martin Heidegger, *The Question of Technology and Other Essays*, trans. William Lovitt (New York: Harper, 1977).

22 See G.W.F. Hegel, *Aesthetics: Lectures on Fine Art*, trans. T.M. Knox (Oxford: Oxford UP, 1975), vol. 2, Introduction to part 3, "The System of the Individual Arts."

23 For discussion of this hypothesis about being, see *Being Singular Plural* (1996), trans. Robert D. Richardson and Anne E. O'Byrne (Stanford: Stanford UP, 2000).

24 Ludwig Wittgenstein, *Remarks on Colour* (1951), ed. G. E. M. Anscombe (Oxford: Blackwell, 1977).

25 For details of this see Martin Heidegger, *Kant and the Problem of Metaphysics* (1928), trans. Richard Taft (Bloomington: Indiana UP, 1986), and *Phenomenological Interpretation of Kant's "Critique of Pure Reason,"* trans. Parvis Emad and Kenneth Maly (Bloomington: Indiana UP, 1997).

26 Jean-Luc Nancy, *The Muses*, trans. Peggy Kamuf (Stanford: Stanford UP, 1996).

27 See Jacques Derrida, "Economimesis," trans. Richard Klein, *Diacritics* 11 (1981): 3–25.

28 See Jean-Luc Nancy, "Vox Clamans in Deserto" in *The Birth to Presence*, trans. Brian Holmes (Stanford: Stanford UP, 1993) 234–48, cited as BP.

29 For Jacques Derrida on the unease this notion of *Sammlung* must prompt, see "Geschlecht II: Heidegger's Hand" in *Deconstruction and Philosophy: The Texts of Jacques Derrida*, ed. John Sallis (Chicago: U of Chicago P, 1987) 161–94, and especially 194.

30 On the translation of logos as *Sammlung* in the discussion of Heraclitus, see Martin Heidegger, *Introduction to Metaphysics* (Tubingen: Max Niemeyer, 1953) 95–103.

31 See Jacques Derrida, "Of an Apocalyptic Tone Newly Adopted in Philosophy" (1981) in *Derrida and Negative Theology*, eds. Harold Coward and Toby Foshay (Albany: SUNY, 1992) 34–35, cited as DNT.

Joanna Hodge
Manchester Metropolitan University
Department of Politics and Philosophy
Geoffrey Manton Building
Manchester M15 6LL
UK
E-mail: j.hodge@mmu.ac.uk

But the disadvantage with sources, however truthful they try to be, is their lack of precision in matters of detail and their impassioned account of events, we refer to a certain internal faculty of contradictory germination which operates within facts or the version of those facts as provided, sold, or proposed, and stemming like spores from the latter, the proliferation of secondary or tertiary sources, some copied, others carelessly transmitted, some repeated from hearsay, others who changed details in good or bad faith, some freely interpreted, others rectified, some propagated with total indifference, others proclaimed as the one, eternal and irreplaceable truth, the last of these the most suspect of all.

david bate

BUNGLED MEMORIES

Louis Althusser gives a surprise definition of art, ranking it not among "the ideologies," but as a relationship to knowledge which he characterises as one of "difference." For Althusser, "the peculiarity of art is to 'make us see [*nous donner à voir*],' 'make us perceive,' 'make us feel' something which *alludes* to reality." Art offers "the form of 'seeing,' 'perceiving,' and 'feeling'" that gives "an 'internal distance'" to the ideology in which it is born.[1]

Freud's work offers us a similar disruption of conscious belief in *The Psychopathology of Everyday Life*. The fact that the *parapraxes*, commonly known as "Freudian slips," show the motivation of other parts of the mind in disrupting conscious actions, speech, gestures, etc. (in short, the whole gamut of human activity), indicates that the unconscious also needs to be ranked amongst the factors of "'seeing,' 'perceiving,' and 'feeling.'"

Cultural and individual memory are intertwined with each other and their collective other: forgetting. As memory of the last century becomes reified, what we remember, how we remember and *if* we remember become crucial issues. But what happens to those things which some, individually or collectively, *wish to forget*. Is it possible that they re-emerge when we least expect them?

note

1 Louis Althusser, "A Letter on Art" in *Lenin and Philosophy* (New York: Monthly Review, 1987) 222 throughout.

ISSN 0969-725X print/ISSN 1469-2899 online/02/010069-03 © 2002 David Bate

Slip of the tongue

Forgetting of a foreign word

henry staten

CLEMENT GREENBERG, RADICAL PAINTING, AND THE LOGIC OF MODERNISM

The collected art criticism of Michael Fried appeared in 1998 with the title *Art and Objecthood*. The centerpiece of the book is the essay by the same name, Fried's most famous statement regarding the art of the 1960s. In this essay, Fried had articulated a critique of the move toward "minimalism" or, in Fried's own preferred term, "literalism" in art. Whereas painting involved the illusion of space and the relation of parts, literalism aimed at a unitary, three-dimensional object. These literal objects would not be sculptures, however; they would have a wholeness and singleness of "shape" inspired by recent painting, above all the work of Frank Stella, that had reduced painting to its most minimal, two-dimensional elements and foregrounded the shape of the support. This new kind of painting, Donald Judd remarked at the time, "overpowers the earlier painting" because it is "nearly an entity, one thing"; but it also exhausted the specific art of painting, with its restriction to two dimensions, and necessitated literalism's opening to three dimensions.

To the arguments of the minimalists/literalists Fried responded that literalism was the "negation of art" because it was, in the terms of a complex argument that I cannot reproduce here, nothing more than "a new genre of theater" (153). In Fried's view, it was imperative for painting to fend off the literalist challenge by observing the distinction between *literal* and *pictorial* shape, thus disproving the charge that the art of painting was now exhausted. The shape of which Judd spoke was "shape as a fundamental property of [literal] objects"; but this sense of shape was distinct from the type of shape with which the painter is concerned, "shape as a medium of painting" (151) – "pictorial" shape. In order for the specificity of the art of painting to remain viable in the contemporary crisis, a painting had to "defeat or suspend its own [literal] objecthood" by the assertion of pictorial shape (ibid.).

In the introduction to the collected work Fried updates, but fundamentally reaffirms, the judgments about contemporary art at which he had arrived when he wrote the earlier work, and notes that he stopped writing art criticism in the 1970s because he was out of sympathy with the direction art had taken and saw no point in continuing to reiterate his opposition.

Just as *Art and Objecthood* appeared, however, *Artforum* (Sept. 1998) carried a review by Fried of monochrome paintings by the New York painter Joseph Marioni. In this remarkable document Fried declared, against all expectation, that Marioni's monochromes were "paintings in

ISSN 0969-725X print/ISSN 1469-2899 online/02/010073-16 © 2002 Taylor & Francis Ltd and the Editors of *Angelaki*
DOI: 10.1080/09697250220142065

73

radical painting

the fullest and most exalted sense of the word," and went on to this conclusion:

> ... I consider Marioni to be one of the foremost painters at work anywhere at the present, and the great and thought-provoking surprise his work has given me is not only that it transcends the previous limitations of the monochrome but also that it is the first body of work I have seen that suggests that the Minimalist intervention might have had productive consequences for painting of the highest ambition. Simply put, the Minimalist hypostatization of objecthood ... seems to have led in Marioni's art to a new, more deeply founded integration of color, amateriality, and support, which is to say to an affirmation of the continued vitality of painting that has something of the character of a new beginning. (149)

Who is Marioni, and what has he wrought that it could cause a theorist as brilliant and polemical as Fried to change his mind in such a fundamental way about the possibilities of monochrome – a type of work that, until he saw Marioni's work, Fried associated with mere literalism and considered "a vehicle for a hackneyed theoretical/ideological stance" (ibid.)? Even more important: could Fried be *right* in his assessment of Marioni's achievement, and, if so, what would this mean for the standard narratives about modernism in painting, and, more broadly, for our sense of the fate of painting (whose "death" has been routinely declared for decades now) and of art as a whole in the era of postmodernity?

I will give a quick introductory account of Marioni and his work, then turn to the metacritical issues raised by his work and its associated theoretical apparatus. Marioni has been living and painting in New York since the early 1970s, but his career for many years was mainly in Europe, especially Germany. His work has special significance in my eyes because it is not an isolated phenomenon, but part of a loosely structured movement that has shown under different names but has most consistently called itself "Radical Painting," and which has been quietly carrying on the project of "reduction to the essence" of the art of painting that Clement Greenberg, and Fried in his wake, did so much to theorize some decades ago – although this project has gone in a direction that might have surprised Greenberg (as it does Fried). Radical Painting has taken widely divergent forms in the course of the two decades I have been following it, and I will not try to survey this variety; but Marioni is, along with his former collaborator, the Cologne painter Günther Umberg, the most theoretically minded of the group, and his paintings manifest in an exemplary way the relation of Radical Painting to the reductionist "logic of modernism."[1]

Now, whereas Greenberg in some famous statements declared *flatness* the irreducible element in the art of painting that modernism had uncovered, Marioni focuses his meditation on the question of *articulated paint* or *painted color* – not paint as it exists in the tube but as it exists when applied to a particular support by a particular means of application.[2] He uses acrylic, applied with a roller to linen on a wooden stretcher, always in a top-down direction, two to six coats of varying hues, but such as to produce a predominantly unitary color-image, each coat monochrome and forming a more or less all-over skin, with the texture of the linen visible to varying degrees through the paint or at the edges. His aesthetic aim is to create a total effect out of the relation between the specific hues he attains, the texture of the paint, the relation of the paint to the linen, and the size and shape of the picture support; this sense of the total physical presence of the painting is what Fried refers to when he mentions the effect on Marioni's work of the "minimalist intervention." However, Marioni is very insistent that his paintings should not cross the line into literalness and become literalist or minimalist "painted objects"; they remain, and are to be judged aesthetically as, paintings, and their predominant effect is of breathtaking color.

The crucial figure in Marioni's sense of the physical presence of the painting as painting, as structure of paint plus support, is, however, not any minimalist but the painter Robert Ryman, without whose work it is impossible to understand Marioni's project. Schematically, then, Radical Painting of the sort done by Marioni is modernism as analyzed by Greenberg's logic, transformed by the achievement of Ryman, and turned toward the exploration of the entire spectrum of painted color.

de duve's interpretation of greenberg

Greenberg's narrative about modernism has recently been massively re-examined and recontextualized by Thierry De Duve.[3] De Duve has heightened the philosophical stakes in this discussion by extensive analysis of the conflicting Kantian elements in Greenberg's problematic – the fact that for Greenberg the beauty of a painting always had to be evaluated by a Kantian judgment of taste, while on the other hand the "logic" of modernism that Greenberg equally derived from (his reading of) Kant implied that judgments of taste were no longer necessary. Greenberg wrote in his 1960 essay "Modernist Painting" that "the essence of Modernism," as observable in Kant, "the first real Modernist," lay "in the use of characteristic methods of a discipline to criticize the discipline itself, not in order to subvert it but in order to entrench it more firmly in its area of competence" (85).[4] Hence modernism in art meant that each art was concerned with "all that was unique in the nature of its medium," and "the task of self-criticism became to eliminate from the specific effects of each art any and every effect that might conceivably be borrowed from or by the medium of any other art. Thus would each art be rendered 'pure' ..." (86). The quest for purity, in the case of painting, yielded the reduction to mere flatness:

> It was the stressing of the ineluctable flatness of the surface that remained ... more fundamental than anything else to the processes by which pictorial art criticized and defined itself under Modernism. For flatness alone was unique and exclusive to pictorial art. The enclosing shape of the picture was a limiting condition, or norm, that was shared with the art of the theater; color was a norm and a means shared not only with the theater, but also with sculpture. ... [F]latness was the only condition painting shared with no other art ... (87)

The logic of this famous argument is considerably less than compelling. Leaving aside its questionable relation to Kant's project, its shakiest assumption is this: that if there is to be an essence of painting, that essence must be absolutely *singular*, there must be *one* characteristic that is the essence and this one characteristic cannot be shared with any other art. By parity of argument, one would have to conclude that sound is inessential to poetry because it is shared with music, and the history of modernist poetry, with its recurrent tendency toward pure musicality, would be an unaccountable mistake.

In any case, this was the conclusion at which Greenberg arrived, a conclusion that, on De Duve's account, led him into an intolerable contradiction. For if mere flatness is the essence of the art of painting, then, as Greenberg remarked in 1962 in "After Abstract Expressionism," a stretched, unpainted canvas could be experienced as a painting or, in the slightly weasally term that he actually used, a "picture," "though not necessarily as a successful one."[5] According to De Duve (and I was surprised to find this out), no one ever presented a mere unpainted canvas as a painting; monochrome or quasi-monochrome was thus the closest thing to the limit-condition of the art of painting at which modernism in fact arrived, "the zero degree of painting" (217). But when Greenberg saw monochrome paintings, rather than thinking that they had arrived at the essence, he dismissed them as "familiar and slick." Monochrome, he judged, had become "almost overnight another taming convention" that "automatically declared itself to be art" (De Duve 251).

If a work automatically declares itself to be art, then no act of aesthetic judgment is required from the viewer; yet Greenberg was irrevocably committed to the necessity of aesthetic judgment. De Duve comments:

> Once an unpainted canvas can be called a picture or a painting, then it is automatically called art. With the dismissal of the very last *expendable convention* of modernist painting – that the canvas be painted at all – the specific [i.e., the art of painting] surrenders to the generic ["art" in general]. The consequences branch out into two possibilities. Either ... the making and appreciation of art require nothing but a mere identification predicated on the conceptual "logic" of modernism, and aesthetic judgment is no longer necessary; ... or aesthetic judgment is

still necessary. But the pressure that the conventions of painting had put on its practice is now nil ... (De Duve 222)

On De Duve's reading, then, if there is a reductive "logic" of modernism, it follows that, once the reduction is complete, there will no longer be any room for judgments regarding the beauty of the work, either on the part of the viewer or on the part of the artist as he creates his work; or, conversely, if there is to be aesthetic judgment, "purism or reductivism is no longer tenable" (ibid.). Hence, Greenberg's choice in favor of aesthetic judgment meant that he had to abandon "modernism" with its progressive paring away of nonessentials from the medium.

De Duve's account, which skillfully exploits the weaknesses in Greenberg's own formulations (importing, however, these same weaknesses into his own argument – as we will see), gains its plausibility not only from its elegant formulation but from the historical sequel, the "Greenbergian anti-Greenbergianism" of Donald Judd and Joseph Kosuth that developed the terms of Greenberg's logic uncompromisingly away from the specificity of the art of painting and toward the negation of aesthetic judgment. Looking at Stella's black paintings in 1962 with Greenberg's doctrine in mind, Judd and his generation of artists had "no alternative other than to pursue the modernist tradition even beyond the literal monochrome where it actually meets its end" (231). Stella's paintings, which seemed to mark the limit to which the modernist reduction could be pushed, were interpreted by Judd as really more like objects than paintings. "[M]ost of the works," Judd wrote, "... suggest slabs, since they project more than usual" (cited in De Duve 236). But Judd argued that three-dimensional "actual space" is "intrinsically more powerful and specific than painting on a flat surface." "Because the nature of three dimensions isn't set, given beforehand, something credible can be made, almost anything" (in De Duve 235). As these remarks indicate, Judd was still awkwardly trying to work with Greenberg's idea of specificity while loosening the traditional constraints to which Greenberg had bound it: Judd's new three-dimensionality in order to open its unlimited new realm of freedom needed to keep clear of the specificity of sculpture as well as that of painting; the new minimalist or literalist art could flourish only in the specificity of the space between the older genres.

Joseph Kosuth went even further than Judd. For him, "the propositions of art are not factual, but linguistic in character – that is, they do not describe the behavior of physical or even mental objects; they express definitions of art, or the formal consequences of definitions of art. Accordingly, we can say that art operates on a logic." This new logic leaves specificity entirely behind, for the artist's true task "now means to question the nature of art. If one is questioning the nature of painting, one cannot be questioning the nature of art. ... That's because the word art is general and the word painting is specific" (in De Duve 245).

In the space of art-in-general, anything whatever could be an artwork; according to Kosuth, the fiat of the artist and not anything intrinsic to the work decreed that something be art. But this was the door to "generic art" that Duchamp had already opened fifty years earlier with his readymades, particularly the famous urinal (hence the title of De Duve's book); the aftermath of the implosion of modernism was thus, according to De Duve, simply the final triumph of Duchamp's intervention.

from ryman to radical painting

The elegance of De Duve's argument conceals a serious flaw, one that becomes evident in light of the retrospective action on the history of modernism of painters like Ryman, Marioni, and Umberg. The flaw is De Duve's assimilation of the monochrome to the blank canvas, as though the conclusion drawn from the possibility of an unpainted painting – "the pressure that the conventions of painting had put on its practice is now nil" – were with equal validity to be drawn from monochrome, so that, in the absence of actual unpainted canvases, the "literal monochrome" would mark the place where the modernist tradition "actually meets its end" (231). It is easy to see how this assimilation could slip, uncriticized, into De Duve's argument on the basis of Stella's early work, which teetered on the edge of the minimalist reduction; more puzzling is how De Duve can praise Ryman as a great painter but quickly assimilate his work, because it "acknowledge[s] the readymade," to the tradition of Duchamp (277). For Ryman's work in fact exploits to an unparalleled degree the pressure that the conventions of painting put on its practice.

Ryman has made an entire career out of paintings that are nominally white, yet each of which is a distinctive exploration of the immense variety of effects of texture, color, and reflectivity that can be achieved within the limits of what language labels univocally (and quite inadequately) as "white"; of the interaction of paint with the immense variety of surfaces to which it can be applied (linen, plastic, paper, metal, etc.); and of the thematization, as part of the formal whole, of the other, previously merely substructural elements, such as the stretcher, the size of the brush and the amount of paint it will hold, the means of attachment to the wall (a very rich element for Ryman, who has used tape, bolts of various sorts, tacks, and so forth, exposing them and making them part of the composition of the painting) – and even the wall itself, which Ryman also calculates as an integral part of the aesthetic structure of the painting. De Duve appears to leap from the fact that brushes, bolts, and so forth are manufactured objects to his conclusion that Ryman's art is properly to be understood as an "acknowledgment of the readymade." There is some interest in linking Ryman in this way to the tradition of Duchamp; but the artistic goal at which Ryman aims could scarcely be more distant from Duchamp's. The thematization of readymade elements in Ryman's work is subordinate to a more comprehensive logic of making than that of the readymade – a logic, older than modernism, that, before it involves their manufactured character, involves acknowledging, and drawing out the consequences of, the materiality of the artwork's component materials.

The characteristically modern critical awareness that there is no pure, raw materiality, that the materials of art come to us already worked over by a long cultural history, becomes for many contemporary theorists, including De Duve, a vision of pure Hegelian *Aufhebung* in which the materiality of art is entirely sublated into the realm of "convention," with convention itself understood as ultimately discursive in nature. The emergence of conceptualism can then be narrated as the logical culmination of the "logic" of modernism. The narrative of sublation cannot, however, do justice to the vital tradition of work within which the unsublated substratum of materiality of even the most readymade materials continues to function. Such work must either be reinterpreted against the grain or rejected as merely naive. Yet the charge of naivety can scarcely be sustained in the face of the fact that Radical Painting is constituted through and through as a continuing critical reflection, carried on within and beyond the terms of the dialectic of modernism developed by Greenberg and Fried, on the techniques and conventional materiality constituting the art of painting at the present moment in culture history.

Ryman, a crucial figure in this alternative tradition, is for his own part unequivocal about the controlling aim of his work: "The basic problem is what to do with paint. What is done with paint is the essence of all painting."[6] The significance of the various material elements of the artwork is wholly reconfigured by their subordination to this aim; and Ryman's work, rather than confirming the tradition of Duchamp, might be more readily understood as the triumph of making, in the entirely *specific* form of the art of painting, over the readymade. Which is to say, not making *ex nihilo*, as the pure originating power of a godlike genius (the model toward which conceptualism gravitates), or as the imposition of form on formless matter, but as the process by which an artist operates the conventional techniques and culturally worked-over materials of a historically evolved *tekhne* and evolves it further. (The crucial philosophical reference for this tradition would then be not Kant – whose aesthetics is the product of the Romantic episode that briefly carried aesthetic theory into the ether of the ineffable – but Aristotle, the original theorist of art as *tekhne* who is much more plausibly considered the predecessor, even if not the actual inspiration, of the modernist idea of the specific medium. I will say more about this at the conclusion of this essay.)

Now, Ryman is often praised for his pragmatic, non-theoretical stance toward his work; yet in his terse way he has situated himself very precisely as working within the selfsame "logic" that was more fully theorized in the 1980s by Marioni and Umberg in their jointly authored account of the nature of Radical Painting.[7] There are, Ryman says, three kinds of painting "procedure": representation, abstraction, and his own, which has "been called by various names, none of them very satisfactory": "There's been 'concrete,' … it's been called 'absolute', 'non-objective', and it's even been called 'abstraction'" (a list to which we can now add "radical"). Ryman prefers to call it "realism," because, unlike the first two procedures, this type of work involves no picture, no illusion, only the perceptual reality of the painting itself.

It is much harder to achieve freedom from representation than one might think. The very fact that "realism" has been confused with "abstraction" (a concept that retains the notion of something represented, only "abstractly") shows that even the idea of purely non-representational painting is not easy to grasp. The notion of a painting's having no picture at all (not even one that is abstractly gestured at), is deceptively simple to state, yet the radical extirpation of representation requires a thinking-through of every conventional and material element of the art of painting – a thinking-through that produces a new logic of form. Realism, says Ryman, "uses all the devices that are used by abstraction and representation such as composition and color complexity, and surface and light, and line and so on," and yet all these terms are transformed when their logic is reconfigured from scratch without the relation to figure. Consider an element as simple and fundamental as *line*: if line is still to be found in the "realist" or radical painting, it cannot be *drawn*, because drawing is a function – classically, for Aristotle as much as for Kant[8] – the defining function, of the procedure of representation. Hence: "I would not actually paint a line, I would paint an area of paint and stop. And then at the edge of the paint would be a line" (Ryman, in Sauer and Rausmüller 64–65).

By contrast with Ryman's endless experimentation, Marioni tinkers only in subtle ways with the format of his paintings, focusing instead on the exploration of an almost unlimited range of hue. And, because the logic of his work is more homogeneously than Ryman's a paint-logic, there is no place in it for composition or line, even as paint-edge (one reason why he paints with a roller). Yet, in part because of what he has learned from Ryman, Marioni's paintings are informed by the most refined awareness of the full physicality of the painting as a composite unity attached to a wall. The successive skins of paint interlock in such a way as to create a highly specific visual effect, as though we were looking into the paint, into a color-space that is not illusionistic but the actual space created between the layers of paint; yet the paint is not laid on thickly, does not create what Greenberg called "furtive bas relief." The successive layers are veil-like in their subtlety, and the weave of the linen shows through (Marioni paints only on linen – eight different kinds depending on the texture and porosity he needs to achieve a specific color-image). Marioni is also acutely attentive to the relation between the color he creates and the shape and size of the painting. The form, or "structure," as he prefers to call it, of the painting, arises, as in Ryman's work – although arguably, as Fried says, "in a wholly different spirit" – out of the interaction of all these elements; hence there is no question of falling into what Harold Rosenberg called mere "matterism," a false sense of aesthetic richness arising from the intoxication of the eye that puts itself to the tracing of raw physical textures in all their endless variety. As always in art, it is a matter of *form*; and yet this is form that is tied in the most intimate way to the materiality of the medium. The "pressure of the conventions of the medium" does not disappear but is transformed; painters are made more conscious of this pressure by their own increasing articulation of the medium's material elements in all their diversity, and this in turn leads to a yet more refined articulation and a yet subtler consciousness.

The difference between Ryman's work and Marioni's, and then again between either of theirs and that of Umberg, shows how vast is the range of possibility of this fundamental or radical or realist exploration of painting. Like the work of the others, Umberg's has evolved through a number of transformations, but in the 1980s when he was collaborating with Marioni he painted intensely black-looking paintings on thin sheets of aluminum, made of dry particles of graphite or ivory black, which he brushed dry onto moist dammar, horizontally and vertically, thirty or forty layers, building up a porous texture that registers the disciplined lines of the brush strokes in the strikingly dry painted surface. This texture is extremely fragile: the merest touch will destroy it. This fragility, together with the thinness of the support – which makes the painting seem at first to be part of the wall – creates a sort of attenuation of materiality, at least in the sense of withdrawal from three-dimensionality. Yet the paint, with its delicately refined yet charcoal-like texture, remains intensely material, and in the absence of any figure, shape, or line, the eye can only perceive the color as bound to this materiality. Black is actualized in a specific painting-medium, and this actualization can only be judged aesthetically in the context of the specific history of aesthetic exploration out of which it comes, the context of fundamental, concrete, absolute, realist, or radical painting.

The increasingly articulate consciousness of the (historically, contextually significant) materiality of painting, the nature of the pressure it exerts on the quest for aesthetic form, and the means by which that pressure can be put to aesthetic account that painters in this tradition have developed, give the lie to Greenberg's own belief that painters had never been, and could not be, explicitly aware of the "logic" that had been guiding their practice throughout the history of modernism.[9] Yet this increased awareness actually has the opposite effect from that inferred by De Duve, moving the art of monochrome farther than ever away from any possibility of producing a painting by mere deduction from a logic.

De Duve creates his dichotomy between aesthetic judgment and conceptual deduction by ignoring the micrology of the painter's practice in its largely tacit interaction with the (materialist) "logic" according to which he works. In his reconstruction of Greenberg's thought De Duve pays lip service to the question of interaction with the medium:

> As to the modernist artist's aesthetic judgment, it has to be suggested, inspired, provoked by or received from the medium itself, for the medium is the only subject matter of modernism and the locus of the artist's aesthetic constraints. (214)

Yet De Duve renders the reference to the inspiration the painter receives from "the medium itself" effectively meaningless when, endorsing Greenberg's narrowest interpretation of the logic of modernism, he sublates the materiality of the medium into the idea of convention. In the context of this sublation, it is easy to conceive monochrome as a bodiless "zero degree" of painting that can provide no further inspiration (only "concoctions" that are produced "automatically"). And the judgment of quality must now hover in the thin air of a generalized or generic "art" that has no palpable relation to the specificity of a given medium, because this relation, if conceived as a logic, would result in the automaticity that renders aesthetic judgment irrelevant. One should pay careful attention to the sleight of hand with the word *medium* that is required for the logic of this argument:

> Between content and form, between the generic value-judgment and the specific self-criticism of the particular medium, there has to be a mediation, but one that doesn't allow for a deduction. If it did, it would mean that content – aesthetic value – could be inferred from the state of the medium. Conversely, it would mean that the medium could be deliberately manipulated so as to produce content or quality, thus allowing for what Greenberg called "concocted" art. (213)

Only the evacuation of materiality from the notion of the medium can justify the imposition of the model of *deduction* on that of "specific self-criticism." If what De Duve has identified is a problem that indeed arose in the conceptualist aftermath of modernism and that might well have

radical painting

been given an essential impetus by Greenberg's "logic," it is not a problem that is intrinsic to the notion of modernism as specific self-criticism, if that notion is going to be construed not in the odd and indefensible form of its reductio in a blank canvas but in the most expansive terms – terms that look to Greenberg's critical practice, which was, as Fried notes, separated by a "gulf" from his theory – and to the history of the modernist reduction since 1962.

an alternative version of greenberg

Greenberg was never in any danger, as De Duve wants to think, of "surrendering" his taste in front of Stella's black paintings (203–04). Greenberg more than once indignantly denied ever having confused the essentialism or purism of a painting with its quality, and any unbiased reading of his work will confirm this. He had a remarkably catholic eye, and in fact confessed a preference for figuration over abstraction. What I want to focus on here, however, is his enthusiasm for color, which shows up repeatedly and which constitutes a sort of second, shadow "logic" leading to a different, and more pregnant, conclusion about the future of modernism than the one that leads to the blank canvas. His remarks on Morris Louis's work, for instance, reveal precisely the kind of eye for "literal" qualities that one needs in order to look at Radical Painting:

> The fabric, being soaked in paint rather than merely covered with it, becomes paint in itself, color in itself, like dyed cloth; the threadedness and wovenness are in the color. Louis usually contrives to leave certain areas in the canvas bare, and whether or not he whitens these afterwards with a thin gesso ... the aspect of bareness is retained. It is a gray-white or white-gray bareness that functions as a color in its own right and on a parity with other colors; by this parity the other colors are leveled down as it were, to become identified with the raw cotton surface as much as the bareness is. (97)

There is clearly a relation between the way Greenberg here reads color and the idea of the reduction to flatness, and there needs to be; the idea of flatness is not simply expendable. But flatness is here fully materialized in the ensemble of constituents that make up the painting, and what Greenberg responds to is not flatness as such but the integration of paint and support. Yet Greenberg, under the influence of his doctrine of pure opticality (another dogma of his theoretical apparatus, and one which I cannot here try to reconcile with the line of thought that leads to the blank canvas), oddly concludes that the color is "disembodied," and argues that the paintings need to be large so as not to be seen as discrete, tactile objects. Thus, the overarching "logic" is not yet that of Radical Painting, but Greenberg's articulation of the physical structure of the painting comes very close.

That a new doctrine of the evolution of modernism is brewing in such observations becomes evident in the very same essay, "After Abstract Expressionism," in which Greenberg makes the remark about the blank canvas. Greenberg here rhapsodizes about the colorism of Still, Rothko, and Newman in terms that continue to resonate today and might be said to presage the onset of Radical Painting (while contrasting sharply with the ambivalent tones in which a little later he speaks of the reduction to mere flatness):

> ... the ultimate effect sought [by Still, Rothko, and Newman] is one of more than chromatic intensity; it is rather one of *an almost literal openness* that embraces and absorbs color in the act of being created by it. Openness, and not only in painting, is the quality that seems most to exhilarate the attuned eyes of our time. ... Let it suffice to say that by the new openness they have attained, [they] point to what I would risk saying is the only way to high pictorial art in the near future. (Emphasis added)

"Openness" is a difficult term to define, and of course Greenberg could not have had in mind quite the sort of thing that is achieved by Marioni (radical painting cannot be *deduced*); yet when he calls it "almost literal" he suggests precisely the direction these painters marked out for Marioni's further development of what he learned from them. "I would like to do for color what Pollock did for line," Marioni remarks in an interview; "I would like to free color from boundary" (Museum Abteiberg Catalog 25).

De Duve passes lightly over this praise of Still, Rothko, and Newman, taking it as somehow restoring Greenberg's confidence in the thesis of flatness and thus as leading up to the remark about a bare canvas; Fried more acutely notes that Greenberg's remarks on color are ironically at odds with the remark about the bare canvas, but argues that "the reductionist logic of Greenberg's theory of modernism meant that color or indeed 'openness' in recent painting could not assume the constitutive or essentialist significance of flatness and the delimitation of flatness …" (39). And it is true that Greenberg now suggests the old logic has expended its impetus as Still, Rothko, and Newman have opened a "second phase" in the "self-criticism" of modernism. In this new phase, the delimitation of flatness is replaced as the central question by that of "the ultimate source of quality in art" (Greenberg 132) – a source that Greenberg identifies as "conception," in the quite traditional sense of "inspiration." But this proclamation of a new phase does not erase from the record the previous remark in which he marks out color and openness as the *exclusive* formal pathway to the future of painting – precisely the role he had formerly assigned to the problematic of flatness (of which, properly conceived, the questions of color and openness are aspects – as I will argue below).

The statement about a new phase confusedly implies both that the old formalist logic is no longer relevant as painting turns from questions of form to questions of aesthetic quality – an implication contradicted by the declaration concerning color and openness; and that the question of quality in painting was not formerly a problem for modernism as it pursued its quest for flatness – an implication that is contradicted by Greenberg's own earlier critical practice, in which he insisted on the distinction between formal means and aesthetic quality. In 1959, for instance, in "The Case for Abstract Art" Greenberg had written that "Abstract painting may be a purer, more quintessential form of pictorial art than the representational kind, but this does not of itself confer quality upon an abstract picture" (82).[10]

It is clear, despite Greenberg's muddled formulation, that the *formal* logic of modernism he had done more than anyone else to define had not all of a sudden shifted course with the achievements in color and openness of Still, Rothko, and Newman; these painters continued to follow out the consequences of the turn in the modern period away from the illusionistic space of representation. Thus, necessarily, they continued to work in a crucial, even an "essential," sense within a "logic of flatness" – the logic of the reduction of representation according to which the form of painting is reconceived in what Ryman calls a realist way. This in fact was how Greenberg himself initially developed his thesis about flatness; what was fundamentally at issue in this thesis was the rejection of representation, figuration, illusionism, "the flat picture's denial of efforts to 'hole through' it for realistic perspectival space," as Greenberg termed it in 1940 (vol. 1, 34). Clearly, this denial must remain at the center of any reflection on the modernist problematic; the work of Still, Rothko, and Newman cannot be understood without it. But because he came to isolate flatness pure and simple as the essence of painting-logic, Greenberg's recoil from flatness seemed to leave him no recourse but to conclude that his problematic, and that of modernism, had shifted in a fundamentally new direction.

If we were to choose one term to replace "flatness" as the best single index of the modernist reduction, at least within Greenberg's work, it should probably be "painterliness." Painterliness is a much richer concept than flatness, more adequately suggesting the complexity of Greenberg's insights into painting, as well as pointing toward the primacy of paint stressed by the radical painters. It is in fact a concept to which Greenberg himself accords centrality (as is indicated, for instance, by his thinking "Painterly Abstraction" was a better name than "Abstract Expressionism" for the phenomenon in question). Painterly qualities are those that pull the viewer's attention away from what the painting represents toward the physical fact of paint-applied-to-a-surface, of paint applied on top of paint, of density and flow and so forth, and the problematic of painterliness therefore calls up as interdependent, intertwined questions the denial of figuration, the physical and perceptual qualities of painted color, and the flatness of the non-illusionistic painted surface.

the painting is the body of color

Now, however, as we move away from representation toward the full materiality of painting, we run up against the other limit of this logic: the limit of objecthood on which Fried has so richly meditated, but which Greenberg already detected. A painting cannot be a literal object, not even a literal painted object. The minimalists were very insistent on the difference between objects and paintings, and their acute investigation of the nature of literal objects is essential to the project of radical painting, a blinking red light that warns the painter how far he can go in this direction and still be making a painting. How can we tell an object that is a painting from a painted object? Only by becoming attuned to the painting-logic that produces the specific type of object that, within a certain history as construed by a certain interpretation of that history, has become as literal in its objecthood as it can be and still be a painting – that has, in fact, become most fully a painting, and nothing but a painting, by the path of its own particular brand of "literalness."

"The radical painter creates an object whose content is dependent on the intrinsic logic of its own material form," claim Marioni and Umberg (*Outside the Cartouche* 22). This logic has to be understood in terms of what they call the *function* of this object (23). "Paintings are not found objects"; they are "manmade" and hence must be understood in terms of the purpose or function that motivates their making (19). Of course paintings can be made for a variety of purposes, including the purpose of representation. But representation would be a purpose external to the "logic of the material form" of the painting. "The material itself has perceptual content that is intrinsic to its function" (24); the support, for instance, "is an object whose specific purpose is to-be-painted" (ibid.). According to this functional definition, then, flatness could not, logically, be the essence of the painting, because everything about the painting has to be understood in relation to what Marioni and Umberg

could easily have called the *telos* of the painting-object or object-that-is-a-painting, which irreducibly involves *being painted*.[11] Unlike, say, a wall that one paints, the painting-support is created purely in view of this function. (Greenberg ignored this fact and thus curiously gave way to literal "literalism" when he started to think of the flatness of the support in abstraction from the purpose for which painting-supports are made.) The function of the whole painting, in turn, is to be *perceived* as a painting, to give human beings the perceptual experience that is the experience of looking-at-a-painting, where the painting, and not the illusion of space or the figure of something in the world, is indeed what is looked at – and where, of course, this entire complex of function, artifact, and experience is constituted "conventionally" by a given society with a given history. The functions of the physical support and its qualities, including flatness, are definable only with reference to the function of the full perceptual unity that is defined by this history, or by a certain appropriation of it, as the finished painting; and the form or essence of the finished painting is the "color-image" that it constitutes. In the final analysis, the "objectness" of the painting is color (ibid.); all the physical parts of which the painting is made are brought into their unity of aesthetic form by their subordination to the color. This does not mean that they are effaced, as was the tendency in representational painting. On the contrary, color is a dimension of materiality and the radical painter is not trying to detach it from materiality. "Aristotle defines color as the 'limit of the translucent in a determinately bounded body.' This is a superb definition for the painter. It locates color within a material (even though it is, in Aristotle's concept, the outermost part of a thing) and it implies the limitation of its form as material" (24). The color of a painting, if it gives the rule to the physical constituents, is itself bound to or determined by their materiality (first of all, that of the paint) as this materiality has historically evolved in relation to the evolving function of painting. But the size and shape and texture and absorptiveness of the support, the relation to the wall, and so forth, must co-operate in an overall perception, the decisive or ruling factor of which is color. Color is the essence of the painting in much the way that for Aristotle the soul is the essence or form of the body. Even though the form is in perception detached from the material, substance or ousia is embodied form; and the radical painting is ousia as embodied color.

How can color be a form? A form is by definition bounded or what gives boundary; Aristotle himself in the *Poetics* used the drawn line as a paradigm of form, but the drawn line is one of the remnants of representation that the radical painter eschews in his search for "openness." But color becomes, or can become, a form when it finds the absolutely specific, bounded body that it reciprocally determines and is determined by. There is no notional answer to the question of how color can function as form, only the historical fact that certain painters have worked out an aesthetic and a painting-practice that treats it as such, and the proof is in the experience of their work (or not).

art vs. craft

If Radical Painting is what gives importance to yet another reconsideration, at this late date, of the logic of modernism, what gives importance to radical painting itself is the act of aesthetic judgment that says "this is good" to the work of Ryman or Marioni or Umberg. And this aesthetic judgment itself, made in the strong form that both Greenberg and Fried emphasize, in which it expresses not just a feeling of pleasure but a judgment of aesthetic quality, is indissociable from knowledge of modernism as a tradition of specific self-criticism. This tradition has not primarily been a matter of conceptual formulations and deductions concerning "conventions" and "the state of the medium," but an *education for the eye*, yet an education that has of course essentially involved the brain and language as well as the hand and the brush, and increasingly so as the tradition has become more articulately self-aware – a self-awareness that has increasingly become, among the practitioners of the art, an explicit logic of purism and reduction to the "essence." Whatever it might be for the theorist, the concept of essence is for the painter not a dogmatic doctrinal simplification but a tool with which to meditate on materiality and objecthood and which through this meditation participates in bringing forth new work. The theorist might, correspondingly, avail himself of the concept in a non-metaphysical, ordinary-language way, as a historically contingent notion, in something like the way Fried already proposed in "Art and Objecthood." Nevertheless, if Greenberg's own dogmatic reduction is too "essentialist" to be useful, Fried's version of a contingent essence of modernism is a little too flexible to capture what is distinctive about Radical Painting.

Greenberg himself suggested that the idea of purity could be "merely an illusion," but a "useful" one, that had led to good new developments among the artists under its spell. The idea of a "mere illusion" functioning in this way, however, is a hangover from nineteenth-century positivism and is inadequate to describe the functional role, within the micrology of radical painting practice, of the idea of reducing painting to its fundamentals. It is necessary to take the idea of an essence of painting seriously in order to understand Radical Painting from within, and even really to *see* it, to see it understandingly in its profound relation, not along one axis but in terms of a myriad of threads, to a tradition out of which this work grows, and which is retrospectively reconstituted once again as a tradition, with a somewhat altered meaning, in view of this new development.

Such conviction of aesthetic quality as may be derived from a radical painting, because specific to the historical-conceptual lineage of the type of artwork in question, is not of the transcendentally compulsory sort implied by De Duve's version of Kantian aesthetic judgment. The version of "specificity" that I am arguing here implies that one can, and indeed ought to, refrain from the judgment "this is art" while making the judgment "this is a good painting." This is not to deny that the generic concept of art is meaningful; only to say that the large questions of art that De Duve raises obfuscate the issue of the logic of reduction in the history of modern painting – at least along the line that leads to Radical Painting. If one knows the most resourceful form of the thesis about reduction to the essence, and if one has spent enough time looking at the most serious work that has been produced either on the basis of this thesis or in a way that supports it, then one can in principle have an aesthetic experience that stands up to the experience one has had of the aesthetic objects that have formed one's sense of optimal aesthetic experience; but it is only as a quite *specific* experience that one can have it. Contrary to De Duve, it is not only not necessary to judge "this is art" before one can judge "this is a painting, and a good one"; it is necessary *not* to do so (though one might go on to the generic judgment afterwards, recognizing that one is now switching language-games in so doing).

As in any other question of aesthetic experience, the judgment of quality in front of a radical painting is not a matter of deduction and it is not compulsory. But Radical Painting has the earmarks of a well-grounded and valid aesthetic movement, and forces a reconsideration of questions that had seemed to be closed when it looked as though the modernist logic had hit a dead end. What all this betokens regarding the larger questions of the "culture wars" is a further question that I will touch on below; for now what I want to stress is that, if we are going to use modernism as an example of anything on the way to a larger argument, we should address it in its fullness as a historically evolving phenomenon, along with the most resourceful statement of its rationale or "theory"; and this involves criticizing and rejecting Greenberg's own dogmatic theses and De Duve's interpretation of them.

Nevertheless, I want to pay tribute to the scope and seriousness of *Kant after Duchamp*, particularly because of the framework of sociopolitical reflection that gives point to De Duve's "genealogical" reconsideration of modernist painting. My remarks here have focused on narrowly aesthetic issues, and I recognize that these issues may appear trivial compared to the question of the cultural and political mission of the artist, in the context of the great upheavals of the twentieth century, which De Duve tries to understand. I am especially troubled by the problem of the esoteric nature of the modernist–formalist aesthetic I have defended here, its seemingly elitist adherence to a refinement of aesthetic taste that can perhaps only ever be the possession of a privileged few. I have no doubt that the ultimate and genuine significance of the debates over essentialism are rooted in the problems of democratization that De Duve addresses.

However, the great democratizing movement that De Duve sees as the legacy of Duchamp – everyone an artist, the artwork as anything whatever – is achieved at the cost of an elision of the *physical labor* involved in making a work of art, and which is the ultimate source of the work's specificity. Duchamp did not make his urinal, but someone or a group of someones did – anonymous workmen in a urinal factory. I am not so worried about the possibility that artworks could be *automatically* created by deduction from a logic (a rather specialized and even artificial problem, in my view) as I am by the fact that the work of their making could then be assigned to someone else, or, in the case of the readymades, has already been done by someone else. One of the things that strikes me most about Ryman's, Marioni's, and Umberg's art is that, for all its conceptual sophistication, it has a strong affinity with *craft* – an affinity that, incidentally, goes back to the roots of modernist art-theory in Baudelaire, that great early debunker of the genius-and-inspiration theory of aesthetics and pioneer of the notion that the specific province of poetry is language as a *material* medium.[12] Marioni and Umberg, in a striking move, compared the purpose and usability of their paintings to that of an ordinary chair (*Outside the Cartouche* 23–24); and Marioni goes so far as to entirely abjure the honorific *art* for his work, defining his work strictly and solely as *painting*.

We are so inured to thinking of painting as art that Marioni's resistance to this assimilation might seem incomprehensible or even senseless. If painting isn't art, what is it? And if it isn't art, why should it have any claim on our attention?

Marioni's stubborn adherence to the specificity of the practice of painting indicates an ethicopolitical resonance of the question of the medium, of its irreducibly material nature, and of the craftsman's attunement to that materiality, which modernity, first in the aftermath of Kant's and Romanticism's infatuation with "genius," later under the spell of the poststructuralist *Aufhebung* of materiality into language, has had trouble keeping consistently in view – in spite of the modernist intervention. The continuing significance of the thesis of specificity is for me grounded in the indissociability it suggests of the labor of the artist from the specific nature of his medium in its complex, socially conditioned materiality – which is the same as the indissociability of art from its craft-aspect. The generic judgment "this is art" is no doubt necessary in the language-game that has developed around art that intentionally wanders away from the constraints of established, specific art-forms. As I have tried to show in this essay, however, this development does not mean that some generic judgment of value has now superseded, wholly and in all contexts, the modernist logic of specificity. Moreover, De Duve's arguments that a picture must be judged to be art before it can be judged to be a picture, and that the judgment "this is beautiful" is identical with the judgment "this is art," strike me as no friendlier to a democratization of art and the creative process than they are to the vacuous cult of art-fetishism of which we already see signs in Kant's almost helpless awe before the inexplicability of genius, and of which the only slightly more foolish descendant is the contemporary worship of the art-superstar.[13]

In this essay I can only indicate the outlines of the full theorization that Radical Painting invites, and to which the current notion of the conventionality of art practices is so inadequate. The convergence once more at this late date in history of the notions of art and craft requires a rethinking of the entire history of the concept of art as this history has been configured by the evolutionary narrative of its emergence – more than once; in ancient Greece and again in the late Middle Ages – in its purity from a more generalized notion of making. Modernism is commonly – and rightly – understood as the final step in the emergence of the pure concept of art, and Greenberg's ideas about the specificity of the individual arts are an important chapter in the history of this emergence. Hence the notion that Radical Painting is a continuation of the logic of modernism, yet an overcoming of the distinction between art and craft, might seem paradoxical.

staten

The paradox is neither illusory nor necessary. The truth is that more than one thread of "logic" traverses the history of modernism, and where we end up depends on which thread we take up. De Duve has articulated for us with great precision the decisive line that is crossed with Duchamp and conceptualism, when, following one development of the logic of specificity, the bond between artistic practice and the specificity of the medium is broken and the concept of art emerges in its own generic rather than specific purity. Once this bond is broken, everything about art begins to dissolve in the universal medium of discursivity, and this marks the final break between the profession of the artist and the guild tradition in which this profession had continued to be, however distantly, rooted. What I have tried to show in this essay is that the terms in which Radical Painting is conceived are terms that lead us ineluctably away from the universal solvent of discursivity and back toward the realm of material practices. I have been concerned to show that there is nothing naive about this turn; that it incorporates as an essential part of its conception and of its practice a reflection on the conventional nature of the materiality of the medium – that this, too, is a rigorous unfolding of the logic of specificity.[14]

I am more inclined to the latter than the former development for two interrelated reasons. First (a point I have stressed), because the sublationist narrative empties most or all of the materiality out of the notion of the medium, in favor of the notion of convention. Radical Painting, by contrast, in its reflection on the materiality of the medium, does not in any way slight the conventional element in this materiality. Second, because the sublationist dematerialization of the medium opens out an unlimited field of critical discursivity about art in which the critic or theorist is authorized to say practically anything since the entire cultural field can now be framed as aesthetic – and art itself in this postmodern regime, as Rosalind Krauss writes, "mimics just this leeching of the aesthetic out into the social field in general."[15] Not everyone will consider this a demerit; and I myself do not believe in any juridical prohibition on the critic's discourse becoming autotelic, nor am I immune to the pleasures of postmodern cultural aesthetics. Nevertheless, there is something *specific* to the painter's, sculptor's, musician's ... practice that is also autotelic, or which might be so conceived, and as so conceived made the basis of that practice, and to which justice can be done only by a critical discourse that does not auto-authorize itself but binds itself as tightly as possible to that practice in the fullness of its conventional materiality.

Here I can only sketch the outlines of the full, historically articulated account of human praxis as a whole that would constitute a more adequate account of artistic convention as grounded in what I have been calling *conventional materiality*.16 Such an account would take as its fundamental reference points, on the one hand, Aristotle's analysis of the teleology of human practices and, on the other hand, Marx's analysis of human productive activity, that is human labor as the foundational fact of social existence.

A fully articulated theory of conventional materiality would begin with the beginnings of human culture in order to excavate the residue of fatality, the unpredictable system of limits, that arises at the point of intersection of multiple acts of individual exertion that are carried on within a social context and leave their residue on the physical world, long before the emergence of even the most rudimentary arts and crafts, and even before the advent of language. The most primordial inscriptions on the world of these residues are the rubbing clear of the ground where a group of humans or proto-humans sits to rest or lies down to sleep, of pathways where one walks after the other, of trees stripped bare of fruit around these inscribed areas so that the people are constrained to move along, fraying new paths and making new clearings. Here is the beginning of history as the simple deposit of accumulated acts within the context of sociality, and the landscape is the incipiently socialized materiality that serves as the support of this inscription. Later on in history, as Marx observes in *The German Ideology*, there will no longer be any nature left; it will all have been absorbed into the network of cultural inscription; in this earlier period there is as yet nothing that can be called a convention, and nevertheless there is already the interaction between sociality and the physical world that leaves a perduring trace that then acts as a partial determinant on the purposeful action of human beings: precisely the fundamental structure that underlies those later features of social activity, more complexly sedimented with the history of a culture, that are properly understood as conventions. Then there begins the making of tools, which are once again initially the residue of repeated acts of fraying, say to make a point or an edge, and the material of which the tool is made – hard or frangible, offering a firm grasp or slippery, etc. – together with the shape with which it has now been inscribed, is henceforth a fatality or system of limits that conditions the further development of the sociality that has brought it into being as just this tool (and even, as some theorists have argued, the further development of the human brain itself). The methods by which the tool is made are themselves the social inscription of historically accumulated individual acts in their effective interaction with the material of the tool, and might have their own further development in interaction with new materials and in combination with methods derived from other contexts. Now labor, craft, and art might begin to be differentiated; but they are part of a matrix that never entirely comes undone – or, rather, that ought never be allowed to come entirely undone.

What is brought to light in such an account, beyond or beneath the question of conventions, is the teleology of social practice that conditions all materiality within culture, and which ordains that praxis must always be grounded in its specificity. It seems to me that an essential beginning toward the thinking-through of this problematic – and at precisely the conjunction between Aristotle and Marx – was made by Georg Lukács in his final work, *The Ontology of Social Being*. "Through labour, a teleological positing is realized within material being, as the rise of a new objectivity. The first consequence of this is that labour becomes the model for any social practice, for in such social practice – no matter how ramified its mediations – teleological positings are always realized, and ultimately realized materially."17

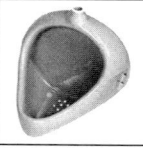

notes

1 The movement was formally baptized in the public eye by a special issue of *Kunstforum International* (Mar.–Apr. 1987), edited by Amione Haase, that focused on "Radikale Malerei." Among the pieces included in this issue are my "Joseph Marioni: Malerei Jenseits Narrativität" and articles on Umberg and other German radical painters who have continued to figure significantly: Ullrich Wellman, Ingo Meller, and Peter Tollens.

2 See the essay on Umberg by Hannelore Kersting, "Painting as Articulated Paint," in the catalogue to the exhibition *Gunter Umberg*, Städelsches Kunstinstitut Frankfurt, 1985.

3 Thierry De Duve, *Kant after Duchamp* (Cambridge: MIT P, 1996). All citations of De Duve refer to this volume.

4 All citations of Greenberg are to *Clement Greenberg: The Collected Essays and Criticism*, vol. 4, *Modernism with a Vengeance* (Chicago: U of Chicago P, 1993).

5 Painting and picture are normally synonymous in art-critical talk, and I won't object to this usage. However, the idea that there can be an unpainted picture seems to me to dissimulate an absurdity that is patent in the phrase "unpainted painting." This absurdity that Greenberg created is exploited at great length by De Duve, who buys into it because it serves his purposes admirably.

6 Stedelijk Museum Catalog, 1975; quoted by Sauer in Christel Sauer and Urs Rausmüller (eds.), *Robert Ryman*, catalog for Ryman exhibition in the Espace d'Art Contemporain, 1991, 31.

7 Joseph Marioni and Günther Umberg, *Outside the Cartouche: Zur Frage des Betrachters in der Radikalen Malerei*. English and German; German trans. Nikolaus Hoffmann and Rolf Taschen (Munich: Neue Kunst, 1986). Umberg's work in the 1990s took new directions; in this essay I refer only to the period of his collaboration with Marioni.

8 Aristotle remarks in the *Poetics*, chapter 10, that in a painting "the most beautiful pigments smeared on at random will not give as much pleasure as a black-and-white outline picture." Aristotle, *Poetics*, trans. Gerald Else (Ann Arbor: U of Michigan P) 28. And Kant comments in the Third Critique that "*delineation* is the essential thing" in all the "formative arts" (61), and painting is the foremost of these arts because "as the art of delineation it lies at the root" of all the others (175). Kant, *Critique of Judgment*, trans. J.H. Bernard (New York: Hafner, 1951).

9 Behind this belief of Greenberg's, once again we might discern Kant, for whom "express rules" cannot be the basis on which an art is transmitted. For Kant, there is no middle term between the pure originating power, granted by nature, of the genius, on the one hand, and the explicit rules that the schools derive from the genius's original works of art in order to train subordinate, unoriginal talents to trudge in his footsteps. An art develops historically by the immediate communication of the inspiring force of nature from one genius to another, without the mediation of "rules." Kant thinks of the *tekhne* of an art only in this sense of "express rules"; he has no concept of the *medium* in the modern or modernist sense – not as a system of explicit rules but as an ensemble of techniques in dialectical interaction with the materiality of a specific material (words, tones, colors, stone, etc.). Third Critique, sects. 45–50.

10 Despite the impression De Duve creates of a sudden choice in favor of quality in 1962, this distinction had been consistently maintained by Greenberg. The remark from 1959 is worth quoting in full: "I still know of nothing in abstract painting, aside perhaps from some of the near-abstract Cubist works that Picasso, Braque, and Leger executed between 1910 and 1914, which matches the highest achievements of the old masters. Abstract painting may be a purer, more quintessential form of pictorial art than the representational kind, but this does not of itself confer quality on an abstract picture. The ratio of bad abstract painting to good is actually much higher than the ratio of bad to good representational painting." "The Case for Abstract Art" 82. And in "After Abstract Expressionism" itself, Greenberg refers to his 1948 refusal of the "dogmatism that held that one species of art must in a given period be better than any other species," and then asserts that Pollock's and Gorky's pictures stayed "further behind their frames than Mondrian's or Picasso's post-1913 pictures did," but that going "backwards in terms of the evolution of style" was at that time "almost the only way to go forward in terms of major quality" (124). The simple statement in 1964 that "form as such is a neutral element as far as quality is concerned" (180) thus reaffirms Greenberg's consistent view. Cf. Fried, who agrees that Greenberg is "right to say that he

never presented flatness and the inclosing of flatness as criteria of quality" (66).

11 The conclusion that a painting must be painted, obvious from the ordinary person's standpoint, and which I am thus slightly embarrassed to draw, has to be argued in the face of De Duve's argument, which keeps alive Greenberg's suggestion that a painting (or "picture") need not be painted (see n. 5 above).

12 See Graham Chester, *Baudelaire and the Poetics of Craft* (Cambridge: Cambridge UP, 1988).

13 I say "almost" helpless because Kant does choose the primacy of rules over mere undisciplined genius.

14 Yet another, deconstruction-based, development of the logic of specificity is that by Rosalind Krauss, who in her reading of Marcel Broodthaers argues that "the specificity of mediums, even modernist ones, must be understood as differential, self-differing, and thus as a layering of conventions never simply collapsed into the physicality of their support." *"A Voyage on the North Sea": Art in the Age of the Post-Medium Condition* (New York: Thames, 1999) 53. Although the artist she discusses, and the theory she elaborates, are very distant from Radical Painting, her essay, like mine, rejects the vulgar idea of the medium as "a layering of conventions ... simply collapsed into the physicality of their support."

15 *"A Voyage on the North Sea"* 56.

16 The earliest stimulus to the interpretation of Radical Painting, and the following reflections on praxis, that I present here was a fascinating essay by Lothar Romain on Analytical Painting, a movement which I interpret as a precursor of Radical Painting. See Lothar Romain, "The Artistic Truth of Things that Exist: Reflections Pertaining to (the Theory of) Analytical Painting," trans. Antony de Nardini and Paul Angus in *A Proposito della Pittura/Bettrefende Het Schilderen/Concerning Painting*, catalogue Museum Van Bommel–Van Dam Venlo/Stedelijk Museum Schiedam/Hedenaagse Kunst Utrecht 1975–76, 27–32.

17 Georg Lukács, *The Ontology of Social Being: Labour* (London: Merlin, 1980) 3. This volume is a translation of the first chapter of Part Two of the larger work.

Henry Staten
Department of English
University of Washington
Box 35436
Seattle, WA 98195
USA
E-mail: hstaten@u.washington.edu

He jotted down this thought, if it can be called that, on a loose sheet of paper, hoping to use it later, perhaps in some pondered statement about the mystery of writing which will probably culminate, following the definitive lessons of the poet, in the precise and sober declaration that the mystery of writing lies in the absence of any mystery whatsoever, which if accepted, might lead us to the conclusion that if there is no mystery about writing, neither can there be any mystery about the writer.

7.2 Zen and the Art of Lock Picking

In order to excel at lock picking, you must train yourself to have a visually reconstructive imagination. The idea is to use information from all your senses to build a picture of what is happening inside the lock as you pick it. Basically, you want to project your senses into the lock to receive a full picture of how it is responding to your manipulations. Once you have learned how to build this picture, it is easy to choose manipulations that will open the lock.

From Ted the Tool, *Guide to Lock Picking*. Chapter 7, "Advanced Lock Picking" (1991). http://www.lysator.liu.se/mit-guide/mit-guide.html

(over left) *I, Digital*, 2001
Digital video, colour, sound 4'18" (for monitor with headphones)

(over right) *SERIES TITLE*, 2000
Digital video, colour, sound 2'40" (for monitor with headphones)

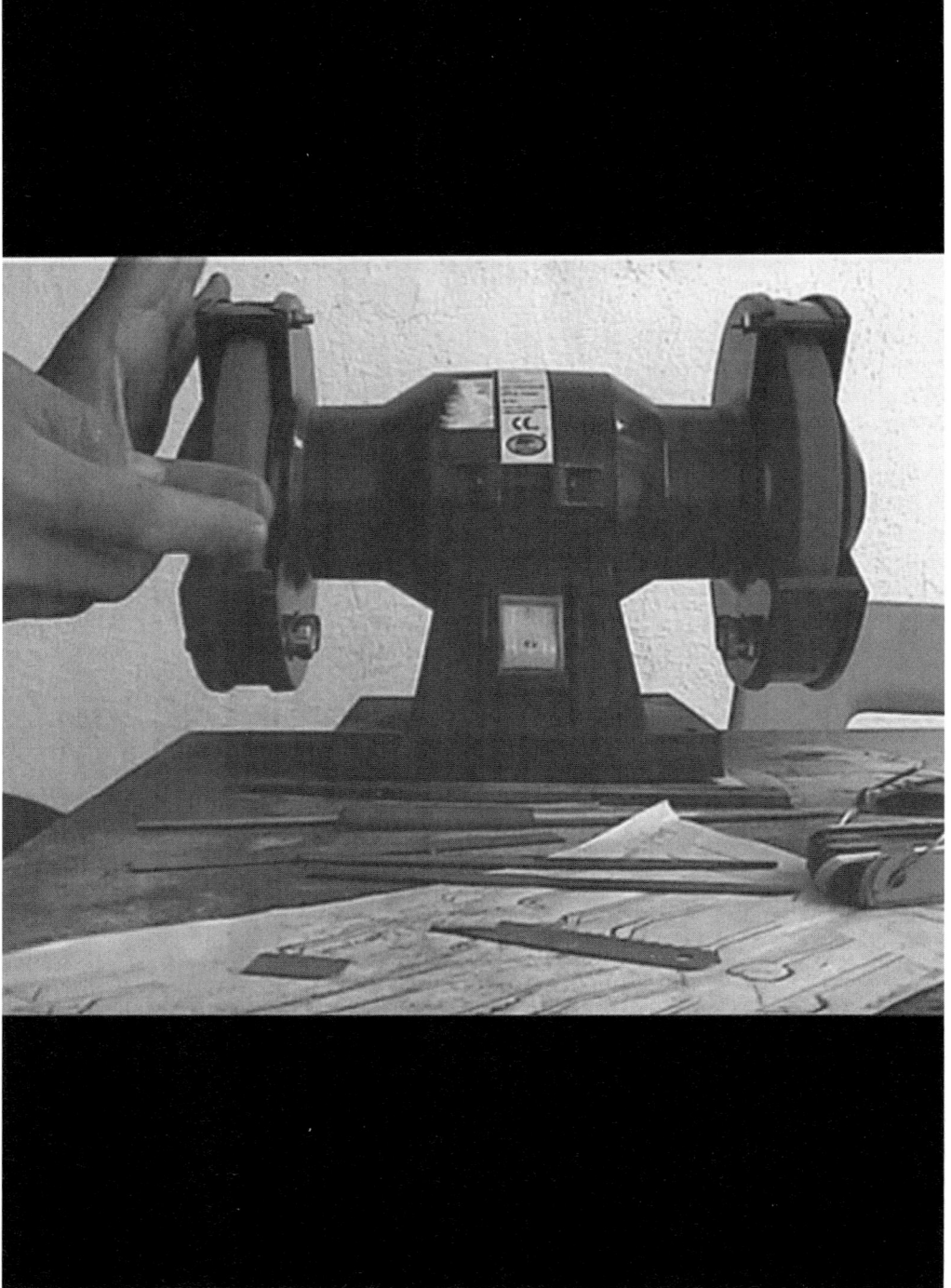

dalia judovitz

DE-ASSEMBLING VISION
conceptual strategies in duchamp, matta-clark, wilson

Among Marcel Duchamp's multiple strategies for challenging the notion and meaning of art in the modern period, his rejection of the retinal aspects of painting and later art has been singled out as one of his most influential gestures.[1] This reaction against a purely visual understanding of painting reflected his attempts to reinvest art with an intellectual dimension that would bring into play its verbal, cultural, and institutional frames of reference. His efforts to strip painting bare of its visual vestments and outward appearance, by making visible its theoretical and institutional givens, redefined decisively the destiny of art as an activity that no longer abides purely in a visual register.[2] Interrogating on intellectual grounds the preeminence accorded to a retinal understanding of art, Duchamp's anti-visual stance also implied a reflection on the mechanisms of sight in the modern period. By elaborating the conceptual and cultural premises that stage the public's consumption of works of art, he decentered the priority of vision as a purely physical operation. His attempt to rethink art as a phenomenon in excess of the optical reflects, as Martin Jay suggested, an anti-ocularcentric impulse that has been central to the development of twentieth-century French thought, art, and culture.[3] What is specific, however, to Duchamp's critique of the "look" is his concerted effort to question spectatorship by de-assembling systematically the givens attached both to the production and consumption of visual forms. His efforts to bring an end to the retinal bias of art have played a crucial role in fueling contemporary debates regarding the possible end of art as conventionally understood.

Gregg Horowitz and Tom Huhn have noted that Marcel Duchamp's anti-retinal stance, understood as a refusal to abide solely in a visual register as the fateful locus of art, brought art face to face with its historical drive for self-definition in visual form and thus its ostensible end:

> Art only needed to have its own lack of visual essence revealed to it to see that its historical drive for self-definition in visual form had been all along a delaying of its rendez-vous with its historical end. ... Duchamp, we might say, brought art to its historical culmination by rendering its commitments visible, by, that is, making visible (not visual) the dialectic of the demand for visuality.[4]

However, to speak about revealing art's lack of a visual essence is not to deny the role of vision and the visible, but rather to question art's

ISSN 0969-725X print/ISSN 1469-2899 online/02/010095-19 © 2002 Taylor & Francis Ltd and the Editors of *Angelaki*
DOI: 10.1080/09697250220142074

de-assembling vision

demand for visuality as a founding premise and as defining destiny. Such an inquiry implies making art's commitment to visuality visible, not only in terms of its outward manifestations, but also its modes of exhibition display and consumption in the public sphere.[5] Duchamp's critique of the retinal involved re-materializing the viewing process of art, thereby restituting its constitutive frames of cultural and historical reference. Rather than liquidating cultural traditions through the cult of the new, as Clement Greenberg has contended, Duchamp brought art face to face with its founding premises, its historical definition in visual form, and its modalities of reception in the modern age.[6] It is this legacy that will prove to be decisive to postmodernity, insofar as the question of the end of art opens up a conceptual reflection on art's conditions of possibility, that is, its historical, cultural, and social premises.

Duchamp's efforts to re-materialize the viewing process implied an interrogation of the art museum that socially frames and institutionally valorizes the reception of works of art. Insofar as forms of museum exhibition display stage the spectator's visual consumption, visual experience also becomes the expression of social and market forces of public consumption that inform the institution of the museum.[7] In the museum, visual contemplation of particular works is supplanted by multiple and rapid exposures fueled by a logic of consumption. Moreover, the expectations that the spectator brings to the viewing of certain works may function as a form of overexposure, insofar as they predetermine and foreclose visual experience by reducing it to yet another vehicle of consumer culture. Marcel Duchamp alluded to this condition by noting that the act of viewing involves an active interchange between the spectator and the work that is minimized, indeed obstructed, by the conditions of display and the public's expectations:

> The exchange between what one / puts on view [the whole / setting up to put on view (all areas)] / and the glacial regard of the public (which sees and / forgets immediately) / Very often / this exchange has the value / of an infra thin separation / (meaning that the more / a thing is admired / and looked at the less there is an inf. t./sep.[8]

According to Duchamp, the visibility of an artwork is attenuated by its exhibition in the public sphere, since the apparatus of display determines the act of seeing. The conditions of display that set up the position of spectatorship glaze over the viewer's look by deactivating engagement with the work.[9] If "seeing" becomes a way of "forgetting," this is because admiration implies less an encounter with an art object per se than its visual foreclosure. It merely functions to confirm some prior knowledge of the object, mediated through its reproduction, market value, or its cultural reputation. Thus the "infra thin" separation that describes visual exchange is eroded, to the extent that looking is overdetermined by forms of social exchange. Interrogating the ostensible transparency of vision, Duchamp redefines the act of viewing in terms of its social and historical determinations. By delaying the immediacy of seeing, he challenges the distinction between vision and visuality understood as the opposition of physical vs. social interpretations of vision.[10] The spectator's "look" thus emerges as a construct, a position that is assembled through the manipulation of the optical and display apparatus that determine the visual exposure and consumption of art objects in the public sphere.[11]

In order to elaborate in more concrete terms Duchamp's anti-retinal critique, this study will begin with a brief examination of his testamentary work *Given: 1. the waterfall, 2. the illuminating gas* (1946–66), one of the earliest examples of installation art. This work explicitly stages the historical and institutional "givens" which inform the exhibition and visual consumption of art objects as an apparatus of projection and display. This mixed-media assemblage will be considered as an installation of the spectator's look, a peephole set-up which reveals through a strategy of overexposure the premises of vision as an apparatus of projection and material consumption in the public sphere. Duchamp's attempt to historicize the position of the observer by disclosing its premises as a technical and social construction implies a critique of the camera

Figs 1 and 2. *Given: 1. the waterfall, 2. the illuminating gas* (1946–66). Philadelphia Museum of Art: Given by the Cassandra Foundation. © 2000 Artists Rights Society (ARS), New York/ADAGP, Paris/Estate of Marcel Duchamp

de-assembling vision

Figs 3 and 4. *Conical Intersect* (1975). David Zwirner Gallery, New York. Courtesy of David Zwirner, NY, and the Estate of Matta-Clark

Fig. 5. *20:50* (1987). The Saatchi Gallery, London. Photograph: Anthony Oliver

obscura as a model for vision. Jonathan Crary has argued that the historic specificity of modernist vision marks a rupture with the conditions of vision presupposed by this device, which legislated for an observer what constituted perceptual truth, as well as delineated a fixed set of relations to which an observer was made subject.[12] Duchamp's efforts to illuminate the seduction of the retinal by undermining its perceptual immediacy and to dismantle the position of spectatorship as subjective mastery mark his seminal contributions to the modernist critique of vision and visuality, as well as his legacy to postmodern installation art.[13] In the wake of Duchamp, installation artists such as Gordon Matta-Clark in the 1970s, and Richard Wilson in the 1980s and 1990s, will interrogate vision by exposing its social and perceptual scaffoldings as an apparatus whose determinations engage with the logic of the museum, as institutional structure and architectural artifact.[14] While different from each other in terms of their outward appearance, Matta-Clark's *Conical Intersect* (1975) and Wilson's *20:50* (1987) share a common conceptual agenda insofar as they seek to dismantle visuality as a necessary "given" or condition for artistic production and consumption. Whereas Matta-Clark will expose the visual "con" of the "look" by dissecting the intersection of the spatial and social scaffolding of spectatorship with the institution of the museum, Wilson will undermine spectatorship by overriding spatial determinations, short-circuiting the detachment of vision through its perceptual overload. Whether enacted from within (Duchamp and Wilson), or from outside (Matta-Clark) of the confines of the museum, these efforts to bring the viewer face to face with the institutional conditions that subtend visuality will result in the redefinition of spectatorship and the deterritorialization of the museum as an autonomous space of consumption.

de-assembling vision

duchamp and the "givens" of the visible

> I am rather uneasy when there is nothing more than this retinal effect.
> *Marcel Duchamp*

Marcel Duchamp's playful denunciation of "retinal euphoria," associated with the effects of conventional painting, marked his radical critique of pictorial vision. Painting's celebration of the visual engendered through a display of manual and artisanal virtuosity is challenged in his works in order to privilege their verbal and conceptual potential. Duchamp's experiments with the readymades (from 1913 onwards) mark the challenge that the exhibition of these mass-produced objects as art objects extends to art and its conditions of possibility.[15] The readymade is a visual lure; it is the perfect copy of an object, since it *is* the object itself.[16] This visual expropriation of the object by its mechanical analogues radically marks a break with both painting and conventional art as a whole, insofar as these objects function as signs that reference simultaneously both their ordinary and artistic conditions. Rather than fetishizing the object as the expression of formal and material artistic concerns, Duchamp appropriates its mechanical analogues, thereby making visible the institutional context that frames, makes legible, and endows objects with value. While the readymades stage the gratuitous conversion of ordinary objects into works of art, they also undermine through this very gesture art's reliance on visual appearance as a defining characteristic.[17]

Through mechanical reproduction, Duchamp discovers a new paradigm for thinking about artistic production, one that expropriates visual appearance of its retinal impact in order to reinvest its potential in strategic interventions that make visible the institutional conventions that define the exhibition and consumption of objects as art objects. The readymades disfigure the mimetic ambitions of painting through the visual redundancy of mechanically reproduced objects. As Walter Benjamin observed, by detaching objects from the realm of tradition and substituting a plurality of copies for unique works, mechanical reproduction undermines the "aura" of works of art as experienced in their original sacred or ritual settings.[18] As Benjamin pointed out, in the modern age the "exhibition value" of the work supersedes the "cult value" of art, since the significance of art objects is defined as a function of their being put on view.[19] However, although they initially appear as the denial or even abandonment of painting, the readymades engage conceptually and draw upon painting insofar as they literally materialize its mimetic ambitions. The readymades thus embody the postponement of art's pictorial becoming, precisely because they restage the question of visual appearance as a belated event, one no longer intrinsic to the fate of painting but rather to its conceptual re-embodiments.

Duchamp's investigations of the notion of spectatorship and the visible, as representations, rather than purely optical constructs, culminate in *Given: 1. the waterfall, 2. the illuminating gas* (1946–66; Philadelphia Museum of Art). Exhibited posthumously, this multi-media installation is a life-size box, constructed as a peep hole apparatus. This work evokes the history of optical, pictorial, and spectatorship experiments in art, alluding to Samuel Van Hoogstraten peep-box, *Perspective Box with Views of a Dutch Interior* (seventeenth century; National Gallery, London).[20] In Hoogstraten's doll-size peep-box, the pictorial depictions of a Dutch interior domestic scene involving several rooms leading off one another is artfully set up so as to create the spatial illusionism of multiple three-dimensional spaces. The constructed illusionism of this display is deliberately emphasized by the presence of a second peephole on the other side, and the additional depiction of a man looking in through the far window.[21] Mimicking the spectator's illicit and intrusive look into this domestic space, the voyeuristic regard of the man outside the window both mirrors and intercepts the spectator's look. The reproductions of pictures, mirrors, and their reflections act to further emphasize an illusionism whose retinal impact is generated through allusions to pictorial renderings. The composite perspectivism of these renderings is artfully combined to deceive the eye into the naive belief that it is "seeing," rather than merely witnessing depictions of its look.

According to Svetlana Alpers this box represents "the accumulated nature of the picturing of the world fit in a peep-box."²² Hoogstraten's peep-box thus functions as a miniature artistic compendium whose depictions of vision constitute a veritable catalogue, a portable museum of pictorial strategies for staging and deceiving the eye. Moreover, by making visible the apparatus of display that structures the act of viewing, Hoogstraten's peep-box exposes the voyeuristic nature of spectatorship.

Given is an assemblage of spectatorship, revealed as an apparatus of viewing and display which stages the spectator's "look" as a form of pictorial consumption. The immobility of *Given* as a permanent installation in the Philadelphia Museum of Art requires the viewer's deliberate displacement to the site. However, it is important to recall that the apparent immobility of this work is deceptive to the extent that it was originally assembled in Duchamp's studio in New York, only to be de-assembled according to his precise instructions, and re-assembled in the space of the museum.²³ In the manual of instructions, *Given* is referred to as an "*aproximation démontable*" (an approximation that can be taken apart, or disassembled), a designation that clearly argues against the visual appearance of solidity and finality engendered by the work.²⁴ The fact that this work is called an "approximation," to be dismantled and re-assembled, captures its provisional nature as an installation whose activation implies the inscription of the viewer/producer. Duchamp's specification that the word "approximation" is intended to convey "a margin of ad libitum in the assembly and disassembly of construction" suggests that this work's attainment of visual form is a function of the viewer/producer's libidinal investments.²⁵ By inscribing a libidinal dimension into the visual production/consumption of this work, Duchamp exposes the visual "con" of the retinal, undermining its pretensions to neutrality and detachment.

The conditions of display of *Given: 1. the waterfall 2. the illuminating gas* (Fig. 1) radically undermine the viewer's expectations of what constitutes a visible exhibit in a museum.²⁶ Its location behind a barred door, at the end of an underlit room, renders this work visually inaccessible initially. The logic of visual consumption that underlies museum exhibits is put into question and delayed. This lack of visual access can be overcome only through the intervention of other spectators whose look initiates the possibility of beholding, restaging spectatorship through the circuit of its social mediation. Before the question of visibility, of what we see in *Given*, can begin to be posed, Duchamp has actively barred and delayed the spectator's gaze by repositioning its perceptual immediacy through its social and institutional mediations. Upon looking, the spectator's detached look is captured by the peepholes, immobilized in a voyeuristic position more akin to carnivals or pornographic shows than to a museum. As John Cage observed, *Given* imprisons the viewer at a particular distance and removes the freedom to look and mobility formerly enjoyed in reference to the transparency of the *Large Glass*.²⁷ However, this attempt to predetermine the spectator's position is a concern that Duchamp expressed, when he mused that "it would be interesting if artists would prescribe the distances from which their work should be viewed."²⁸ First denied visual access, the spectator is then invited to look through the peepholes, which set up and fix the spectator's view from a predetermined distance. The spectator's predicament as voyeur, imprisoned in a particular position and way of looking, reflects Duchamp's deliberate gesture to hold the viewer at bay, all the while setting up spectatorship for view as an apparatus of display.

Looking through the peepholes the viewer is startled by the blinding illumination of the scene (which has the effect of a photographic overexposure) and by the sense of visual constriction and violence produced by a gaping aperture through a brick wall (Fig. 2). In his manual of instructions, Duchamp specified that black velvet curtains are to be used as a way of creating a "black chamber" between the door and the wall of bricks, thereby mimicking the effects of a photographic chamber. This photographic allusion emphasizes the logic of exposure associated with vision at issue in this work.²⁹ The brick wall delays the viewer's gaze, it undermines the urgency of the look by inscribing it into a narra-

de-assembling vision

tive of potential violence associated with the physical breach of the brick wall. Through this irregular breach, the spectator is confronted with the display of a cropped, mock nude who defiantly holds up a gas lamp, while lying spread eagle in a hyper-realistic landscape with a running waterfall in the background. Described by Joseph Masheck as "startlingly gross and amateurish," this diorama view of the spread-eagle nude staged by the peephole apparatus startles by mirroring back the spectator's look.[30] This exposure of genitalia, which has conventionally been veiled in the pictorial traditions of the nude, is here defiantly displayed and offered up for view.[31] The spectator's intrusive gaze that seeks to probe the reality of sex is projected back upon itself, thus becoming itself the object of scrutiny. The violence of this work appears to lie less in its manifest sexual exhibitionism and voyeurism, than in the fact that the spectator is put face to face with his or her desire to look, to be fascinated by the consumption of sexuality as an image. Despite this work's overt sexual display, or rather, because of its exaggerated display, which is emphasized by blinding illumination of the scene, the equation of sexuality and vision is sundered. Duchamp undermines the logic of voyeurism by questioning the coincidence of sight with visual pleasure. In so doing, he moves away from equating sexuality with forms of visual essentialism, towards redefining it as a construct of mechanisms of cultural and social projection.

The sense of visual discomfort and violation that *Given* engenders is less the expression of its explicit sexual content than the shameless exposure and confrontation of the viewer with the apparatus of spectatorship. What *Given* exposes is less sexuality per se, than its modalities of representation and consumption as perpetuated by the artistic traditions of the pictorial nude. Attempting to find a way out of painting, Duchamp reproduces and makes visible its conventions, through a strategy where the installation of the mocking figure of the nude emerges as a rhetorical trace of painting dispossessed of its outward appearance. Staging its complicity with the viewer's gaze, with painting understood in the mode of the peep show, *Given* de-assembles the spectator's gaze, freeing it from its objectifying constraints by delaying its impact. Appealing to conceptual strategies that defer the perceptual priority of vision, Duchamp de-essentializes the visual impact of painting. In so doing he undermines the referentiality of gender, as well as the artistic modes that sustain it, since their facticity is provisional on spectatorship understood as public spectacle. As an "installation" that exposes the objectifying and dead-end character of the spectator's look, *Given* stages the mortality of the "nude" as pictorial genre and of art as a visual form. Ensconced in the museum, this anti-monument or cenotaph undermines its visual and institutional logic. By decentering the priority of vision through a strategy of delay that postpones *Given*'s retinal becoming, Duchamp resituates its potential meanings and conceptual legacy within a postmodern horizon.

matta-clark's anarchitectures: the museum as ruin

> The determining factor is the degree to which my intervention can transform the structure into an act of communication.
> Matta Clark

While informed by Duchamp's anti-retinal stance and interrogation of the museum, Gordon Matta-Clark's works redeploy these issues in a different sphere, since they seek to radicalize and ultimately challenge the relation of art and architecture. Matta-Clark used decayed urban buildings, which he called "throwaway environments," as the strategic medium for interventions whose lack of visual appeal, disposability, and precarious existence outside the sphere of the museum restaged the ideology of modernism in the modality of a disposable ruin. Subject to impending demolition and even destruction, the record of his works captured in drawings, photographic, and filmic documentation proves more lasting than the actual pieces themselves. It is precisely the inability of these works to endure, to be preserved, monumentalized, or enshrined that attests to their resistance to an artistic ideology that would objectify and reduce them to a spectacle of consumption. Matta-Clark's efforts to break away from conventional notions of art and architecture involve the expansion of the historical and social understandings of space, by releasing the "power of the positioned interrelationship of things beyond form and function."32 The formal and functional concerns regarding space are redirected into an inquiry regarding the passage of time, notably the disintegration of space through lived time. This effort to reconceptualize architectural space as an always already lived site, whose urbanity is explored in the modality of decay, constitutes a radical departure from the formal and artistic logic of the museum. Matta-Clark deterritorializes the institutional ambitions of the museum by relocating works within the logic of debris and demolition that inhabits zones of urban decay. The structures of ruined buildings he operates on are the visible symptoms of social decay, of a breakdown of notions of community that underlie the production of lived space.

While relying on already extant architectural structures, Matta-Clark's interventions put the notion of architecture itself under erasure, insofar as he challenges its conditions of possibility.33 His works remind us of Heidegger's injunction that "the essence of the erecting of buildings cannot be understood adequately in terms either of architecture or of engineering construction, nor in terms of a mere combination of the two."34 Matta-Clark's violent reframing and rethinking of architectural and engineering practices involves exposing buildings as exoskeletons of modalities of dwelling in order to reveal the lived traces of their social history. Matta-Clark intervenes in the urban landscape by cutting up and disfiguring already abandoned and ruined buildings, thereby putting the social and institutional presuppositions of architecture on display. He inverts the idea of sculpture by not filling in spaces but making holes whose breaching thrust exposes the hidden violence intrinsic to purely formal and functional understandings of building. By making visible the layers of lived sediment associated with dwelling, these voids activate the reinfusion of socially determined meanings.35 His strategies of intervention mark the radical rupture with all functional constraints, severing the logic of construction through engineered acts of deconstruction.

judovitz

Matta-Clark's "anarchitectural" works thus excavate within the building ethos of modernist architecture the moribund, melancholic condition of urban decay.

In his original plan for *Conical Intersect* produced for the Paris Biennial, Matta-Clark proposed to make an enormous hole in the new building of the still unfinished Pompidou Center, the controversial museum of Modern Art which was under construction in a large area under demolition in Les Halles.36 Jean-Hubert Martin notes that Matta-Clark's initial plan was surprising since it involved doing the reverse of what he usually did: "That is, he wanted to make one of his works before the completion of a building, rather than before its demolition."37 However, since this project was not deemed viable, he was given two weeks' use of two adjacent townhouses dating back to the seventeenth century at 27–29 Rue Beaubourg, which were among the last buildings left standing in the modernization of the district. Matta-Clark described *Conical Intersect*, also called *Etant d'art pour locataire* (1975) (Fig. 3), as follows:

> The work was interesting as a non-monumental counterpart to the grandiose bridge-like skeleton of the center just behind. For two plaster-dusty weeks people watched us measuring, cutting and removing the debris from the truncated conical void. The base of the cone was a circle four meters in diameter through the north wall. The central axis made an approximately forty-five-degree angle with the street below. As the cone diminished in circumference, it twisted up through the walls, floors and out of the attic roof of the adjoining house. This hollow form became a *Son et Lumière* for passers-by or an extravagant new standard in sun and air for lodgers.38

A demolition slated anti-monument to the rising bridge-like scaffolding of the newly erected Pompidou Center, this provisional ruin stages the drama of urban decay as visual counterpoint to the ostensible desires for modernization and urban renewal entailed in the construction of the new museum of modern art.39 *Conical Intersect* takes on the social and institutional presuppositions of the museum, on the ground level, as it were. It focuses attention on the construction of the edifice, as a gesture of deliberate violence that relies upon the destruction and grandiose reconstruction of the social and community fabric of an entire neighborhood. Visually reframing, and partially blocking the side view of the Pompidou Center rising beyond it, the ruined façade of the two buildings at once bars and realigns the view for passers-by. Mimicking the gaping wound of an eye, the conical aperture (Fig. 4) opens downwards towards the spectacle of the street below, as well as provides an exposure of the building's hollowed form for the passers-by. The eruption of sun and air engineered through the cut in the roof and the circular opening in the front disrupts the building's functional closure through its visual exposure. Depending on the position of the viewer, this work becomes a "sound and light show" (*son et lumière*) for the passers-by, or a "new standard in sun and air for lodgers."[40] Fracturing the unity of vision, by not allowing for a "single or overall view," and thus defying the "category of a snapshot project," *Conical Intersect* interrogates the structures that determine visual consumption.[41] Alluding to Duchamp's *Given* (*Étant Donnés*), a reference reinforced by this work's punning subtitle *Étant d'art pour locataire* (which can be translated as *Given Art for the Dweller* or *Standard for the Dweller*), *Conical Intersect* dismantles the apparatus of spectatorship by introducing the point of view of the absent dweller. It is precisely this historical position, voided by the erection of the nascent museum, which marks the blinding gap at the heart of visual consumption. The illusion of visual mastery fostered through spectatorship is radically disrupted through an appeal to notions of dwelling whose historical and social underpinnings defy reduction to conventional visual and architectural forms.

The overt associations of this work with Duchamp's critique of spectatorship and the logic of the museum are spelled out in Matta-Clark's alternative designation of this work as "*Quel Con*," as presented by Gerry Hovagimyan:

> The other name was *Quel Con*, which he knew was a very wry play on Duchamp's *L.H.O.O.Q.* (Gordon also called it at various times, "Quel Can," "Cal Can.") Duchamp's title when said aloud letter by letter, means in French, "she has a hot behind." Gordon's pun says both "what a cone," and "what a – " – I don't know quite how to say this, "lady's genitals, a cunt."[42]

Matta-Clark's reference to Duchamp's *L.H.O.O.Q.* (1919) is not surprising given that this readymade stages, through its comic disfiguration of a commercial print of the Mona Lisa, Duchamp's critique of pictorial vision and his mockery of the masterpiece as the embodiment of the institutional aspirations of the museum.[43] Matta-Clark reappropriates Duchamp's barb at the museum in order to redirect the spectator's look at the condition of the newly nascent museum as an edifice that entails the violent erasure, the "shave" of the edifices that surround it. The reversibility of Mr and Mrs Leiseville (1699) "his and hers" townhouses, which constitute the site of Matta-Clark's interventions, playfully alludes to the gendered reversals operated by Duchamp on the Mona Lisa through the discrete addition of a mustache and goatee. If Duchamp undermines the facticity of sex by suggesting that it may be a function of the reversibility of the spectator's look, Matta-Clark redeploys this playful rhetoric to hold up a mirror to the monumentality of the art museum in order to reverse its logic as ruin in the making. By setting up the visual lure of an eye and mimicking its optical functions through mechanisms of conical projection, Matta-Clark exposes the museum's visual "con," the institutional and ideological set-up at work on the unsuspecting passer-by spectators. Countering the spectacle of the erection of the new museum, he redirects their look to the vacant, eye-like aperture that bears witnesses to the townhouses' demolition as that blind spot in urban architecture that will continue to haunt its modernist ideals.

Conical Intersect thus captures the "transitional nature of the urban environment" and the "implicit violence of social displacement."[44] As disposable ruins of our times, the townhouses' pathos is to be found not in their formal structure, but in the loss of their temporal function, since they no longer reflect an adequate embodiment of either lived space or an ideal of community. These twin houses emerge as mnemonic reminders of social displacement, a transition that must be literally erased by demolition in order to enable a new modernist ideal of community to come forth. By recasting this modernist ideal as an obsolescent ruin, Matta-Clark temporalizes its postmodern becoming in the modality of decay. Viewed from the inside, the introduction of light into the building functions less to illuminate the structure than to scramble its internal coherence. The light reveals the sedimented layers of lived meaning or memory attached to the dwelling. Light here references not vision but time, since it illuminates the internal surfaces of the building so that walking through becomes an encounter with traces of other people's histories. The marked surfaces, screen memories of individuals now departed, redefine the building as an apparatus for restaging collective memory. The inscription of the inhabitant's presence is figured by the eerily void premises, which recall the evidence of human life as a haunting absence. As Matta-Clark explains in reference to *Splitting* (1975): "I just wanted to get back to whatever the empty rooms were made of, like the layers of the linoleum on the floor, or whatever there was of surfaces. The shadows of the persons who had lived there were still pretty warm."[45] As memorials or tombs of urban life, these abandoned buildings capture the traces of human dwelling as perceptible absence. The positivist construction and manipulation of space that characterizes architecture as it attempts through building to set up forms of dwelling is here unveiled in terms of its effects of reification. The abjection of the twin townhouses illuminates the trace of the living subject as alienation, as subjection to the violence of the urban sprawl. As both a symptom of and apparatus for forms of human sentience, *Conical Intersect* displays the alienating gap of the human, as a subject estranged from the conditions of living.[46]

Matta-Clark's *Conical Intersect* thus challenges the meaning of both architectural and artistic modes of production. Instead of activities whose performance seek realization as finished structures, his anartistic operations redefine production as a process that brings forth the specific social and cultural meanings attached to notions of dwelling. His interventions involve

judovitz

"unbuilding" objective structures so as to reveal their social and cultural underpinnings, as conditions that inform the phenomenological and conceptual appropriations of space.[47] In *Conical Intersect*, as in his subsequent works that challenge the edifice and institution of the museum, Matta-Clark derealizes the intent of architectural notions of reference, through conceptual redeployments that violate the visual semblance and viewing space of the museum.[48] These include his plans for cutting-up a seminar room into two-by-two square pieces that would be stacked in the middle of the exhibition space for the "Idea as Model" show at the Institute of Architecture and Urban Studies in New York (1976). His blueprint for *Meander* (1976) involved making three diagonal cuts through the edifice of Georgia Museum of Art in order to create a "free passage from ground to sky."[49] In *Office Baroque* (1977; Antwerp), he reconfigured the space of a building directly across a military museum, along the explosive axis of two interlocking semi-circular areas of cuts. In his last work, *Circus or The Caribbean Orange* (1978), commissioned by the Museum of Contemporary Art in Chicago in an adjoining townhouse slated for its expansion, he generated a series of circular cuts whose spherical shape unfolds like a ball thrown into space along an ascending diagonal axis.[50] Like *Conical Intersect*, these works keep the museum in sight in order to challenge its visual and institutional logic through the violent activation of modes of viewing that shatter the ostensible transparency of both vision and space. Referencing the ideology of modernist architecture, his works apply a radical wedge to the idea and edifice of the museum deterritorializing its visual premises and modernist ambitions through the temporalizing register of the ruin.[51]

wilson's space transformers

> To think between the center and the edge of things.
> *Robert Smithson*

Richard Wilson's *20:50* (1987; used sump oil, steel, dimensions variable) exhibited at the Saatchi Gallery, London (Fig. 5), alludes to both Duchamp's and Matta-Clark's interrogations of the apparatus of visual consumption, while pursuing a different agenda. This work addresses less the object of vision than the spectator's perceptual horizon whose activation is orchestrated through conceptual interventions. As this study will show, *20:50* both staggers and speeds up visual consumption by creating a perceptual overload, a delirium of vision that serves to short-circuit its impact, thereby dismantling its immediacy. Like *Given*, direct visual access to this work is barred. A narrow aperture opens out of the gallery space leading off without precise indication as to the nature of the installation hidden from view to the right. As the viewer draws closer an overwhelming smell of oil overpowers the senses, an olfactory euphoria akin to stench, that brings to mind the residual presence of large industrial spaces. A security guard stands at the threshold of the entry into the installation, not to protect the piece, as it turns out, but rather to protect the spectator. The access to the large rectangular room filled with 10,000 gallons of used sump oil is mediated through a metal jetty that projects obliquely into the space. This jetty is protectively walled in on three sides coming up to the waist, constituting a metal trench or well suspended in the heavy oil. Its outline tapers inward with a slight upwards incline dead-ending within the installation. At its edges, the surface of the oil disturbed by the viewer's movement threatens to spill over and violate the integrity of both the viewer's body and that of the spectatorial platform. It is precisely when the viewer activates the piece by physically stepping into it that the function of the security guard is revealed. The guard attempts to protect the beholder from this work, which threatens to spill over and contaminate the viewer's body. Thus from its very inception, the neutrality of beholding is threatened and exposed as a gesture that has potential physical consequences.

This threat of physical contamination is not merely about the physical interplay between the viewer and the piece, since it also involves forms of visual exposure and disorientation that are so radical as to question the viewing subject's position and orientation in space. The visual and reflective properties of oil as a shimmering pool create a kind of visual delirium subverting the sense of spatial orientation. The reflective surface engenders a play of mirrors, confusing the viewer's sense of what constitutes reflection as opposed to what can be seen in depth through the transparent medium of the oil.[52] This undecidable play of surface and depth as an experience of the "reversibility" sets space free of its rational connotations by imploding the logic of vision.[53] This loss of spatial orientation, which impacts on the sense of grounding of the beholder, enacts a fundamental subversion of figure/ground relations. In *20:50*, it is the viewer who is the medium acted upon and ungrounded, and not painting, which conventionally functioned as the privileged medium for staging figure/ground relationships. Commenting on the public's interaction with his installation, Wilson underlines the violence of its impact: "I watched some people go into that room and walk halfway up the corridor and grab the sides – they thought the floor had gone. They got oil on them ..." (*DYD* 4). This, however, was not a momentary experience, since this radical sense of disorientation persisted beyond the immediate scope of the installation. The sense of vertigo resulting from vertiginous loss of spatial orientation, as a physical sense of grounding, dispossesses the viewer of the conventional neutrality of beholding. It transforms the spectator into a performer, an unwitting actor whose agency and subjective position has been restaged by the experience of the installation.

This sense of spatial expropriation engendered by the play of reflections is also echoed by the visual expropriation of the beholder. The experience of seeing is activated by stepping into the work. However, the waist-high metal walls of the viewing trench preempt the spectators from seeing their reflections. The physical impediment of the well prevents self-reflection, disrupting the desire to see oneself represented on the mirror surface of the oil pool. Vision is sundered from the temptations of self-reflexivity, since the beholder is dispossessed of his or her visual reflection. Disabled from visually inscribing him or herself into the work, the visual lure of the play of reflections only serves to emphasize the position of the beholder as the blind spot in the installation. This visual disenfranchisement of the seeing subject reveals a "moment of non-visual 'belonging,'" that pertains to and inhabits the very experience of seeing.54 In *20:50*, this condition is made perceptible as the expression of the positional nature of the viewer's body, of its enforced invisibility in the midst of the reflective oil.

20:50's visual overload is paradoxically achieved through this work's invisibility to the extent that the sump oil that fills the tank is molded to the dimensions of the room, thus fudging visual boundaries and form/content relations. According to Wilson: "It brought me right back to the perfect solution of making a piece of work which is almost invisible, ... except that in this case the room was the mould and the liquid remained liquid" (*DYD* 4). Alluding to techniques of mechanical reproduction, Wilson treats the room as a mold whose shape is first reproduced by the tank within it, only to be once again "reproduced" by the sump oil whose fluid illusionism divests the room of its architectural solidity.55 Wilson thus undermines the architectural reference of the gallery site through a strategy of technical delays, which confuse its spatial and formal logic.56 Wilson explained that his choice of oil was driven precisely by its anti-sculptural character and the fact that its "liquidity" was technically mediated and socially regulated: "I was also interested in using a material which was so anti-sculpture, a material which you could be arrested and fined for if you poured it down the drain" (*DYD* 4). If oil is anti-sculpture, this is not simply because it is a liquid, and thus a material that only achieves shape in response to forms of containment, but also because it is a contaminant (with "environmentally unfriendly connotations") that threatens the physical well-being of the spectator.

Wilson's choice of sump oil – a material equated with industrial residues from mechanical engines – is also motivated by its derivative and hence transformative character: "... what better way to deal with the idea of transformation than to deal with a material that has been through its own transformation?" (*DYD* 4). But the latent transformation of oil into residue or sump oil is merely a stage in a set of metamorphoses that oil undergoes starting from its geological origin as a fossil fuel to its later chemical refinements into modern fuels. When Wilson notes that "Oil is very much a material of our century" (*DYD* 4), this is not merely because of its associations with wealth and the wars fought over it, but also because oil as a substance incarnates in its transformations temporal history and its liquidation in modern times. As a material that has been through its own transformations, sump oil not only has a geological and technological history, but it also tells a story about the fate of history in the modern and postmodern period. And, perhaps, the story that it tells both as liquid medium and as olfactory residue references the history of art as well. The oil's dilatory presence both as liquid and as invisible smell or gas suggests a allusion to painting, to the materiality of an absent medium present here in its conceptual evocations. However, this earlier historical condition of art is evoked only to be sublated by its subsequent conceptual transformations. Like the sump oil that functions as recorded history, so does *20:50* reference its own art historical past. According to Wilson, "it seemed to touch on its immediate past: Op Art, Land Art, Field Painting, Installation – so many of those other 'isms' from the sixties and early seventies were suddenly pulled together" (*DYD* 4). However, *20:50* does not only pull these various art "isms" together in a compendium that acts as a totalizing corpus, but it conceptually restages and transforms them inasmuch as this work is virtual, multiple, and variable in its displayed manifestations.

The designation of variable dimensions used to describe *20:50* refers to the fact that this is a work of multiple incarnations. Each time it was exhibited, first at Matt's, then in Edinburgh, at Saatchi's and at Meto Japan, its visual appearance changed, reflecting the specific constraints of the site. In his interview with Richard Wilson, Steve Rushton compares Charles Saatchi's buying of this work to the relationship between Richard Hamilton's *Large Glass* and Duchamp's *Large Glass*, that is the acquisition of a record of the original event at Matt's. Richard Wilson, however, clarifies his own position by specifying that what Saatchi bought was the rights to the work, to its conceptual framework, rather than its objective incarnations: "What he actually bought were the rights to that piece of work which meant that every time it is shown it has to be rebuilt. Each time it is shown the focus changes. It can only be shown with the owner's permission and in every case so far it has had my agreement … it is very much a chameleon piece" (*DYD* 5). By selling the rights to the work, rather than the work itself, Wilson clarifies the status of his intervention as one that bears on the ideas that govern its construction. Selling the rights to the work involves a transfer of ownership that references a conceptual blueprint, rather than a distinct and unique object. Despite its site-specific manifestations, this work is virtual since its multiple physical embodiments are both variable and contingent. Each site introduces its own contingencies thereby modifying the physical realization of the work's conceptual blueprint, since the work's reflective properties change in respect to the specific sources, position, and quantity of light. As Wilson explains in reference to *Sheer Fluke* (1985): "The influence of the room was important, because the room was doing all the informing via me" (*DYD* 6). By recognizing the contingently "appropriative" aspects of the site that inform the display and physical appearance of this work, Wilson expropriates himself as an artistic agent by relegating himself to the status of an intermediary negotiating the givens of a specific site.[57] The so-called "appropriation" of the work by the site, in the case of Wilson's *20:50* and Duchamp's "appropriation" of the museum room by his installation, implies the "expropriation" of these spaces from the institutional logic of the museum. The space of the gallery exhibit is "reappropriated" through the installation and put on display in a manner that subverts the decontextualizing effects of the museum as an autonomous space intended to accommodate multiple displays.[58] Enacted from within (Duchamp and Wilson), or from outside (Matta-Clark) the confines of the museum, this strategy of deterritorialization references its underlying apparatus of visual consumption and display as a terrain of continued contestation.

As this study has demonstrated, the question of the end of art in its definition in visual form that Duchamp inaugurated does not merit summary conclusions regarding art's final demise or discouragement regarding its prospects for the future. Rather, it implies the radical redefinition of art through the elaboration of conceptual considerations that interrogate the historical, cultural, and social premises of art's demand and reliance on visuality. The question of what becomes of art, when it no longer considers itself as an activity that abides purely in the visible, necessitated an inquiry into how it gives itself to be seen. It is in this context that an examination of spectatorship proved crucial, since it brought under scrutiny the viewing conditions at work in the display and consumption of art.[59] Based on Duchamp's de-assemblage of the "look" that exposed the retinal bias of art, Matta-Clark and Wilson re-appropriated its apparatus by redeploying its implications through a critique of visuality at the strategic juncture of art and architecture. Exploring the intersection of sight and site, their installations put both art and architecture on notice in terms of their visual, spatial, and ideational content. Defying the constraints of conventional artistic genres, their interventions decisively disrupted the dominance of vision through conceptual strategies that reactivated its historical, cultural, and social frames of reference. By re-materializing the viewing processes of art, their installations challenged art's demand for visuality in terms of its outward manifestations, and its modes of display and consumption. Whereas Matta-Clark took a jackhammer to the idea and edifice of the museum in order to expose its visual "con," Wilson short-circuited spectatorship through a visual overload that ungrounded the subjective appropriation of architectural space. Exposing the "givens" that underlie visual display and consumption, Matta-Clark and Wilson de-assembled the operational logic and scaffolding of spectatorship by reinfusing it with social and historical considerations. Decentering the priority of vision through conceptual strategies, their installations mark the decisive shift from modernism to postmodernism insofar as they enable the emergence of forms of unartistic production that challenge art's visual essence and aesthetic mandates.

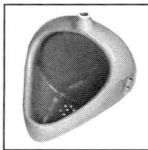

notes

1 These include Duchamp's efforts to question the distinction between art and non-art, to move toward a conceptual understanding of painting and art, and to redefine authorship in the mode of appropriation, that is, gestures that have also played an influential role in the development of postmodernity.

2 See Octavio Paz, *Marcel Duchamp: Appearance Stripped Bare* 4–60; Thierry de Duve, *Pictorial Nominalism: On Marcel Duchamp's Passage from Painting to the Readymade* 31–44 and his *Kant After Duchamp* 174–96, 378–81; and also my *Unpacking Duchamp: Art in Transit* 24–26, 56–73, 230–31.

3 See Martin Jay's influential account in *Downcast Eyes: The Denigration of Vision in Twentieth-Century Thought*, and particularly his comments on Duchamp (160–70).

4 See Horowitz and Huhn's introduction to Arthur C. Danto, *The Wake of Art: Criticism, Philosophy, and the Ends of Taste* 23–24.

5 For an analysis of exhibition as a system of display, see Marry Kelly, "Re-viewing Modernist Criticism" in *Art After Modernism: Rethinking Representation* 99–101. For questions concerning consumption and art audience, see Martha Rosler, "Lookers, Buyers, Dealers and Makers: Thoughts on Audience" in *Art After Modernism* 312–23.

6 See Clement Greenberg, "Counter Avant-Garde" in *Marcel Duchamp in Perspective* 123–24.

7 For an analysis of the museum as a way of seeing and mode of display, see Svetlana Alpers, "The Museum as a Way of Seeing" in *Exhibiting Cultures: The Poetics and Politics of Museum Display* 25–32. See also Michael Baxandall, "Exhibiting Intention: Some Preconditions of Visual Display of Culturally Purposeful Objects" in *Exhibiting Cultures* 33–41.

8 This note was produced in the 1930s and 1940s, and collected under the rubric of "Infra thin"; see *Marcel Duchamp, Notes*, n. 10.

9 As Pierre Bourdieu points out, the consecration of art objects in the confines of the museum corresponds to both their economic and visual "neutralization"; see *Distinction* 273.

10 For a more detailed account of the distinction of vision and visuality, see Hal Foster, "Preface" in *Vision and Visuality* ix.

judovitz

11 To invoke the notion of apparatus here is to draw attention not just to the physical processes, but to the mechanisms involved in the production of vision both as perceptual and social fact. My use of this term alludes to Jean-Louis Baudry's "Ideological Effects of the Basic Cinematographic Apparatus" in *Cinematographic Apparatus: Selected Writings* 25–37.

12 See Jonathan Crary, "Modernizing Vision" in *Vision and Visuality* 29–32.

13 For the influence of Duchamp's gestures on the development of installation art, see Nicolas de Oliveira, Nicola Oxley and Michael Petry, "Preface" in *Installation Art: With Texts by Michael Archer* 11. See also Julie H. Reiss, *From Margin to Center: The Spaces of Installation Art* 6–7.

14 Corinne Diserens noted that Duchamp's readymades and the Dadaist disruptions of convention were an important source of inspiration for Matta-Clark; see "The *Greene* Street Years" in *Gordon Matta-Clark* (Valencia: IVAM Centre Julio González) 359. Wilson acknowledged his interest in the works of both Matta-Clark and Duchamp – see Wilson's interview with Lynne Cooke in *Heatwave* 10; also see his interview with Steve Rushton on the World Wide Web (1994), "By Digging you Discover" 2–3, 5; henceforth abbreviated in the text as *DYD* with page number.

15 Initially relegated to the privacy of Duchamp's studio, these works took several years to emerge in the public sphere, in terms of being properly named and recognized for their conceptual potential to usurp conventional art objects. For instance, in 1916 Duchamp exhibited "Two Readymades" at the Bourgeois Gallery, New York, *Exhibition of Modern Art*, 3–29 April 1916, no. 50, without specifically identifying them.

16 Roger Dadoun, "Rrose Sschize: Sschize d'un Portrait Théorie de Marcel Duchamp en Jésus Sec Célibataire," *L'Arc* 25. Arthur C. Danto understands this perfect likeness between the object's ordinary and artistic condition as crucial towards redefining the meaning of art independently of visual criteria; see "The Philosophical Disenfranchisement of Art" in *The Wake of Art* 74–75.

17 See Octavio Paz, *Appearance Stripped Bare* 20–22.

18 See Walter Benjamin, "The Work of Art in the Age of Mechanical Reproduction" in *Illuminations* 221.

de-assembling vision

19 Benjamin observed that the value of ceremonial objects is defined by their "existence, not their being on view," "The Work of Art" 224–25.

20 Like Hoogstraten's box, Duchamp's *Box in a Valise* (1941–68) reproduces a compendium assemblage not only of his works but also of his conceptual strategies to question the traditions and conventions of picturing. For a discussion and inventory of this seminal work, see Ecke Bonk, *Marcel Duchamp: The Box in a Valise*.

21 See Svetlana Alpers's discussion of this work in the context of experiments with optical illusion in *The Art of Describing: Dutch Art in the Seventeenth Century* 58–64. For a further elaboration of the analogy of vision and painting as image-making processes, see Celeste Brusati, *Artifice and Illusion: The Art and Writing of Samuel Van Hoogstraten* 169–201.

22 Alpers, *The Art of Describing* 62. See also Brusati's analysis of the camera obscura as a paradigm for painting in *Artifice and Illusion* 70–71.

23 It is important to note that the terms of agreement of this work specify that no photographs of the interior construction, or of the notebook of instruction, were to be published by the Philadelphia museum for a period of at least fifteen years.

24 See the manual of instructions, *Marcel Duchamp: Étant Donnés: 1) La chute d'eau, 2) Le gaz d'éclairage*, title page.

25 Cf. Jean-François Lyotard, who emphasizes the directive nature of Duchamp's instructions for the re-assemblage of this work; see *Les transformateurs Duchamp* 126–27.

26 For a more detailed discussion of issues of visual consumption and spectatorship in this work, see my *Unpacking Duchamp* 199–208.

27 Moira and William Roth, "John Cage on Marcel Duchamp: An Interview" in *Marcel Duchamp in Perspective* 155.

28 Moira and William Roth, "John Cage on Marcel Duchamp" 155.

29 For a more detailed account of these photographic analogies, see Lyotard, *Les transformateurs* 130–33.

30 See Masheck's description of *Given* in "Introduction: Chance is zee Fool's Name for Fait" in *Marcel Duchamp in Perspective* 23, which reflects his discomfort with what he calls the "veristic" aspects of this work.

31 For an extensive analysis of Duchamp's critique of essentialist representations of sexuality, see my *Unpacking Duchamp* 205–11.

32 Elaine A. King, "Architecture/Art" in *The Architect's Dream: Houses for the Next Millennium* 2. However, her interpretation of Matta-Clark's works as prototypes of postmodern architecture overlooks his radical critique of architecture in the temporalized modality of the ruin.

33 Cf. Yves Alain-Bois, "Threshole" in *A User's Guide to Entropy* 60–61.

34 Martin Heidegger, "Building Dwelling Thinking" (1951) in *Basic Writings* 337.

35 For an elaboration of the social in Matta-Clark's works, particularly as regards loss of community and social memory, see my "Unpacking the House: Architectural Transformers," *Art Papers* 22–25.

36 Jerry Hovagimyan explains that the idea for this piece came from Anthony McCall's film *Line Describing a Cone*, which began with a dot of light that the throw of the projector enlarged into a cone of light; see his comments in *Gordon Matta-Clark: A Retrospective* (Chicago: Museum of Contemporary Art, 1985) (exh. cat.) 88.

37 See Jean-Hubert Martin's comments in *Gordon Matta-Clark: A Retrospective* 89.

38 For Matta-Clark's comments, see *Matta-Clark* (Antwerp: Internationaal Cultureel Centrum) (exh. cat.) 12.

39 Matta-Clark's intervention constitutes a bridge between the Pompidou Center, the rising new monument to French architecture and culture, and the nineteenth-century monumentality of the Eiffel Tower, with which it is visually aligned. It temporalizes their shared modernist ideals in the context of the neighborhood which was also known as the "Quarter of the Clock" ("*Quartier de l'Horloge*").

40 The phrase "sun and air for the lodgers" recalls the reaction of a Parisian concierge to Matta-Clark's work. See his interview with Donald Wall in "Matta-Clark's Building Dissections," *Arts Magazine* 79.

41 For Matta-Clark's comments, see his interview with Judith Russi Kirshner in *Gordon Matta-Clark* (Valencia: IVAM) 367.

42 See *Matta-Clark: A Retrospective* 88–89. Joan Simon describes in her note the punning play of "*Quel Con*" ("what a cunt") with "quel con" ("what a cone") with "*quel conque*" ("whatever" or "more or less") in *Matta-Clark: A Retrospective* 89.

43 *L.H.O.O.Q.* is also a bilingual pun on "look," the work's title when pronounced in English. For an analysis of this work in reference to Leonardo's masterpiece and the institution of the museum, see *Unpacking Duchamp* 142–48, 169–73.

44 See Joshua Decter's comments in *Arts Magazine* 104–05.

45 See, *Gordon Matta-Clark* (Marseilles: Musées de Marseilles, 1993) (exh. cat.) 376.

46 Cf. Anthony Vidler's discussion of the "modern unhomely," documenting the incongruence between building and home, between a space intended for habitation, and a place for dwelling in his *Architectural Uncanny: Essays in the Modern Unhomely*; see "Introduction."

47 For an insightful analysis of the tension and possible conflation of the phenomenological and conceptual readings of Matta-Clark's works, see Pamela M. Lee, *Object to be Destroyed* xix, 135–42.

48 Brian Hatton observed that Matta-Clark's works were increasingly "aimed at museums"; see "Anarchitect," *Art Monthly* 15.

49 Quoted in *Matta-Clark: A Retrospective* 94.

50 For a detailed analysis of *Office Baroque* and *Circus or The Caribbean Orange*, see Pamela M. Lee's comprehensive study in *Object to be Destroyed* 142–60, 220–32.

51 See Douglas Crimp's elaboration of the mortality of the museum and the end of modernism in *On the Museum's Ruins* 44–64.

52 Michael Archer noted that this had the effect of dematerializing space, since whether one looked up or down, "one simply looked at light"; see his "Richard Wilson at Matt's Gallery," *Artforum*, review section.

53 My discussion of Wilson's use of depth and issues of reversibility is informed by Maurice Merleau-Ponty, "Eye and Mind" in *The Primacy of Perception* 178–80.

54 See Hans Blumemberg, "Light as a Metaphor for Truth: At the Preliminary Stage of a Philosophical Concept Formation" in *Modernity and the Hegemony of Vision* 45.

55 Wilson's allusion to sculptural techniques of casting liquid metal into dies in order to achieve solid form recalls Duchamp's explorations of the "mould" as a mode of impression. For his comments on casting, see his interview with Lynne Cooke, *Heatwave* 8. In *20:50*, the casting of the oil into the mold of the room preempts further solidification, thus breaking up the sculptural analogies that it stages.

56 Cf. James Roberts's comment that Wilson's architectural works involve two related issues: the interplay between the way things appear and are actually built and the function of architecture as creator of space; see "Richard Wilson: Assembly Required," *Terskel* 100.

57 See Douglas Crimp's analysis of the political implications of site specificity in "Redefining Site Specificity," *On the Museum's Ruins* 150–86.

58 For a critique of the gallery space as spatial design and set-up for visual consumption, see Heidi Tikka, "The Space of the Gallery: Undoing the Place of the Spectator" in *Haunted Spaces* 15–25.

59 Thierry de Duve underlines Duchamp's break with the spectatorial gaze as phenomenological support and founding premise of aesthetic experience by noting that "Paul Klee's 'visible' is not Duchamp's *viewable*"; see *Kant After Duchamp* 407.

bibliography

Alain-Bois, Yves with Rosalind Krauss. "Threshole." A User's Guide to Entropy. Special issue. *October* no. 78 (Fall 1996).

Alpers, Svetlana. *The Art of Describing: Dutch Art in the Seventeenth Century*. Chicago: U of Chicago P, 1983.

Alpers, Svetlana. "The Museum as a Way of Seeing." *Exhibiting Cultures: The Poetics and Politics of Museum Display*. Ed. Ivan Karp and Steven D. Levine. Washington, DC: Smithsonian Institution P 1991.

Archer, Michael. "Review of Richard Wilson at Matt's Gallery." *Artforum* no. 10 (Summer 1989).

Baudry, Jean-Louis. "Ideological Effects of the Basic Cinematographic Apparatus." *Cinematographic Apparatus: Selected Writings*. Ed. Theresa Hak Kyung Cha. New York: Tanam, 1980.

de-assembling vision

Baxandall, Michael. "Exhibiting Intention: Some Preconditions of Visual Display of Culturally Purposeful Objects." *Exhibiting Cultures: The Poetics and Politics of Museum Display*. Ed. Ivan Karp and Steven D. Levine. Washington, DC: Smithsonian Institution P, 1991.

Benjamin, Walter. "The Work of Art in the Age of Mechanical Reproduction." *Illuminations*. Ed. Hannah Arendt. Trans. Harry Zohn. New York: Schocken, 1978.

Blumemberg, Hans. "Light as a Metaphor for Truth: At the Preliminary Stage of a Philosophical Concept Formation." Trans. Joel Shapiro. *Modernity and the Hegemony of Vision*. Ed. David M. Levin. Berkeley: U of California P, 1993.

Bonk, Ecke. *Marcel Duchamp: The Box in a Valise*. Trans. David Britt. New York: Rizzoli, 1989.

Bourdieu, Pierre. *Distinction*. Trans. Richard Nice. Cambridge: Harvard UP, 1984.

Brusati, Celeste. *Artifice and Illusion: The Art and Writing of Samuel Van Hoogstraten*. Chicago: U of Chicago P, 1995.

Crary, Jonathan. "Modernizing Vision." *Vision and Visuality*. Ed. Hal Foster. Dia Foundation, Discussions in Contemporary Culture, no. 2. New York: New P, 1988.

Crimp, Douglas. *On the Museum's Ruins*. Cambridge: MIT P, 1997.

Dadoun, Roger. "Rrose Sschize: Sschize d'un Portrait Théorie de Marcel Duchamp en Jésus Sec Célibataire." *L'Arc* no. 59 (1974).

Danto, Arthur C. *The Wake of Art: Criticism, Philosophy, and the Ends of Taste*. Ed. Gregg Horowitz and Tom Huhn. Amsterdam: G+B Arts International, 1998.

De Duve, Thierry. *Pictorial Nominalism: On Marcel Duchamp's Passage from Painting to the Readymade*. Trans. D. Polan. Minneapolis: U of Minnesota P, 1991.

De Duve, Thierry. *Kant After Duchamp*. Cambridge and London: MIT P, 1996.

De Oliveira, Nicolas, Nicola Oxley and Michael Petry, "Preface." *Installation Art: With Texts by Michael Archer*. London: Smithsonian Institution P and Thames, 1994.

Decter, Joshua. "Splitting: Four Corners." Exhibit, Holly Solomon Gallery: New York, 20 Nov.–15 Dec. 1990. *Arts Magazine* no. 65 (Feb. 1991): 104–05.

Diserens, Corinne. "The Greene Street Years." *Gordon Matta-Clark*. Valencia: IVAM Centre Julio González, 1993 (exh. cat.).

Duchamp, Marcel. *Marcel Duchamp, Notes*. Trans. Paul Matisse. Preface Anne d' Harnoncourt. Boston: G.K. Hall, 1983.

Duchamp, Marcel. *Marcel Duchamp: Étant Donnés: 1) La chute d'eau, 2) Le gaz d'éclairage*. Introduction Anne d' Harnoncourt. Philadelphia: Philadelphia Museum of Art, 1987.

Foster, Hal. "Preface." *Vision and Visuality*. Ed. Hal Foster. Dia Foundation, Discussions in Contemporary Culture, no. 2. New York: New P, 1988.

Greenberg, Clement. "Counter Avant-Garde." *Marcel Duchamp in Perspective*. Ed. Joseph Masheck. Englewood Cliffs: Prentice Hall, 1975.

Hatton, Brian. "Anarchitect." *Art Monthly* no. 169 (Sept. 1993): 12–15.

Heidegger, Martin. "Building Dwelling Thinking." *Basic Writings*. Ed. David Farrell Krell. Trans. Albert Hofstadter. New York: Harperm, 1977.

Internationaal Cultureel Centrum. *Matta-Clark*. Text Florent Bex. Antwerp: Internationaal Cultureel Centrum, 1977 (exh. cat.).

IVAM Centre Julio González. *Gordon Matta-Clark*. Valencia: IVAM Centre Julio González, 1993 (exh. cat.).

Jay, Martin. *Downcast Eyes: The Denigration of Vision in Twentieth-Century Thought*. Berkeley: U of California P, 1993.

Judovitz, Dalia. *Unpacking Duchamp: Art in Transit*. Berkeley: U of California P, 1995.

Judovitz, Dalia. "Unpacking the House: Architectural Transformers." *Art Papers* 20.2 (1996): 22–25.

Kelly, Marry. "Re-viewing Modernist Criticism." *Art After Modernism: Rethinking Representation*. Ed. Brian Wallis. Foreword Marcia Tucker. New York and Boston: New Museum of Contemporary Art and David R. Goodine, 1984.

King, Elaine A. "Architecture/Art." *The Architect's Dream: Houses for the Next Millennium*. Cincinnati: Contemporary Arts Center, 1994.

Lee, Pamela M. *Object to be Destroyed*. Cambridge and London: MIT P, 2000.

Lyotard, François. *Les transformateurs Duchamp*. Paris: Galilée, 1977.

Merleau-Ponty, Maurice. "Eye and Mind." Trans. Carleton Dallery. *The Primacy of Perception*. Ed. James M. Edie. Evanston: Northwestern UP, 1964.

Musées de Marseilles. *Gordon Matta-Clark*. Marseilles: Musées de Marseilles, 1993 (exh. cat.).

Museum of Contemporary Art. *Circus: The Caribbean Orange*. Text Judith Russi Kirshner. Chicago: Museum of Contemporary Art, 1978 (exh. cat.).

Museum of Contemporary Art. *Gordon Matta-Clark: A Retrospective*. Mary Jane Jacob; with an essay by Robert Pinkus-Witten; and interviews conducted by Joan Simon. Chicago: Museum of Contemporary Art, 1985 (exh. cat.).

Paz, Octavio. *Marcel Duchamp: Appearance Stripped Bare*. Trans. R. Phillips and D. Gardner. New York: Viking, 1978.

Reiss, Julie H. *From Margin to Center: The Spaces of Installation Art*. Cambridge and London: MIT P, 1999.

Roberts, James. "Richard Wilson: Assembly Required." *Terskel* 4.9 (1993): 88–100.

Rosler, Martha. "Lookers, Buyers, Dealers and Makers: Thoughts on Audience." *Art After Modernism: Rethinking Representation*. Ed. Brian Wallis. Foreword Marcia Tucker. New York and Boston: New Museum of Contemporary Art and David R. Goodine, 1984.

Roth, Moira and William Roth. "John Cage on Marcel Duchamp: An Interview." *Marcel Duchamp in Perspective*. Ed. J. Masheck. Englewood Cliffs: Prentice Hall, 1975.

Tikka, Heidi. "The Space of the Gallery: Undoing the Place of the Spectator." *Haunted Spaces*. Ed. Eeva Kurki. Working Papers. Helsinki: University of Art and Design, 2000. 15–25.

Vidler, Anthony. *Architectural Uncanny: Essays in the Modern Unhomely*. Cambridge: MIT P, 1992.

Wall, Donald. "Matta-Clark's Building Dissections." *Arts Magazine* 50.9 (1976): 74–79.

Wilson, Richard. Interview with Lynne Cooke. *Heatwave*. Birmingham: Ikon Gallery, 1986.

Wilson, Richard. Interview with Steve Rushton. "By Digging you Discover." Available <www.backspace.org/everything/e/hard/text/wilson.html>, 1994

judovitz

Dalia Judovitz
Department of French and Italian
Emory University
Atlanta, GA 30322
USA
E-mail: djudcvi@emory.edu

How the time has passed quickly, that other time, this one into which he had suddenly been launched, would give him the illusion of allowing himself to slow down, a pause sustained on a vibration, his right hand appearing to tremble slightly as it rests on the paper.

Artificial Life ~ Virtual Worlds

These exposures were made by traffic cams. I took them off the Internet and reformatted them. In this way I became familiar with the intersections represented. Now when I drive these highways, I feel I'm a player in a performance.

Cheryl Sourkes

ANGELAKI
journal of the theoretical humanities
volume 7 number 1 april 2002

Robert Mapplethorpe's career as an artist spans the period 1970–89. During these years a number of important and divergent schools attempted to engage with the nature of art and its relationship to aesthetics, and a recurrent reference was the work of Marcel Duchamp, not least due to his presentation of "readymades." This encounter with the work of Duchamp both facilitated and encouraged conceptualist understandings of art. This type of response to art was thought to sever the philosophy of art from aesthetics.[1] Since the author taken to have provided the major treatment of aesthetics was Immanunel Kant, it is perhaps not surprising that one recent author has placed Kant and Duchamp into relation and attempted a representation of Kant's enquiry not on the grounds of a critique of taste but rather through the prism of a critique of art.[2] In this article I intend to insert Mapplethorpe as a third partner to this encounter between Duchamp and Kant, in the process indicating reasons for thinking that whilst Kant's enquiry needs to be engaged with anew, the basis for this will be through providing a wider sense to the term "aesthetics" than is traditionally done. It is my hope that the result of this enquiry will be a newly inclusive understanding of the place of photography in the comprehension of the ends of art.

the readymade as photograph

Whilst much has been written about Duchamp's readymades there has been scant attention to the fact that there is a signal condition for the discussion of these objects: that they be reproduced. The manner of the reproduction has been threefold: casts were made of the originals by Duchamp himself in the construction of his

gary banham

MAPPLETHORPE, DUCHAMP AND THE ENDS OF PHOTOGRAPHY

Boîte en Valise (1941–49) (reproduction in miniature of works to be displayed in a case in limited editions), Duchamp signed and often selected replicas, and many of the readymades are re-presented to us by photographs. Whilst the first mode of presentation was limited owing to the artisanal labour required to construct the boxes and their contents, and the second mode of presentation is only of use when within an art gallery, the third is the mode by which the majority of those familiar with Duchamp's readymades encounter them.

Not only is it the case that readymades are usually encountered as photographs, there are also good reasons, as I have explained elsewhere, for assuming in at least one case (and this case is the one which has been most significant in the

ISSN 0969-725X print/ISSN 1469-2899 online/02/010119-09 © 2002 Taylor & Francis Ltd and the Editors of *Angelaki*
DOI: 10.1080/09697250220142083

119

history of art) that the photographic reproduction of the work is itself the readymade in question.³ This is the case of *Fountain* (1917). Since the object in question (a urinal) was lost in mysterious circumstances shortly after it was first presented, the photograph of the object by Alfred Stieglitz has taken on the status of "original." The work has a peculiar status as it is reproduced in works on Duchamp and not in works on Stieglitz.⁴ The "original" is, despite this, a work by Stieglitz and the circumstances of lighting and the placing of the urinal above a painting were undertaken by him. It should be added, however, that there are some reasons for thinking that Duchamp was involved in this episode. Dalia Judovitz in a discussion of the earlier *Nude Descending a Staircase, No. 2* states:

> What is at issue here is a challenge of the pictorial medium through sequential photography: a critique of vision as a cognitive medium that conflates spectatorship and pleasure. ... Functioning neither descriptively nor prescriptively, the title *Nude Descending a Staircase* inscribes a temporal delay that interferes with the visual consumption of the image. This strategy of delay also redefines and defers notions of visual reference that are traditionally associated with photography.⁵

If *Nude Descending a Staircase, No. 2* is taken to have photographic elements for two reasons, due to both its presentation of sequential and yet still elements and also due to the delay of reception of the work imposed by its caption, then the relation of this work to the readymade *Fountain* seems close. *Fountain* also includes an element of "delay" in the insertion of the title into the reception of the work and, like *Nude Descending*, the photograph of *Fountain* by Stieglitz includes a number of compositional elements that have the effect of imposing on the still image a sequential effect.

Whilst the confluence of *Fountain* and *Nude Descending* occurs through the understanding of both as including photographic elements, there is an important difference between them, which is that the former work's "original" has survived as a photograph. The question of who "produced" *Fountain* is made unclear by the manner of its survival: is the person who signed the urinal or the one who photographed it the author of the work? Since there seems no clear way of answering this question the object seems to have transcended the standards of authorship we usually expect to be able to claim for art works. The nature of the readymade as a representation of elements, which were not created by the artist but merely arranged in a certain form, seems, however, almost to be a definition of the photograph. Since we can see that the practices Duchamp engaged in involved an intrinsic dependence on photography it is clear that photography is the condition for the existence of his work. This suggests that rather than enabling a claim that his works dissociate art from aesthetics, they require instead a rethinking of how interrelation and interdependence of art forms is possible.

photography as sculpture (1): mapplethorpe's early works

Before undertaking a return to the description of fine art in Kant and attempting a redescription of the relation between different art forms on the basis of a new reading of the relations between art and aesthetics, it will be instructive to provide some reasons for relating Mapplethorpe to Kant and Duchamp. At the beginning of Mapplethorpe's career as an artist he had no special commitment to photography and his early works have a collage form. In *Cowboy* (1970) we have a mixed media collage in which a heavily retouched male nude has a Cyclops eye superimposed on his face whilst an adjoining panel contains a painted grey surface and a disjointed white panel is presented at right angles to the image. The whole ensemble is displayed against the backdrop of an oak panel that the artist has signed whilst framing the work with a heavy black border. Other early works also employ mixed forms: *Jay Kiss* (1973) features a reclining male nude photographed against a pillow with a scarf loosely disarranged. The more startling aspect of the work, however, is its framing, as the small photograph is enclosed within a frame – which is indicative of a hand-held mirror – and just below the photograph a peg is inserted into the frame from which hangs a scarf akin to the one photographed. Finally, *The Slave* (1974) features a photograph of pages of a book that reproduce images of Michelangelo's sculpture of this title. Resting upon the photograph is a real knife, underneath which Mapplethorpe has affixed a panel that has written on it "Mapplethorpe." The backdrop to the work displays the interior of the frame in expansive manner. This work is described by William Hood as a sculpture.6 Like its predecessors it utilises a method that, since its inception with the Cubists, has tended to ensure that painting approximates to the condition of sculpture. Since *The Slave* also presents a photograph of a photograph of a sculpture we might well suspect that Mapplethorpe was well aware of the possibilities of "mixing" art forms in precisely the manner we have noted in Duchamp. Furthermore, since the elaborate use of the frame demonstrates that Mapplethorpe is conscious of the importance of the means by which a photograph is presented, he turns the collage element which he has utilised to present a photograph of a photograph of a sculpture into a demonstration that the visual condition of photography is dependent upon conditions of en-framing that precede the medium and render it possible.

If we turn to the later and better known works of Mapplethorpe this relation of his photographs to sculpture may seem less evident. But Janet Kardon, at the conclusion of an interview with Mapplethorpe for the catalogue of his show *The Perfect Moment*, stated of his photographs: "A stillness surrounds each of them, as if each image were a piece of sculpture with its own space around it."7 To this interpretation of Mapplethorpe's photographs William Hood has responded by making an even larger claim: "it is not so much the figures in Mapplethorpe's photographs that are sculptural as the photographs themselves."8 Whilst Hood's claim is based on relating Mapplethorpe's work to Clarence Kennedy's photographs of Renaissance sculptures, I would like instead to relate Mapplethorpe to the traditions of modern sculpture and particularly to his reception of the sculptural possibilities of photographing readymades.

The first claim, that Mapplethorpe's works can be related to modern sculpture, will be illustrated

banham

in a consideration of his pictures of human figures, relating these figures to sculptural portrayal of human forms. The second claim, that Mapplethorpe's work is informed, and made possible by, the sculptural nature of photographed readymades, will then be illustrated by reference to both his practice of photographing works of sculpture and by relating this practice to a theoretical argument for the convergence of sculpture and photography. Looking at Mapplethorpe's portrayal of figures is the first step towards understanding the sculptural nature of his work and corresponds to Kardon's restricted claim. Comprehending the claim that Mapplethorpe's work is made possible by the practice of photographic reproduction of readymades is the second step towards understanding the sculptural nature of his work and corresponds to Hood's general claim, though not just by reference to a tradition of photographs of sculpture as Hood intends but rather by reference to an even more general claim than he makes, to wit, that sculpture and photography have become mutually implicated art forms.

photography as sculpture (2): mapplethorpe's figures

In thinking about Mapplethorpe's portrayal of figures I would like to begin by examining *Larry & Bobby Kissing* (1979). This work can be compared to many sculptural precedents but I would like here to presume on the widespread knowledge of Rodin's *The Kiss* (1886) to make the point about the sculptural nature of this image. In *Larry & Bobby Kissing* we have a close-up portrayal of two leather-clad men, one of whom is indicated to be placed above the other. The taller figure bends down towards the lips of the lower figure whilst the neck of the lower figure is presented in prominent outline as he reaches upwards to connect with the face above. The hand of the taller figure rests upon the shoulder of the one below. The hair of the taller figure is presented squarely and the crown of his head strengthens the frontal unity of the composition. The lower figure has a resplendently white face and the fleshiness of his neck connected to a wholly absorbed facial expression conveys a stillness, which appears rapturous. The contrast between the lightness of the lower figure and the darkness of the upper one is increased by the shadow cast upon the upper figure's face due to the action of bending and the concomitant hiding of the upper figure's neck within the folds of his jacket. A blank background that frames the two men and forces them into relief assures the compositional unity of the figures.

Rodin's *The Kiss*, which was carved in marble, lacks the full contrast in colouring that we can see in the figures which make up *Larry & Bobby Kissing*. But whilst the colour of the sculpture is uniform and there is an important difference in the embrace as conveyed by Rodin – who has the lower female form drawing down the head of the higher male figure in order to present the connection between the two faces – there is an important relation nonetheless between these two works. Rodin's figure is full scale. We are given an appreciation of the whole forms of the two figures right down to their toes and even get an appreciation of their posture by a carved bench on which they embrace. By contrast, Mapplethorpe's foreshortened image presents merely the upper part of the figures from above the elbow to the peak of the head. But in both images there is an extraordinary concentration of depiction with the enveloping kiss serving to cut the figures off in both cases from contact with any other figures. Rodin's higher figure, like Mapplethorpe's, bends and confirms his posture by a strategically placed hand, which connects him with the lower form as firmly as in Mapplethorpe's photograph. The representation of the heads in Rodin is caught at a different angle from that in Mapplethorpe's picture and the insistence on a full portrayal of heads and hair plunges both faces in Rodin into an obscurity which contrasts markedly with the frontality of Mapplethorpe. The fuller portrayal of the bodies of the figures in Rodin allows a firm portrayal of hips and thigh in the lower form but the resulting lack of facial invigoration in his sculpture diminishes the sense of personal involvement in the embrace and turns the figure into a type. Both the sculpture and the photograph decisively isolate the figures from a background, isolation emphasised heavily in photographic representations of *The Kiss*, which frequently portray the work having a black backdrop of precisely the type we have noted in *Larry & Bobby Kissing*. Photographic reproduction of *The Kiss* assimilates the condition of its viewing to that of viewing a photograph and ensures that only one aspect of the work is visible: the frontal aspect, precisely the aspect rendered so emphatic by Mapplethorpe in *Larry & Bobby Kissing*.[9]

If we turn from *Larry & Bobby Kissing* to *Tim Scott* (1980) we are confronted with a figure that finds a very different sculptural analogue. Whilst *Larry & Bobby Kissing* compels comparison with earlier works evocative of tender passion, the pose of *Tim Scott* is reminiscent of earlier toilet scenes, scenes that are normally occupied by female figures. A sculptural correlate for the work can be seen in Brancusi's *Princess X* (1916). Whilst Mapplethorpe's picture displays a tight unity that centres on the connection between hand and head, the Brancusi (which exists in both marble and bronze) only intimates this connection with the hand of the figure vestigially represented and leading to the paradoxical consequence of giving a phallic shape to a feminine scene. The nature of Brancusi's achievement and the number of connections it has to the Mapplethorpe picture become clearer if we recall its emergence from the earlier *Narcissus Fountain* (c.1914). *Tim Scott* presents a head which, like the upper figure in *Larry & Bobby Kissing*, is angled downwards with a concentration here, however, on a distant horizon where we might anticipate a mirror. The sharp curve of the head illuminates the back of the neck, which is displayed as fully and vigorously as with the lower figure in *Larry & Bobby Kissing*. The sharp angle of the arm occupies a large and central part of the picture and focuses attention on the figure's tattoo. The dark top of the man corresponds with his dark hair and renders the light of his arms, hands and face more vigorous. The shading of the one eye in the frame allows the face to taper out with an angled and sharp nose and permits the head to fade insensibly into the arm. The hand on top of the head curves sharply and takes on a largeness enhanced by the jutting, frontal presence of the thumb. The figure's concentration and rapt aloneness is once again given great emphasis due to the backdrop of the picture being a blank greyness that gives the form a sharp relief.

By contrast to *Tim Scott*, *Princess X* is caught in a single line of perspective with a sharp angle from the frontal arm upwards to the head. The delicacy of the figure is given in its radical treatment of form, which refuses to supply a real musculature and forces a balance on a plinth. Nevertheless, *Princess X* is caught in the same action as *Tim Scott* and with the same downward tilt of the head forcing a strong portrayal of the neck. Whilst the bronze form of the sculpture has an appearance of greater sinuosity it loses the phallic grace of the marble version. *Narcissus Fountain* is more overtly connected to *Tim Scott* as the appearance of the figure is given in fuller profile and the downward tilt of the head is indicated to be concentrating on a reflection just as we suspect that the figure in *Tim Scott* may have a mirror within his range of vision. The sharp angles portrayed in *Tim Scott* find a clear parallel in the outstretched arm that balances the figure in *Narcissus Fountain* and the self-absorption, which is involved in the toilet scene, is sharply indicated in the very title of this sculpture. As with *The Kiss*, the appearance of the two Brancusi pieces in books is dependent upon a photographic art, and the standard reproductions of both *Narcissus Fountain* and *Princess X* are in a profile view, which corresponds to the perspective from which we view the figure in *Tim Scott*.[10]

photography and sculpture (3): mapplethorpe's photographs of sculpture

Towards the end of his life Mapplethorpe initiated a practice of photographing sculptures. Two aspects of this practice are important for the general argument I am developing here: firstly, the sculptures he photographed were usually reproductions and, secondly, the photographs he took of these works correspond very closely to general reproductions of sculpture in books on sculpture, which also ensures that these works relate in their turn to his photographs of live models. Mapplethorpe's use of reproductions is commonly stated to be due to his concern with the fragmentary state of the originals.[11] Whilst there is biographical evidence to support this claim it is also the case that classical art works, like all art works, are usually seen in reproduction form and classical statuary is now known to consist mainly of Roman reproductions of Greek originals. Not only is this the case but the angle of view, which Mapplethorpe chooses for these portrayals, is also derivative of that provided in books on sculpture, books whose illustrations are provided by photographs.

If we look for an example at *Apollo* (1988) we will be able to see a number of comparisons both with conventional photographs of sculpture and with Mapplethorpe's earlier treatment of live models. The figure in *Apollo* is viewed in frontal profile, just like the figures in *Tim Scott* and *Larry & Bobby Kissing*. The face of this figure is set against a blank backdrop which forces it into relief in exactly the same way as occurs in the above-mentioned photographs. The brightness of the marble surface is made even more manifest and whiter by the prevailing darkness of the backdrop. The effect of focusing attention on only part of the figure, which is removed from its support, is again deployed and it has been argued by some that the effect of this when photographing a sculpture has been to make the figure lifelike.[12] The figure portrayed in *Apollo* certainly appears very focused and the effect of the profile view is to give us a sense of the forceful purposes of the figure portrayed. The inward repose of the figure contrasts with the outward action of the figures represented by Rodin and Brancusi but the modernity of vision, which renders the lips of Apollo as sensual as those of *Larry & Bobby Kissing*, tells us that the appreciation of photographic depiction has a clear relation to the conditions of sculpture's dependence on photography. William Hood's reproductions of the photographs of Renaissance sculpture by Clarence Kennedy show that there is a central tradition of depiction of sculptures which precisely concentrates on frontal or profile view, bringing the figure into relief and isolating it from supports.[13] This renders sculptures themselves readymades and illustrates that Duchamp's discovery of the condition of possibility for the readymade is convergent with the modern condition of sculpture.

the "mixing" of art forms and the ends of aesthetics

In section 52 of *The Critique of Judgment* Kant turns his attention to the "Combination of the Fine Arts in One and the Same Product." His comments are ambiguous and face in different directions:

> the exhibition of the sublime may, insofar as it belongs to fine art, be combined with beauty in a *tragedy in verse*, in a *didactic poem*, or in an *oratorio*; and in these combinations fine [*schön*] art is even more artistic. But whether it is also more beautiful [*schön*] (given how great a variety of different kinds of liking cross one another) may in some of these cases be doubted. But what is essential in all fine art is the form that is purposive for our observation and judging, rather than the matter of sensation (i.e., charm or emotion). For the pleasure we take in purposive form is also culture, and it attunes the spirit to ideas, and so makes it receptive to more such pleasure and entertainment ... (Ak. 5, 325–26)[14]

Whilst in this passage Kant presents fine art as dependent not on sensation but upon judgement, he doesn't here make clear in what way this judgement works to allow appreciation. Elsewhere in the work he is clearer: "the harmony of a thing's manifold with an intrinsic determination of the thing, i.e., with its purpose, is the thing's perfection" which gives the consequence, "that when we judge artistic beauty we shall have to assess the thing's perfection as well" (Ak. 5, 311). In understanding how these remarks relate to the art forms of photography and sculpture we need to look at Kant's account of visual arts. Kant divided visual art into two types: arts of sensible truth and arts of sensible illusion. Kant also denoted the former types as "plastic" arts, the latter as "painting" (a large designation which includes landscape gardening). Sculpture belongs under the heading of "plastic" or truthful art and of it Kant states:

> *Sculpture* is the art that exhibits concepts of things corporeally, as they *might exist in nature* (though, as a fine art, it does so with a concern for aesthetic purposiveness). ... In sculpture the main aim is the mere *expression* of aesthetic ideas ... the *sensible truth* in it must not be carried to the point where the work ceases to look like art and a product of choice. (Ak. 5, 322)

What enables sculpture to be understood as an art of sensible truth is its corporeal extension, its occupation of real space (as opposed to the flat surface of painting). But this aspect of sculpture has a definite limit: if a work of sculpture were to appear lifelike it would no longer appear as a work of art, that is not as something which had been *chosen*. In defending the notion of the readymade, Duchamp referred also to the fact that what was exhibited under this title had been *chosen*:

> Since the tubes of paint used by an artist are manufactured and ready-made products we must conclude that all paintings in the world are "readymades aided" and also works of assemblage.[15]

Whereas Kant sought to separate sculpture from painting by referring to the fact that sculpture extends into space and thus has real corporeality, Duchamp assimilates painting to sculpture in producing sculptural works, which depend, as painting did, on pre-given materials that are not supplied by the sculptor. This divergence between Duchamp and Kant can be accounted for by the invention of photography.

This is not to suggest that the transcendental enquiry conducted by Kant is reduced to empirical conditions but rather to argue for an expanded sense of "aesthetics." In discussing sculpture as projected into space, Kant assimilated the conditions for judging it as an art form to those provided in the Transcendental Aesthetics' delimitation of conditions of perception. This form of treatment of "aesthetics" is, however, distinct from that provided in other places in Kant's work. We can distinguish at least another two senses of the aesthetic: practical and reflective. Practical aesthetics is the least investigated of Kant's senses of the term and is meant to indicate the affective grounds of morality as given in an initial form in the Second Critique and greatly expanded elsewhere.16 But the sense of the aesthetic that the *Critique of Judgment* is primarily devoted to is a reflective aesthetic or aesthetic of judgement. This requires a revisiting of the conditions of perception as given in the Transcendental Aesthetic, a revisiting neglected by Kant when he explicates the fine arts. In the Analytic of the Sublime, Kant indicates a form of sublimity entitled by him the "mathematically sublime" which consists of two forms of apprehension which defeat the conditions of the Transcendental Aesthetic as supplied in the First Critique: the vanishingly small and the inordinately large. Further, in the treatment which Kant gives here of the conditions of spatial awareness it becomes clear that the possibility of relating to shapes and corporeal figures is dependent on a basic measure provided by the embodied viewer (Ak. 5, 251). Since this entails that space is not only given *to* us as a basic condition but also given *by* us as this, it follows that the apprehension of magnitude alters with the conditions of our placement.

This is as much as to say that if, as I am claiming, the condition of possibility of sculpture alters with the invention of photography, this is not a merely empirical claim but part of the a priori condition of there being a reflective aesthetic. This would suggest that the relation of organic beings to their embodiment is essentially part of their relationship to technicity.17 If we apply these observations to the notion of sculpture as defined in the course of this investigation we reach the following formula: the condition of possibility of "modern" sculpture is that there are readymades and the condition of possibility of readymades is that photography exists. It remains to ask what the ends of photography themselves are.

the ends of photography

In this section I want to suggest that there are a number of ends we can ascribe to photography and to relate these ends to the multiple and extended sense of the "aesthetic" we can derive from Kant if we cease being guided by some of the more restrictive comments in the *Critique of Aesthetic Judgment*. As I have suggested else-

banham

where, I think there are four senses we can give to the term "ends."18 These four senses are: end as limit of range of something, end as purpose, end as final destination or inherent value, end as co-determination of parts. I want now to specify how these types of end can be described as applicable to photography with reference to what I have described as operative in the work of Mapplethorpe. The *limits* of photography are given in the changing conditions of its technical possibility. These limits affect photography's mapping of space.19 Photographers are now in a position to radically alter images without the crudities of superimposition previously resorted to. The *purposes* of photography are supplied, as Kant noted to be true of fine art in general, by cultural conditions. These supply photography with content in relation to advertising, political agitation and documentary reportage. These purposes are, however, generally given to photography from "without" whilst the practice of integrating photography with other art forms in the production of "mixed media" allows photography to operate as part of an immanent system of art. The *ultimate value* of photography, as is illustrated in the pictures of Mapplethorpe discussed here, is the depiction of humanity to itself. This brings us to the *co-determination* of the self-presentation of the human with the purposes of culture that are imposed upon photography. This co-determination occurs through the condition we have uncovered as integral to photography: "mixing" the technical with the human so that each becomes enmeshed in the other. This "mixing" ensures that humanity's self-presentation in photography is part of a self-overcoming.

duchamp after mapplethorpe

If reflecting on the place of Mapplethorpe's photography in a choreographed encounter between Duchamp and Kant helps to reformulate the comprehension of the aesthetic within Kant, what does this reformulation in its turn do to Duchamp? Rather than seeing Duchamp as involved in an "anti-aesthetic" gesture in the presentation of the readymades we can now understand his work as involved in a redefinition of the conditions of sculpture, a redefinition which frankly acknowledged that the sculptural work does not exist primarily as located in a particular place of installation but instead in its partial viewing in photographic reproduction. *Fountain*'s placement in a carefully posed position which long survived the initial "object," and which replaced the initial "object," is a frank confession of the sculptor's dependence upon mechanisms of reproduction over which he has little control. If we compare *Fountain* to *The Slave* we note a striking connection and an equally telling divergence. Whilst *Fountain* is the reproduction of one art form by another, which latter becomes the mode of transmission of the former, *The Slave* involves a frank claim of one art form over another. Just as Duchamp did not sign *Fountain* with his own name and is dependent for its reproduction upon Stieglitz (who in a sense becomes its maker), so Mapplethorpe affixes his name to the picture of Michelangelo's sculpture, hence claiming it (and framing it).

The two works mark two ends of a process and the culmination of the relation inaugurated by *Fountain* is with the arrival of the authority of the photographer as the one whose control of art forms is ensured precisely at the time when photography's claim to truth (the means by which Kant demarcated sculpture from painting) is at an end. This does not entail that the work of the photographer is thus to be understood as no longer accountable but it does entail that what this work is accountable for is not accuracy to a pre-given reality but the shaping of a reality to come. For a vision of a futurity that is both one of an order of desire and affirmative of the conditions of making that enable a relation to the self-overcoming of the human, can we do better than an alliance of Duchamp with Mapplethorpe? I would prefer to conclude with an image and its analysis rather than a further explication of this future.

Ken and Tyler (1985) displays two bodies in harmony. They are both angular, curved and in a tense repose. The harmony between the bodies is structural. The forward thrust, the reach upwards of the arms and the gentle arch of the legs with a culminating move of a slight toe-hold on the ground being balanced by a straight back leg. The difference arises only with the reflection on each leg, which appears to be from a window. This reflection provides a low shadow on the white leg, and much higher shadings on the black legs. The two forms stand out in high relief against the backdrop owing to its complete blankness. In their harmony they not only portray a gentle beauty but also a forceful control over limbs that have been cast into art. The art of the figures combines with that of the photographer to enable a still and yet sweeping gesture of acceptance of a finite condition, which captures its futurity in its finitude.[20]

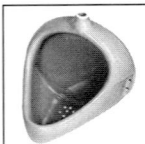

notes

1 For a work that is particularly key in this regard see Arthur Danto, *After the End of Art: Contemporary Art and the Pale of History* (Princeton: Princeton UP, 1997).

2 Thierry De Duve, *Kant After Duchamp* (Cambridge and London: MIT P, 1996).

3 See Gary Banham, "Duchamp's 'Mechanistic Sculptures': Art, Nudes and the Game of Chess," *Angelaki* 4.3 (1999): 181–90. For a lengthy examination of the status of *Fountain* see De Duve, op. cit., chapters 1 and 2.

4 One reason for its lack of appearance in works on Stieglitz is likely to be because of the curious fact that it lacks a negative. Owing to this lack of a negative there is no conclusive way of demonstrating that Stieglitz in fact took the photograph.

5 Dalia Judovitz, *Unpacking Duchamp: Art in Transit* (Berkeley and London: U of California P, 1995) 29.

6 William Hood, "A Lazy Man's Approach: Robert Mapplethorpe and the Language of Sculpture" in *Sculpture and Photography: Exhibiting the Third Dimension*, ed. G.A. Johnson (Cambridge: Cambridge UP, 1998) 208.

7 Janet Kardon, *Robert Mapplethorpe: The Perfect Moment* (Philadelphia: Institute of Contemporary Arts, 1989) 29.

8 Hood, op. cit. 201.

9 For a fine example of photographic representations of *The Kiss* and indeed of Rodin's sculpture generally see Sommerville Story, *Rodin* (London:

Phaidon, 1951). The photographs are by Ilse Schneider-Lengyel.

10 For a standard photographic reproduction of these works and of Brancusi's work in general see Sidney Geist, *Brancusi: A Study of the Sculpture* (London: Studio Vista, 1968). Christian Zernos is responsible for the majority of the photographs.

11 Cf. Patricia Morrisroe, *Mapplethorpe: A Biography* (London: Papermac, 1995) 334.

12 Arthur Danto, *Playing with the Edge: The Photographic Achievement of Robert Mapplethorpe* (Berkeley and London: U of California P, 1996) 125–26.

13 Hood, op. cit., *passim*.

14 Immanuel Kant, *Critique of Judgment*, trans. Werner Pluhar (Cambridge and Indianapolis: Hackett, 1987). Citations give *Akadamie* (Ak.) pagination.

15 Marcel Duchamp, "A Propos of Readymades" in *Salt Seller: The Writings of Marcel Duchamp*, eds. Michel Sanouillet and Elmer Peterson (Oxford and New York: Oxford UP, 1973) 142.

16 See Gary Banham, *Kant and the Ends of Aesthetics* (London: Macmillan; New York: St. Martin's, 2000) chapters 1, 2 and 10.

17 For a more extensive discussion of this question see Gary Banham, "Teleology, Transcendental Reflection and Artificial Life," *Teknehma: Journal of Philosophy and Technology* 6 (2000): 52–71.

18 These senses of ends are traced at much greater length in *Kant and the Ends of Aesthetics*.

19 For the ever-changing condition of photography see H.V. Ameluxen et al. (eds.), *Photography After Photography: Memory and Representation in the Digital Age* (Amsterdam: G&B Arts, 1996).

20 This account of photography differs from those that would be suggested by a Greenbergian insistence on formal properties but is not equivalent to the positions standardly attributed to Benjamin or Barthes. Further work on photography will address the relationship between the account presented here and that in the work of these authors. I would like to thank my referees for supportive comments and Don Milligan for his help and advice.

Gary Banham
Manchester Metropolitan University
Department of Politics and Philosophy
Geoffrey Manton Building
Manchester M15 6LL
UK
E-mail: g.banham@mmu.ac.uk

Forgive my handwriting, my style, my spelling. I don't dare reread myself when I write in a rush! I know very well that one shouldn't write in a rush. But I have so much to say. It comes surging like wave.

anne ramsden

ANASTYLOSIS

Anastylosis describes a set of principles used in restoration, whose goal is to reconstruct an object from its surviving fragments. Although the rules of anastylosis were developed in the context of archeological structural reconstitution – minimal intervention, exclusive use of all surviving parts, visible filling of gaps or integration of segments added for purposes of stability and security – the procedure can be applied to the restoration of all artifacts.

1 introduction

isabelle wallace

FROM PAINTING'S DEATH TO THE DEATH IN PAINTING
or, what jasper johns found in marcel duchamp's tu m'/tomb

Much has been written about the link between Jasper Johns' *According to What* (Fig. 1) and Marcel Duchamp's *Tu m'* (Fig. 2), yet the connection forged between them is nevertheless reducible to a word: homage.[1] Indeed, for almost all of Johns' commentators, it is the admiration of Johns for Duchamp that suffices to explain substantial affinities between *According to What* and the Duchamp painting that is its presumed source and prototype. The essay that follows takes Johns' admiration, moreover, his indebtedness to Duchamp as a given (is anyone/anything not indebted in some way to ideas that found expression in Duchamp's oeuvre?), and raises in its place the additional possibility that affinities at the level of pictorial concept and form are in fact the manifestation of a larger and, to this author, a more interesting commonality, namely, the engagement of each artist with the possibility of art's demise. Thus, without diminishing either the admiration that engendered or the commonalities that emerged from *According to What*'s revisitation of *Tu m'*, this essay aims to take up where the record seems determined to leave off, asking if one can see *more* in Johns' nod to the notorious Duchamp.

Arguing that *Tu m'* and *According to What* are deeply entwined meditations on the viability and vitality of art, I propose that they are ultimately linked by a shared *but crucially divergent* interest in the still more specialized subject of painting's relation to death. Indeed, as I argue in the following essay, Johns' appropriation of Duchamp is both a revival and re-thinking of terms already in play in the Duchamp painting Johns seeks to re-vision. Those terms, I suggest, are art, painting and death, and it is Johns' subtle re-negotiation of the relation between them that is the subject of the essay below. Taking seriously the impulse of Johns to make *again* (i.e., to make differently) the painting with death in its title (*Tu m'*/tomb), this essay takes seriously, too, the reception of Johns' appropriative act within art historical discourse, believing that a larger picture may emerge from a critical examination of the homogeneity of scholarship which takes, interestingly, the sameness of Johns and Duchamp to be its primary point and theme.[2] In sum, this essay considers both Johns' representation of Duchamp and the representation of Duchamp's relation to Johns, certain that there is in both the visual and verbal record the nascent elements of a story not yet told. The essay that follows is that story.[3]

painting, death

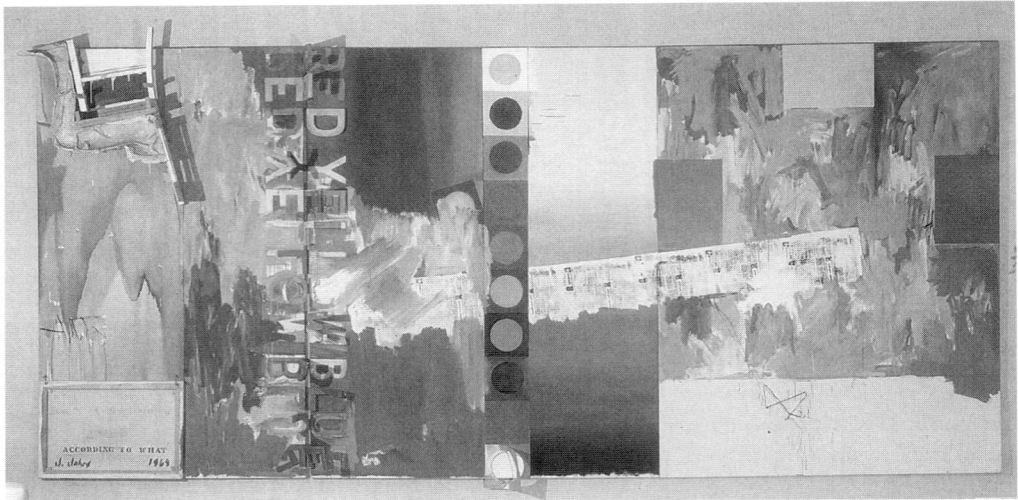

Fig. 1. Jasper Johns, *According to What*, 1964, oil on canvas with objects, 88 × 192″.
Photograph provided by Gagosian Gallery, NYC.
© Jasper Johns/Licensed by VGA, New York, NY

II crossroads

Painted in 1964, *According to What* bears an obvious relation to *Tu m'* (1918), owing to its prototype a substantial and admitted debt. As scholars have observed, there are several features of the work which lead us to Duchamp, the most straightforward of which is the inclusion of Duchamp's initials and purloined profile on the underside of a small canvas appended via hinge to the lower left-hand corner of Johns' colossal assemblage.[4] In addition, Johns' work also shares with its predecessor an exaggerated horizontal format, enlisted by both Duchamp and Johns for the shared purpose of cataloguing the artists' work at a mid-point in their careers.[5] This impulse to catalogue – i.e., to revisit and reflect – is one that periodically recurs in the work of Duchamp and Johns.[6] It is a curious feature of their oeuvres, one that indicates not only their thoughtfulness – after all, what is a retrospective if not the occasion for thoughtful review? – but also, I think, their sense of a moment's gravity. Indeed, what I wish to stress before turning to a more specific discussion of these two paintings is the cautious hesitation of the retrospective, its need to carve out from the present a space for review of the past. In 1918 and 1964, respectively, Duchamp and Johns had need of this space, and it is my contention that the desire of it derived from the knowledge that each had arrived at a crossroad whose navigation required some thought.

Given *Tu m*'s collection of readymade imagery, and given also its morbid title and accepted status as Duchamp's last painting, it's easy to imagine that the crossroad reached by Duchamp had something to do with painting's viability in the aftermath of his experimentation with the readymade.[7] Given in comparison the interrogative title of Johns' piece – *According to What* – and given also Johns' life-long career as a painter, it seems unlikely that the crossroad reached by Johns maintains any significant relation to the one reached by Duchamp some 46 years in advance. Yet, as an analysis of these works will bear out, the crossroad reached by Duchamp and Johns is one and the same, as is the path by which they arrive at this considerable fork in the road. As Duchamp's experimentation with readymade imagery brings him to this fork in the road first, I begin with his *Tu m'*, as it is a brief description of this work which will set the stage for Johns' return to both the readymade and the crisis it is said to have engendered.[8]

Looking at *Tu m'*, there is little doubt that "readymade" is the crucial term for Duchamp in the period that *Tu m'* surveys. Consider the

wallace

following inventory of its contents: at left, the shadowy outline of *Bicycle Wheel, 1913*, one of three such tracings in *Tu m'*, all of which were made by copying the outline of a readymade's shadow as it fell across *Tu m*'s elongated surface;[9] then, immediately below, in the work's lower left-hand corner, an elaboration on the familiar (i.e., already extant and thus readymade) motif of the three *Standard Stoppages*, and above, aside the shadow left by *Bicycle Wheel*, the traced outline of a second readymade – this time, the never "executed" corkscrew, an object which never did take its intended place alongside Duchamp's bottle rack and urinal as one of the Dadaist's "sanctioned" readymade objects. Above all of that, extending from the canvas's upper left-hand corner to its exact center, a simulated set of commercial color samples – for Duchamp, even life's unruly and irrational counterpart is at essence readymade[10] – the last of which appears to be "fastened" to the canvas by an *actual* metal bolt. Immediately below the "bolted," right-most sample, next to the corkscrew's "handle," a hand that may or may not have been painted by a commercial sign painter, whose signature – A. Klang – the sign painter may or may not have affixed to the canvas's surface beneath the hand he is said to have "authored."[11] Left of that, the spidery trace of Duchamp's *Hat Rack, 1917* – the third and last of the traced shadows – and finally, atop it, in the painting's right-most quadrant, an additional elaboration of the three *Standard Stoppages*.[12]

Many of these details are clearly in need of interpreting, and I will return to much of this later in the essay; here, let it suffice to say in summary that virtually every element in Duchamp's mid-career retrospective can be described as "readymade" in so far as each of the motifs therein is either an *actual* readymade object – the bolt, for example – or the effect of a readymade object enlisted in service of the work's execution – the traced shadow of the bicycle wheel and hat rack, for example. To this generalization, there is the notable, and to this point unremarked, exception of the *trompe l'oeil* tear at the work's center, a simulated rip in the canvas' surface here "repaired" by the aid of

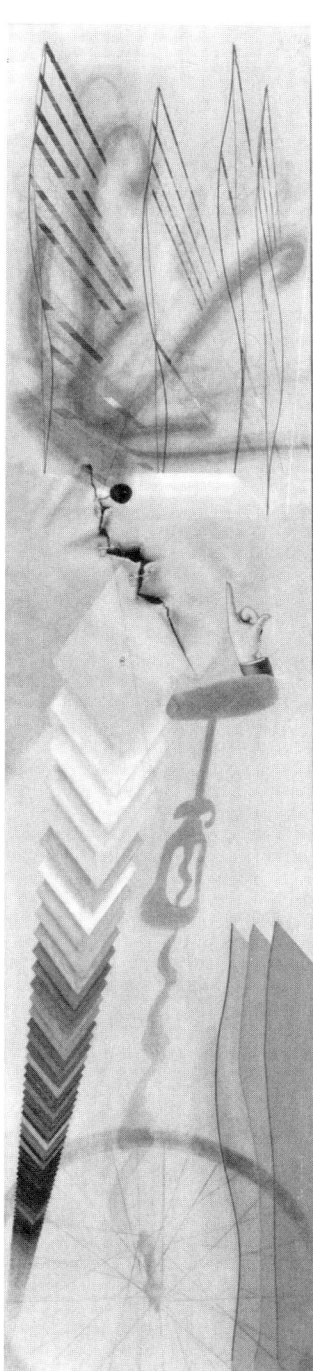

Fig. 2. Marcel Duchamp, *Tu m'*, 1918, oil on canvas with objects.
© 2001 Artists Rights Society (ARS), New York/ADAGP, Paris/Estate of Marcel Duchamp.
Yale University Art Gallery. Gift of the Estate of Katherine S. Dreier

three *actual* or, if you like, *readymade* safety pins. Complicated further by the presence of an *actual* bottle brush which projects out from the safety-pinned hole, this motif is as unprecedented within Duchamp's oeuvre as it is meaningful, at least in the context of the argument to be plotted here, though an analysis of its meaning will be temporarily deferred in favor of introducing the reader to *Tu m'*'s mid-century appropriation.

If *Tu m'* is with one exception a catalogue of readymade images, so too, is *According to What*. A colossal work comprised of seven discrete panels, *According to What* conforms to the Duchampian model elaborated above, as Johns also uses an exaggerated horizontal format to summarize work to date. Again, moving left to right, there is a panel that recycles Johns' *Watchman, 1964*, next to a panel that recycles Johns' *Field Painting, 1963*, next to a band of color samples that recall the work of Johns and Duchamp simultaneously (several of Johns' early works are inscribed with the names of the primary colors, as is plainly evident from the adjacent panel), next to a panel that recalls among other things the gray gradations of Johns' *Diver, 1962*, next to a panel that quotes almost exactly the format of his earlier *Arrive/Depart, 1963-4*, next to a panel whose only imagery is, interestingly enough, the spidery shadow cast by a "real" bent coat hanger which hangs before the bare canvas. Finally, atop all of this, there is the motif that simultaneously conjures the color samples and tear of *Tu m'* while at the same time alluding to Johns' own engagement with the process of collage: a silk-screened (*not* collaged as one might expect) newspaper swath that travels diagonally across two-thirds of *According to What*'s considerable length.

Thus, as in *Tu m'*, the images and objects assembled in *According to What* are, for the most part, readymades twice over. First, they are readymades in the sense that they are quotations of compositions already conceived and executed by Johns. Second – and this the more provocative level of readymade-ness at work in *According to What* – the paintings quoted by *According to What* are *themselves* readymade. In other words, as with Duchamp, it isn't simply that Johns is quoting Johns; rather, it is that Johns is quoting *Johns' quotation* of elements that were extant even in the moment of their "debut" within Johns oeuvre – and here it must be noted that these elements are both verbal (the word red, for example) and visual (the abstract expressionist brushstroke, for example) in nature.

A recurrent strategy within Johns' work – one need think only of the painting that established Johns' reputation: *Flag, 1954* – the tendency to employ motifs that exist in an established form, while occasionally *revealing* established forms where none were thought to exist (Johns' dispassionate and thus devastating use of de Kooning's "signature" brushstroke would be the best example of this sort of subversion), clearly aligns Johns with Duchamp in ways that justify Johns' initial reception under the label "Neo-Dada."[13] Of course, labels such as these are always problematic, especially in a context that aims to privilege analysis over description. "Neo-Dada," for example, correctly identifies Johns' resuscitation of Duchamp, yet it is nevertheless indifferent to the possibility that Johns' return to Duchamp may function *strategically*. As this possibility is in some sense the subject of this essay, I am wary of the elision performed by a label like "Neo-Dada," even as I note that terms such as this are emblematic of the problem to which this essay is addressed. That problem is the minimization of, indeed the *de-strategization* of, Johns' relation to Duchamp – a phenomenon that is itself highly strategic. Indeed, as we shall see, there is a great deal at stake in the return of Johns to Duchamp.

III the argument

I am arguing that *Tu m'* and *According to What* are best read as indices of an aesthetic crossroad – one reached by both Duchamp and Johns through an engagement with readymade objects, images and words. Moreover, I am proposing that this crossroad had something to do with the issue of painting's viability given the readymade's affront to a set of ideas most closely linked to the enterprise of painting under modernism: originality, immediacy, unity, authenticity and so on. To say here that Duchamp and Johns take different paths at the crossroad gives nothing away –

as is well known, Duchamp claims to abandon painting in 1918, while Johns perseveres, insisting not only on painting, but on painting *as readymade.*

Given this pointed opposition between the one who refuses to paint and the one who later insists, it is tempting to imagine that Johns returned to Duchamp for the simple purpose of exploring the road less traveled. But again, though this may be an accurate *description* of events given Johns' ongoing commitment to painting, it seems to me inadequate as explanation. As I see it, Johns returned to the fork in the road not so much to rethink or correct Duchamp's choice, but rather to foreground that choice as function of *desire.* After all, in retrospect it has to be said – and really, what said it better than Johns' iconic conjunction of painting and readymade image? (flags, maps, numbers, etc.) – that Duchamp's experimentation with the readymade resulted in painting's en-*Tu m'*/tomb-ment because Duchamp *wanted it to.* Indeed, how *did* the crisis of the readymade end up being a crisis for painting when the readymade's critique of authorship and originality applies equally to sculpture and poetry?[14]

Questions such as these, I suggest, are exactly the point of Johns' return to *Tu m'* – a fact we might have guessed given the interrogative nature of the title Johns bestowed on the painting most closely linked to his ongoing examination of Duchamp. Yet it isn't only the question of authorship that Johns pursues within the painting whose title seems oriented toward that issue – as I've already begun to suggest, it is also less thinkable questions, ones that involve the isolation of painting from the larger category of art. Thus as I begin a consideration of Johns' turn at a crossroad already traversed by Duchamp, I ask one further question – one that's expressly prompted by an oeuvre whose conjunction of painting and readymade image immediately manifests the *vitality* of conjunction once assumed to be lethal. Indeed, given an entire series of such works (*Flag, White Target, Gray Alphabets, White Numbers,* etc.) – a series many hold responsible for *renewing* a medium made moribund by the readymade in 1918 – the question to ask can only be this: if the death of paint-

ing in 1918 was purely rhetorical, for whom and for what was this rhetoric performed?

It is often said that the 1960s witnessed a crisis within the field of representation brought on by the experimentation of the 1950s (read: Johns and Rauschenberg) with readymade imagery (read: Duchamp). A basic narrative about the emergence of postmodernism, this story is most often told in the interest of explicating the present, as it provides a basic lineage for concerns we associate with visual culture post-war. Yet, looking back, one wonders: how and why did the readymade's emergence in the 1950s produce the epistemological break we call postmodernism, when its emergence in 1913 (the date attributed to *Bicycle Wheel,* Duchamp's first readymade) did very little to disrupt either modernism or the medium with which it is associated?

The onslaught of postmodernity – the reasons for, the timing of – is an extraordinarily complicated topic involving factors beyond the scope and grasp of this paper. Thus, what I offer by way of explanation is a creative and schematic interpretation of facts which beg creative and schematic analysis.[15] I do not imagine that what follows is the whole story, though it is, perhaps, an aspect of the story that is unlikely to be told elsewhere, given some of the leaps it entails. In a nutshell, my theory is this: the impact of the readymade in 1913 was diffused and deferred because Duchamp engineered, out of necessity and ingenuity both, a distraction meant to divert himself and his audience from the true nature of readymade's critique. This distraction was accomplished, as it had been accomplished before in the context of the photograph's traumatic "invention."[16] through a false or symptomatic discourse about the death of painting – a discourse emblematized most readily in the homophone that is the title of Duchamp's final work in this medium.[17] What this resurgent rhetoric about the death of painting allowed was the following: first, it temporarily obscured the real impact and meaning of readymade, at least as it would be constructed mid-century when the readymade and its crisis would again appear; and, second, it allowed painting to be reborn independent of the readymade's critique – hence the vitality of high-modernist abstraction, a movement which was nothing if not the suppression of readymade-ness.[18] Indeed, here it must at last be said that what was truly embalmed within Duchamp's tomb/*Tu m'* was not painting – a medium that's never not been vital – but rather the readymade and the crisis it would have engendered, for what could not be acknowledged in the moment of the readymade's "invention" were, as we will discuss in the paper's latter half, the implications of the readymade not merely for painting, and moreover, not merely for art, but also the implications of the readymade object for the subject who gazes upon it.

As for Johns, I have a hunch about him. I believe Johns knew that the crisis of the readymade, as it had been constructed in the moment of the readymade's debut, was a false one. Moreover, I believe that Johns also understood (whether consciously or unconsciously) that the readymade's real impact had been deferred, and that he set out to prove (again, whether consciously or unconsciously) both the falseness of the original crisis and the deferred-ness of the genuine crisis with a series of paintings that explicitly conjoined two terms whose incompatibility was widely assumed under modernism: painting and the readymade. Indeed, as a painter committed to painting, and as a philosopher committed to an understanding of the visual image, Johns felt compelled, I think, to demonstrate that no special relationship exists between the readymade and painting: not only is their combination *not* lethal, it is also unavoidable, as Johns made painfully clear by revealing in this same body of work that even abstract expressionist brushwork – modernism's sign of all that the readymade was not – was nothing more than a readymade sign of expressiveness and authenticity. Thus, if Duchamp had imagined that painting could deliver culture from the crisis of the readymade by assuming for representation at large the role of the sacrificial lamb, it would become all too apparent, given artworks like Johns' *Flag*, that painting could also be the vehicle by which that crisis was delivered to culture. Before turning to a direct consideration of *Flag* and the crisis it engendered, a word about scholarship and sources. Anyone familiar with the literature on Duchamp will recognize in the above a debt owed to the scholarship of Thierry De Duve. In the first of two influential books on Duchamp – *Pictorial Nominalism: On Marcel Duchamp's Passage from Painting to the Readymade* – De Duve argues that the readymade signifies and *is* the abandonment of painting, as articulated by Duchamp outside the painterly idiom. In this same text, De Duve also argues that hindsight has allowed us to see that this abandonment, the abandonment of painting, should be understood as a "stand in" for a larger and, at that point, a less speakable loss: namely, the loss of art as defined by the idea of the beautiful. The account offered here takes no issue with the idea that the readymade signals a new conception of art (an argument also advanced by Dalia Judovitz), nor does it take issue with the idea that the readymade is in some sense linked to the abandonment of painting. Indeed, one might say that it is precisely this link that interests me, for it is in the service of re-thinking the connection between the readymade and painting's so-called "abandonment" that this essay in part addresses.

In short, I am suggesting that we think less of the role that the readymade played for painting (bringing it to a crisis, announcing that crisis, etc.), and more of the role that painting, specifically the rhetorical insistence on its abandonment, played for both the readymade and the epistemological shift it seems to have signaled. As noted, I'm imagining that Duchamp's (staged) abandonment of painting, along with public proclamations to that effect, in fact *made possible* Duchamp's engagement with the readymade and all its later-to-be-acknowledged repercussions. Drawing on Freud's notion of the fetish as that which makes possible an otherwise unbearable experience of lack, I'm proposing that talk about the "abandonment of painting" served to disavow a more fundamental loss, and that it in this way worked to facilitate Duchamp's engagement with the very thing he could not (and yet did) face: the possibility of a differently conceived art.

That Duchamp's ability/willingness to engage the readymade *required* this phantasmatic rhetoric about the death of painting is borne out by the well-rehearsed – i.e., the sanctioned – facts of Duchamp's early years.[19] Indeed, it is interesting to note that Duchamp's adoption of longstanding rhetoric about the death of painting begins in 1912 on the eve of the readymade's invention (in October of this year he writes the following note to himself: "Marcel, no more painting; go get a job"), and later culminates in 1918 with the painting that signaled *simultaneously* the end of traditional painting for Duchamp *and* the end of his rigorous investigation of the readymade *as such*. Seen in this light, it is perhaps clear that for Duchamp the one was never without the other: the readymade was never without the idea of "painting's abandonment" (in fact, the latter preceded the former), and conversely, the idea of "painting's abandonment" was never without a contemplation of the readymade – after all, what purpose would this morbid rhetoric have served once Duchamp concluded his rigorous investigation of readymade-ness?[20] Read in this way, the Duchamp chronology would seem to imply that there are in fact *three* things en-*Tu m'*/tomb-ed in Duchamp's painting of 1918, as it was not only painting and the readymade that Duchamp would "abandon" and/or encrypt in this year, it was also a no longer relevant discourse about the imminence of painting's demise. Marking the apex and end of this rhetorical and fetishistic strategy, the title of the work said to be Duchamp's last – *Tu m'* – is at one and the same time a vehement and ultimate expression of a discourse that will not again resurface until Johns retrieves from Duchamp's crypt *all* of its moribund contents. Of course, Johns' decision to renew the readymade in the form of a *painted* American flag is one that will have serious consequences for the fetishistic structure that originated with and around Duchamp. Indeed, as a *painted* readymade, *Flag* renders impotent and nonsensical the idea that the topic of painting's death could be used to distract from the losses implicit in the readymade and, as such, it would soon become apparent that the crisis forestalled by Duchamp could not be so easily or successfully deferred.

To sum up, then, this paper is in one respect an elaboration upon Thierry De Duve's brilliant framework for connecting "Duchamp" to the larger dynamics of twentieth-century art (something I didn't quite realize until I was significantly immersed in the present text). Yet in another sense my reading departs from De Duve's, in that it complicates his reading of Duchamp's decision to abandon, or talk about abandoning, painting. My suggestion that we rethink the relation between the readymade and painting is one that may be interesting to consider within the immediate context of Duchamp scholarship – a context where, again, I'm not entirely at home – but it may also have implications for the way in which art history gets told, in that it points to a pattern (one in which Duchamp scholarship partakes) in which painting takes on the role of sacrificial lamb, but also *because of that*, the role of facilitator for culture at large (the fetish obscures, but in the end it makes possible the sex act). It is this phenomenon, rather than the already crowded and brilliant field of Duchamp studies that my sights are ultimately set on, even if in the *present* context I remain focused on the way in which some of this gets played out in the undertheorized relation between Duchamp and Johns.

IV by the dawn's early light ...

As we make our way to a discussion of *Flag*, the work which returned culture to the critique from which it was temporarily distracted in 1918, I would like to say a bit more about the rejuvenation of painting post-readymade, as I think a consideration of this phenomenon will allow us to understand not only the relative invisibility of the readymade between Duchamp and Johns, but also the force of its reappearance mid-century. If the sacrifice of painting was the most immediate means of distracting attention from the readymade's critique of aesthetic object and maker, the aesthetics of high-modernism can be understood as a more systematic and effective means of achieving the same. Indeed, in retrospect, it seems likely that the readymade is in no small way related to the subsequent popularity of an "ism" which privileged in the extreme concepts like originality, expressivity, authenticity and unity. Without suggesting that readymade "invented" either modernism or an early twentieth-century anxiety over the issue of the representation's efficacy, I *am* proposing that the readymade's emergence was nevertheless instrumental in the fortification of both, in the sense that the readymade made all the more urgent the codification of already extant views about the importance of authenticity within an aesthetic context.[21] In short, I am arguing that the fortification of modernism as it occurred in the writing of Greenberg and others in this period is best understood as a function of a larger cultural desire, namely the desire to reinforce the *Tu m'*/tomb in which the readymade and its crisis had been installed.[22]

By way of example, consider modernism's insistence on the mutual reflexivity of aesthetic subject and object. Does it not bear a curious relation to the readymade's prior insistence that the two are related *in name only*, and occasionally not even then (think of R. Mutt's "signature" on Duchamp's *Fountain*)? Consider, too, the insistence of high-modernism on the unity of the visual field.[23] Does it not bear a similarly defensive relation to the readymade's earlier insistence that an artwork is, by virtue of its inevitable reference to the external and prior, a riven object whose unity is only ever a function of the spectator's desire? As these examples instantiate, modernism never really responded to or assimilated the readymade's critique – something I attribute both to *its* resistance and, to a lesser degree, to the resistance of Duchamp himself (should we call it a loss of nerve?), who claimed to have abandoned not only painting but art *at large* as early as 1923. Whatever the reasons for this failure, it's clear that modernism declined to rethink its position in the face of the readymade's debut, opting instead to bolster those elements most threatened by the readymade's initial appearance.[24] Ironically, this strategy unwittingly worked to secure the crisis of the readymade's return mid-century, for when the readymade *did* at last resurface not only were the consequences more profound and more visible given a system built in anticipation of its arrival, they were also less dismissible given the coherence and interconnectivity of high-modernist ideas about the nature of art and authorship.

Add to this the fact that the readymade returns in the medium of paint, and one has a situation of dire consequence for a tradition convinced of the readymade's irrelevance. Indeed, it wasn't simply that *Flag* returned culture to the repressed fact of the readymade, it's that it also revealed by virtue of its medium and style the inextricability of the readymade from the very tradition assumed to exclude it. In other words, because *Flag* made abstract expressionist brushwork and readymade imagery indistinguishable aspects of the *same image* (an image that was at one and the same time the sign of the readymade and the sign of high-modernist aesthetics), *Flag* revealed that the story of high-modernism *had always been* the story of the readymade – and not only because high-modernism emerged in the name of the readymade's suppression. What *Flag* demonstrated in addition – and this was the more devastating implication of the *Flag*'s unprecedented conjunction – was that high-modernist paintings were, for all their theoretical opposition to the nihilistic aesthetic of the readymade, themselves an assortment of readymade signs. As such, Johns' dispassionate use of modernism's sign for passion (the abstract expressionist brushstroke) brought to light what Derrida would soon articulate: the necessary iterability, and thus the inevitable extant-cy, of any and all communicative signs.[25] Indeed, whether visual or verbal, passionate or dispassionate, abstract or representational, no form of representation is exempt from the repetitious logic of readymade-ness – and in the aftermath of Jasper Johns' *Flag* everyone knew it.

Thus, though at essence no different from *Bicycle Wheel* or *Fountain*, *Flag* nevertheless realized the readymade's critique to greater effect, for in addition to being the traumatic sign of the readymade's inevitable return, *Flag* was also the *kind* of readymade that refused to be labeled irrelevant. In the case of a *Bicycle Wheel* or *Fountain* it had been easy to speak of exceptions, as these works seemed utterly divorced from both the look and the enterprise of art as it was understood at the time these works were conceived. In 1954, however, the exception ended up looking very much like the rule and, as such, it forced a consideration of art's intersection with ideas once isolated to that exceptional category of objects known as Duchampian readymades. Was it difficult to accept in 1954 that *Bicycle Wheel* had no identifiable author? No. Was it difficult in 1954 to accept that this made *Bicycle Wheel* the kin of abstract expressionist painting? Absolutely, but *this* was the legacy and leap of *Flag*.[26]

Acknowledging the theatricality of abstract expressionism's opposition to the readymade (and also the theatricality of the readymade's opposition to painting), *Flag* thus dissolved a second false antagonism, and did so with dire consequences for the tradition devoted to the readymade's suppression. Marking in this way the end of high-modernism, *Flag* was also a return and point of departure.[27] Indeed, if *Flag* is to be credited with prying open the crypt in which readymade and its crisis had been en-*Tu m'*/tomb-ed, it must also be credited with inaugurating the critique once deferred by Duchamp. Moreover, in so far as it accomplished all this in the medium of paint, *Flag* can also be said to have rendered ineffective diversionary rhetoric about "the death of painting," and as such there was little in 1954 to distract from the trauma of the readymade's resurgence.[28]

Like clockwork, a crisis took shape (some have called it postmodernity), and alongside it new means of mitigation. Given the latter, the challenge for Johns post-*Flag* was providing a space for the readymade's review such that an understanding of its meaning and import could at last be achieved. As you may have guessed, I am proposing that *According to What* would function as this space, and as such I argue in the text's remaining pages that this painting worked to force a confrontation with the implications of the readymade art object, while at the same time deflecting and foregrounding the kinds of strategies employed to avoid exactly this sort of scenario.

V according to ... what?

Needless to say, one of the issues raised most forcefully by the readymade's contemplation is authorship – *According to What*'s inclusion of Duchamp's profile and initials is enough to signal that, as is *Tu m*'s equally pointed inclusion of

A. Klang's commercially painted and centrally located hand. Explicit challenges to the notion that an artwork is the product of a singular, original consciousness, these aspects of *According to What* and *Tu m'* aggressively thematize what the readymade imagery therein had been working to manifest all along: the untenability of modernism's faith in the originality and singularity of its signatories.

Consider a work like *Bicycle Wheel*, for example. Like all readymades, it poses a double threat to the modernist conception of authorship: on the one hand, it multiplies the author in that it increases to infinity the number of hands and/or minds involved in the work's execution (how many people *did* it take to make a work like *Bicycle Wheel*?); on the other hand, it divides the author, in that it inevitably stages the dependence of its maker on that which is either external or prior or both. Given a work that manages thus to divide and double its author simultaneously, it makes little sense to speak of "an artist" and his "originality" – which artist? What origin? – and, undoubtedly, questioning the relevance of these terms to the enterprise of art was always part of the point of artworks which were defiantly readymade.

As the artist credited with the readymade's return, Johns evidences a clear understanding of the critique his work reinstates: inaugurating his career with an image that "belongs" equally to everyone in his immediate audience (what American hasn't at some point drawn an image of the American flag?), he then summarizes that same career with a work that foregrounds his indebtedness to Duchamp (here, the author's division), while underscoring in this work's title – *According to What* – the centrality of authorship's critique to both his work and the broader tradition of readymades on which his work depends. Indeed, if it can be said that *According to What* is in some sense a catalogue of all that was repressed by Duchamp and renewed by *Flag*, then here it must be stressed it prioritizes among the repressed contents of Duchamp's *Tu m'* the effect of the readymade art object on its artist, and that it does this for good reason. After all, in a sense everything would follow from this, for if the artist was the figure in whom art found its ultimate meaning and justification under modernism, if he was indeed "the thing according to what," then surely the mid-century discovery of his long-forgotten death was to be an event of unparalleled consequence for the making and meaning of art.[29]

As I aim to demonstrate now, the readymade's return did a great deal more than multiply and diffuse the notion of *an author* – though this alone had been enough to ensure the readymade's initial encryption in the period between Duchamp and Johns. In addition, the readymade also made manifest by virtue of this inauthorability the impossibility of a unified visual field. Bear in mind that Johns returns culture to a consideration of authorship at a moment when the unity of the visual object was understood to be a function of its relation to *an artist* whose vision it sought to convey.[30] As such, the readymade's challenge to the author's singularity was something that had consequences for the integrity of the object as well – a fact thrown into sharp relief mid-century, given the insistence of high-modernism on the absolute reflexivity between an aesthetic subject and the objects which bear his name.

Indeed, if this reflexivity was invisible (though extant) in 1913, it was all too apparent in 1954.[31] Returning once again to the notion that modernism unwittingly participated in its own destruction, it seems important to note that it was the insistence of high-modernism on the connection between artist and art object – an insistence it offered to counter the readymade's assertion that there is none – which ultimately ensured that the readymade's critique of authorship was understood as a critique of the visual field's unity. As such, we might conclude that it was high-modernism's theory of mutual reflexivity that ended up revealing the incoherence of the visual object it sought to unify – and *this* at a moment when Lacan had already made clear the profound importance of that unity for the spectator who gazes upon it.

Writing in 1936, Lacan famously asserts that the unity of the visual field – its boundedness and coherence – is crucial for the spectating subject, as it is that aspect of the specular image which allows the infant to maintain the illusion that he or she is a comparably unified entity. Leave aside Lacan's insistence on the inevitable *failure* of this relation – on his account the identification between disorganized infant and coherent specular illusion inevitably produces a sense of alienation – and one is left with a theory about the relation of subject and visual object that sounds a great deal like the theory implicit within high-modernist discourse, in the sense that there, too, one finds a spectator who is comparably invested in the presumed unity of the visual field.[32] If Lacan is right and at all relevant, then one can imagine that paintings which are manifestly riven, either by tradition or the readymade or both, are paintings which compel immediate repair by those who gaze anxiously upon them.

It goes with out saying, perhaps, that *According to What* is one such painting: not only is the work *literally* riven in the sense that it is comprised of seven irreducible canvases, it is also conceptually riven by the here interchangeable presence of tradition and the readymade, each of which threatens to disrupt the imaginary unity of the picture plane by pointing to conflicting and irrecuperable sites outside the bounds of the visual field. Thus, just as the title of *According to What* alerts us to the consequence of the readymade's return for the aesthetic subject, so the physical construction of *According to What*, along with the irreducible heterogeneity of its contents (a chair, some letters, a color scale …), alerts to the consequence of that return for the aesthetic object. As it has been the contention of this essay that *According to What* revisits the readymade's *Tu m'*/tomb for the purpose of dramatizing the consequences of the readymade's resurgence, I note here that the visual field's fragmentation is the second consequence revealed by Johns' painting, and like the inauthorability from which it derives, it remains to this day a difficult, if apparent, aspect of the visual image.

Enter here the interpretive concept "homage" – indeed, what better way to transcend the problem of multiple authors and the threat their presence poses to the notion of a unified visual field? Because it subjugates one author to the will of another, the concept "homage" allows the interpreter to maintain his or her belief in a solitary authorial consciousness whose relation to tradition is that of controlled selection.33 Seen from this perspective, the pervasiveness of the concept "homage" within the literature on *According to What* seems more than convenient or trendy. A means of disavowing not only the insistence of *According to What* on the undecidability of its author, but also the related and more explicitly Freudian problem of the work's fragmentation, the interpretive strategy "homage" is yet another fetishistic structure, this one a function of interpretive desire to avoid the losses and lacks foregrounded by the experience of a work like *According to What*.34 After all, it's by virtue of this interpretive strategy that the disruptive presence of Duchamp in Johns' work is transformed into an index of Johns' (and, ultimately the interpreter's) mastery over that which is most unruly: the divisive visibility in an aesthetic present of either the readymade or tradition, or both.35 Thus, if Duchamp seems to me the sign and agent of *According to What*'s fragmentation, then he seems to others no less than the means of the work's reparation.

Of course, in defense of Johns' interpreters, it must be said that Johns *is* consciously invoking and manipulating Duchamp's legacy: "I have deliberately taken Duchamp's work and slightly changed it" (Coplans 30–31). Yet, as the cagey Johns is surely aware, the presence of tradition always exceeds the intentions of the one who invokes it – both because of the infinite regress its presence implies (*According to What* may refer to *Tu m'*, though needless to say, not only to *Tu m'*, but *Tu m'* necessarily refers to elsewhere and so on, ad infinitum) and because there is, as always, the uncontrollable element known as the "spectator's share."36 As such, Johns' documented intention to include Duchamp does little to alleviate the work's affront to modernist notions of authorship; as the remainder of Johns' statement insists – "I thought to make a kind of play on whose work it is, whether mine or (Duchamp)" – the issue of the work's author remains obdurately undecidable in ways that exemplify and anticipate Derrida's theorization of this concept in 1972.37

For this interpreter – an interpreter who writes after Johns and Derrida both, the literature's insistence on Johns' control over *According to What*'s Duchampian elements is a compelling testament to the painting's critical success, for on this account it is precisely the undecidable, and thus irrecuperable nature of the work's authorial "origin" that makes necessary and ubiquitous the insistence on the work as an act of "homage." Indeed, I would argue that it is ultimately the *impossibility* of the work's repair, the impossibility of any work's repair, that makes all the more urgent its discursive performance, as it is through this rhetorical drama that spectators (art historical and otherwise) are able to maintain, however precariously, the primary illusion on which the modernist subject insists: that of a specular field which reflects and confers not only the artist's unity but also the unity of the I/eye who looks.

Not surprisingly, *According to What* seems to have something to say about all this: indeed, as promised, *According to What* thematizes not only the modernist presumptions it interrogates but also the means by which modernism aims to mitigate the challenge summed up in the entity and phrase: *According to What*. In other words, in addition to dramatizing modernism's faith in the relation of author to object, *According to What* also anticipates and foregrounds the response of the spectator/art historian when confronted with a work that fails to conform to the desired image of unity.

As noted, a small canvas is appended via hinge to the lower left-hand corner of *According to What*. One side of this canvas features Duchamp's profile and initials, while the other side features the work's stenciled title, and in handwritten form, both Johns' name and the year of the work's execution. When the hinged canvas is in an upright position, which is to say when it's attached to the main portion of the work by two hook and eye fasteners, only Johns' name and the date is visible. When the hinged canvas hangs freely, Johns' name is obscured, and the blank, lower left-hand corner of the work is left exposed by the release of the hinged canvas which now reveals Duchamp's profile and initials.

painting, death

It's clear immediately that Johns' use of the hinge (itself a Duchampian motif) dramatizes on behalf of all post-readymade art the undecidability of an artwork's author.[38] What may be less obvious is that the hinge also dramatizes the familiar consequences of that undecidability for the integrity of the aesthetic object. Consider the hinged canvas a second time: when placed in an upright position such that Johns' name is alone visible, and the unity of the visual field seems uncompromised – i.e., the rectangle remains a unified and coherent shape. Now allow the hinged canvas to hang such that Duchamp's name is visible, and the unity of the visual field is broken in ways that are both literal and symbolic – i.e., the coherence of the visual field is broken by the manifest presence of a supplement that is at one and the same time a physical and conceptual appendage. Seen in this light, the hinged canvas dramatizes the undecidability of *According to What*'s author, while also articulating *as untenable fantasy* one of modernism's most fundamental assumptions: namely, the inextricable link between the picture plane's coherence and the originality and/or singularity of its author.

Indeed, it's important to stress here that the illusion of a unified subject and object is thematized *but transparent* in Johns' work: when the hinged canvas is in its upright position such that *According to What* "reads" as the unified product of a single author, the viewer is nevertheless left with haunting traces of the repression on which this illusion depends. Not only are the hook and eye fasteners still visible, but there is also the difficult presence of a "back-turned" canvas – as straightforward a sign as any that something is being obscured in the service of this illusion. A clear symbol of the suppression required by the modernist fictions of unity and originality, the back-turned canvas – a recurrent motif in Johns' work of this period – tells us more concretely than any other element in Johns' work that he understands full well the nature of this relation, but cannot himself forget the omissions on which it depends. An articulation of the fantasy *and its impossibility, According to What* thus reveals on behalf of the readymades it assembles not only their target (modernist myths about the link between artist and artwork), but also the various implications of their release from the *Tu m'*/tomb to which Johns' painting returns.

Thematizing the link between unified artist and artwork in ways that acknowledge the threat the readymade and tradition pose to each (remember that in *According to What* they are brilliantly collapsed in the figure of Duchamp), *According to What* can also be seen to thematize and deflect a purported means of this threat's mitigation. Looking again to the hinged canvas, we see that it is also a pictorial analogue for the "mechanics" of recuperation as performed by critics and scholars of Johns' work. Indeed, part of what the hinge demonstrates is the process by which culture contends with objects which too manifestly bear the signs of the tradition on which they depend. A dominant art historical method at the time of *According to What*'s execution, source scholarship – the broader category in which one would locate an interpretive insistence on homage – is that process, and schematically relayed its procedure sounds something like this: first, identify the artwork's referent and/or source; second, enframe the referent and or source such that it refers only to itself; third, bring this contained entity into the context that is your immediate concern; fourth, enjoy the resulting illusion of bounded plenitude.

Now, does *According to What* not stage a procedure of exactly this sort? Does it not (1) identify Duchamp as its prototype and source, (2) isolate and enframe that prototype so that it refers only to itself (hence the indexical portrait of Duchamp by Duchamp), (3) bring that referent into the larger context of *According to What* via the mechanism of the hinge, and (4) allow the subsequent illusion of originality and plenitude in the form of a unified visual field whose authorship has been effectively reduced to a single, authoritative consciousness? A literalization of the interpretive method it was bound to attract, *According to What* takes as a given the modernist desire to contain tradition within the unbroken boundaries of the pictorial field, and thus demonstrates not only the need but also the means of restoring to the frame's confines the fragments of a past it must elide in the name of unity in the present.

Of course, as always, Johns gives us the fantasy as well as its failure to compel: as noted, the resulting image of unity is hardly convincing, given both the back-turned canvas and the basic irony a work which thematizes with uncanny accuracy the terms of its own reception. Moreover, it has to be said that even if source scholarship *were* an effective means of restoring unity to the pictorial field, even if the chain of signification *could* be arrested in this way such that one could restore to a painting all its wayward fragments – and again I wish to be clear in saying that this is not the view I see embedded in *According to What* – there is still, in this particular case, the problem of Johns' chosen interlocutor. After all, what would it mean to "recuperate" a figure like Duchamp? Further, what would it mean to "recuperate" a source like *Tu m'*? For reasons I turn to now, "mastery" of Duchamp – whether by Duchamp or Johns or interpreters of either – is an impossibility, as Johns clearly understood. Yet, as always with Johns, it will be an impossibility that makes of the exception a rule. Indeed, as we shall see, the irrecuperability of Duchamp and *Tu m'* is in the end the irrecuperability of *all sources*, and as such the reference of *According to What* to each is the means by which Johns will at last enforce an un-mitigatable engagement with the unexceptional and insurmountable fact of a visual field that is readymade, inauthorable and fragmented.

VI according to what, indeed!

Needless to say, there are several problems with positing Duchamp as *According to What*'s restorative passe-partout.[39] First, from the vantage point of the 1960s, Duchamp is the artist most closely associated with subverting the author-function under modernism, as it was his revived experimentation with (al)readymade imagery that threatened to expose the symbolic (and not necessarily indexical) nature of the relationship between an artist and the artwork which bears his name. Thus before delving any deeper into Duchamp's legacy, we can already say of his invocation in *According to What* that it leads Johns' interpreters to the very place they aimed to avoid, for in their attempt to establish a one-to-one relationship between artist (Johns) and artwork (*According to What*), they inevitably confront the idea that this relation is nothing more than a violent assertion of ownership and legitimacy in the symbolic form of a proper name.[40]

Moreover, having been forced to consider the idea that authorship is an arbitrary function of language, these interpreters *also* have to contend with Duchamp's demonstrated interest in revealing the unreliability of the connection between an artist and his name, for if Duchamp's experimentation with readymade imagery focused attention on the importance of the artist's name (what else is left to link artist and artwork when all trace of the artist's hand has been removed?), it also focused attention on the unreliability of the name as a means of securing artist to artwork.[41] *Fountain*, the urinal signed by Duchamp with name R. Mutt, exemplifies in the extreme this simple but devastating point: as a work which eschews entirely the importance of the artist's traditional "signature" – style – *Fountain* forces attention on the artist's signature as the sign of presence within, and connection to, the work. Yet having oriented the spectator's attention toward the artist's *literal* signature (the only sign of the artist's presence in the work), *Fountain* then reveals that the relation between the artist and his name is as arbitrary and uncertain as the relation between an artist and his or her artwork. Indeed, *so* arbitrary is this relation that one can simply change it at will, adopting as it suits one the name Rrose, the name Marcel, the name R. Mutt.

Thus, if the resuscitation of Duchamp threatened to reveal the arbitrary (not essential) relation between artist and artwork, it also threatened, by virtue of Duchamp's fascination with aliases, the faith of modernism in a second relation: namely, the one assumed between the person we call an artist and the name that is the sign of his presence. Indeed, this is the second and perhaps more intractable problem associated with a mid-century "recuperation" of Duchamp – a fact Duchamp seems to have anticipated in a work of 1923 (Fig. 3).[42] A comedic take on the genre of the old-time fugitive poster, *Wanted*

painting, death

Fig. 3. Marcel Duchamp, *Replica of: Wanted $2,000 Reward, New York*, form *Boite-en-Valise*, 1923, color lithograph, 8 1/8 × 6 3/8."
© 2001 Artists Rights Society (ARS), New York/ADAGP, Paris/Estate of Marcel Duchamp.
Philadelphia Museum of Art: The Louise and Walter Arensberg Collection

Duchamp is both missing and wanted – and not only because the artist had fled the scene of representation at a moment when an author's absence from this arena would have been conceived as a criminal offense.[43] Indeed, even when present, "Duchamp" proves hard to find.

Masquerading as Rrose and R. Mutt, to name only two, Duchamp's adoption of aliases makes "Duchamp" an uncertain target of *any* investigation, be that investigation the fictive one staged by the artist in *Wanted*, or be it the one less self-conscious investigation undertaken by source-hungry interpreters of *According to What*. Indeed, were Duchamp's work not *itself* so problematic, there would still be the matter of the artist's performed difference from himself. As such, it's fair to say that *According to What* sends its commentators to an artist and body of work that is nothing, if not irrecuperable: not only are Duchamp's works fragmented and unauthored,

$2,000 Reward features two indices of the artist – one photograph in profile, one dead-on – along with the following text:

> Wanted. $2,000 reward for information leading to the arrest of George W. Welch, alias Bull, alias Pickens etcetry, etcetry. Operated Bucket Shop in New York under name HOOKE, LYON and CINQUER. Height about 5 feet 9 inches. Weight about 180 pounds. Complexion medium, eyes same. Known also under name RROSE SÉLAVY.

There is great deal one could make of this work, but here let it suffice to say that absence and desire are the key words here, for what we have in this work is a dramatization of the idea that

their "author," whose name might have functioned fetishistically to disavow that fact, is known to us only as a series of names, none of which are fundamentally and/or essentially "Duchamp." As such, the idea of recuperating either Duchamp or the works made in his name(s) becomes a ludicrous proposition, as Johns no doubt knew.

Of course, *Tu m'* is *According to What*'s *specific* point of reference, and thus it should come as no surprise that it is, like the body of work for which it speaks, a dramatically irrecuperable entity. Indeed, as a collection of readymades "made" by the man who refused to concede his relation to the works which bear his name(s), *Tu m'* is irrecuperable for all the familiar reasons – a fact it elects to thematize in the motif that dominates its center. Anticipating another centrally placed and gendered gash within another work that is said to have been Duchamp's "last" – here, I speak of *Given*'s far more explicit thematization of the pictorial field as violated female body – *Tu m'*'s "ripped" and safety-pinned surface acknowledges the traditional conception of the picture plane as that which is penetrated both by the spectator's gaze and by the interpreter's quest for knowledge of something which is assumed to be both interior and unknown. Yet having lured the spectator to the image in ways that foreground the metaphorics that continue to structure our engagement with the mater-ial space of painting, *Tu m'* then complicates the conventions it invokes by adding to the culturally feminine space of representation a phallic element (the bottle brush) which serves to repel the viewer from the recessive space he had hoped to master (Fig. 4).[44] Summarizing in this way a body of work that is as enticing as it is impenetrable, *Tu m'* thematizes its own irrecuperability, while marking in this same motif a subtle difference between it and *According to What*.

Indeed, if we look once again to the core imagery of *Tu m'*, juxtaposing it against the comparable motif within the work that is its compulsive repetition, we see that for all the sameness of these two works (a sameness I embrace as one more sign of Johns' engagement with the topic of art's relation to death, repetition being, after all, the death drive's visible manifestation) there is nevertheless a significant difference here – one that is as much a product of the work's imagery as it is a product of the artists' inscription within an apocalyptic and theatrical discourse about the imminence of painting's demise. Indeed, when we contrast *Tu m'*'s tear with the newspaper swath that is its compliment in *According to What*, we see that Duchamp, for all his irony and iconoclasm, still operates within a metaphorics Johns has learned to reject.[45] That is to say, even though one's access to *Tu m'* is ultimately blocked by the bottle brush which extends out from the painting's "torn" surface, and even though that tear is ultimately only an illusion that *refers to* rather than *is* a point of literal and metaphoric access for the would-be spectator, *Tu m'* and its author nevertheless still

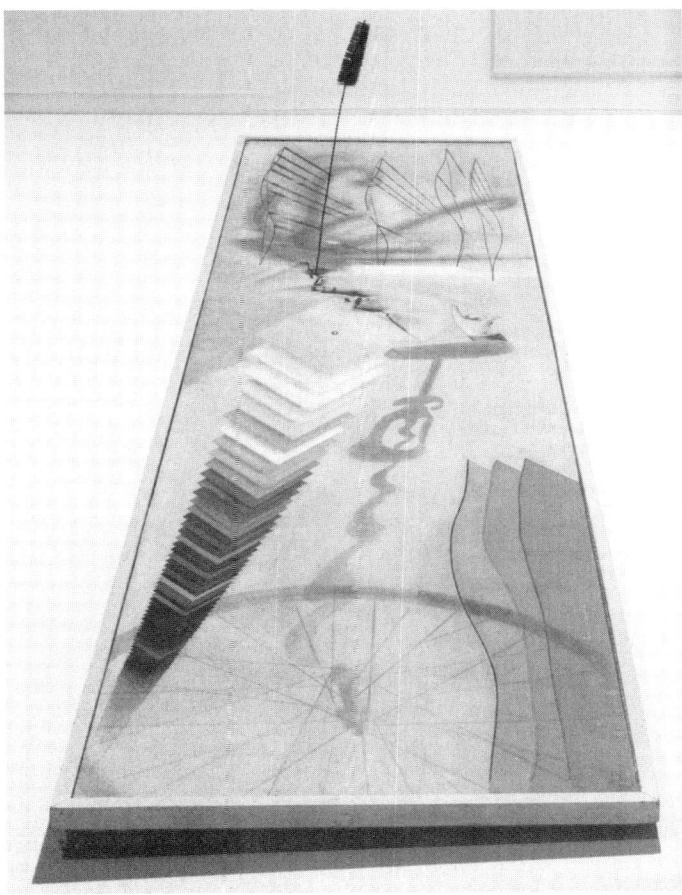

Fig. 4. Marcel Duchamp, *Tu m'*, 1918, o l on canvas with objects.
© 2001 Artists Rights Society (ARS), New York/ADAGP, Paris/Estate of Marcel Duchamp.
Yale University Art Gallery. Gift of the Estate of Katherine S. Dreier

participate within a paradigm in which things are known and not known, penetrated and not penetrated, accessed and not accessed.[46] In contrast, *According to What*'s silk-screened swath of newspaper suggests Johns' assimilation of an alternative vision: surface where there was the suggestion of depth, meanings where there was the possibility of meaning, deferral where there was the promise of knowledge, and reference's endless chain where there was once a would-be referent.[47] An index of the paradigm shift brought on by the readymade's return, this juxtaposition is perhaps our best example of Johns' difference from, and debt to, Duchamp.

If the central imagery of *Tu m'* thus alerts us to a central difference between it and *According to What*, and if that difference is yet another sign of Johns' ability to see in Duchamp what even Duchamp was unwilling to picture, *Tu m'*'s central imagery nevertheless continues to impress upon us the deep similarities that mark the artists' understanding of the representation's essential properties. Indeed, if we look one last time to the "ripped" and safety-pinned surface of *Tu m'*, we see in its central motif a succinct articulation of the conclusion that we, the interpreters of *According to What*, have been approaching and resisting all along: neither diligent scholarship nor eloquent hermeneutics can repair the picture plane's eternally riven surface, for in the aftermath of the readymade's irrepressible return the imaginary unity of the picture plane is, like the subject it expresses, always already torn from the pressure of its ties to a tradition that is both infinite and irrecuperable.[48]

VII death drive[49]

So where does that leave us, the tired interpreters of *According to What*? Confronted with a fragmented work of ambiguous origin whose readymade contents refer us to another manifestly riven and irrecuperable work, we who are without recourse are at last forced to consider the irrepressible fact of the readymade along with *According to What*'s itemization of its unmitigatable effects, the last of which, the most devastating of which we endure only after we have performed the irrecuperability of *According to What*'s impossible referent. Indeed, having failed to recuperate either "Duchamp" or *Tu m'*, we have no choice but to see in the fractious surface of *According to What* the thing that Duchamp surely saw at the moment of *Tu m'*'s completion: the horrifying image of his own mortal finitude, as reflected in the fragmented "face" of a work whose insistence on the readymade-ness of expressive signs had already spoken of death in symbolic terms.

As such, it's now clear to us, as surely it was clear to both Johns and Duchamp, that the death of *painting* was never really at stake here – a fact Duchamp both acknowledges and denies in the homophone that is *Tu m'*'s title.[50] More than a morbid play on the English word for "tomb," *Tu m'* is of course also a grammatical fragment – one which alerts us to the dynamic that has been at issue in this moribund conjunction of terms all along, namely the relation of the object to the mortified subject who gazes upon it. Indeed, when seen through the mid-century eyes of Jasper Johns, the meaning of this assembled but fragmented corpus is all too clear, as are the reasons for our initial diversion from the truth that was nevertheless implicit in Duchamp's title: the encounter of the subject with the object *is always* the encounter thematized in both *Tu m'* and *According to What*, as this relation is always at essence the spectator's experience of a fragmented and inauthorable corpus which reflects back to the spectator his or her own fate as a body in pieces inside a *Tu m'*/tomb that is and is not the container for the unruly fragments that each of us inevitably are and will be.[51]

Much more than homage, *According to What*'s revisitation of *Tu m'* is thus rather more like the process of analysis in which the analyst (Johns) provides the context necessary (*According to What*) for the analysand's (Duchamp) expression of that which has been manifest only as hysterical symptom (*Tu m'*). That symptom, I have claimed, is the insistence of *Tu m'* on the death of painting at the hands of the readymade – an insistence whose phantasmatic nature was irrevocably revealed by Johns' own insistence on readymades executed in the medium of paint. Revealing in this way that *painting*'s death was never at issue, works like

Flag and *According to What* revealed that the apocalyptic rhetoric of *Tu m'* was in fact nothing more than the displaced articulation of a different discovery, one that also concerned the relation of painting to death. Indeed, it was Johns' mid-century return to the readymade that forced an examination of painting's death as *Tu m*'s hysterical *symptom*, and as such it was also Johns who finally made manifest that the issue at hand in both 1918 and 1964 was not the death *of* painting, but rather the death *therein*. Whether the death of the unified object whose referent is forever deferred in the process of its symbolization, or the death of the expressive and spectatorial subject who sees in that symbol his own riven and mortified reflection, Johns' resurrection of the readymade revealed that painting was less death's *victim* than it was its unwitting participant. In other words, because it reinforced the relationship between representation and the living death we all experience as mortified subjects of an inherited symbolic code, *According to What* allowed us to see that the readymade had implications for subject and object alike, even if Duchamp and many of his critics have preferred to speak only of the readymade's implications for painting. Indeed, "preferred" is the operative word here for, as noted, the issue of the readymade's effect on the subject was implicit in *Tu m*'s title all along, as was the unanswerability of the question Johns posed in the title of the work that is *Tu m*'s compulsive repetition: if Johns' summary painting asks a question it knew it could not answer (the question of authorship), then Duchamp's summary painting poses a question it knows it cannot ask (the question of spectatorship – i.e., the question of the relation implied between tu/you, the spectator and m'/me, the readymade object). *Tu m'*: a grammatical fragment with homophonic implications for the relation it cannot in the end articulate, Duchamp's title speaks not only of his silence, but also of his reasons.[52] As we have seen, those reasons find their belated expression in an oeuvre summarized in 1964, their deferral a testament to, and instance of, the trauma they dared not speak.

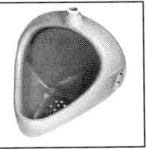

notes

Because it goes without saying, here it will be said what my work owes to the generosity and intelligence of my mentor, Steven Z. Levine. In addition, I would like to acknowledge the debt this essay owes to the scholarship of Thierry De Duve; I was fortunate to study with him at the University of Pennsylvania in the Fall of 1997 and Spring of 1998. I would also like to recognize Gary Banham and the anonymous *Angelaki* readers; their comments made this essay better.

1 Several studies have addressed the links between these two works and artists. See Max Kozloff, "Johns and Duchamp," *Art International* 8.2 (Mar. 1964): 42–45; Max Kozloff, "Art and the New York Avant-Garde," *Partisan Review* 31.4 (Fall 1964): 535–54; Rosalind Krauss, "Jasper Johns," *Lugano Review* 1.2 (Mar. 1964): 94–95; John Tancock, "The Influence of Marcel Duchamp" in *Marcel Duchamp*, eds. Anne d'Harnoncourt and Kynaston McShine (New York: Museum of Modern Art, 1973) 165–66; Peter Higginson, "Jasper's Non-Delimma: A Wittgensteinian Approach," *New Lugano Review* 10 (1975): 53–60; Walter Hopps, "Jasper Johns – Fragments – According to What," *Print Review* 1 (Mar. 1973): 41–50; Patricia Kaplan, "On Jasper Johns' *According to What*," *Art Journal* 35.3 (Spring 1976): 247–50; Barbara Rose, "Decoys and Doubles: Jasper Johns and the Modernist Mind" 68–73; Barbara Rose, "Jasper Johns: The Tantric Details," *American Art* 7.4 (Fall 1993): 54ff.; Francis Naumann, *Jasper Johns: According to What & Watchman* (New York: Gagosian Gallery, 1992). Though these accounts contain several interesting observations, they fail to assess the essential point of Johns' return to Duchamp. Rather, taken as a whole, these analyses are more interested in the *fact of Johns' return* than they are in either the reasons for, or the ramifications of its occurrence. Barbara Rose comes closest to avoiding this phenomenon. Acknowledging the dominant reading of *According to What* as a homage to Duchamp – "*According to What* has been correctly construed as an homage to Duchamp" – she goes on to say that "it is also much more," that it is, among other things, "an affirmation of the continuing significance of painting as a carrier of meaning" (Decoys and Doubles 71). Though I agree that Johns' revisitation of Duchamp has everything to do with the viability of painting, I read *According to What* and the entirety of Johns' oeuvre as an acknowledgment that painting need not be, nor *can it be* "a carrier of meaning."

2 Duchamp was very interested in puns and homophones, especially those that played one language – usually French – against another – usually English. For a discussion of Duchamp's use of puns, see Dalia Judovitz, *Unpacking Duchamp: Art in Transit* 87–119 and Thierry De Duve throughout his two influential books on Duchamp: *Kant After Duchamp* and *Pictorial Nominalism: On Marcel Duchamp's Passage from Painting to the Readymade*.

3 The reader will notice that psychoanalysis plays an important role in the telling of this tale. Not only does the present account speak of culture in psychoanalytic terms – e.g., the return of the readymade mid-century will be the return of that which the West repressed – it also employs psychoanalytic terms in its description of individual paintings – e.g., Duchamp's *Tu m'* will be interpreted as if it were itself a subject who/which holds things both above and below the threshold of conscious awareness. The prominence of psychoanalysis here should be taken as an indication of two interconnected things: (1) my belief that there is a cultural consciousness that is related to but in excess of individual consciousness whose structures and strategies mirror on a grander scale that of the individual, and (2) my belief that the telling of art's history, indeed the telling of any history, is only ever a displaced narration of one's own psychoanalytically informed tale.

4 The profile is in fact a copy of a work by Duchamp entitled *Self-Portrait in Profile, 1958*.

5 Duchamp describes *Tu m'* in terms that are equally applicable to *According to What*: "It is a kind of inventory of all my preceding works, rather than a painting itself." See Schwarz (1997, 2, 658).

6 Barbara Rose reads Johns' interest in cataloguing his work as an index of his desire for a seamless totality; my own essay argues the exact opposite. See "Decoys and Doubles: Jasper Johns and the Modernist Mind," *Arts Magazine* 50.9: 68. For an account of Duchamp's interest in cataloguing his work, see Judovitz, *Unpacking Duchamp* 4ff.

7 David Joselit argues with characteristic nuance that the readymade allowed Duchamp to invert his earlier cubist preoccupations, in that the readymade made possible a movement from a practice which revealed the body's dissolution within a libidinal economy, to a practice that revealed the subject's multiplication within the flow of capital. See *Infinite Regress*, chapter 2.

Thierry De Duve has also written extensively on the subject of the readymade's relation to the abandonment of painting. I address this later in this essay. Also, it needs to be said that *Tu m'* is not literally Duchamp's last work in the medium of paint. Nevertheless, it has come acquire that tag within the Duchamp literature.

8 There are several compelling interpretations of *Tu m'*, most of which are uninterested in its relation to *According to What*. David Joselit reads the work as a meditation on the theme of measurement, which is itself a clear metaphor for the knowability of things. For him, *Tu m'* takes "the cycle of semiotic measurability and immeasurability to its logical extreme" in that every element of the work is both an "object to be measured and a standard of measurement" (Joselit 61–70). Though my own account will not concern itself with the particular trope of measurement, it does correspond to the idea that *Tu m'* represents something in the extreme. For me, that something is best articulated in semiotic and psychoanalytic terms (terms I don't think Joselit would reject), in that I imagine *Tu m'* to simultaneously represent the limit of signification and subjectivity. Put otherwise, the limit or impossibility of reference – which is to say the limitless-ness of reference is also the impossibility of unmediated being: hence a work about representation that is also a tomb/*Tu m'*. Rosalind Krauss reads *Tu m'* in terms of its relation to the idea of the index, observing that as Duchamp is retreating from abstract painting, he is also engaged with something like its opposite: indexicality, which *is*, she notes, the essence of photography. Rosalind Krauss, "Notes on the Index: Part I" in *The Originality of the Avant-Garde and Other Modernist Myths* (Cambridge: MIT P, 1985) 197–209. Judovitz builds on Krauss's account of *Tu m'*, arguing that readymade must also be associated with nomination such that the gesture of reference (the photograph, shadow or finger that points elsewhere) is transformed into a gesture of *self*-reference in which it points also itself in the act of reference. See Judovitz 221–26.

9 Duchamp describes his process as follows: "I had found a sort of projector which made shadows rather well enough, and I projected each shadow, which I traced by hand, onto the canvas" (Cabanne 60). Also, this is as good a place as any to note that the unusual format of *Tu m'* – $22\frac{1}{2} \times 122\frac{3}{4}''$ – was designed to accommodate a long, narrow space above a door in the study of the woman who

commissioned the work: Katherine Dreier (Lebel 43).

10 Thierry De Duve has written extensively on this issue, arguing that Duchamp's turn to the readymade is inextricably linked to the invention of mechanically reproduced paint. See De Duve, *Kant After Duchamp* (Cambridge: MIT P, 1996) 147–96.

11 There is some debate about this within the Duchamp literature even though the artist is on record as saying "right in the middle, I put a hand painted sign by a sign painter, and I had the good fellow sign it" (Cabanne 60).

12 I take the significance of this last motif (a three-dimensional rendering of the standard stoppages and their shadows?) – admittedly the most curious in *Tu m'* – to be the impossibility of reifying the readymade. In other words, even though the readymade introduces to the realm of art the idea of a necessary iterability, it does not follow that representation is now finite because already known. As Barthes and others will eventually insist, there is always in addition the uncontrollable and unanticipatable remainder – the tenor of the voice, the repetition of the sound, the smear of the ink, etc. As a distortion of a unit of a linear measurement (as always the Duchampian irony …), which was itself already distorted, this motif is the symbol of that remainder, a reminder that the readymade's critique *does not* result in an utterly mechanized or systematic conception of representation.

13 The term "Neo-Dada" first appears in 1957 in a review of a group exhibition that included Johns' *Flag* (Rosenblum 53). Also, I should note that though the term Neo-Dada can be applied to a number of artists, my engagement with the term in this essay is restricted to its application to Johns and Rauschenberg.

14 Of course, one could argue that Duchamp eventually acknowledges the universal applicability of the readymade's critique, and is thus forced to abandon not merely painting, but art altogether – a step Duchamp claims to have taken after completion of the *Large Glass* in 1923. Also, I mention poetry here to stress the link between Duchamp and Eliot, both of whom were (wittingly or unwittingly) anticipating the author's death as it would be theorized by Barthes and Foucault in the course of the 1960s. On this aspect of Eliot, see Maud Ellman, "Eliot's Abjection" in *Abjection, Melancholia and Love: The Work of Julia Kristeva*, eds. Johns Fletcher and Andrew Benjamin (New York: Routledge, 1990) 179–201.

15 Here, a general disclaimer. "Duchamp" refers to Duchamp, but it also refers here to a larger cultural phenomenon he seems to have embodied. As such, there are moments in this text when his name is used as a place-holder in a larger, more general theory about the phenomenon of modernism – its endurance and sudden collapse. I am not a Duchamp scholar by training, and I have not produced a document that intends to "compete" with those produced by eminent minds in this field Thierry De Duve and David Joselit foremost among them. Rather, what I offer here is a creative explanation for the dynamics of a culture which has rendered things both above and below the threshold of conscious awareness. "Duchamp" is one such thing, and it is the mid-century revitalization of this term/phenomenon/persona that is the fundamental concern of my essay.

16 Here I use the term "invention" advisedly. As Geoffry Batchen has forcefully argued, the photograph's invention was a product of widespread desire, rather than fortuitousness. See *Burning with Desire: The Conception of Photography* (Cambridge: MIT P, 1997).

17 A theme that this paper cannot fully explore is the way in which painting is routinely employed as a scapegoat when there is a fundamental challenge to dominant ideas about representation. The "invention" of photography is a case in point: even though the index cality of the photograph posed a challenge to representation at large, its "invention" in the 1820s would result in a series of proclamations about the death of painting. See n. 23.

18 Duchamp himself returns to painting in this period, though not without a great deal of irony.

19 Again, here I wish to be clear that this argument is as much about the "Duchamp" constructed by art historical discourse as it is about the intentions or biography of an unknown and unknowable man.

20 Add to this De Duve's observation that the "abandonment of painting" coincided with the abandonment of the figure – i.e., with the early twentieth-century move to abstraction – and it becomes increasingly obvious that it is the status

of the subject and, more specifically, his or her body, that is at stake in Duchamp's experimentation with the readymade.

21 Terms like originality and expressivity were much in the air at this time, as is clear from several early twentieth-century manifestos – see, for example, the insistence of Marinetti on tradition's irrelevance in the First Futurist Manifesto of 1909.

22 Greenberg's most vehement attacks on Duchamp follow upon his revival by Johns and Rauschenberg, whom he also dismisses on ideological grounds. In a sense, it is the almost complete absence of Duchamp's name from Greenberg's early, voluminous writing that is most striking, for there's a way in which *all* Greenberg's criticism is in dialogue with the ideas that are attached to Duchamp's name at a later date. In terms of Duchamp's absence, it's as if his name is nowhere and everywhere, as is the name of a mentor to whom you write, but about whom you say nothing. For an example of Greenberg's criticism of Duchamp, see "Avant-Garde Attitudes: New Art in the Sixties" in *Clement Greenberg: The Collected Essays and Criticism*, vol. 4 (Chicago: U of Chicago P) 292–303. For a discussion of the antagonism between Duchamp and Greenberg, see Rosalind Krauss, *The Optical Unconscious* (Cambridge: MIT P, 1993) 95–146.

23 The notion of a unified visual field is central to high-modernist aesthetics. Two examples of the way in which high-modernist discourse prioritizes notions of unity, wholeness and fullness are found in the writing of Greenberg, the preeminent critic of that moment: see "On Looking at Pictures: Review of Painting and Painters: *How to Look at a Picture: From Giotto to Chagall* by Lionello Venturi" and "Review of *Cezanne's Composition* by Earle Loran" in *Clement Greenberg: The Collected Essays and Criticism*, vol. 2, ed. John O'Brien (Chicago: U of Chicago P, 1986) 34–35, 46–49.

24 If high-modernism is codified in the 1930s, then what's not accounted for in this history is the 1920s, a decade marked equally by the daring of the surrealists and the conservatism of those we lump under the phrase "the call to order." My own account of this moment is that it constitutes the first wave of modernism's bolstering post-readymade in that, despite their differences, surrealist works of art and their conservative opposites nevertheless share a desire to suture representation and referent: be that referent the beautiful woman realistically drawn, or the artist's unconscious skillfully tapped by the practice of automatic writing etc. Again, this is schematic and there are, as always, exceptions – de Chirico foremost among them.

25 The key essay here is "Signature, Event Context" in *Margins of Philosophy*, trans. Alan Bass (Chicago: U of Chicago P, 1982) 307–30.

26 Of course, not everyone was prepared to make that leap – neither Johns' initial critics who interpreted *Flag* in exclusively formal terms, nor the readymade's own "inventor" were willing to consider the implications of the readymade for the issue of authorship at large. As I have argued throughout, it was Duchamp's resistance to this very idea that made necessary both the "abandonment of painting" and the encryption of the readymade within a work that was also its *Tu m'*/tomb.

27 It is often said that *Flag* was something of a death knell for high-modernist abstraction, both because it returned art to the issue of reference, and because it refused, given the readymade-ness of its motif, necessary deference to the sacred concepts of originality and authenticity.

28 Interestingly, this moment *did* witness a resurgence in apocalyptic rhetoric concerning the fate of painting, but given painting's role in the readymade's return, it was difficult to sustain the notion of painting as the readymade's victim. On the death of painting mid-century, see Yve-Alain Bois, "Painting: The Task of Mourning" in *Painting as Model* (Cambridge: MIT P, 1990) 245–59; Thomas Lawson, "Last Exit: Painting," *Artforum* (Oct. 1981) 40–47; Douglas Crimp, "The End of Painting," *October* 16 (Spring 1981): 69–86.

29 Part of my argument here is that Duchamp and Johns acknowledged *avant la lettre* the death of the author, and that their readymades in some sense made possible the subsequent theorization of the author's death as it would take place in the writing of Barthes, Foucault and Derrida.

30 Harold Rosenberg popularized this notion. See his "American Action Painters," *Art News* (Dec. 1952) 22–23, 48–50.

31 Invisible but operative nonetheless: an operative assumption in this essay is that the human subject and visual image are parallel structures, even if they are dynamic by virtue of their historical constitution.

32 See Lacan, "The Mirror Stage as Formative of the Function of the I as Revealed in Psychoanalytic Experience" in *Écrits* 1–7. Michael Fried and Clement Greenberg are the modernist critics most closely associated with privileging the notion of a unified visual field.

33 On tradition, see Norman Bryson, *Tradition and Desire from David to Delacroix* (Cambridge: Cambridge UP, 1984).

34 Barbara Rose offers the most striking example of this tendency, interpreting Johns' entire oeuvre in the following terms: "Constantly reflecting on its own history – a mental world of related perceptions, memories and images shuttling back and forth across time – Johns' aggregate picture of a continuous consciousness uninterrupted in its analytic self-reverie has its closest analogue in Proust's *Remembrance of Things Past*, which sets as its goal the externalization, in a work of art, of overlapping and interweaving themes and leitmotifs: that is, the representation of the totality of consciousness" (Rose 68).

35 Interestingly, this strategic repositioning of Duchamp as *According to What*'s passe-partout mirrors an earlier and continued relation between Duchamp scholars and the *Green Box* vis-à-vis both *Tu m'* and the *Large Glass*.

36 As the title of his impressive study suggests, "infinite regress" is the central trope in David Joselit's account of Duchamp. There, as here, the notion of limitless regress is applied to the semiotic chain (meaning), and to the similarly dynamic subject, each refers at the moment that they are referred to.

37 Undecidability is a concept borrowed from Derrida, who finds the term a useful way to signify the movement of différance. See Derrida, *Positions* 41–42. On Johns' relation to "undecidability," see Fred Orton, *Figuring Jasper Johns* (Cambridge: Harvard UP, 1994)131–46. Also, here I might note that Johns also "shares" the position of author in *4 the News*, which he signs "Peto Johns" as a homage to John F. Peto, the American *trompe l'oeil* artist. In particular, Johns seems to be referencing a work entitled *The Cup we all race 4, 1890*. On the relationship between these two paintings, see John Yau, *The United States of Jasper Johns* (Cambridge: Zoland, 1996) 56–57. The most extreme example of Johns' interest in the undecidability of authorship is the 1971 multiple, *Target (Do it yourself)*, in which a lithograph of a not-yet-painted target is accompanied by three disks of watercolor pigment and a brush. Underneath the target are two blank spaces joined by the word "and"; Johns has signed the first and the second is left blank.

38 Duchamp had a documented interest in the hinge: "Perhaps make a hinge picture (folding yardstick, book …) develop the principle of the hinge" (Schwarz 1969, 80, n. 41). And there is ample evidence to suggest Johns' awareness of Duchamp's interest. First, in 1960 Johns acquired an inscribed copy of the 1934 *Green Box* from which the latter quotation is taken. See Kirk Varnedoe (ed.), *Jasper Johns: A Retrospective* (New York: Museum of Modern Art) 70, n. 27. Second, Johns notes in a discussion of the hinged canvas in *According to What*: "There is in Duchamp a reference to a hinged picture, which of course is what this canvas is" (Coplans 30). The concept of the hinge also interests Derrida, who uses the term to suggest the ontology of the "neither/nor." See *Positions*, trans. Alan Bass (Chicago: Chicago UP, 1982) 40–41.

39 Dalia Judovitz clearly outlines Duchamp's critique of both the conventional art object and the conventional art maker. She sums the impact of Duchamp in this way: "Mechanical Reproduction becomes the paradigm for a new way of thinking about artistic production, one that recognizes that creativity operates in a field of givens, of ready-made rules" (Judovitz 7).

40 See De Duve, *Kant After Duchamp* 389.

41 David Joselit has read Duchamp's play of identities in relation to the artist's pictorial themes of dismemberment; utterly convincing is the idea that Duchamp's play of aliases is yet another analogue for the subject's fate within what Deleuze and Guattari call "the deterritorialized flow of capital" (Joselit 96–109).

42 On *Wanted*, see Richard Brilliant, *Portraiture* (Cambridge: Harvard UP, 1991) 171–74.

43 Interestingly, criminal rhetoric is a commonplace within the literature on Johns. See, for example, Patricia Kaplan, "On Jasper Johns According to What," *Art Journal* 35.3 (1976): 247–50.

44 Duchamp's work is consistently interested in the ambiguity of gender – both in terms of his artistic persona (Rrose Sélavy) and in terms of his work (*Fountain*, for example). Also, it seems important to note that Duchamp's invocation of sex in the context of this moribund painting bears

a compelling relation to Freud's theory of the death drive as expounded in *Beyond the Pleasure Principle* – a work originally published in 1920, just two years after *Tu m'*.

45 It should be noted that there are works in Johns' oeuvre which toy with the notion of an inaccessible "interior" space. Yet I would insist that what they hide is less a meaning or referent, than meaning's impossibility.

46 David Joselit reads *Tu m'* differently, noting that the work thematizes the disappearance of the object world into its own multiple and unstable representations.

47 As always, Johns' implication in this paradigm shift will only make more vehement his insertion within the system his work rejects – by way of example I need only note that Johns' early work (encaustic collages made of newspaper fragments) was once subjected to the process of infrared photography in 1977 in the hopes that his interpreters might at last *see through* the work's opaque surface. See Joan Carpenter, "The Infra-Iconography of Jasper Johns," *Art Journal* 26.3 (1981): 221–27.

48 That Duchamp and Johns each make this point in the context of works that function as retrospectives is a fact worthy of consideration. Because the retrospective unwittingly manifests both the object's separation from its origin and the subject's difference from him or herself, the retrospective is, as the interpreter, beholden to the unifying presence of the artist's name as that entity capable of linking decontextualized objects to their absent origin in ways that suggest that the origin in question is both singular and indivisible. In this regard, *Tu m'* and its mid-century repetition are profoundly sinister works, in that they conjure the need for an artist to have a place that seems oriented toward dramatizing precisely the impossibility of his or her presence – whether to the work or to himself.

49 Given Freud's insistence on the link between repetition and death – repetition being on his account the sign of the death-drive's presence, it seems important to note that Johns performs his conclusions about the link between art and death in the context of a work that is itself a repetition of another.

50 Rosalind Krauss interprets Duchamp's title in ways that complement my own reading; see Krauss, "Notes on the Index: Part I" in *Originality of the Avant-Garde*.

51 The implications of the idea of readymade-ness for the subject were already implicit in Duchamp's commentary: "Let's say you use a tube of paint, you didn't make it. You bought it and used it as a readymade. Even if you mix two vermilions together, its still a mixing of two readymades. So a man can never start from scratch – he must start from readymade things like even his own mother and father."

52 Duchamp is on record as saying of his title that one can add whatever verb one wants as long as it begins with a vowel (Cabanne 60). "Tu m'es" would fit this requirement while establishing the reflexivity of the relation between subject and object.

bibliography

Cabanne, Pierre. *Dialogues with Marcel Duchamp*. Trans. Ron Padgett. New York: Viking, 1971.

Coplans, John. "Fragments According to Johns: An Interview with Jasper Johns." *The Print Collector's Newsletter* 3.2 (1972): 29–32.

Derrida, Jacques. *Positions*. Trans. Alan Bass. Chicago: U of Chicago P, 1972.

Derrida, Jacques. *Margins of Philosophy*. Trans. Alan Bass. Chicago: U of Chicago P, 1982.

De Duve, Thierry. *Pictorial Nominalism: On Marcel Duchamp's Passage from Painting to the Readymade*. Minneapolis: U of Minnesota P, 1991.

De Duve, Thierry. *Kant After Duchamp*. Cambridge: MIT P, 1996.

Joselit, David. *Infinite Regress: Marcel Duchamp 1910–1914*. Cambridge: MIT P, 1998.

Judovitz, Dalia. *Unpacking Duchamp: Art in Transit*. Berkeley: U of California P, 1995.

Krauss, Rosalind. *The Originality of the Avant-Garde and Other Modernist Myths*. Cambridge: MIT P, 1985.

Krauss, Rosalind. *The Optical Unconscious*. Cambridge: MIT P, 1993.

Lebel, Robert (ed.). *Marcel Duchamp*. Trans. George Head Hamilton. New York: Grossman, 1959.

Orton, Fred. *Figuring Jasper Johns*. Cambridge: Harvard UP, 1994.

Rose, Barbara. "Decoys and Doubles: Jasper Johns and the Modernist Mind." *Arts* 50.9 (May 1976): 68–73.

Rosenblum, Robert. "Castelli Group." *Arts* 31.8 (May 1957): 53.

Schwarz, Arturo. *Notes and Projects for the Large Glass*. New York: Harry Abrams, 1969.

Schwarz, Arturo (ed.). *Complete Works of Marcel Duchamp*. 2 vols. New York: Delano & Greenridge, 1997.

Isabelle Wallace
Department of Fine Arts
University of New Orleans
New Orleans, LA 70148
USA
E-mail: iwallace@uno.edu

I am starting this booklet not just as a favour to my future biographer, although with my prospects for immortality I can be sure I shall have one. It shall be a notebook of my heart, which, true to the tones my heart sets, will preserve them for my delight in future years.

I have never kept a diary before, because I could never see the benefit of it. But now that I am concerned with the development of my own faculties, I shall be able to judge from a diary the progress of that development.

ANGELAKI
journal of the theoretical humanities
volume 7 number 1 april 2002

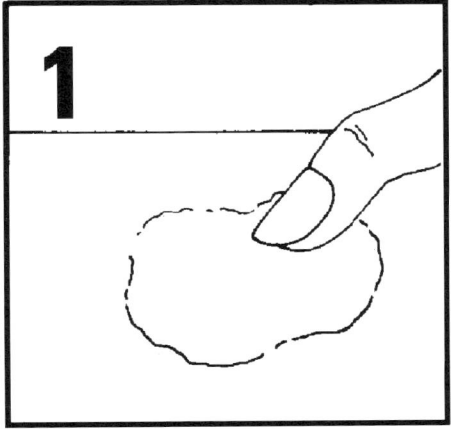

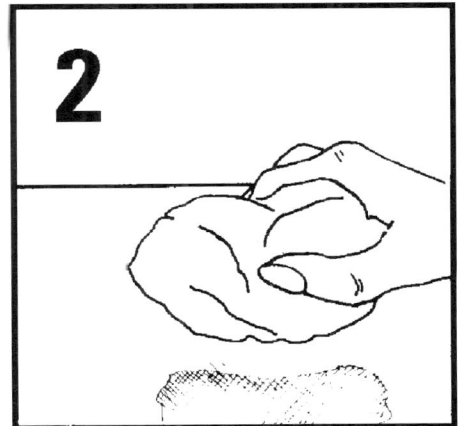

ISSN 0969-725X print/ISSN 1469-2899 online/02/010157-03 © 2002 Pavel Buchler

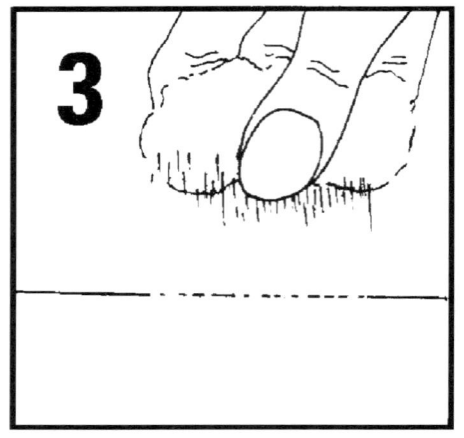
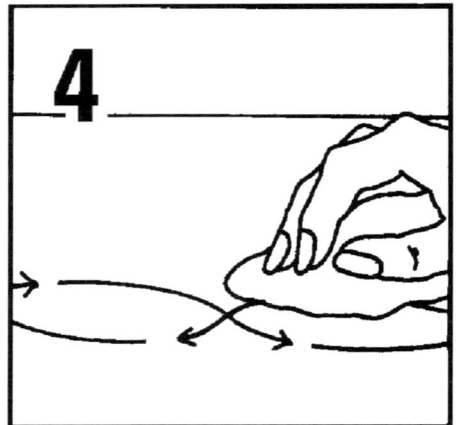
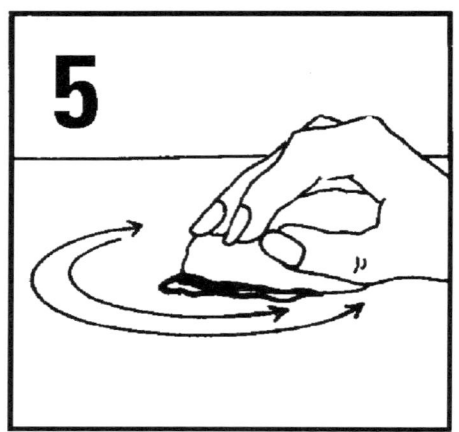
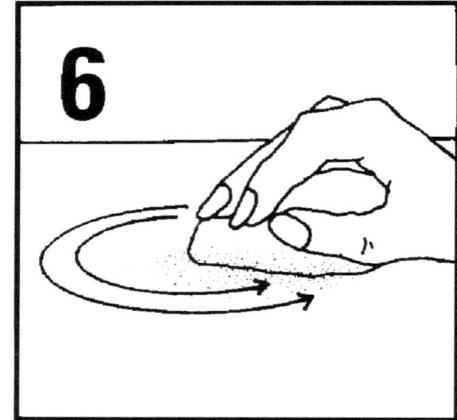
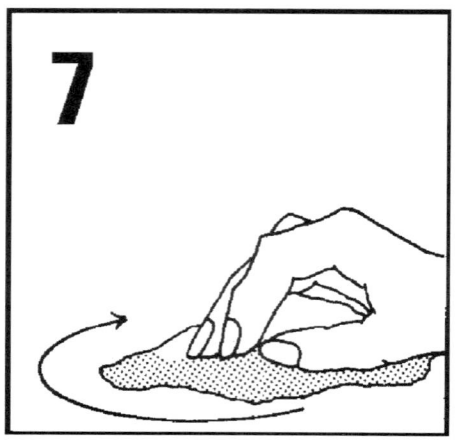
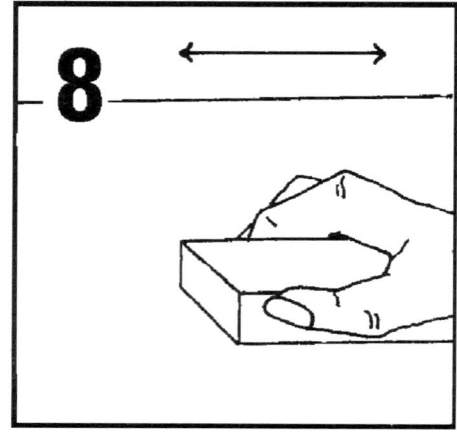

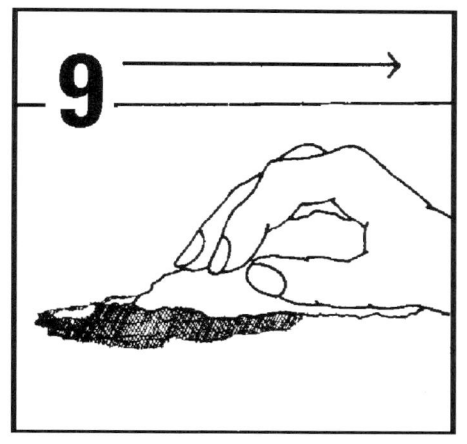
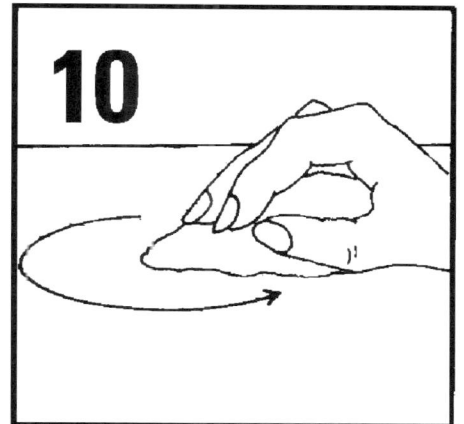
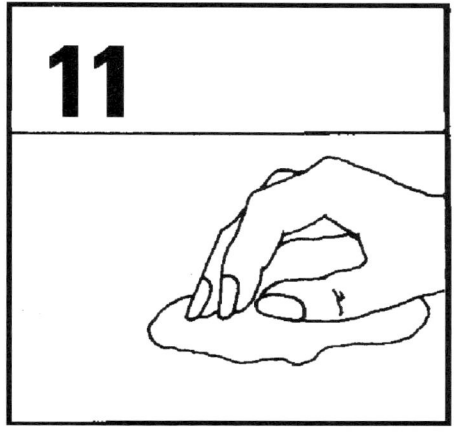
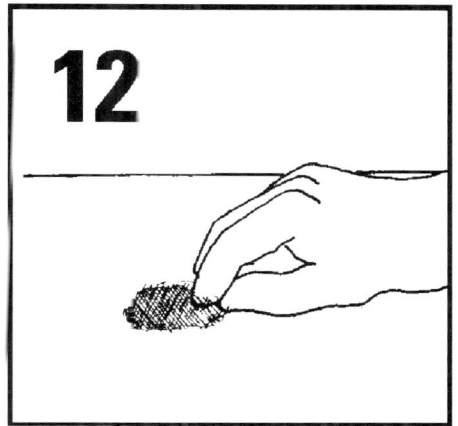
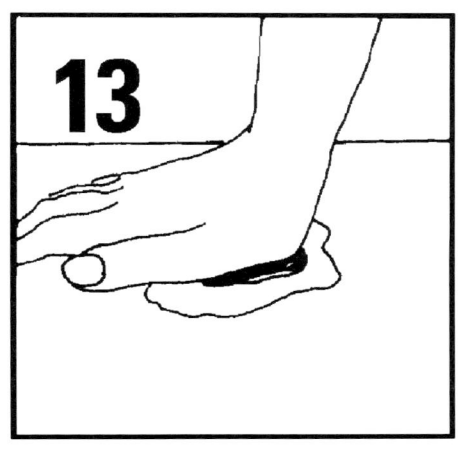
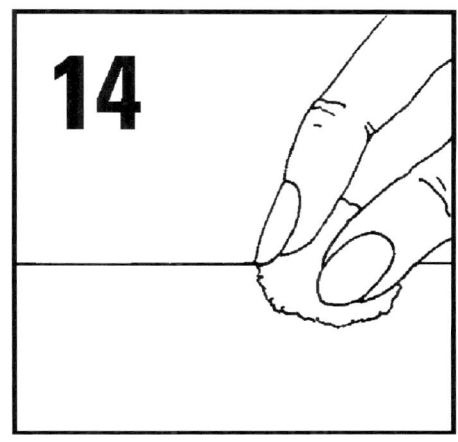

robert j. yanal

DUCHAMP AND KANT
together at last

"What would have provoked Duchamp to madness or murder … would be the sight of aesthetes mooning over the gleaming surfaces of the porcelain object he had manhandled into the exhibition space: 'How like Kilamanjaro! How like the white radiance of Eternity! How Arctically sublime!' (Bitter laughter at the *Club des artistes*.)"[1] Marcel Duchamp, of course, is one of Arthur Danto's artworld heroes, primarily because Duchamp, through his readymades, most famously the porcelain urinal coyly titled *Fountain*, managed to throw off art's "bondage to prettiness." "I owe to Duchamp the thought that from the perspective of art aesthetics is a danger," Danto acknowledges.[2] But if art is to avoid "prettiness," what should art seek? According to Danto, Duchamp's work implies "that art already is philosophy in a vivid form, and has now discharged its spiritual mission by revealing the philosophical essence at its heart."[3] The philosophical essence of art is its "aboutness."[4] Sometimes Danto says that artworks have "semantic character."[5] "To see an artwork without knowing it is an artwork is comparable in a way to what one's experience of print is, before one learns to read; and to see it as an artwork then is like going from the realm of mere things to a realm of meaning."[6]

A story that has heroes also has villains, and one of Danto's is Immanuel Kant, specifically the Kant of the *Critique of Judgment*. "If we wish to decide whether something is beautiful or not," Kant tells us at the outset of his book on beauty and art, "we do not use understanding to refer the presentation to the object so as to give rise to cognition; rather we use imagination (perhaps in connection with understanding) to refer the presentation to the subject and his feeling of pleasure or displeasure" (sect. 1).[7] The feeling of pleasure that signals the beautiful, however, is to be "disinterested," by which Kant meant "a delight … independent of all interest" (sect. 2). "When a judgment of beauty is pure, it connects liking or disliking directly with the mere *contemplation* of the object, irrespective of its use or any purpose" (General Comment on the First Division).

Suppose someone asks me whether I consider the palace I see before me beautiful. I might reply that I am not fond of things of that sort, made merely to be gaped at. Or I might reply like that Iroquois *sachem* who said that he liked nothing better in Paris than the eating-houses. I might even go on, as Rousseau would, to rebuke the vanity of the great who spend the people's sweat on such superfluous things. I might, finally, quite easily convince myself that, if I were on some uninhabited island with no hope of ever again coming among people, and could conjure up such a splendid edifice by a mere wish, I would not even take that much trouble for it if I already had a sufficiently comfortable hut. The questioner may grant all this and approve of it; but it is not to the point. All he wants to know is whether my mere presentation of the object is accompanied by a liking, no matter how indifferent I may be about the existence of the object of this presentation. (Sect. 2)

Disinterested pleasure is brought about by the "free play of the presentational powers," by which Kant meant the play of the imagination (our faculty for perception) and the understanding (our faculty for conceptualization) (sect. 9). Specifically, it is the "form" (or "design" or "composition" or "shape") of objects that puts our mental faculties into free play. "All forms of objects of the senses ... is either *shape* or *play*; if the latter, it is either play of shapes (in space, namely, mimetic art and dance), or mere play of sensations (in time). The *charm* of colors or of the agreeable tone of an instrument may be added, but it is the *design* in the first case and the *composition* in the second that constitute the proper object of a pure judgment of taste" (sect. 14).

Danto's objection to Kant's theory centers on disinterested pleasure. "It immediately follows," Danto comments, "that aesthetic considerations are extruded from the realm of function and utility."[8] Kantian disinterested pleasure, denounced by Danto as a "tepid gratification" and a "narcoleptic pleasure," was the foundation for any number of philosophical theories – Schopenhauer, Bullough, Bell, Vivas, Greenberg – that contrasted and hence "extruded" art from the "topical urgencies in real life."[9]

However, it seems less the concept of disinterested pleasure and more Kant's remarks on how judgments of beauty concern "form" or "design" or "composition" or "shape" that might inspire aesthetes to moon over *Fountain*'s gleaming surfaces. For example, "When we judge free beauty (according to mere form) ... our imagination is playing, as it were, while it contemplates the shape ..." (sect. 16). In any case, Danto thinks that Kant's aesthetics cripples both art theory and art by failing to distinguish between "aesthetic objects and works of art," a distinction "which Duchamp made central to his enterprise." Danto thinks the disdain such critics as Clement Greenberg and Hilton Kramer have shown to Duchamp's work is traceable to Kant, for theirs is a criticism that "pivots precisely on the issue of 'quality in art,' which Kramer identifies specifically with aesthetic quality but which Duchamp and his followers – and I [Danto] must count myself among them – would identify in some other way."[10]

In brief, Danto holds Kant responsible for the widely held view that art had to be, by definition, beautiful or aesthetically pleasing. When Danto speaks of aesthetics or beauty he means roughly what Kant meant in the *Critique of Judgment*. Any object of sense perception – a paperclip, a gemstone, a parrot, a tree in full autumn foliage, a painting by Cézanne – would deliver aesthetic satisfaction (and hence would ground a judgment of pure beauty) just in case it delivers disinterested pleasure by virtue of its form alone. And when Danto asserts that art need not be aesthetic, he means that something whose form is not especially pleasing can still be genuine art – can even be great art. It's not that Danto thinks art isn't beautiful. "There are doubtless works of art, even great works of art, which have material counterparts that are beautiful, and they are beautiful in ways in which certain natural objects would be counted as beautiful – gemstones, birds, sunsets – things to which persons of any degree of aesthetic sensitivity might spontaneously respond."[11] It's rather that beauty on Danto's view is not essential for art – a point demonstrated by Duchamp.

It is undeniable that certain aspects of the *Critique of Judgment* are the groundwork for the Schopenhauer-to-Greenberg line of art theory according to which an artwork is minimally and essentially an object with an aesthetically pleasing form. Now crucially for Danto, an artwork is minimally and essentially an object with semantic character – "aboutness" – and a work of art need not be beautiful, or have some other aesthetic merit, to have semantic character.

(Compare: the statement, "The cat is on the mat," need be poetically eloquent to impart information.) This is why Duchamp is so important in Danto's history of art:

> The ready-made objects were seized upon by Duchamp precisely because of their aesthetic nondescriptness, and he demonstrated that if they were art but not beautiful, beauty indeed could form no defining attribute of art. The recognition of that, one might say, is what draws so sharp a line between traditional aesthetics and the philosophy of art, indeed the practice of art, today. ... Even members of Duchamp's immediate circle, like Walter Arensberg, thought Duchamp was drawing attention to the white gleaming beauty of the urinal. ... There is an argument recorded between Arensberg and the artist George Bellows in 1917, in which the former said, "A lovely form has been revealed, freed from its functional purpose, there a man has clearly made an aesthetic contribution."[12]

Duchamp himself took umbrage at the suggestion that he was presenting beautiful form. "When I discovered readymades, I thought to discourage aesthetics," Danto quotes him as having written. "I threw the bottle rack and the urinal in their faces as a challenge, and now they admire them for their aesthetic beauty."[13]

I want to urge that it is more Kant's successors then Kant himself who applied his theory of free beauty to works of art. Noël Carroll has a brief but convincing account of how Kant's theory of beauty came to be appropriated into theories of art.[14] Basically, Carroll finds an equivocation on the concept of disinterestedness. Kant used it to specify the *state of mind* an observer should put himself in to render a pure judgment of beauty: the observer should not judge whether an object is beautiful based on whether it meets such practical concerns as private or social utility. Post-Kantians applied the concept of disinterestedness to *works of art* which, they urged, need not play any part in our practical concerns. For twentieth-century formalists, for example Clive Bell or Clement Greenberg, art is form and form alone, and form alone has little practical consequence except to deliver aesthetic satisfaction.

However, it bears repeating that Kant is defining pure or free *beauty* – not art – as that which arouses disinterested pleasure as the mental faculties play with "intuitions" of form or shape. The examples Kant mentions tend more to be "free natural beauties" such as "flowers" and "birds (the parrot, the humming-bird, the bird of paradise) and a lot of crustaceans in the sea," and the artifacts he mentions are sometimes borderline instances of works of art, "designs à la grecque, the foliage on borders or on wallpaper," sometimes the subclass of artworks that "represent nothing" such as "fantasias in music" (sect. 16). It is true that if we start with the premise that all works of art are intended to be free beauties, and if we agree with Kant's analysis of free beauty, then we will think of works of art as objects designed to deliver disinterested pleasure on the basis of form alone. And we may then decide that Duchamp has failed to make art or has made bad art – or we may misguidedly moon over *Fountain*'s gleaming surfaces. But there is reason to think *Kant* didn't agree with the starting-point.

Up to section 43 of the *Critique of Judgment* Kant is writing about the beautiful and the sublime. At section 43, he begins a theory of fine art that does not urge us to think of artworks as merely instances of beautiful design. The purpose of the fine arts is "that the pleasure should accompany presentations that are *ways of cognizing*." "Fine art ... is a way of presenting" possible or actual objects that has as its purpose "social communication." The purpose of the agreeable arts (e.g., a table setting) is "that the pleasure should accompany presentations that are mere *sensations*." The pleasure engendered by fine art, on the other hand, is "a pleasure of reflection rather than one of enjoyment arising from mere sensation" (sect. 44). The fine arts "must necessarily be considered arts of *genius*," and one of the "powers of the mind which constitute genius" is "spirit." The artist, by dint of spirit (and other talents), having created an artwork, is thereby able to "animate" the minds of those who view, hear, or read his artwork. "Spirit [*Geist*] in an aesthetic sense is the animating principle in the mind. But what this principle uses to animate [or quicken] the soul, the material it employs for this, is what imparts to the mental powers a purposive momentum, i.e., imparts to them a play which is such that it sustains itself on its own and even strengthens the powers for such play" (sect. 49). The artist animates the minds of his audience by his "ability to exhibit aesthetic *ideas*." An aesthetic idea is "a presentation of the imagination which prompts much thought, but to which no determinate thought whatsoever, i.e., no [determinate] *concept*, can be adequate, so that no language can express it completely and allow us to grasp it" (sect. 49).

Kant may have been wrong in thinking that *every* work of art expresses aesthetic ideas, just as Danto may be wrong in thinking that every work of art has semantic character.[15] Nevertheless, this is certainly a Kant more congenial to Duchamp than the villain of Danto's story. The proper consideration for whether something is art is not whether its form is beautiful but whether it expresses aesthetic ideas. Clearly the sense of "aesthetic" Kant is using here in the theory of fine art does not necessarily depend on pleasing form or design. What makes an idea aesthetic is its indeterminate nature and the way it "animates the soul." An aesthetic idea must be expressed by something material, and that material something must have some form or other – it may even have a beautiful form – but its form is simply the medium for communication, and its aesthetic delightfulness (or aesthetic insipidness) is neither here nor there as far as communication is concerned.

There is a strong similarity between how Kant and Danto tell us works of art communicate. "When Napoleon is represented as a Roman emperor," Danto writes, "the sculptor is not just representing Napoleon in an antiquated get-up. ... Rather the sculptor is anxious to get the viewer to take toward the subject – Napoleon – the attitudes appropriate to the more exalted roman emperors – Caesar or Augustus ... That figure, so garbed, is a metaphor of dignity, authority, grandeur, power, and political utterness."[16] One of Kant's examples is rather close: "Jupiter's eagle with the lightning in its claws is an attribute of the mighty king of heaven" (sect. 49). In both cases, something is taken to signify something else – Napoleon to signify power and political utterness, the lightning in Jupiter's eagle's claws to signify that god's awesome power. I've used the term "signify," though for both Kant and Danto the mode of communication is not straightforwardly denotation, and what is communicated is not a straightforward proposition.

Art, for Danto, communicates metaphorically – art has the structure of a metaphor – and he draws a lesson from Aristotle's *Rhetoric* to explain how metaphors communicate. A metaphor, Danto thinks, has "something of the dynamism" of the enthymeme, which is a syllogism with a missing conclusion, a rhetorical device that invites the listener to "draw his own conclusions." The listener participates in a process "rather than just being encoded with information as a tabula rasa. Explicitness is the enemy of this sort of seductive cooptation the enthymematic forms ideally exemplify."[17] Danto thinks that the metaphor is a kind of enthymeme, and explains the process of understanding a metaphor as that of "finding a middle term t so that if a is metaphorically b, there must be some t such that a is to t what t is to b. ... The important observation here ... has less to do with whether Aristotle has successfully found the logical form of the metaphor than with the fact that he has pragmatically identified something crucial: the middle term has to be found, the gap has to be filled in, the mind moved to action."[18] Additionally

> if the structure of artworks is, or is very close to the structure of metaphors, then no paraphrase or summary of an artwork can engage the participatory mind in at all the ways that it can; and no critical account of the internal metaphor of the work can substitute for the work inasmuch as a description of a metaphor simply does not have the power of the metaphor it describes, just as a description of a cry of anguish does not activate the same responses as the cry of anguish itself.[19]

Philosophers, like everyone else, take their inspiration from what moves them, though if Danto had repaired to Kant's third *Critique* rather than to Aristotle's *Rhetoric* he would have found a more congenial partner. In particular, in accounting for metaphorical communication Danto would not have to backpedal away from two of the main consequences of Aristotle's account of the enthymeme, which is that the (unexpressed) conclusion is both *determinate* and *logically implied* by the (expressed) premises. "All men are mortal" and "Socrates is a man" logically imply the determinate (and let's assume, unexpressed) conclusion, "Socrates is mortal" (though I can't resist mentioning Woody Allen's joke, "Therefore, all men are Socrates"). A metaphor, or rather the meaning of a metaphor, as Danto himself holds, is neither determinate nor logically implied. (I might mention that on this point there is substantial agreement from contemporary philosophers. Max Black wrote, "There is an inescapable indeterminacy in the notion of a given metaphorical statement."[20] Donald Davidson states that "there is no limit to what a metaphor calls to our attention, and much of what we are caused to notice is not propositional in character."[21])

Kant comes very close to Danto's account of how art communicates (though he speaks in terms of aesthetic ideas, not metaphor). Fine art is a way of cognizing the world; its pleasures are the pleasures of reflection not sensation; it "animates" the mind of its hearers by its expression of aesthetic ideas which "prompt much thought" but which cannot be expressed "determinately" since no linguistic formulation seems adequate. The meaning of a work of art is in the words of Kant, "immense" and "indeterminate" (sect. 49).

But Kant is more than just a proto-Danto. Kant has, I shall argue, a bridge between the aesthetics of form and aesthetic ideas, though Kant's initial statement on the matter is confused. At section 51 he writes, "We may in general call beauty (whether natural or artistic) the *expression* of aesthetic ideas." Now it is hard to see how a natural beauty – a seashell, say – can express aesthetic ideas. Even if we look at the neglected teleological second half of the *Critique of Judgment*, the most we can get out of an "idea" in nature is that nature seems to have a purpose, though we cannot tell what purpose.

Suppose, though, we take Kant to have said something a bit weaker, not that *every* beautiful thing expresses aesthetic ideas, which seems manifestly false, but rather that the expression of aesthetic ideas is (or can be found to be) beautiful. Aesthetic ideas can be found beautiful because *coming to discover them* mimics the same mental processes as judging natural beauty. Kant's remarks suggest that he found a deep similarity, which he did not fully spell out, between the grasping of aesthetic ideas and the perception of beautiful form. In section 49 Kant tells us that when we "arrange" our thoughts "in the aesthetic mode" then they can have a unity signaled by a feeling, a feeling, we might assume, of pleasure. At section 51 he suggests that the grasping of aesthetic ideas involves "reflection" with the possibility of the "harmony" of sensibility and understanding, the very sort of harmony that presages a judgment of beauty. It is, I think, the latter that ties Kant's theory of aesthetic ideas with his theory of pure beauty: both stimulate the mind to some sort of play which delivers pleasure based on the harmony of the mental faculties, though in the case of semantic-less but beautiful things, such as flowers, the only thing we feel is a sense of disinterested pleasure (a liking, as Kant would put it, based on form alone), while in the case of a work of art we experience pleasure from the discovery and play of aesthetic ideas (what Stanley Cavell has called "a burgeoning of meaning"[22]). Not a complete bridge, perhaps, but, as Kant himself might put it, a prolegomena to an aesthetics of communication.

This, of course, brings us back to pleasure, though a pleasure that often hinges on the contemplation of the very things that Danto calls "topical urgencies in real life." Kant nowhere acknowledges that something could (a) count as a genuine work of fine art and (b) fail to be beautiful in design or form, and I rather doubt that he even considered the possibility of such a thing. To be sure, Kant himself occasionally – but only very occasionally – endorsed the application of his theory of beauty to works of art, and even asserts at one point that beautiful design is necessary for art: "In painting, in sculpture, indeed in all the visual arts ... *design* is what is essential; in design the basis for any involvement of taste is not what gratifies us in sensation, but merely what we like because of its form" (sect. 14). However, this is more a passing thought, reflective of Kant's inability to see beyond his art-historical position – Köningsberg, Prussia, 1790 – but not forced on him by his theory. His *theory*, though Kant himself did not realize it, implies that (a) and (b) can both be true together. In sum, Duchamp has not effected quite so radical a departure from Kantian aesthetic theorizing as Danto thinks. In fact, Duchamp, whether he was aware of it or not, acted out Kant's thoughts on fine art in a very pure fashion.

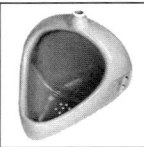

notes

1 Arthur Danto, *The Transfiguration of the Commonplace* (Cambridge: Harvard UP, 1981) 94.

2 Arthur Danto, *The Philosophical Disenfranchisement of Art* (New York: Columbia UP, 1986) 13.

3 Danto, *The Philosophical Disenfranchisement of Art* 16.

4 Danto, *The Transfiguration of the Commonplace* 52.

5 Danto, *The Transfiguration of the Commonplace* 68.

6 Danto, *The Transfiguration of the Commonplace* 124.

7 Immanuel Kant, *Critique of Judgment* (1790), trans. Werner Pluhar (Indianapolis: Hackett, 1987). Section references are given in the text.

8 Arthur Danto, *After the End of Art: Contemporary Art and the Pale of History* (Princeton: Princeton UP, 1997) 82.

9 Danto, *The Philosophical Disenfranchisement of Art* 11.

10 Danto, *After the End of Art* 84, 85.

11 Danto, *The Transfiguration of the Commonplace* 105.

12 Danto, *After the End of Art* 84.

13 Danto, *After the End of Art* 84. Duchamp's remark is referenced as "Letter to Hans Richter, 1962" in Hans Richter, *Dada: Art and Anti-Art* (London: Thames, 1966) 313–14.

14 Noel Carroll, *A Philosophy of Mass Art* (Oxford: Clarendon, 1998) 89–109. Carroll is wrong on one point, however. He states that Kant did not have a theory of art.

15 For counterexamples to Danto's "aboutness" theory of art see George Dickie, "A Tale of Two Artworlds," and Noël Carroll, "Essence, Expression, and History," both in Mark Rollins (ed.), *Danto and His Critics* (Oxford and Cambridge: Blackwell, 1993).

16 Danto, *The Transfiguration of the Commonplace* 167.

17 Danto, *The Transfiguration of the Commonplace* 170.

18 Danto, *The Transfiguration of the Commonplace* 171.

19 Danto, *The Transfiguration of the Commonplace* 173.

20 Max Black, "More About Metaphor," *Dialectica* 31 (1977): 438.

21 Donald Davidson, "What Metaphors Mean" in *On Metaphor*, ed. Sheldon Sacks (Chicago: U of Chicago P, 1978) 44.

22 Stanley Cavell, *Must We Mean What We Say?* (New York: Scribner's, 1969) 79.

Robert J. Yanal
51 W. Warren – Philosophy
Wayne State University
Detroit, MI 48201
USA
E-mail: r.yanal@wayne.edu

It's as well that this diary is intended for my eyes alone as some queer passages would excite the risible faculties of the most sober-minded; or, if they should fall into the hands of some of my gossip-loving friends, would afford them many subjects of mirth.

Here I pour out my heart when it is overly oppressed; for certain things one can tell no one.

journal of the theoretical humanities
volume 7 number 1 april 2002

The two images presented here are components of a larger series of work provisionally titled, "it is occupied," following the Penguin Freud Library translation of Freud's writings where "cathected" is used to translate what may otherwise have been "occupied." They are a continuation of my obsession with and investigation of snapshots and domestic family photography. My search for what it is that is so captivating in these images has recently led me to turn to the house itself as a site for work. The images in this series were taken in the space below the floor in my mother's house.

ISSN 0969-725X print/ISSN 1469-2899 online/02/010169-03 © 2002 Stephen Cornell

journal of the theoretical humanities
volume 7 number 1 april 2002

introduction

This article considers "net art" and argues that there is a developing aesthetic of failure in many online works. In general terms, this aesthetic of failure can be defined as the ways that net artists reflexively quote and misuse the programmed aspects of the computer. Jodi's *%20Wrong*, Peter Luining's *D-TOY 2.502.338*, and Michaël Samyn's *The Fire from the Sea* represent distinct aspects of this aesthetic. These works have been described as formalist. However, they offer a stance that goes beyond formalist considerations of the medium because their employment of misquotation, misdirection, and interface breakdown can offer a distance from the Internet's effects and a critical commentary on its vernacular.

Similar visuals are not a necessary part of this aesthetic. It is conveyed by the ways that net art performs and malfunctions. This aesthetic is produced by particular kinds of spectatorship and of course the corollary to this is that cultural tastes and values inform viewer reactions to this work. Aesthetics is related to the spectatorial positions that are scripted by individual works but this does not necessarily provide the spectator with the ideal or cohesive view. In many cases, the net art spectator's empowered position and ability to gaze upon the whole work are disturbed by the ways that net art cannot be interacted with or controlled. The use of the term "spectator" is intended to suggest the history of art and media spectatorship, the ways that people have been structured to look, and the particular relationship between computer viewer and interface. This term is also meant to indicate that net art highlights and enacts viewing limits. The disruption of spectatorial mastery, which

michele white

THE AESTHETIC OF FAILURE
net art gone wrong

produces a distinctly different user from the one promised by computer "interactivity," can encourage computer spectators to read Internet technologies differently.

The net art aesthetic also calls into question the possibility of maintaining unique "objects" and authorship online. Museums and other websites, which seek to maintain the aura of objects, struggle with the copied and quoted aspects of net art and the issues introduced in Walter Benjamin's "The Work of Art in the Age of Mechanical Reproduction."[1] Benjamin, whose work has influenced a group of contemporary theorists and many net artists, argued that the value of art objects dissipates with mechanical reproduction. Varied aspects of the computer setting contribute to this destabilization of singu-

ISSN 0969-725X print/ISSN 1469-2899 online/02/010173-21 © 2002 Taylor & Francis Ltd and the Editors of *Angelaki*
DOI: 10.1080/0969725022014219

lar and specific works. Different computers, monitors, browsers and connection speeds produce contrary views. Such problems encourage an interrogation of traditional reading and viewing positions. They also suggest that computer-facilitated material is produced through a variety of technologies as much as an individual author generates it. However, there is the possibility that net art authorship will remain elevated and intact because of the significant ways in which spectators are scripted to fail.

All of this suggests that computer facilitation and specific net art works require a rethinking of art aesthetics and the production of setting-specific theories of spectatorship. A detailed study is necessary in order to describe the ways that spectators look as well as how artists can still be seen through such failures as misdirection, misquotation, and crashes. This can be elaborated upon by considering the relationship between aesthetics and net art, the different definitions of the term "net art" and its "history," the critical and popular uses of the conception of failure, and the ways that failure is employed in specific net art works. An aesthetic of failure can encourage a critical look at technology or become no more than a style. This article addresses ongoing theoretical and political "problems" with the position of the spectator and artist and offers a theory of net aesthetics.

aesthetics and net art

A better understanding of net art aesthetics can be reached by considering some of the critical and political questions about the cultural role of aesthetics. The *Oxford English Dictionary* defines aesthetics as "the philosophy or theory of taste, or of the perception of the beautiful in nature and art."[2] Aesthetics has been understood as a "coherent system of criteria, which can be purely visual, moral or social, or any combination of these, used for evaluating works of art."[3] However, some more recent arguments insist that the "social," in the form of cultural values and beliefs, always informs aesthetics.

Feminist aesthetics has encouraged spectators to acknowledge the cultural aspects of aesthetics. This political project has clearly influenced some contemporary art practices, including net art. "The emergence of feminist aesthetics in the 1980s" has "resulted in a broader and deeper understanding of the many social and cultural variables that contribute to prevailing notions of taste, aesthetic value and artistic genius."[4] Feminist aesthetics "is not a way of evaluating art or our experience of it, but rather examines and questions aesthetic theory."[5] Hal Foster's "anti-aesthetic" establishes a similar practice. His anti-aesthetic is not meant to suggest a "negation of art or of representation as such."[6] Instead, he is resisting ongoing beliefs, which are often associated with Immanuel Kant, that aesthetic judgment, or deliberations about what is beautiful and pleasurable, are universal.[7]

This article is politically aligned with feminist aesthetics and a version of Foster's anti-aesthetics. It considers the cultural aspects of aesthetics as well as such "taste"-oriented issues as color and composition. Aesthetic engagement is related to spectatorship because objects are understood through particular embodied positions, cultural values, beliefs, and points of view. All of these aspects of aesthetics are an important part of contemporary criticism. People and other components of the environment are understood through aesthetic criteria. For instance, power is delivered to certain individuals through seemingly universal codes of beauty, such as body shape and skin color.

Contemporary artists may seem to have resisted aesthetics by downplaying bodily representations as well as beautifully and skillfully produced works in favor of a more theoretical project, or an anti-aesthetic. However, these artists still employ a set of aesthetic conventions, including the copied (Sarah Charlesworth, Sherrie Levine, and Richard Prince), and low (Mike Kelly, Karen Kilimnik, and Paul McCarthy). The net artists discussed here also employ an anti-aesthetic because they critique art aesthetics and produce sites that are intertwined with varied forms of web culture. However, such potentially critical strategies as copying aspects of the web and quoting popular culture can become solely an aesthetic style when they are consistently repeated without political intent.

net art

Net art is sometimes described as "net.art" or even "art on the net." It usually includes e-mail projects, text-based performances, and other Internet-based forms. Website projects are probably the most common type of net art.[8] It has been widely discussed on listservs and other e-mail-based communication forums, including 7-11, Rhizome, The Thing, Museum-L, nettime, and the World Wide Web Artist's Consortium.[9] The term "net art" suggests that there is a consistent set of aesthetic guidelines for producing and evaluating these cultural works. The varied producers and critics that engage with net art have also tried to establish a vocabulary and set of expectations for this form through discussions and production practices. Some of the reoccurring attributes of net art, which have been mentioned in these discussions, are collaboration, interactivity, formalism, and reflexivity.

The works of Jodi, Luining, Samyn, and many other net artists share a loose set of visually and politically aesthetic properties. However, there are also online and net art practices with different aesthetic criteria. Describing a completely unified net aesthetic is stymied because many of the artists resist fully delineated categories and stable terms. In fact, this "slipperyness," in which artistic identity is challenged, the relationship between a title and the content of a work shifts, and display strategies are used to make "new" works, may be an aspect of this aesthetic.

Net art has been associated with a number of essential aspects of the web. According to Brett Stalbaum, net art's formalism "involves the exploration of the HTTP protocol, HTML, and browser specific features as a unique medium in a Greenbergian sense."[10] Stalbaum and other critics of net art have been referencing more traditional understandings of formalism:

> Formalism usually refers to an over-emphasis in ethics or aesthetics on form over content. ... Formalism has been used to describe a twentieth-century view in aesthetics, art history, and literary criticism that values artistic form over artistic content and that is therefore opposed both to representationalism and realism in the arts.[11]

However, net art can do more than employ the structural elements of the medium. Many net art works visualize the web's language, a code that often remains hidden, and re-represent the elements of the web in countless reflexive configurations. These net artists pastiche and critique their medium in ways that are significantly different from formalist art.

Net art is often described as an alternative to traditional art concepts and the limiting aesthetics of the gallery system. To some extent, it must move the viewer away from the confines of the physical gallery and the object-oriented focus of traditional art forms because of its means of delivery. Steve Dietz may argue that "rather than trying to assimilate net art into our existing understanding of art history" it could "problematize many of the very assumptions we take to be normal, if not natural."[12] However, there are a variety of artistic movements that have significantly challenged art conventions and then been incorporated into the canon.

It is quite ironic that art remains a part of the discourse and is embedded in the movement's name, because many net producers and critics have been ambivalent about calling these works "art." This is a familiar strategy. Jay David Bolter and Richard Grusin argue that "popular culture often wants to deny traditional high art a claim to superior status, but still to appropriate its cachet and vocabulary, as it does, for example, with the terms *digital art* or *computer art*."[13] Through their strategy of quotation and denial, net artists manage to elide their relationship to such high art "problems" as class privilege, hierarchical evaluation, claims of mastery, and the exclusion of other voices while still marking the importance and cultural worth of their work. However, the occasional resistance to the art label produces new versions of incomprehensibility, because these works are difficult to understand and culturally locate, as well as high-art exclusivity, because net art sites like hell.com were once only available by invitation. Spectators who are familiar with contemporary art and its debates have an advantage in engaging with these net-based works.

It is certainly the case, particularly with new kinds of works and aesthetic strategies, that art is more easily recognized when such contextual devices as museums and gallery-like structures demarcate it. In 1996, Alexei Shulgin and the Moscow WWWArt Centre commented on the different ways that art and aesthetics could function online and founded an award for Internet web pages that provided an "art feeling" rather than having intentionally been produced as works of art.[14] Their accompanying manifesto states that the "internet is an open space where the difference between 'art' and 'not art' has become blurred as never before in XX century. That's why there are so few 'artists' in this space."[15] They suggest that an artist's identity is reliant on institutional affiliations. "There is possibility of misinterpretation and loss of 'artistic' identity here. This might be welcome. There are no familiar art institutions and infrastructures." However, familiar institutions and infrastructures have been appearing on the web in escalating numbers.

Net artists have had the opportunity to present their works in different ways online and to have seemingly different relationships to art structures. Early online organizations like äda'web, which released its first project in 1995, offered the spectator access to works by Heath Bunting, Jodi, Jenny Holzer, Michaël Samyn, Julia Scher, Alexei Shulgin, and Lawrence Weiner but the term "art" was never mentioned.[16] Of course, for some spectators, a number of these names would have immediately marked this as an art site. In any case, the Walker Art Center incorporated these net works into its virtual museum presence after äda'web lost its funding. Jodi also appears on the Rhizome site where the term "art" has been frequently employed. Rhizome is a nonprofit organization that "presents new media art to the public, fosters communication and critical dialogue about new media art," and offers a web-based "artbase." This artbase provides access to a featured number of "art objects" and an alphabetically organized database of documented works.[17] Organizations like Rhizome may actually counteract the indeterminacy of online identification by calling these varied representations "art objects" and by providing spectators with label-like details.

These works may be called "art" but there are still problems in conceptualizing net art's relationship to traditional forms because of the unfamiliar aspects of the medium and the ways that space and display, two key ways that viewers understand their encounter with art, have been skewed online. The structure of the web and the difficulty in determining the borders or limits of a website make it difficult to identify individual net art works or to describe where these works end. The "edge" between works of art and the surroundings are almost impossible to conceptualize online because there is little physicality. We could include the browser frame, e-mail interface, or other supporting structures as well as surrounding sites, computer screen, and the computer "box" itself as part of net art.

There has been a continuing drive to collect and show net art within the museum structure even though its attributes make it difficult to physically display and some net art relies on its position "outside" the art market for its impact. The possibility that net art will present new formal and political aesthetic strategies has become increasingly unlikely with the growing influences of such traditional structures as the gallery and museum. The larger functions of net art and its shifting identity and address are curtailed by its containment within more familiar art structures. Luther Blissett maintains that net art is "Everyone with his own site, everyone with his own domain, everyone with his own gallery, they are throwing themselves into the trammels of traditional art."[18] However, even the traditional museum and other structures for displaying and selling art face new challenges online because they cannot fully transform digital reproductions into original and aura-imbued works of art.

The museum and other websites, which seek to maintain the aura of objects, still struggle with the issues introduced in such articles as Benjamin's "The Work of Art in the Age of Mechanical Reproduction." Benjamin suggests that the authority of the object dissipates when it can be mechanically reproduced:

> One might generalize by saying: the technique of reproduction detaches the reproduced object from the domain of tradition. By making many reproductions it substitutes a

plurality of copies for a unique existence. And in permitting the reproduction to meet the beholder or listener in his own particular situation, it reactivates the object reproduced. These two processes lead to a tremendous shattering of tradition.[19]

The shattering of tradition that Benjamin describes is only intensified in the online environment where the material basis of the museum and its possession of objects are continually challenged.

Directors and curators of a number of leading museums, including David Ross who is the director of the San Francisco Museum of Modern Art, believe that museums should play a significant part in the development of net art. Ross is interested in linking net art to more canonical forms of art production, in order "to develop standards and a critical evaluation framework for looking at net art based on our idea of what art should act like or do."[20] Yet his goals appear to be different from some net artists who want to challenge the art system through their online production practices. SFMOMA has certainly played a part in authorizing this form by establishing a Webby prize for "Excellence in Online Art."[21] Their Webby symposium panel on "The Artwork in the Age of Online Communication" acknowledges "The Work of Art in the Age of Mechanical Reproduction" and the problematic of copying online. It also appears to replace these challenges to the traditional system and materiality with a visceral presence or a new aura in the form of human interaction.[22] Of course, online communication is often delivered textually. It is copied when portions of e-mails are reposted and individual users save their chat session logs.

There have been a variety of constituencies interested in publicizing and commodifying net art. Art.Teleportacia, which describes itself as "The First Real Net.Art Gallery," has worked to define the worth and originality of this form. Art.Teleportacia's insistent use of the terms "first" and "real" and Artcart's claim to be "the first net.art_shop" indicate that there are problems with maintaining aura online.[23] Douglas Crimp could have been thinking about these online institutions when he suggested that "if the withering away of the aura is an inevitable fact of our time, then equally inevitable are all those projects to recuperate it, to pretend that the original and the unique are still possible and desirable."[24] Art.Teleportacia may be concerned with establishing ways that individuals and institutions can own some kind of original net art and Artcart may offer the "original print" along with screen-based works but they also confront a dilemma because there is reason to believe that the "one thing mechanical reproduction cannot, by definition, reproduce is authenticity."[25]

Attempts to authenticate and market net art have instead highlighted such "problems" as the lack of clearly official agencies online, the easy downloading and transferring of simple html-oriented web-based projects to other sites, and the inability to fully archive works outside the Internet. Online works can be transferred to more stable and clearly defined formats like CD-ROMs but this transfer irrevocably alters the work and web-based links are usually lost.[26] This destroys the webbed quality of these works and their relationship to the larger structures that many of these works are commenting on and quoting. To some extent, net art is viable only within the particular "environment" in which it has been situated. In other words, net art requires some supporting online structure to facilitate its full functioning. The multiple and reproducible aspects of net art, which can be understood as its distinct lack of uniqueness and originality, have also been part of its character. In this sense, the concept of uniqueness hasn't fully dissipated.

However, reproducibility is still a problem for the various constituencies that want to make net art into a commodity. Art.Teleportacia argues that original net art works can be identified by the "location bar" or url address.[27] "One can copy HTML code and images of simple net project, but URL can't be doubled."[28] Of course, there are certain instances where the url can be faked. Art.Teleportacia's argument suggests that the originality of net art is based on the uniqueness of its supporting address, which would presumably allow for the authentication of net art within virtual galleries or other institutional structures, rather than any unique attributes of the work.

aesthetic of failure

Location-based originality and the existence of authorizing urls would allow online galleries a heightened control over net art works. Not surprisingly, a variety of artists have argued that this connection between net art and the address, which performs as a kind of physical location, is ill conceived. Michaël Samyn does not "think location is of much importance. The network has become a place on its own"[29] It might be more accurate to say that the network has insistently remained a non-space where exact and fixed locations are inconceivable. The identity of specific supporting servers has been supplanted by other internal net relationships that are established through hypertextual links, search engine listings, listserv conversations, and user browsing.

Art.Teleportacia proposed that unique addresses substantiated original works of net art after their *Miniatures of the Heroic Period* web "show," which included a number of for sale web pieces, was manipulated and reposted to another site by 0100101110101101.org.[30] This collaborative has resisted the continued institutionalization and commercialization of net art. Their comments evoke the political aspects of Benjamin's work on mechanical reproduction and underscore why an aesthetic, which stresses the problems with original works of art, might be employed online:

> Theoretically every work of art can be reproduced, but with Net art the reproduction is absolutely identical to the original one. It follows that it becomes a "non-sense" to perpetrate such concepts that seemingly functioned in the real world. The notion of author in general, [and] therefore concepts like authenticity and plus-value, are strictly connected to the economic, institutional, and juridical aspects of traditional art. ... Net art requests new production, preservation, and fruition criteria that often conflict with the old rules of the art system, like the necessity of critics and museums.[31]

Net artists like 0100101110101101.org sabotage other sites or make them "fail" in order to encourage a more critical look at what technology delivers.[32] They are invested in reproducibility because making an exact copy of something on the web negates the originality of net art works.

However, the claims for the critical work that these copies can perform, as well as the celebration of other reproduction media, can also ironically establish a kind of unique status for them. It is possible that reproductions can hold their own kind of aura for academics, artists, intellectuals, and Marxists through such devices. For instance, the dismissal of authenticity, rejection of traditional forms of aura-imbued art, and acknowledgment of indistinguishable copies may increase net art's worth in art markets where postmodern appropriation has been institutionalized. It is certainly ironic that value and a different kind of aura are produced through critical strategies that are seemingly designed to resist such effects.

These tactics have promoted the copy, which according to Benjamin could politically reconfigure art and culture by allowing the masses access into a system of exchange and power that had previously excluded them. However, these strategies have not necessarily made net art comprehensible to all viewers. For instance, in hypertext and web-based works, users are often unsure what will occur when they "follow" particular links or paths. This may suggest that previous conceptions of user navigation are inadequate. Surfing has provided one understanding of the Internet. It has been "used by analogy to describe the ease with which an expert user can use the waves of information flowing around the Internet to get where he wants."[33] However, hypertextual documents may also produce unintended connections and mistaken paths. A more appropriate term for encountering material online might be "blundering." Such a term suggests the difficulty in recognizing net art and other online materials and the ways that these sites are open to various interpretations. In some cases, this may be the intention of the artists and programmers.

an aesthetic of failure

The hypertext critic and enthusiast George P. Landow has favored the productive aspects of linked computer documents. However, he has also suggested that computer breakdowns, coding errors, and the disorientation of viewers are important, and sometimes positive, aspects of the medium.³⁴ He traces this interest in disorientation to modernist and postmodernist tendencies in the arts and literature. "Joyce's *Ulysses*, T.S. Eliot's *Waste Land*, and William Faulkner's *The Sound and the Fury* – to cite three classics of literary modernism – all make disorientation a central aesthetic experience."³⁵ Such aesthetics can be designed in order to encourage the viewer to perceive differently.

Feminist aesthetics and anti-aesthetics have invited such alternative perceptions by attending to the social structures through which we see objects. In a similar way, the intermingled formal and political aesthetic of net art encourages the spectator to address the ways that technology is understood. Jonathan Crary suggests that the acknowledgment of failure and the disjunction between streamlined technology and rot is one way to induce an awareness of aesthetics and the underlying presumptions that accompany technology. He argues that society will increasingly engage with such conflicting terrains as Paul Virilio's high-technology world of "absolute speed" and "the decaying, digressive, terrain of the automobile-based city."³⁶ For him, "any sense of breakdown, of faulty circuits, of systemic malfunction" can begin to disrupt the production of a "fully delusional world." Crary's call to highlight and even produce failure, which he identifies with such writers as Philip Dick and David Cronenberg, is also achieved by the actions of some net artists.³⁷

The incompatible contemporary settings that Crary highlights also appear in many literary and critical writings about technology. William Gibson, Bruce Sterling, Neal Stephenson and other cyberpunk authors depict male characters who must correlate the almost omnipotent power that they can gain by "jacking in" to the machine with the limits of their physical environments and corporeal bodies.³⁸ The artist Lee Bul also tries to understand the "contradiction between the growing faith in the creed of new technology and the chastening reality of things constantly breaking down."³⁹ According to Bul, Korea is a "place of casual catastrophes: bridges and department stores collapse, subterranean gas mains explode, and the jumbo jets of Korean Air, the national carrier, routinely go down." Of course, an examination of international events indicates that the reliance on certain kinds of technologies and the failures of both human and machine readings are "global" issues. Bul's list of breakdowns has no national borders.⁴⁰

Popular entertainment has also provided a fascinated and terrified audience with innumerable representations of technological failures. These include airplane disaster films like *Alive* (Frank Marshall 1993), *Airport* (George Seaton 1970), *Airport 1975* (Jack Smight 1975), *Airport '77* (Jerry Jameson 1977), and *The Concorde: Airport '79* (David Lowell Rich 1979); other transportation failures such as *The Poseidon Adventure* (Ronald Neame 1972) and *Runaway Train* (Andrei Konchalovsky 1985); architectural horrors such as the *Towering Inferno* (Irwin Allen and John Guillermin 1974); and computer-oriented failures such as *2001: A Space Odyssey* (Stanley Kubrick 1968), *The Net* (Irwin Winkler 1995), and *War Games* (John Badham 1983). In many of these films, instances of sabotage or other improper human interventions reveal poor construction practices and other technological insufficiencies. These films may confirm the spectator's concerns about technology or encourage the viewer to see the technological infrastructure in new and uneasy ways.

The familiarity, if not outright fascination, that contemporary culture has with such narratives of technological failings suggests why "recent media art is preoccupied" with "fallibility, limits," and rupture.⁴¹ The net artists who are engaged with failure use a series of strategies that are similar to those employed in disaster films. Sometimes they shock the viewer with breakdowns, technological confusion, and illegibility in order to warn the viewer against believing that technology is highly functional. Terry Winograd and Fernando Flores argue that breakdowns "serve an extremely important cognitive function, revealing to us the nature of our practices and equipment, making them 'present-to-hand' to us, perhaps for the first time. In this sense they function in a positive rather than a negative way."⁴² Winograd and Flores's argument underscores the important work that net artists can perform by rendering "accidents."

aesthetic of failure

These highlighted and simulated failures encourage the viewer to more carefully attend to the functional and aesthetic properties of the Internet. However, another group of spectators can never engage with this political aesthetic because its codes remain incomprehensible or invisible.

jodi

The artists Joan Heemskerk and Dirk Paesmans, who collaborate on Jodi, produce an aesthetic of failure by intentionally misusing the properties of html. They quote such common website blunders as improperly written html, broken forms, and malfunctioning java. When it first appeared on the web, this work produced a number of productive conversations on listservs about the parameters of net art. The work was particularly challenging because spectators had to visually confront a version of web programming:

> We use certain elements, like a virus, whether a virus is present, or whether things go wrong with somebody's "cache," somebody's personal computer. A lot of these elements are collages of things that are found on the net. The natural environment of us, of Jodi, is the net and you can find a certain condensed form of the net in Jodi.[43]

Heemskerk and Paesmans disassociate Jodi from an art context by describing the Internet as its "environment."

Jodi has disrupted the familiar aspects of web pages by literally overwriting them with all sorts of incomprehensible material. Part of this material is the support code for all web pages that has now been revealed to the spectator. On the web, this code is masked and yet also available through the use of the browser's "Page Source" menu option, which allows the spectator to see the html for any given page, or through error messages and other malfunctions, which make the programming of any individual site visible. Jodi's work suggests that the usual structure of the web has somehow been turned around. This can produce a kind of panic or trauma in the spectator who mistranslates these texts and believes that the computer has crashed. When following links from the Jodi site, the spectator is likely to misidentify coding errors and other glitches as part of Jodi's project. Through this process, the spectator is encouraged to read all web material in a different way after engaging with the Jodi site.

Jodi's work rejects a literal reading of html and print media in favor of a more visual presentation of text. Blocks and shaped units of words as well as other aspects of the web are offered up for the spectator's aesthetic contemplation. The revealed snippets of html on various Jodi sites suggest that the documents are transparent. However, spectators who are not familiar with html or who cannot imagine why a web page would intentionally be written "wrong" will fail in their contemplation because the underlying content layers are not accessible to all viewers:

> *Jodi.org*'s pulsing green and black blankness is not so blank as it seems, that is; one just needs to know where to look. In the browser's tool bar menu, there is a command to view "Document Source." The source code comes up as a text document, and what is revealed is that there is a whole layer of pictorial, ASCII text art "below" the surface of *jodi.org*.[44]

Jodi's work is as much about blindness as it is about visibility. It operates by shifting the spectator between confusion and comprehension:

> We get a lot of email. In the first couple of weeks after we put up the site we got a lot of complaints. People were seriously thinking that we made mistakes. So they wanted to teach us. They sent us emails saying: You have to put this tag in front of this code. Or: I am sorry to tell you that you forgot this or that command on your page.[45]

Jodi suggests that some spectators are unwilling to give up certain forms of programming logic and control. Ironically, it is Jodi's work that encourages these spectators to perform such "spectatorial limitations." These spectators may be alienated or they may eventually be inculcated into the codes of net art and read web materials differently. In either case, satisfaction in navigating Jodi's site is unfortunately based on the knowledge that such spectators fail to comprehend. Jodi and some other net art works, perhaps unintentionally, operate by creating an "inside"

white

and "outside" online in the same way as such categories as "newbie" and "guest" consolidate power in virtual communities by labeling users who are not a part of the system.

Readings of Jodi's site as confusing or error-riddled code are certainly suggested by the front page of *%20Wrong*, which greets the viewer with a 404 message. It evokes the common web error message "404 Error – File Not Found" that occurs when a user tries to access a file that is not available. The 404 message usually marks the end of a "path" or the termination of the user's progression through a series of pages and links. However, in Jodi's work the 404 message is on the first page of their *%20Wrong* site and thus marks the beginning. The spectator who detects the link can access the site despite the error message but has been warned that proper files, clearly marked links, and exact meaning are not available "within."

There are a number of sites that explore the history, aesthetic, and collect unusual versions of 404 messages.46 The codes of the web have become so established that most of these sites refer to certain 404 messages as "classic." This suggests that 404s are an integral part of the web. Stuart Moulthrop argues that 404 error messages "may be the most profound thing one can say about the World Wide Web – the best representative for all its shifting multiplicity."47 These 404 messages act as a stand-in for the larger structure of the web where addresses and styles are temporary. Sarah Papesh's 404 message advises, "Oops! You didn't find the file you were looking for, but LOOK, here's all of those socks you lost in the clothes dryer!"48 She implies that 404s provide a substitute for the expected material at the same time that they remind us about what has been lost.

Jodi's, Papesh's, and other designers' error messages evoke loss or a missing gap in the web. They highlight the ways that the system functions and malfunctions. Speaking about hypertext, Terry Harpold argues that the navigation of links and paths "presumes displacement, separation and loss, departures and farewells."49 The missing gaps that Jodi foregrounds and the potentially melancholic sense of absence that they evoke are a crucial part of the Internet.

Absence, according to Derrida and other writers, is also an aspect of writing.50 There is the "absence of the sender, the addressor from the marks that he abandons, which are cut off from him and continue to produce effects beyond his presence and beyond the actuality of his meaning, that is, beyond his life."51 Online texts contain and intensify these absences by making it more difficult to locate authorship or even articulate the physical location of the text.52

The sense that something is missing does not necessarily have to produce a completely negative experience. The 404 error messages and other kinds of disappearances that happen online may offer an erotic of the medium. Roland Barthes suggests that the "intermittence of skin flashing between two articles of clothing (trousers and sweater) between two edges (the open-necked shirt, the glove, and the sleeve); it is this flash itself which seduces, or rather: the staging of an appearance-as-disappearance."53 Versions of this online erotic flickering, such as the downloading of web pages, the delivery of sequential webcam images, the flashing of banners, the occasional staccato of Flash images, and the qualities of the screen, are a significant part of online spectatorship and may keep users engaged because they are always waiting for more.

There are also other kinds of intermittence online. N. Katherine Hayles argues that information technologies create "*flickering signifiers*, characterized by their tendency toward unexpected metamorphoses, attenuations, and dispersions. ... When a text presents itself as a constantly refreshed image rather than a durable inscription, transformations can occur that would be unthinkable if matter or energy, rather than information patterns formed the primary basis for the systemic exchanges."54 However, there are also ways that these absent and shifting elements stabilize and even become a form of online materiality. The highlighted error messages by Jodi and 404 fan sites change disappearances into appearances. They reconfigure the non-site of incorrectly typed addresses and missing material into desired destinations.55 With this restructuring of the 404, spectators see something that is meant to inform them that there is nothing there. This produces a significant rift between the intended conventions of the web and the ways that this material is read by some spectators.

There are alternative renditions of many Jodi projects. A version of the web-based *%20Wrong* piece on the Rhizome site presents a completely different opening page.[56] In this piece, the processes of failure and breakdown are evoked by the flickering background that abruptly shifts from black to gray, the "Transfer interrupted!" message, the visibility rather than functionality of certain sections of html code, the "accessDeniedPage" warning, the malfunctioning forms, and the "%Diconnecting%Host%20wrong.htm" notice at the bottom of the page. Failure, or the spectator's inability to identify Jodi's work, also occurs because its position as art was repressed. As Heemskerk and Paesmans argue, there is "no 'art'-label on it." However, Jodi's work also does not follow the conventions of web design, which "is not about art, it's about making money. To make money, you don't want to design a site that might confuse someone."[57]

The work of net artists like Jodi is linked to recent feminist theory through its tactics of disorientation, ideological failure, and a rupturing of the "law." Judith Butler argues that repetition and a failure to master certain identity categories may offer the "other" a unique form of agency:

> My recommendation is not to solve this crisis of identity politics, but to proliferate and intensify this crisis. This failure to master the foundational identity categories of feminism or gay politics is a political necessity, a failure to be safeguarded for political reasons. The task is not to resolve or restrain the tension, the crisis, the phantasmatic excess induced by the term, but to affirm identity categories as a site of inevitable rifting, in which the phantasmatic fails to preempt the linguistic prerogative of the real.[58]

Butler calls for the rifting of categories as a way of reconceptualizing identity politics.[59] She continually repeats or rehearses aspects of certain arguments until they fail. Net artists also use exacting repetition of technologies, sites, and styles and the failure to master craft as a way of reworking traditional ideas about artistic identity.

Butler's proposal and the work of net artists like Jodi suggest a postmodern celebration of fragmented identities. Butler wants to "resist both the claim that feminism is being 'ruined' by its fragmentations … and the claim that fragmentation ought to be overcome through the postulation of a phantasmatically unified ideal."[60] These practices are antithetical to "existential literature and psychoanalytic theorizing" that presumes that the divided self is "in need of unification and reintegration."[61] Jodi employs failure for its political and disrupting effects rather than as a way of achieving a more readable and coherent work. There is rarely a move to achieve a reintegration of sites or identities.

However, Jodi and other net artists have disrupted their own politics by constantly employing and repeating ruptures, breakdowns, and confusion so that they are instituted as a more formal aesthetic. So many net artists now work in this way that it has become a conventional web strategy:

> Immitators of the Jodi style abound. From Hotwired's recent RGB feature (www.hotwired.com/rgb/opp/++++++++++ ++++++++/) to the design group e13 (www.e13.com), from San Francisco's superbad.com to Brooklyn's experimental performance space Fakeshop (www.fakeshop.com), net art these days is taking a giant step away from print-oriented graphic design and toward an aesthetic of the machine, of code, of the crash.[62]

In discussions about net art, on lists like Rhizome and nettime, Jodi is often used to contextualize other net art works. There has also been a tendency to collapse Jodi's name with other rupture-oriented net art. Eryk Salvaggio's *Absolut Net.Art* project, which included a Jodi simulation, has often been mistaken for Jodi's work. His "favorite comment in response to the work was: 'I don't care who made it, its still JODI.'"[63] Salvaggio's work and such comments underscore the problems with establishing authorship and specific categories online but they also suggest that artistic originality has been transmuted into a style rather than overturned.

Jodi's processes of confusion, which resist such things as legibility, linear reading, conventional culture, "high" art, and authorial mastery, are related to avant-garde art practices like Dada and Surrealism. However, like these other practices, Jodi's constant association with net art has institutionalized and legitimized the work.[64] The Rhizome site describes *%20Wrong* as "A nice tidbit from the kids who invented net.art."[65] By being anointed as "inventors," Jodi is incorporated back into a series of art discourses, net art is provided with a lineage, and its worth is validated. Jodi's work becomes "a literal origin, a beginning from ground zero, a birth" and originality and aura are recreated online even though the Internet setting is still conceived of by some as a site in which mechanical and digital reproduction have destabilized the very possibility of originality.[66] Spectators have become familiar with and accepted the "rightness" of an aesthetic that was once wrong and relied on the strange. The aesthetic of failure has faltered because critical distance can no longer be maintained with the incorporation of this material into the art canon.

peter luining

Peter Luining produces an equally troubled aesthetic of failure by juxtaposing and misquoting computer games and post-painterly abstraction in *D-TOY 2.502.338*.[67] This work presents the spectator with a series of colored squares that move inside a larger square grid. The movement of the square units is accompanied by a pulsating noise that seems to be produced by their progression. The color, composition, and the accompanying sound change when the computer spectator "catches" and "clicks" on the moving elements.

Luining establishes and denies the work's formalism. For instance, the grid-like arrangement and hard-edged quality of the colored units evoke post-painterly abstraction, but this formalist aspect is disturbed because the underlying "material" is code rather than paint. A white background emphasizes the flatness of the image. Yet this rendering of flatness and computer immateriality is contradicted by the sound effects that accompany the shape's progression through the composition. In one part of the sequence, each shift of the units within the maze-like structure produces a reverberating sound as if the moving square is hitting against hollow walls. In another sequence, a static-like sound suggests that the moving square "object" is scraping along an uneven channel that remains invisible to the eye.

It may be difficult for the spectator to establish a relationship to these works or to read them "properly" because of these conflicting messages. In many of his works, Luining contradicts the viewer's visual and auditory perceptions. Interestingly, Luining dismantles the spectator's ability to determine things by actually allowing a high level of engagement or "interactivity." This contradicts various theories, from Barthes's work on the writerly text to Landow's arguments for hypertext, which imagine that reader agency occurs with the ability to control the materials. Instead, the work renders a bodily disorientation in which signals can no longer be taken as reliable.

Despite this problem, the work continues to provide the spectator with varied effects. Its frenetic sound and speed seem to duplicate the intense fascination and immersion of computer games. Luining underscores this connection by calling many of his pieces "toys." Their design, which lets spectators manipulate simple abstract representations as if they were objects, may seem to suggest games like Pong. However, in Pong the user identifies the white "blips" as paddles and ball, and Luining's work does not make any such stable references.

The limited instructions provided on the *D-TOY 2.502.338* site may be called a "manual," which suggests that this is a game with rules and parameters, but there is no detailed explanation of the game play:

> manual: click on the moving blocks
> for maximum effect: put monitor brightness 50% & contrast 50%
> soundvolume 20%

The aesthetic of Luining's instructions, with its focus on terse commands and numerical adjustments, removes his works from the realm of art. Yet, his "toys" fail to deliver a clear set of rules or a standard form of game play. There is no apparent success achieved through interaction,

aesthetic of failure

clear directions about the ways to navigate, or obvious ending. Instead, each of these quotations acts as a false clue or misdirection. The shifting functions of the work, in which it can be read alternately as a form of art or computer game, suggest the computer technique of morphing, or the "transformation of one image into another by computer."[68] The spectator's decision to engage with one of the conflicting elements effects the reading of the work.

The work's function is purposefully kept in an unfixed state by the hosting site. Both Luining's *D-TOY 2.502.338* and Samyn's *The Fire from the Sea* are part of the Lifesaver project that is sponsored by the Dutch television station VPRO:

> Lifesavers are small interactive programs exclusively made for the Internet, and aim to occupy the user for approximately five minutes. They are situated somewhere between popular and avant-garde culture, and are created by young producers who operate in the hazy area between media, art, and subcultures.[69]

These pieces, like Jodi's works, are not fully identified. However, they do have some physical existence because they are represented by a "half-page graphic design in the VPRO television guide" that is designed by the producer and appears when the Lifesaver is released.

Luining's design is worth noting for the way that it depicts the spectator.[70] In the ad, an abstracted female figure contemplates a large straight-edged abstract work so that only her back is revealed. This depiction of aesthetic consideration and transcendent contemplation, with the spectator waiting for her revelation in front of the work of art, is troubled in a number of ways. The originality of Luining's image and the possibility of online authenticity are disturbed because the image seems to reference a female figure from Oskar Schlemmer's *Bauhaus Stairway*, c.1932. In Schlemmer's work, the female figure shifts her body in space as she navigates new architectural and educational environments. However, Luining's figure is pushed to the periphery of the composition rather than centered in front of the work. She appears to be embedded in an abstract "art work" that is like Luining's compositions. This suggests that immobility is an aspect of Internet spectatorship and engagement with Luining's toys.

Luining's depicted spectator is intimately close to the contemplated object. The computer user is also bound to the computer screen rather than repeating the ideal spectatorial and critical distance of traditional Hollywood film. Mary Ann Doane has suggested that women film spectators are often arranged in intimate connection with their own images on the screen.[71] If nearness to the screen is a feminine position then computer users are feminized. "Problems" with the gender position of computer users are also underscored by the portrayal of male nerds, geeks, and other obsessive computer users as abnormal and not "appropriately" masculine.[72]

It seems unlikely that this was Luining's intent but it may be possible to reprieve the negative effect of women's closeness to their bodies and representations based on the ways that this image and new technologies function.[73] Unfortunately, it seems likely that computer spectatorship will become a more stable experience as Internet and computer technologies become an ever more central aspect of culture. Before a newly solidified form of empowered male spectatorship is facilitated through closeness, there are some unique opportunities to intervene in the ways that certain versions of gender, race, class, and sexual difference are produced through spectatorship. Luining's work might contribute to this by showing the spectator how interactivity does not necessarily lead to an empowered position.

More traditional ideas about art, like that of the individual and unique work, are also disturbed by the ways that *D-TOY 2.502.338* can be manipulated. The "final" work is presented as a discrete abstract composition that is framed against a white ground, but the work's edge or limits become increasingly hard to delineate as the spectator interacts. The work can be changed into a series of similar pieces through the "zoom in," "zoom out," "play," and other Flash Player menu options. The zoom in option produces a series of micro works, since it is clear that this is an enlargement of a section, which are the same size as the first view. These are both details and completely different works in which each view becomes an abstract composition reminiscent of Kenneth Noland's or Ellsworth Kelly's paintings. Yet these views have no autonomy outside the spectator's manipulation.

The possibility of identifying an original or unified structure is destabilized by the ways that each of these parts becomes a whole that is centered within the browser window. The browser-based setting is like André Malraux's "Museum without Walls," which is produced through photographic books and "has created what might be called 'fictitious' arts, by systematically falsifying the scale of objects; by presenting oriental seals the same size as the decorative reliefs on pillars, and amulets like statues."74 In the Internet setting, there is no constancy to a work's height or depth. The dimensions of the screen and other settings, rather than the more typically stable aspects of the work, determine the ways that viewers see things online.

Online art is largely reliant on such display techniques as the framing operations of browser windows and already established museum vernaculars for its context. Of course, these aspects may also cause a work's coherency to fail. Luining tries to displace the stability of his site and the parameters of his art by changing the display technique instead of the work:

> I don't think it is exciting always to present my work in the same way. By often presenting the work anew, by adding variety, one gets a different experience. When you visit my site in two weeks, you see the work presented completely differently, so to speak. I think it is important to not always present work in the same way, even if the work is the same.75

If net art is often difficult to detach from its supporting display structure, in the same way that site-specific installations are sometimes difficult to distinguish from their surroundings, then presenting the work differently allows Luining to destabilize its constancy. He cites but does not deliver the expected conventions for art and computer games. The ability to read these works as original and authentic is disturbed by the quotation of disparate styles. Luining puts pressure on a variety of irreconcilable aesthetic styles or "movements" so that their codes fail. His

white

aesthetic may avoid the canonization and institutionalization of other online works if the display mechanism through which spectators encounter these works continues to evolve. However, the spectator's ability to engage with these works through other sources suggests that this aesthetic of disorientation, misquotation, and spectatorial limitations is also being incorporated into a net art canon.

michaël samyn

Michaël Samyn's *The Fire from the Sea* is more visually complex and painterly than Jodi's or Luining's work.76 Its depiction of running children, walls of fire, and fluttering butterflies appears to be aligned with a romantic vision and a traditional kind of art production. However, Samyn's work also acknowledges its means of delivery and critiques the properties of the computer. *The Fire from the Sea*, like Jodi's work, begins with a warning. "This piece is not user friendly and deliberately counter-intuitive: roll over to load, click to unload. It can even bring a fast computer to its knees. That is exactly the point."77

Such warnings suggest the ways that the spectator's physical body is impeded throughout *The Fire from the Sea*. Moulthrop indicates that spectatorial disturbances are a common occurrence in hypertexts:

> "Profound shock" could describe the conditions from which these texts emerge as well as the effect they address, and perhaps aim to reproduce. Hypertext may be a technology of trauma, reflexively figuring its own assault on the textual corpus in terms of insults to the physical body.78

A kind of spectatorial trauma is produced in Samyn's work since he does not let the spectator master the interface. His instructions are unreliable because the spectator must "click" rather than "roll over" the word "Enjoy" in order to engage the piece and its promised programming. Yet some spectators insist on believing that his instructions provide the correct way to access the work.79 This can lead to a frustrated reloading of the opening screen, which is particularly painful when using a slow computer and connection.

aesthetic of failure

Samyn and his partner Auriea Harvey emphasize the unpleasant or even traumatic encounter of the spectator with interfaces in their *Sixteenpages* search engine.[80] In this net art work, the user must manipulate an avatar through a maze and "work" in order to gather information. When this representation of a fleshy body is improperly steered into a "wall" it makes strange sounds of pain or despair. This may provide a gripping reinterpretation of the user's interaction with interfaces.

Samyn's work does critique and even occasionally sabotages the expectations of spectators with expensive technologies and high-bandwidth access but his work can be frustratingly inaccessible to spectators with outdated technologies and more limited Internet access. For instance, *The Fire from the Sea* has a tendency to stall slow computers and dial-up connections even though it can also slow computers with faster processors and connections. Thus, his critique and resistance to a certain Internet and technology economy is most readily available to those who are a part of that system.

The Fire from the Sea, unlike Jodi's and Luining's work, employs a fairly traditional form of overlapping translucent layers and a dark ground as a way of rendering depth. The browser window acts as a frame through which the spectator gains access to this spatial world. Points of light seem to render a night sky that is seen through the browser/window. However, the spectator is forced to contend with the means of delivery as well as the content. The spectator must engage with the work's illusionistic window onto another world, which is a familiar painting convention and "reads on the picture plane in correspondence with the erect human posture," and the computer's mouse navigation and menu-based controls, which suggest different bodily orientations.[81] A version of Leo Steinberg's "flatbed" subject position is produced by these different elements. This flatbed position, which disorders the traditional vertical relationship between viewer and art object, offers new spectatorial positions such as floating over flat icons and topographical maps. However, the difficulties of the interface and the slow processing speed mean that the flatbed position can also generate fractured, disabled, or even illegible views.

The spectator cannot access the coherent narrative that Samyn's animation might imply or even manipulate the elements according to a familiar set of computer codes. Of course this displacement has already been foregrounded by his warning at the beginning of the piece. Rolling over what seems to be a translucent torso at the beginning of the work allows the spectator to manipulate a series of visual and sound elements, which includes a tangle of octopus legs. However, this "bodily" control quickly changes into a representation of a throbbing organ-like mass of flesh that is covered in blood red spots. This is one of the many failures and "insults" to the corporeal body that this work evokes. The pulsing image suggests the catastrophic toll of AIDS more than it does computer viruses or codes. It is only by "touching" each mark, engaging on some metaphorical level with the viral body, and changing its sores from dark burgundy to bright red that the spectator gains some level of control over the piece.

The bottom register of marks, which function as "buttons," provide a fairly clear set of effects that include (from left to right) clouds, a pair of woman's lips, butterflies, and a wall of flames. A layered soundtrack, which includes ocean noises and a woman's slow melodic singing, accompanies these images. The date stamp on some of the images, which evokes the low-tech of camera snapshots, contradicts the complex visual and aural effects. Playing children, fluttering butterflies, and other captured instamatic moments may seem to provide the spectator with a nostalgic past, but navigating the buttons means that an animated wall of flame or scorching sun often burns out these possibilities. The nuanced qualities and the non-narrative composition encourage navigation without providing the spectator with a final destination.

Through such effects, Samyn renders both aesthetically attractive compositions and some kind of critique of the medium. He works to keep himself between fixed and expected positions by describing himself as a "bad designer and an ex-artist."[82] Samyn and Harvey have often resisted their individual authorial role by identifying their combined projects as entropy8zuper.org.

Samyn's work borrows from the computer vernacular but it is critically and aesthetically positioned in a slightly different way than the work of many other net artists. He uses these differences to distinguish his work and to establish a different position for his production. In an interview with Alex Galloway of Rhizome, Samyn notes that it is strange to "be appreciated by someone @rhizome. We always have the feeling that Rhizome is interested in a totally different kind of Art, you know the kind of art that *looks* conceptual and only uses code as an aesthetic element and is never about anything but itself."[83]

Samyn's critique of net art suggests that politics is always linked to an aesthetic. He states that during the online reaction to the Communication Decency Act "when every website made its homepage black as a protest against censorship, I made the homepage of FFF black too with the text 'This page is black as a result of aesthetic considerations.'"[84] What Samyn's critique does not address is that aesthetic strategies can also enable political projects. Samyn and "the typical 'blinking pixel' net artists abuse this technology" and embrace failure.[85] His critical project may be to use these technologies "to make something poetic and beautiful that is about human things rather than machines."[86] However, his opening warning in *The Fire from the Sea* suggests that he is also engaged with the aesthetic of code. Samyn's aesthetic of failure, including his misuse of computer conventions, clearly engages with and resists the aspects of other net art.

conclusion

In the work of Jodi, Luining, Samyn, and a variety of other net artists, clear navigational markers and links are suspended in favor of moving the spectator towards a cacophony that, at least for some spectators, is never fully realized. Turning the ruptures in this work into more elaborate site-wide, browser, or system failures is a problem because at least some spectators must be engaged for net art to maintain an audience. Net art works quote and perform failures while also keeping a precarious relationship with functionality. The net art works discussed here contain a white version of Roland Barthes's punctum. These works contain "that accident which pricks me (but also bruises me, is poignant to me)."[87] However, the poignancy and pain of interacting with individual works eventually dissipate as the spectator grows acclimated to the site and discovers the highly constructed aspects of the failures. This may even be a necessary aspect for net art to function.

However, Barthes has suggested that no punctum can be intentionally produced, persist over time, or be shared by viewers. In the photographs that he discusses in *Camera Lucida*, the shocks from individual aspects of the photos eventually disappear. Some other point of interest may replace these but there is no way to recapture the flashes of blindness and confusion. Changing sites and aspects of the work can keep the spectator in a more prolonged period of blundering. However, as the spectator becomes more familiar with the work, clear and less critically oriented navigation probably replaces an attention and consideration of particular interface tools and representations. It is ironic that net art most clearly engages with "accomplished" Internet users and those who are familiar with art conventions. These spectators can find an entrance point and understand the quotations of the sites, and yet it is just these spectators who will probably quickly decode all of the failures that these works perform. It seems likely that the spectators who engage are most safe from the destabilizing effects of these works.

All of this suggests a problem with the kinds of failures that occur in this work and the forms of repetition through which they are achieved. Judith Butler indicates that repetition can be used to unravel dominant cultural beliefs. However, the forms of repetition that occur in these net art works and the ways that they have become institutionalized suggest that repetition may also reinstall traditional categories and forms of power. This problem with the politics of repetition is certainly indicated by the ways that Jodi's repetitions have become a stylistic convention rather than encouraging further interrogations of programming and technology.

Repetition of particular phrases and ideas (which may admittedly be different from Butler's

aesthetic of failure

repetition of the law) also negates the political messages in other net art works. For instance, Jennifer Ley's *Catch the Land Mine!* quotes a click and catch form of online ad campaign to call attention to the catastrophic loss of life and body parts that occurs because of the proliferation of land mines.[88] However, the initially disturbing effect of being blown up after trying to "catch" a mine is not intensified with repetition. The reoccurrence of the same page and ironic texts about our poor sense of body image seem to cause apathy rather than concern after any lengthy engagement.[89]

There are certainly situations in which repetition can be a critical strategy; however, the ongoing viability of such instances remains unclear. According to Rose, the trends in recent media art, such as a focus on "insufficiency" and "fallible corporeality," is "an acknowledgment of the limits of performativity."[90] Rose suggests that Butler's performative repetition is not a successful strategy for producing politically productive works. The relationship between disruptive reiteration and reinscription needs to be more carefully articulated. In the meantime, the problem of ongoing repetition should warn political groups and theoreticians against solely organizing their work around such effects.

Despite the critical writings about the political effects of failure, this strategy also presents some problems. The ongoing recognition of net art online and the interest of many traditional art institutions in this form indicate that the aesthetic of failure will become increasingly more stylistic. The institutionalization of the aesthetic of failure as a common kind of online style threatens to compromise its "wrongness" and provide instructions for spectators who previously engaged with the strange and unfamiliar properties of these works. The challenge for net artists, software producers, technology critics, and spectators may be to find new critical strategies rather than relying on repetition to highlight the ways that technologies have been constructed. Perhaps with such effects and aesthetics we can continue to read carefully as well as differently.

notes

This article could not have been written without the generous support of the Institute for Advanced Study and the National Endowment for the Humanities. My colleagues at the Institute were helpful in addressing the relationship between net art and Internet studies. Maggie Morse was particularly kind in listening to some of the ideas represented here. Gary Banham, who edited this issue, and Richard Hamilton and Saul Ostrow, who refereed this article, also provided insightful comments. Important revisions to this article were supported by an NEH summer seminar that Kate Hayles led at UCLA. The critical thinking about hypertext that developed in this seminar was invaluable to my own conception of the relationship between hypertextual reading approaches and net art failures. Conversations with Kate Hayles and a number of seminar participants, most notably Jenny Bay and William Gardner, allowed me to reconceptualize aspects of this article.

1 Walter Benjamin, "The Work of Art in the Age of Mechanical Reproduction" in *Illuminations*, ed. Hannah Arendt (New York: Schocken, 1983).

2 James A.H. Murray, Henry Bradley, W.A. Craigie and C.T. Onions (eds.), *Oxford English Dictionary*, vol. I (Oxford: Clarendon, 1961) 148.

3 "Xrefer-Aesthetic," *The Thames and Hudson Dictionary of Art Terms* (London: Thames, 1984), available <http://www.xrefer.com/entry.jsp?xrefid=647986&secid=.->, 24 May 2001.

4 Mary Devereaux, "The Philosophical Status of Aesthetics," available <http://www.aesthetics-online.org/ideas/devereaux.html>, 24 May 2001.

5 Sarah Worth, "Feminist Aesthetics" in *The Routledge Companion to Aesthetics*, eds. Berys Gaut and Dominic McIver Lopes (London and New York: Routledge, 2001) 437.

6 Hal Foster, "Postmodernism: A Preface" in *The Anti-Aesthetic: Essays on Postmodern Culture*, ed. Hal Foster (Port Townsend, WA: Bay, 1983) xv.

7 Immanuel Kant, *Critique of Judgment*, trans. J.H. Bernard (New York: Haffner, 1951).

8 Some critics have suggested that there are political implications to the terms that are used to describe online art works. Josephine Bosma argues that "replacing the term 'net art' by 'web art' causes a negligence of art history within a

political and economic environment. The radical implications of net art are replaced by the much less threatening aspects of web art." Josephine Bosma, "Text for Moscow: Between Moderation and Extremes. The Tensions Between Net Art Theory and Popular Art Discourse," *Switch* 6.1, available <http://switch.sjsu.edu/web/v6n1/article_b.htm>, 19 July 2000.

9 Not all of these lists approach the issue of net art in the same way. Josephine Bosma has argued that nettime has largely evacuated net artists from its forum and disrupted critical exchanges. "Now that nettime has chosen to mostly close the door to art, the development of net art has lost a central point for critical cross disciplinary thought from a multicultural perspective." Josephine Bosma, "Text for Moscow: Between Moderation and Extremes. The Tensions Between Net Art Theory and Popular Art Discourse," *Switch* 6.1, available: <http://switch.sjsu.edu/web/v6n1/article_b.htm>, 19 July 2000.

10 Brett Stalbaum also argues that it "is both productive and ironic that these sites turn to a specific historical manifestation of modernism as an escape avenue." Brett Stalbaum, "Conjuring Post-Worthlessness [excerpt]," online posting, 20 Aug. 1999, Rhizome, available <http://rhizome.org/object.rhiz?1543&q>, 31 July 2000.

11 Peter Saint-André, "The Ism Book: 'F,' The Ism Book: A Field Guide to the Nomenclature of Philosophy," available <http://www.monadnock.net/ismbook/F.html#Formalism>, 31 July 2000.

12 Steve Dietz, "Why Have There Been No Great Net Artists?," *Webwalker* 28, 23 Apr. 2000, available <http://www.walkerart.org/gallery9/webwalker/index.html>, 23 July 2000.

13 Jay David Bolter and Richard Grusin, "Digital Art" in *Remediation: Understanding New Media* (Cambridge: MIT P, 1999) 142.

14 Moscow WWWArt Centre, "WWWArt Award," available <http://www.easylife.org/award/>, 23 July 2000.

15 Vuk Cosik and Alexei Shulgin, "Who Drew the Line?," *Net Criticism, ZKP2 Proceedings*, June 1996, available <http://www.nettime.org/desk-mirror/zkp2/theline.html>, 23 July 2000.

16 Benjamin Weil, "Untitled (äda'web)," *Walker Art Center: Gallery 9*, available <http://www.walkerart.org/gallery9/dasc/adaweb/weil.html>, 2 Aug. 2000.

17 Rhizome, "Rhizome.org Info," available <http://rhizome.org/info/>, 22 July 2000. Through Rhizome's search function the user can also gain access to its artbase:

> The Rhizome ArtBase is an online archive of Internet art projects. The goal of the Rhizome is to preserve Internet art projects for the future, and to provide a comprehensive resource for those who are interested in experiencing and learning more about Internet art.

Rhizome, "Rhizome ArtBase: The Net Art Resource," available <http://rhizome.org/artbase/>, 22 July 2000.

18 Luther Blissett, "0100101110101101.ORG--art.hacktivism," online posting, 26 June 1999, Rhizome, available <http://rhizome.org/cgi/query.cgi?a=query&q=jodi&f=&start=10&target=12>, 17 July 2000.

19 Benjamin, "The Work of Art" 221.

20 David Ross as quoted in Reena Jana, "David Ross: Director. San Francisco Museum of Modern Art," *Flash Art International* Jan./Feb. 1999: 34.

21 For a press release from the first SFMOMA prize in May 2000 see SFMOMA, "SFMOMA Press Release," available <http://www.sfmoma.org/info/press/press_webby.html>, 5 Aug. 2000.

22 SFMOMA, "SFMOMA Press Release," available <http://www.sfmoma.org/info/press/press_webby.html>, 14 June 2001.

23 Art.Teleportacia, "FAQ," available <http://art.teleportacia.org/art-ie4.html>, 17 July 2000. Artcart offers works by Peter Luining and a number of other net artists. Artcart, "Artcart – Be Avantgarde – Buy Net.art," available <http://artcart.de/>, 3 Aug. 2000.

24 Douglas Crimp, *On the Museum's Ruins* (Cambridge and London: MIT P, 1993) 112.

25 Bill Nichols, "The Work of Culture in the Age of Cybernetic Systems," *Screen* 29.1 (1988): 23.

26 Discussions about this issue have occurred at a SFMOMA panel on net art as well as in other forums:

> One of the most forward-thinking SFMOMA curators, Betsky came under fire for his white

"butterfly-pinning" method of archiving websites, in which he burns them onto a CD and renders links dead. While Betsky said that the work maintains its beauty without active links, artists and new media enthusiasts in the audience expressed their discontent with giving privilege to form over function.

Marisa S. Olson, "Weighing In on Net Art's Worth," *Wired News* 15 May 2000, available <http://www.wired.com/news/culture/0,1284,363 20,00.html>, 4 Aug. 2000.

27 Art.Teleportacia, "FAQ," available <http://art.teleportacia.org/art-mac.html>, 9 Sept. 2000.

28 Art.Teleportacia, "FAQ," available <http://art.teleportacia.org/art-ie4.html>, 17 July 2000.

29 Michaël Samyn, as quoted in Art.Teleportacia, "Under Construction," available http://art.teleportacia.org/art-ie4.html>, 17 July 2000.

30 For a discussion of this issue see Luther Blissett, "0100101110101101.org--art.hacktivism," online posting, 26 June 1999, Rhizome, available <http://rhizome.org/cgi/query.cgi?a=query&q=jodi &f=&start=10&target=12>, 17 July 2000.

31 This site is a parody of Britannica.com. 0100101110101101.org, "Britannica.com," available <http://www.britannica.com/bcom/original/article/0,5744,8800+2,00.html>, 2 Aug. 2000.

32 "Xrefer-machine aesthetic" in *Bloomsbury Guide to Art* (London: Bloomsbury, 1996), <http://www.xrefer.com/entry.jsp?xrefid=439085 &secid=.->, 24 May 2001.

33 Free On-Line Dictionary of Computing (FOLDOC), "Surfing from FOLDOC," available <http://foldoc.doc.ic.ac.uk/foldoc/foldoc.cgi?surfing>, 14 June 2001.

34 George P. Landow, *Hypertext 2.0: The Convergence of Contemporary Critical Theory and Technology* (Baltimore: Johns Hopkins UP, 1997).

35 Landow, *Hypertext 2.0* 118. Of course these linkages are also an attempt to relate computer-based works to more canonical forms of production.

36 Jonathan Crary, "Eclipse of the Spectacle" in *Art After Modernism: Rethinking Representation,* ed. Brian Wallis (New York: New Museum of Contemporary Art, 1984) 290.

37 Crary, "Eclipse" 291.

38 See, for instance, William Gibson, *Neuromancer* (New York: Ace, 1984); Neal Stephenson, *Snow Crash* (New York: Bantam, 1992); and Bruce Sterling, *Holy Fire: A Novel* (New York: Bantam, 1996).

39 Lee Bul, "Beauty and Trauma," *Art Journal* 59.3 (2000): 106.

40 For instance, the work of James Der Derian highlights such "accidents" as "A U.S. EP-3E Aries II aircraft on a routine reconnaissance flight is in a mid-air collision with a Chinese fighter plane" and a "CIA-contracted surveillance plane [that] detects a suspicious plane flying over the Amazon and alerts the Peruvian Air Force, which shoots down a Cessna carrying not drugs but U.S. Baptist missionaries and their two children." James Der Derrian, "Global Events, National Security, and Virtual Theory" in *Information, Technology, and Society: Proceedings,* Institute for Advanced Study, 8–10 June 2001, 2.

41 Christine Rose, "The Insufficiency of the Performative: Video Art at the Turn of the Millennium," *Art Journal* 60.1 (2001): 29.

42 Terry Winograd and Fernando Flores, *Understanding Computers and Cognition: A New Foundation for Design* (Reading: Addison Wesley, 1985) 77–78.

43 Dirk Paesmans, as quoted in Josephine Bosma, "Interview with Jodi," online posting, 16 Mar. 1997, nettime, *The Beauty and the East,* ZKP4 Proceedings, May 1997, available <http://www.ljud-mila.org/nettime/zkp4/38.htm>, 23 July 2000.

44 Peter Lunenfeld, "The World Wide Web: In Search of the Telephone Opera" in *Snap to Grid: A User's Guide to Digital Arts, Media, and Cultures* (Cambridge: MIT P, 2000) 84.

45 Jodi, as quoted in Tilman Baumgärtel, "Interview with Jodi," *Telepolis* 10 June 1997, available <http://www.heise.de/tp/english/html/result.xhtml? url=/tp/english/special/ku/6187/1.html&words= Baumgaertel>, 19 July 2000.

46 See, for instance, "404 Error," available <http://www.sendcoffee.com/minorsage/404error.htm>, 31 July 2000; Jenni Ripley, "404 Research Lab," Plinko.Net, available <http://www.plinko.net/404/>, 31 July 2000; and "404 Not Found Homepage," available <http://www.mindspring.com/~isixtyfive/404page/404.html>, 31 July 2000.

47 Stuart Moulthrop, "Error 404: Doubting the Web" in *The World Wide Web and Contemporary Cultural Theory*, eds. Andrew Herman and Thomas Swiss (New York: Routledge, 2000) 261.

48 Sarah Papesh, "sarahpapesh.com:: online portfolio:: 404," available <http://sarahpapesh.com/404.html>, 31 July 2000.

49 Terry Harpold, "The Contingencies of the Hypertext Link," available <http://www.lcc.gatech.edu/~harpold/papers/contingencies/index.html>, 5 July 2001.

50 For a discussion of this see Terry Harpold, "The Contingencies of the Hypertext Link," available <http://www.lcc.gatech.edu/~harpold/papers/contingencies/index.html>, 5 July 2001.

51 Jacques Derrida, "Signature Event Context" in *Margins of Philosophy*, trans. Alan Bass (Chicago: U of Chicago P, 1982) 313.

52 What we read isn't on the screen, under the glass, or distinctly located on the hard drive.

53 Roland Barthes, *The Pleasure of the Text*, trans. Richard Miller (New York: Hill and Wang, 1995) 10. Of course, these glimpses of flesh or webcam images can also repulse the spectator.

54 N. Katherine Hayles, "Virtual Bodies and Flickering Signifiers" in *How We Became Posthuman: Virtual Bodies in Cybernetics, Literature, and Informatics* (Chicago: U of Chicago P, 1999) 30.

55 Usually all mistyped addresses on a specific site will produce the same effect.

56 Jodi, "%20Wrong," online archive, 1 Jan. 1996, Rhizome, available <http://rhizome.org/artbase/1678/wrong.html>, 1 Aug. 2000. Other sites with versions of this work include "%20Wrong," available <http://www.502.org/404.html>, 2 Aug. 2000.

57 Vincent Flanders, "Web Pages that Suck – Bad Navigation," available <http://webpagesthatsuck.com/badnavigation.html>, 4 June 2001.

58 Judith Butler, "The Force of Fantasy: Feminism, Mapplethorpe, and Discursive Excess," *Differences: A Journal of Feminist Cultural Studies* 2.2 (1990): 121.

59 Strangely, Butler's call to performativity always seems best resolved by her own critical practice and repetition of texts.

60 Butler, "The Force of Fantasy," *Differences* 2.2: 124, n. 7.

white

61 David Payne, "Failure and Personal Identity" in *Coping with Failure: The Therapeutic Uses of Rhetoric* (Columbia: U of South Carolina P, 1989) 34.

62 Alex Galloway, "browser.art," online posting, 30 Jan. 1998, Rhizome, available <http://rhizome.org/cgi/query.cgi?a=query&q=jodi&f=&start=30&target=12>, 19 July 2000.

63 Eryk Salvaggio, "*Absolut NetArt*: Project Description," online archive, 5 Nov. 1998, Rhizome, available <http://rhizome.org/object.rhiz?1690&q>, 30 July 2000.

64 Jodi, as quoted in Tilman Baumgärtel, "Interview with Jodi," *Telepolis* 10 June 1997, available <http://www.hese.de/tp/english/html/result.xhtml?url=/tp/english/special/ku/6187/1.html&words=Baumgaertel>, 9 July 2000.

65 Jodi, "%20Wrong," online archive, 1 January 1996, Rhizome, available <http://rhizome.org/artbase/1678/wrong.html>, 1 Aug. 2000.

66 Rosalind Krauss, "The Originality of the Avant-Garde" in *The Originality of the Avant-Garde and Other Modernist Myths* (Cambridge: MIT P, 1994) 157.

67 Peter Luining, *D-TOY 2.502.338*, online archive, 9 Mar. 1999, Lifesavers, available <http://www.vpro.nl/data/lifesavers/10/index.shtml>, 4 Sept. 2000.

68 AllWords.com, "AllWords.com-Dictionary, Guide, Community and More," available <http://www.allwords.com/query.php?SearchType=3&goquery=Find+it%21&Language=ENG&Keyword=morphing>, 14 July 2001.

69 VPRO, "VPRO Aflevering," available <http://www.vpro.nl/lifesaversmanualuk>, 15 Sept. 2000.

70 VPRO, "VPRO Aflevering," available <http://www.vpro.nl/lifesaversmanualuk>, 20 Sept. 2000.

71 According to psychoanalytic and apparatus theory, male cinema viewers achieve an ideal spectatorial position because of their physical distance and intellectual detachment from the screen. However, female spectators are conceived as being inextricably bound to their bodily processes and tied to a version of their image within the screen. Women's nearness to the cinema image is less than ideal. According to Noël Burch, such an intimacy prevents the spectator from a comprehensive understanding:

> If he is too close, so close that his field of vision does not include the whole screen, his

eyes must change focus as the centers of visual interest shift, and he will never be able to grasp the total visual effect created by the framed image.

Noël Burch, "Editing as a Plastic Art" in *Theory of Film Practice*, trans. Helen R. Lane (New York: Praeger, 1973) 35. Mary Ann Doane argues that it is the "opposition between proximity and distance, control of the image and its loss, which locates the possibilities of spectatorship within the problematic of sexual difference." Mary Ann Doane, "Film and Masquerade: Theorizing the Female Spectator" in *Femmes Fatales: Feminism, Film Theory, Psychoanalysis* (New York: Routledge, 1991) 22.

72 The difference between these identity positions is usually explained as "geeks must be born, nerds are made." Internet and Unix Dictionary, available <http://www.msg.net/kadow/answers/n.html#nerd>, 12 Apr. 2001. Geek is defined as "One who eats (computer) bugs for a living. One who fulfills all the dreariest negative stereotypes about hackers: an asocial, malodorous, pasty-faced monomaniac with all the personality of a cheese grater." "The Jargon Lexicon (4.2.3)," available <http://tuxedo.org/jargon/html/entry/nerd.html>, 12 Apr. 2001. Of course, these positions may now be viewed as desirable with the economic and social rise of the programmer. Films such as Hackers (Iain Softley 1995), with its portrayal of hip teenage computer users, have also changed the way that computer users are conceived.

73 I presented a longer discussion of this concept in Michele White, "Too Close to See: Men, Women, and Webcams" in *Information, Technology, and Society: Proceedings*, Institute for Advanced Study, 8–10 June 2001.

74 André Malraux, "Museum Without Walls" in *The Voices of Silence: Man and His Art*, trans. Stuart Gilbert (Garden City: Doubleday, 1953) 24.

75 Peter Luining, as quoted in Josephine Bosma, "Interview with Peter Luining." Online posting, 3 May 2000, Rhizome, available <http://rhizome.org/cgi/query.cgi?a=query&q=jo&target=12&search=+search+>, 17 July 2000.

76 Michaël Samyn often works with Auriea Harvey on their collaborative website. They won the first SFMOMA Webby Prize for Excellence in Online Art in May 2000. Michaël Samyn and Auriea Harvey, "if (1+1==1) {e87=true;};" Available <http://www.entropy8zuper.org/>, 24 Sept. 2000.

77 Michaël Samyn, *The Fire from the Sea*, available <http://www.vpro.nl/data/lifesavers/16/index.shtml>, 21 Apr. 2000.

78 Stuart Moulthrop, "Traveling in the Breakdown Lane: A Principle of Resistance for Hypertext," available <http://www.ubalt.edu/ygcla/sam/essays/breakdown.html>, 7 July 2001.

79 I have encountered this insistence more than once while presenting *The Fire from the Sea* to students at the University of California Santa Cruz. This "problem" with the instructions has also produced interesting conversations.

80 Michaël Samyn and Auriea Harvey, "sixteenpages.net," *Sixteenpages*, available <http://sixteenpages.net/>, 20 July 2001.

81 Leo Steinberg, "Other Criteria" in *Other Criteria: Confrontations with Twentieth-Century Art* (New York: Oxford UP, 1972) 82.

82 Michaël Samyn and Auriea Harvey, "*g*e*n*e*s*i*s*," available <javascript:parent.genesisF.go('biographies.html');>, 4 Aug. 2000.

83 Michaël Samyn, as quoted in Alex Galloway. Online posting, 18 Apr. 2000, Rhizome, available <http://www.rhizome.org/fresh/>, 24 Sept. 2000.

84 Michaël Samyn, as quoted in fokky, "Art and Design – An Interview with Michael Samyn," online posting, 3 Oct. 1997, Rhizome, available <http://www.rhizome.org/cgi/to.cgi?q=871>, 24 Sept. 2000.

85 Michaël Samyn, as quoted in fokky, "Art and Design – An Interview with Michael Samyn," online posting, 3 Oct. 1997, Rhizome, available <http://www.rhizome.org/cgi/to.cgi?q=871>, 24 Sept. 2000.

86 Michaël Samyn, as quoted in Alex Galloway, online posting, 18 Apr. 2000, Rhizome, available <http://www.rhizome.org/fresh/>, 24 Sept. 2000.

87 Roland Barthes, *Camera Lucida: Reflections on Photography*, trans. Richard Howard (New York: Hill and Wang, 1981) 27.

88 Jennifer Ley, "Catch the Land Mine!! – Win a Free Prosthetic …" *Catch the Land Mine!*, available <http://www.heelstone.com/banner/>, 17 July 2001.

89 Jennifer Ley, "Catch the Land Mine!! – Win a Free Prosthetic …" *Catch the Land Mine!*, available <http://www.heelstone.com/banner/pic3.html>,

17 July 2001. My observation of people using this net art work in lab situations suggests that movement through the piece is escalated in attempts to "win" the game. The meaning of the texts seems to give way through such engagements.

90 Rose, "The Insufficiency" 33.

Michele White
Department of Telecommunications
108 West Hall
Bowling Green State University
Bowling Green, OH 43403
USA
E-mail: mwhite@bgnet.bgsu.edu

Because I am alone. It is my dialogue, my society, my companion, my confidant. It is also my consolation, my memory, my scapegoat, my echo, the reservoir of my intimate experiences, my psychological itinerary, my protection against the mildew of thought, my excuse for living, almost the only useful thing I can leave behind.

journal of the theoretical humanities
volume 7   number 1   april 2002

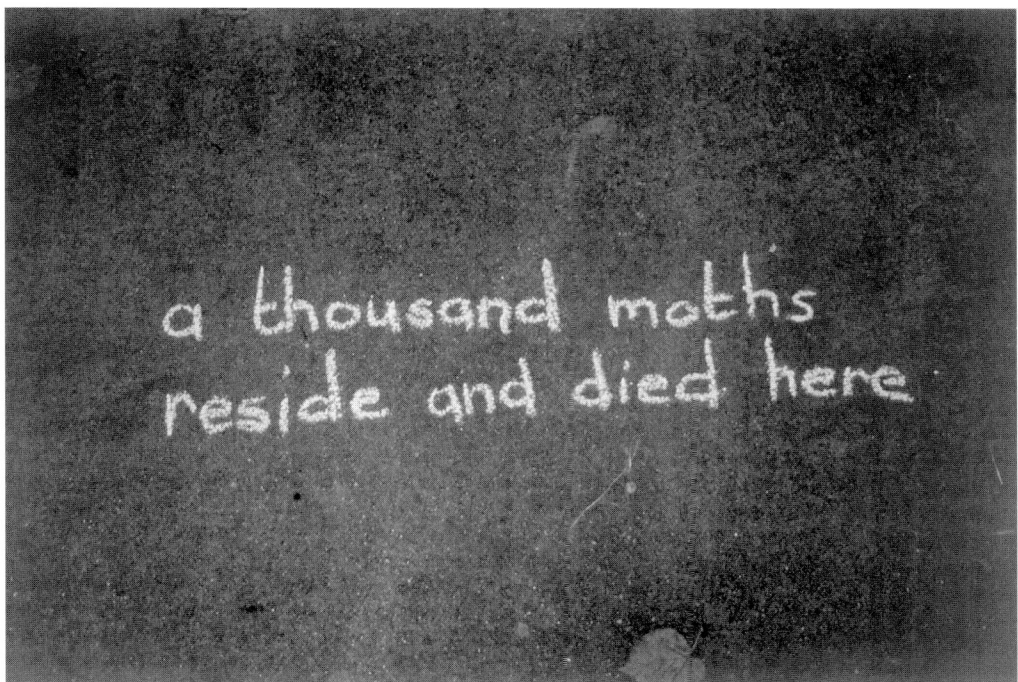

ISSN 0969-725X print/ISSN 1469-2899 online/02/010195-03 © 2002 Maria Fusco

simon malpas

SUBLIME ASCESIS
lyotard, art and the event

"One paints for very few people," writes Cézanne. Recognition from the regulatory institutions of painting ... is of little importance compared to the judgement made by the painter-researcher and his peers on the success obtained by the work of art in relation to what is really at stake: to make seen what makes one see, and not what is visible.[1]

More than any other contemporary theorist of aesthetics, Jean-François Lyotard has interrogated the relationships that obtain between philosophical arguments about the importance of the aesthetic and the work of modern artists. Since the beginning of the 1970s, Lyotard has written as extensively on art as on any other subject, discussing artists such as Daniel Buren, Paul Cézanne, Marcel Duchamp, Jacques Monory, Sigmar Polke and Barnett Newman. Rather than simply using works by these artists as examples to illustrate independently generated theoretical positions, responses to their work tend frequently to be the stimuli that set Lyotard thinking. To cite just one example, Lyotard's extended work on and discussions with Monory provide a series of key impulses for the movement of his thought that ranges from the break with Marxist critique in the late 1960s, through his analyses of libidinal economies in the 1970s, right up to the focus on postmodernity and the politics of the sublime in the 1980s and 1990s.[2]

Despite this sustained interest in art, the Lyotard familiar to the majority of English-speaking readers is not the art critic but the political and social philosopher. For Lyotard, however, there is no radical distinction to be drawn between art, philosophy and politics: the three genres are, and in modernity have always been, inextricably intertwined in a series of encounters in which none is able to dominate or escape the influence of the other two. Consequently, art, and avant-garde art in particular, becomes a site where the disruption of systems of instrumental thought and control are able to emerge as questions of presentation force themselves into the conceptual and political realms. The avant-garde artist breaks with traditional cognitive and representational structures, experimenting with the materials of art (line, colour, space, etc.) to produce new ways of seeing and feeling which, in turn, might open the possibility of new ways of thinking and acting.[3] Without an acknowledgement of Lyotard's work on art, then, what is at stake in his political philosophy is difficult to grasp.

Since the beginning of the 1980s, this analysis of the avant-gardes has tended to link them with

ISSN 0969-725X print/ISSN 1469-2899 online/02/010199-13 © 2002 Taylor & Francis Ltd and the Editors of *Angelaki*
DOI: 10.1080/09697250220142128

that discourse for which Lyotard is most widely known: the postmodern. It is his drive to retain a sense of the avant-garde's transformative potential that differentiates Lyotard's account of the postmodern most decisively from other analyses such as Baudrillard's discussion of technological innovation and communicational simulation or Jameson's Marxian notion of the weakening of resistance to global capitalism in an almost schizophrenically self-ironising contemporary culture. Lyotard's formulation of the relation between artistic experimentation and the postmodern is well known, but nonetheless worth re-quoting to set the context for what I want to argue:

> I shall call modern the art which devotes its "little technical expertise" (*son "petit technique"*), as Diderot used to say, to present the fact that the unpresentable exists. To make visible that there is something which can be conceived and which can neither be seen nor made visible: this is what is at stake in modern painting. ... The postmodern would be that which, in the modern, puts forward the unpresentable in presentation itself; that which denies itself the solace of good forms, the consensus of a taste which would make it possible to share collectively the nostalgia for the unattainable, that which searches for new presentations, not in order to enjoy them but in order to impart a stronger sense of the unpresentable.[4]

The postmodern artist thus seeks to disrupt conventional forms, to challenge established consensus and to search for new presentations that point to the possibility of a future that differs from what appears permissible for thought and action in the present. Immediately this draws the artist (or her or his surrogate – the postmodern thinker) to the centre of the social and political stage.[5] The question arising here is thus, in what way can art achieve this apparently transformative vision?

What Lyotard is gesturing towards in this account of the postmodern is the ability of art to disrupt established ways of viewing and conceiving reality, to challenge what he calls the "realism" of everyday perception and representation that aims to "stabilise the referent, to arrange it according to a point of view which endows it with a recognisable meaning, to reproduce the syntax and vocabulary which enable the addressee to decipher images and sequences quickly," and thereby to "preserve consciousnesses from doubt."[6] What this entails is disrupting form: presenting the possibility that discursive, representational or categorical schemes do not adequately map the world or the possibilities open to thought. All realisms exclude certain possibilities of presentation from their representational structures: voices are silenced; things, feelings and ideas are refused. The artist's task is to bear witness to the fact and the processes of this silencing exclusion. As Lyotard states in the quotation which opens this piece, the point is "to make seen what makes one see": to reveal those structures of the realisms that give the world to consciousness in a pre-packaged form with all the presumptions, prejudices and possibilities already mapped out.

This disruption of the forms of presentation has a name within Lyotard's aesthetics: the sublime. This aesthetic figure was central to his thought throughout the 1980s and 1990s, and is the key to his analyses of art, history and politics during this period. For Lyotard, the sublime challenges representational norms by alluding to that which disrupts them. In the sublime nothing appears, there is no solution or resolution, but rather an iteration and solicitation of common conceptual understanding. It is thus for Lyotard the most vital way of thinking the possibilities open to the present and their places in the imbrication between modernity and the postmodern.

The sublime plays a central role in *The Differend*, Lyotard's most philosophically sophisticated analysis of the postmodern. A differend between phrases – in which one is silenced, disqualified or reduced to the generic conventions of another – is signalled in a feeling of the sublime. These differends, however, are not open to immediate political correction: "In the deliberative politics of modern democracies ... the transcendental appearance of a single finality that would bring it to a resolution persists in helping forget the differend, in making it bearable."[7] The task of the postmodern thinker-artist consists in refusing to "forget" the sublime feeling that is evoked, in testifying to its existence as a means of opening up that deliberative politics to critique.

This politics of the differend has drawn criticism from a number of Lyotard's most recent commentators. For James Williams, the differend is simply not reliable enough to form the basis of a politics: "it cannot guarantee that its judgements will last any longer than a given 'experience' of the feeling of the sublime. ... Due to its dependence on unpredictable occurrences of the feeling of the sublime, the politics of the differend cannot be well defined in terms of what it stands for."[8] Similarly, Gary Browning argues that "the upshot of a valorisation of this non-discursive sublime feeling is taken to constitute a universal limit, precluding the possibilities involved in individuals making and experiencing an inter-subjective world in which their different interests can be satisfied along with their common interests in participating in public deliberations over the pursuit and distribution of goods."[9] For both Williams and Browning, the unpredictability of the sublime feeling elicited by the differend is an unstable basis for political action as it precludes an empirical definition of goals or an inter-subjective consensus about interests. These are accurate and perceptive criticisms whose accusations appear quite plausible, and yet, judged from the perspective of Lyotard's arguments in *The Differend*, both might seem somewhat beside the point. For Lyotard, "common interest" and "public deliberation" are part and parcel of contemporary politics, and yet exclusion is still too often the order of the day. The task of thinking in terms of differends is to draw out the fault lines in even the most apparently benign political orders. A politics of the differend must be unpredictable: its unpredictability, its potential to disrupt consensual norms after the manner of avant-garde artistic experimentation, is precisely what is at stake. Just because one might not ask a Picasso or a Klee to give "well defined" advice about the "common interest in participating in public deliberation over the pursuit and distribution of goods" doesn't mean that a *Guernica* or a *Senecio* cannot generate political insights. Like the avant-garde work, the feeling elicited by the occurrence of a differend calls for a response without determining in advance what that response will be. Like the work of art, the differend emerges in a culture, and raises questions about the possibility of responding adequately to it in terms of that culture's customs and rules. And just as the work of art calls for criticism, the differend calls for judgement.

What both Williams' and Browning's accusations have in common is the ways in which the respective arguments that generate them sideline Lyotard's engagements with avant-garde art.[10] In order, therefore, to grasp properly what might be at stake in the political thrust of Lyotard's avant-garde-inspired notion of the postmodern, it seems important to examine his discussion of the artistic sublime in detail. What I want to do in this paper is to focus closely on one specific case: the construction of a relation between avant-garde art and the sublime in Lyotard's two essays on Barnett Newman: "The Sublime and the Avant-Garde" (from 1983) and "Newman: The Instant" (from 1985). Through a detailed reading of these essays, I hope to open up the question of what might be at stake for a politics of art that is thought in relation to Lyotard's account of the differend. I shall begin by setting out Newman's impact on the American art scene of the 1950s, and then develop a reading of Lyotard's response to his work.

barnett newman's disruptions

Lyotard's interest in Barnett Newman is not entirely fortuitous: as well as being an important abstract expressionist artist, Newman was a frequently incisive theorist of aesthetics and an accomplished writer about the innovations of post-war American art. Within the ad hoc group of experimental New York artists that came to the fore in the 1940s (others included Willem de Kooning, Robert Motherwell, Mark Rothko and Jackson Pollock), Newman's discussions of innovation and the contemporary sublime became key ideas, even guiding principles. Together, these artists developed a specifically American-based avant-garde to challenge what was then felt in the USA to be the hegemony of European art. Writing programmes for exhibitions by members of this group, as well as a series of articles, letters

sublime ascesis

and polemics for the American art journals of the time, Newman became the chief theorist and spokesperson for abstract expressionism.

However, despite this position, his first one-person exhibition at the Betty Parsons Gallery in January 1950 confused and even alienated many of his colleagues who had accepted his theory as a description of their work but were baffled by what he produced in practice. In a sense this response is hardly surprising. Newman's paintings for the 1950 exhibition were completely new: rather than the expressive art that had drawn upon indigenous American themes and designs during the early 1940s, the new works with their single blocks of colour and straight, vertical lines appeared to push the notion of abstraction to a limit that rivalled such works as Malevich's infamous squares.11 Even now, Newman's art continues to disturb: the visual effect is often startling, and yet on closer inspection of the canvas there just seems so little to it. Lyotard captures this apparent emptiness in his description of responses to the paintings:

> A canvas by Newman draws a contrast between stories and its plastic nudity. Everything is there – dimensions, colours, lines – but there are no allusions. So much so that it is a problem for the commentator. What can one say that is not given? It is not difficult to describe, but the description is as flat as a paraphrase. The best gloss consists of the question: what can one say? Or the exclamation "Ah." Of surprise: "Look at that." So many expressions of a feeling which does have a name in the modern aesthetic tradition (and in the work of Newman): the sublime.12

Lyotard's comments are apt: one can describe a Newman piece all too easily, there seems little hidden in the physical presentation, little trickery – all that it is, is on display – and yet that seems really to tell us nothing of why the painting is effective or what it might be "about."

The first piece of Newman's that captured this new style was entitled *Onement* (later *Onement I*). It is, at least compared to some of his later works, a relatively small painting, measuring only twenty-seven by sixteen inches, and consists of an orange stripe (or, more specifically, one of cadmium light red) running vertically down the middle of the canvas, above a single-coloured (cadmium dark red – or, roughly, a sort of red-brown sienna) background. This background, instead of being made up of any texture that expresses the physical materiality of the paint or the plane of the canvas, is an even, "blank," abstract wash of solid colour. The cadmium dark red adheres to the surface of the canvas in a way that suggests the texture of a mural or poster reproduction, and the orange stripe stands above it, anchored to the vertical strip of masking tape that runs the length of the picture. Instead of expressing a motion across the surface, it is an instant divider, a "zip" as Newman referred to it and the other vertical elements in his work. If motion is suggested at all, it is the motion of a bolt of lightening that leaves a jagged after-image on the eye. The paint is applied messily, almost slapdash, and yet the measurement is precise: it splits the painting absolutely symmetrically. As Thomas Hess (Newman's biographer and probably the chief commentator on his work) says,

> By using symmetry, by placing the zip dead centre in the painting, the constricting apparatus of composition was wiped away at a sweep. ... [Symmetry, according to traditional art criticism,] was supposed to stiffen a composition, to kill its sense of spontaneity, naturalness, variety. Newman discovered in *Onement I* that whatever the perils of monotony might be, symmetry more than compensated for them by destroying the whole art-look, art-object convention.13

If Hess is correct here, Newman's *Onement*, in its symmetrical abstraction that destroys the "whole art-look, art-object convention," recalls very closely Lyotard's notion of the disruptive nature of the postmodern sublime. It "denies the solace of good forms" as it breaks the rules by seeking new possibilities of presentation that are not subject to a hitherto established "consensus of taste."

the sublime is now

In 1948, Newman published a highly polemical article in *Tiger's Eye* bearing the striking title "The Sublime is Now," in which he considers the relationship between classical and romantic aesthetics and contemporary artistic experimentation. The discussion is based upon a central question:

> if we are living in a time without legend or mythos that can be called sublime, if we refuse to admit any exaltation in pure relations, if we refuse to live in the abstract, how can we be creating a sublime art?14

For Newman, the mythological, exalted, sublime is that of European Romanticism and Christianity. It is the sublime that is laid out in Hegel's *Aesthetics*: the mythical or technological sublime in which the idea is either too underdetermined or too complex for sensible plastic presentation – either art at its inception as a representation used by a proto-social culture to ward off the anger of gods it does not understand, or the post-mythological society whose gods are too theologically and psychologically complex for plastic presentation and are better represented through philosophical reason.

According to Newman, this sort of account of the sublime, an account that he claims has remained pervasive throughout Western thought, is unsatisfactory as it conceives sublimity as a subset of the beautiful. Since the "invention of beauty by the Greeks," he argues, the understanding of artistic presentation has remained tyrannically centred on the ideal of beauty, with the effect that:

> Man's natural desire in the arts to express his relation to the Absolute became identified and confused with the absolutisms of perfect creations – with the fetish of quality – so that the European artist has been continually involved in the moral struggle between notions of beauty and the desire for sublimity.15

Because of the relation that aesthetics has set up between beauty and sublimity, the desire to express the possibility that there is something more than the quotidian becomes confused and imbricated with the ideals of pictorial perfection, of artistic quality. According to Newman, this state of affairs has remained fairly constant in philosophical aesthetics, from Longinus onwards. The only exception to this tradition that he finds is Edmund Burke, who "insisted on a separation" between beauty and the sublime, and whose writing, "reads like a surrealist manual."16

In the sphere of artistic production, the effect of the subservience of the sublime to the beautiful reached its zenith with the influence of Greek aesthetics on the art of the Renaissance. In search of a Christian Absolute, Renaissance artists set about the depiction of Christ in terms of the "ideals of Greek beauty," which Newman dismisses as the ideals of "eloquent nudity or rich velvet" that make up the "beauty cult" of Renaissance painting.17 And this cult of beauty did not end in the Renaissance, but rather continued to influence modern artistic experiments from impressionism to cubism. The responses to Renaissance painting that came from modern artists in Europe have been, according to Newman, attempts to destroy the established rhetoric of beauty. And yet, because European art, however experimental, has always remained within "a framework of pure plasticity (the Greek ideal of beauty, whether that plasticity be a romantic active surface or a classic stable one)," it has continually found itself "incapable of creating a new sublime image" and remained "unable to move away from the Renaissance imagery of figures and objects except by distortion or by denying it completely for an empty world of geometric formalisms."18 What Newman calls for is a fresh start, a different modality of sublime presentation that breaks away from the Greek beauty cult and its inheritors:

> We do not need the obsolete props of an outmoded and antiquated legend. We are creating images whose reality is self-evident and which are devoid of the props and crutches that evoke associations and outmoded images, both sublime and beautiful. We are freeing ourselves from the impediments of memory, association, nostalgia, legend, myth, or what have you, that have been the devices of Western European painting. Instead of making *cathedrals* out of Christ, man, or "life" ... [t]he image we produce is the self-evident one of revelation, real and concrete, that can be understood by anyone who will look at it without the nostalgic glasses of history.19

This is a statement typical of the avant-garde artist throughout the twentieth century: the turn away from myth, nostalgia and the traditions of the West, even from history itself, is presented as the basis for a new creation. It is a challenge to established doctrines and categories of artistic production, an assault on traditional form and an affront to the public. But Newman's is not a turn away from Western aesthetics as such; rather, he proposes a reappropriation of that key aesthetic category, the sublime. Published in 1948, this article (even manifesto) set the tone for his work from that time onwards: the work that began with *Onement*.

Newman's reappropriation of the sublime in his work and theorising is tied up with the attempt to reconfigure the relationship between artistic presentation and time. The sublime is "now" not just in the sense of its modernity or relevance, but also in terms of its impact on sensory perception and cognition. For Lyotard, Newman's sublime is the basis for a perceptual ascesis that opens presentation to the possibility of the inexpressible:

> When [Newman] seeks sublimity in the here-and-now he breaks with the eloquence of romantic art but he does not reject its fundamental task, that of bearing pictorial or otherwise expressive witness to the inexpressible. The inexpressible does not reside in an over there, in another world, or another time, but in this: in that (something) happens. In the determination of pictorial art, the indeterminate, the "it happens" is the paint, the picture. The paint, the picture as occurrence or event is not expressible, and it is to this that it has to witness.[20]

the time of the sublime

Newman's and Lyotard's notions of the sublime are thus intricately tied up with a thinking of time. In an unfinished piece from 1949, provisionally entitled "Prologue to a New Aesthetic," Newman claims that "The concern with space bores me."[21] Although this is an apparently strange comment when one looks at his work, which is almost draughtsman-like in its physical precision, it is not an insignificant one. He continues, "I insist on my experiences of sensations of time – not the *sense* of time but the physical *sensation* of time."[22] Time replaces space as the focus of painting, and yet it is a particular time: the "sensation" of time. This distinction between sense and sensation is crucial, and it is one that Lyotard focuses on in detail in order to rework the accounts of the sublime presented in his earlier writings on the postmodern.

Of course, the representation of time in art is nothing new: art has been concerned with time for a long while. The work of art captures not just a moment of time but a temporal dynamic or formation. Each work brings together past, present and future in a particular modality that generates meanings and affects. To go back just three centuries, Holbein's *The Ambassadors* famously places behind the two figures of the ambassadors a clutter of scientific instruments, including the sundial on whose faces one can simultaneously read both nine-thirty and half past ten. This discrepancy between the times points, presumably, to the fact that time moves irretrievably forwards, even during the act of painting, and the anamorphosis of the skull that appears at the base of the picture alludes to time's inevitable precipitation towards the end of life. Even medieval tableaux pictures with their series of related scenes (or "snapshots" from a progress) present the development of narrative in a way that has been taken up for more temporal ends in contemporary cartoon strips. These examples can be multiplied almost indefinitely. Art, be it a painting, sculpture or even a video installation, illustrates or depicts changes in time, the idea of its indefatigable progression or simply a captured moment, for our consideration. However, all of these examples are of *senses* of time. In the reading or viewing of the work, time is given to our consciousness as a sense, a conceptual relation that has been mapped and described by the work or, at the very least, its critical appreciation.

But if this is the "sense," what does Newman mean when he distinguishes the "sensation" of time from it, and posits the latter as the focus of his interest? Newman's essay is a fragment: it breaks off at the point that this distinction is posited and does not explain it. Lyotard, however, maps out the possible implications of "sensation" by returning to the works of art.

In "Newman: The Instant," Lyotard draws a distinction between Newman and Duchamp, whose work (however disruptive of the tradition it might be) still presents time as a mapable sense. In many of Duchamp's works, particularly *The Large Glass* and *Etant Donnés*, a reference is made to events: in the former the possibility of the bride being stripped bare by the bachelors is held in abeyance as an anticipation, and in the latter it is clear that something scandalous has already happened by the time we come to view the naked female torso through the peephole. According to Lyotard,

> The two works are two ways of representing the anachronism of the gaze with regard to the event of stripping bare. ... Duchamp organised the space of the *Bride* according to the principle of "not yet" and that of the *Etant Donnés* according to that of "no longer". ... Duchamp's great pieces are a plastic gamble, an attempt to outwit the gaze (and the mind) because he is trying to give an analogical representation of how time outwits consciousness.[23]

In contrast to this, Lyotard argues that Newman does not represent a Beckettian account of interminable anticipation or even a Proustian idea of "lost time," does not employ analogy at all, but rather that in his work "time is the picture itself," in other words, that a "painting by Newman is an angel. It announces nothing; it is in itself the annunciation."[24] And it is this "annunciation" that forms the basis of a presentation of time as sensation: the physical flash of the zip on the retina, the exclamatory "Ah!" of surprise. Lyotard again:

> The titles of many of [Newman's] paintings suggest that they should be interpreted in terms of a (paradoxical) idea of *beginning*. ... The paradox [of the beginning] is that of performance, or occurrence. Occurrence is the instant which "happens," which "comes" unexpectedly but which, once it is there, takes its place in the network of what has happened. Any instant can be the beginning, provided that it is grasped in terms of its *quod* rather than its *quid*. Without this flash, there would be nothing, or there would be chaos. The flash (like the instant) is always there, and never there. The world never stops beginning. ... If, then, there is any "subject-matter" [in Newman], it is immediacy. It happens here and now. What (*quid*) happens comes later. The beginning is *that* there is – *quod*.[25]

The quiddity of this instant is not pictured, represented, by Newman; rather the *quod* occurs in the viewing of the painting: something happens, takes place, but what the painting refers to or means is impossible to determine. The flash of the instant, the vertical zip of the painting, disturbs but does not represent. It announces without defining or distributing senses, symbols or allusions to develop meaning. The annunciation is crucial for Lyotard's reworking of sublimity: following Burke's notion of the sublime as being brought up suddenly by a recognition of the possibility that this is the last moment, that nothing else might happen, nothing will follow this "now" – something happens: the painting.[26] This sublime moment does not suggest or hold open any possibility of transcending the quotidian after the manner of Romantic aesthetics. Rather, what flashes up is the *quod* of the quotidian: the occurrence, the isolated "it happens" that has always been immanent in what happens but has remained occluded by realist representations.

In "The Sublime and the Avant-Garde," Lyotard refers to this flash as "*ein Ereignis*." This is a significant move: despite his frequent scepticism about Heidegger's philosophy (in, for example, *Heidegger and "the jews"* and *The Differend*) and his insistence during a discussion with Derrida that the "interest in phrases" that forms the basis of his thinking "is not on the side of ontology," Lyotard suddenly takes up a key Heideggerian term as a basis for his reworking of the sublime.[27]

ereignis and the instant

In "The Sublime and the Avant-Garde," Lyotard relates the presentation of the instant in Newman's work to Heidegger's *Ereignis*:

> Newman's *now* which is no more than *now* is a stranger to consciousness and cannot be constituted by it. Rather, it is what dismantles consciousness, what deposes consciousness, it is what consciousness cannot formulate, even what consciousness forgets in order to consti-

tute itself. What we do not manage to formulate is that something happens, *dass etwas geschieht*. Or rather, and more simply, that it happens – *dass es geschieht*. Not a major event in the media sense, not even a small event. Just an occurrence. ... An event, an occurrence – what Martin Heidegger called *ein Ereignis* – is infinitely simple, but this simplicity can only be approached through a state of privation. That which we call thought must be disarmed.[28]

Lyotard's appeal to *Ereignis* here is far from being a flip analogy or a casual aside. In order to appreciate the impact of this notion of the event, however, it is crucial to trace its provenance in Heidegger's philosophy.

The term *"Ereignis"* plays a central role in Heidegger's later writing. Broadly speaking, it presents the separation and relation between Being and beings or entities. This separation and relation is what Heidegger calls the ontological difference: the difference that Western philosophy has left unacknowledged since Plato, which means that for all its analyses of entities, philosophy has never enquired into the fundamental meaning of their existence, the question of why there is something rather than nothing. He describes the ontological difference in *Being and Time* as "the basic theme of philosophy, [Being] is no class or genus of entities; yet it pertains to every entity. ... Being and the structure of Being lie beyond every entity and every possible character which an entity may possess," and yet it is instantiated only in entities and discernible only to one entity: Dasein.[29] The task that *Being and Time* sets itself is thus to uncover the meaning of Being through an existential and phenomenological analysis of Dasein. This is not an entirely straightforward process, however, as Being is something that remains concealed: as that which is closest to us, Heidegger argues, it is that which is hardest to grasp.

After *Being and Time*'s focus on Dasein and phenomenology has begun to withdraw into the background of his thinking, the key figure in which Heidegger argues that the relationship between Being and beings can be addressed becomes the event. One of the clearest descriptions of *Ereignis* is Otto Poggeler's in *Martin Heidegger's Path of Thinking*: "Event refers to Being as the occurrence of a truth which is not at one's command, a truth which needs man's thinking and is thus 'identical' with him, which lets beings be seen in their Being historically, and which therefore tears open the 'difference' between Being and beings. This difference is the 'basis' for thought about Being."[30] *Ereignis* thus opens the possibility for thinking about Being, and yet it cannot itself be contained in metaphysical or logical conception. Heidegger argues in the *Contributions to Philosophy* that: the "setting free" of thought in *Ereignis* as it is "grasped out of the clearing of the t/here [*Da*], is simultaneously the *withdrawal* of enowning [*Ereignis*], namely that it withdraws from any re-presenting-calculation and holds sway as refusal."[31] *Ereignis* is unpresentable – irreducible to conscious thought or calculating reason – as its grasping occurs precisely in the "rift structure" of earth and world that Heidegger introduces in "The Origin of the Work of Art."[32] And yet it is not a "beyond," either transcendent or transcendental: it is what gives thinking and entities in the first place; it is the separation and relation of Being to beings and beings to their Being.

This ontological argument is not without its political interests and implications. For Heidegger, one of the dangers that contemporary society faces is the forgetting of this Being: the world is conceived only in terms of the collection of entities that are set off as distinct from the subject. The description of existence in terms of a subject–object relationship that focuses exclusively on theoretical contemplation (how does one bridge the gap between consciousness and the world?) tends to obscure certain ontologically significant aspects of, and events in, human activity and experience. To give only the most often cited example, Heidegger argues that the technological-scientific view of nature as mere material is what opens the possibility of our appropriating it solely for production and consumption.[33]

Although Lyotard doesn't appear to share Heidegger's interest in the ontological status of *Ereignis*, his employment of the term bears important resemblances to Heidegger's questioning of the instrumental rationality of subject–object-based epistemologies. For Lyotard, it is the instrumental structure of capitalist speculation in which the "experience of the human subject – individual and collective – and the aura that surrounds this experience, are being dissolved into the calculation of profitability" that *Ereignis* stands to unsettle.34 If a work of art can hold within itself the minimal instance of an event, it retains something that is irreducible to speculative comprehension. In Lyotard's appropriation of Heidegger, these occluded aspects and possibilities are what he calls differends: moments where something cries out to be put into phrases but, because of the calculative-technological structure of the hegemonic discourses of society, there is no language in which they can be spoken. In terms of avant-garde art, the *Ereignis* holds out against the constant threat of art's being reduced entirely to the laws of technological innovation and the marketplace:

> The occurrence, the *Ereignis*, has nothing to do with the *petit frisson*, the cheap thrill, the profitable pathos, that accompanies innovation. … Through innovation the will affirms its hegemony over time. It thus conforms to the metaphysics of capital, which is a technology of time. The innovation "works". The question mark of the "*Is it happening?*" stops. With the occurrence, the will is defeated.35

Art's *Ereignis* is not based simply on innovatory technique or form employed by the artist. Rather, in the *Ereignis*, a work of art opens the question of art's possibilities and potential to transform established forms of perception and thinking. The aim of art, then, is to bear witness to this *Ereignis* that is continually under threat of being subsumed within, but is always potentially there to disrupt, the instrumental rationality of techno-scientific calculative thinking.

Both artist and viewer can engage with this witnessing, but only at a cost. Lyotard again:

> These elementary sensations are hidden in ordinary perception which remains under the hegemony of habitual or classical ways of looking [realism]. They are only accessible to the painter, and can therefore only be re-established by him, at the expense of an interior ascesis that rids perceptual and mental fields of the prejudices inscribed even in vision itself. If the viewer does not submit to a complementary ascesis, the painting will remain senseless and impenetrable to him.36

sublime ascesis: *lema sabachthani*

Between 1958 and their exhibition at the Guggenheim in 1966, Newman completed a series of fourteen paintings that were entitled *The Stations of the Cross: Lema Sabachthani*. This title recalls a classical religious theme: artistic representations of the Stations of the Cross date back to the rise of the Franciscan influence on art in the fourteenth century. The Stations are still commonly seen in the naves of churches and on the progresses that lead to certain shrines and sanctuaries (particularly in Italy). They depict the series of halts, the fourteen key moments, in Christ's progress towards Golgotha. Newman takes this traditionally sublime subject, Christ's final journey, and strips the moments that are depicted of their representational status as emblems of the Christian mythos to present, instead, a series of occurrences, events, that revolve around the cry: "*Lema Sabachthani*," "why have you forsaken me?"

Newman follows closely the structure of the traditional series in presenting fourteen stations that form a progress around the gallery. However, his version of this progress dispenses with all subjective representation: Christ isn't pictured, and neither are the cross or the other figures from the story. Instead, each picture is restricted to raw canvas, black and white paint, and a series of vertical zips or flashes. In each of the fourteen pictures, a number of black verticals cut the canvas into sections: some sections are blocked in with the black paint, some washed; some of the vertical lines are painted ruler-straight, some jaggedly, energetically brushed. In each picture, everything is stripped down to a bare minimum: there is no representation, no colour, even the canvas itself remains un-primed. And yet the relations between these presentations generate an urgent sense of energy and anticipation. Describing the *First Station* in the exhibition catalogue, the critic Barbara Reisse comments, "The skinny un-primed zip on the right seems to screech like fingernails up and down a blackboard of dry-brushed edges, as if in terror of the solid vertical band which seems to move with ominous slowness into the painting's space. This painting almost shrieks vital terror in the face of death as an inevitable absolute."37 Each of the other thirteen paintings presents, in its own way, an analogous sublime terror as the same group of constituents, the raw canvas and its black zips, arrest the gaze of the viewer.

Each painting in the series is a gesture, an instant that reflects and refracts the presentations in the thirteen other works. And yet they do not make up a story: any possibility of pictorial allusion to the traditional plot of the Christian Stations is withheld; all that links them to the Biblical narrative is their number and the title. Under the expectation of seeing the Stations, the paintings themselves appear as a lack, a withdrawal of meaning and representation. So, stripped as they are of all reference, what presents itself in these pictures?

Newman offers the following gloss in a programme note to the original exhibition:

> *Lema Sabachthani* – why? Why did you forsake me? Why forsake me? To what purpose? Why? This is the Passion. The outcry of Jesus. Not the terrible walk up the Via Dolorosa, but the question that has no answer. ... This question that has no answer has been with us so long – since Jesus – since Abraham – since Adam – the original question. *Lema?* To what purpose – is the unanswerable question of human suffering. The first pilgrims walked the Via Dolorosa to identify themselves with the original moment, not to reduce it to a pious legend; nor even to worship the story of one man's agony, but to stand witness to the story of each man's agony: the agony that is the single, constant, unrelenting, willed – world without end.38

What both Newman's comments and his pictures strip out of the Stations is their mythical content. The journey along the Via Dolorosa is presented only as an absence: suggested by the title of the series, there is nothing in the paintings that pictures it. The passion is no longer Christ's alone, but that of every person at every instant: in this Hebrew version of the Passion, there is no reconciliation between existence and meaning, no resolution of, or answer to, the question "why?"

This "*Lema?*" is both original and eternal: it is the question of meaning opened up in the *Ereignis*, the "Is it happening?" If each picture presents us with the possibility that the "it happens" might at any moment cease to happen, with the threat of being irrevocably forsaken by meaning and signification, the exhibition as a whole presents in the series a simultaneous set of releases, moments of happening, *Ereignisse*.

Along with the fourteen *Stations*, Newman's exhibition included another picture, which was entitled, quite simply, *Be*. This picture, a larger canvas painted white with a black zip running down its right-hand side and one of cadmium light red on its left, does not offer a resolution to, or confer a meaning upon, the series. Rather, it presents existence as an imperative: be. For Lyotard, it is just this imperative which emerges in the *Ereignis*:

> This *Be* is not concerned with the resurrection in the sense of the Christian mystery, but with the recurrence of a prescription emanating from the silence or from the void, and which perpetuates the passion by reiterating it from its beginnings. When we have been abandoned by meaning, the artist has a professional duty to bear witness that *there is*, to respond to the order to be. The painting becomes evidence, and it is fitting that it should not offer anything that has to be deciphered, still less interpreted. ... The work rises up [*se dresse*] in an instant, but the flash of the instant strikes it like a minimal command: *Be*.39

The *Ereignis*, the unpresentable that is put forward in presentation itself, which Lyotard finds in Newman's art, takes the form of an imperative. There are no unpresentable, transcendent contents in the sublime instant of the paintings; rather, from the disruption of presentation there emerges the imperative, as minimal and ascetically reduced as it is, to act. The rules for action, for the decision, aren't given in advance to be interpreted according to any pre-established system. Instead, the *Ereignis* signals that the necessity for action will always be in excess of any rules or system, will always be the possibility of the system's failure.

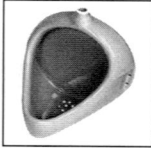

notes

1 Jean-François Lyotard, "The Sublime and the Avant-Garde" in *The Inhuman: Reflections on Time*, trans. Geoffrey Bennington and Rachel Bowlby (Cambridge: Polity, 1993) 102.

2 This movement appears most clearly in the relationship between the two essays, from 1972 and 1981, which make up Lyotard's book, *The Assassination of Experience in Painting – Monory*, ed. Sarah Wilson, trans. Rachel Bowlby (London: Black Dog, 1998).

3 This conception is not entirely original to Lyotard, and has in fact played a major role in a range of radical (and not so radical) theories of art. The notion of art's ability to break with an established cultural consensus and open thought to the future is a keystone of G.W.F. Hegel's aesthetic theory:

> if the essential world-views implicit in the concept of art, and the range of content belonging to these, are in every respect revealed by art, then art has got rid of this content which on every occasion was determinate for a particular people, a particular age, and the true need to resume it again is awakened only with the need to turn *against* the content that was alone valid hitherto; thus in Greece Aristophanes rose up against his present world, and Lucian against the whole of the Greek past, and in Italy and Spain, when the Middle Ages were closing, Ariosto and Cervantes began to turn against chivalry. (Hegel, *Aesthetics: Lectures on Fine Art*, vol. 1, trans. T.M. Knox [Oxford: Clarendon Press, 1975] 604–05)

For Hegel, then, art has the potential to break with an established world order, and provides the first glimmers of an issuing in of the new. What is at stake in Lyotard's reading of Newman is, I want to argue, a much more complex notion of disruption than this developmental conception – which is frequently identified as postmodernist by those critics who see the postmodern as a historical field that follows on from the modern. The aim of this essay, then, is to trace the stakes of Lyotard's notion of sublime disruption.

4 Jean-François Lyotard, "Answering the Question: What is Postmodernism?," trans. Régis Durand, in *The Postmodern Condition: A Report on Knowledge*, trans. Geoff Bennington and Brian Massumi (Manchester: Manchester UP, 1984) 78, 81.

5 For Lyotard's comparison between the tasks of the artist, writer and philosopher, see *The Postmodern Condition* 81–82.

6 Lyotard, "Answering the Question" 74.

7 Jean-François Lyotard, *The Differend: Phrases in Dispute*, trans. Georges Van Den Abeele (Manchester: Manchester UP, 1988) 147.

8 James Williams, *Lyotard and the Political* (London: Routledge, 2000) 118.

9 Gary Browning, *Lyotard and the End of Grand Narratives* (Cardiff: U of Wales P, 2000) 163–64.

10 Interestingly, Williams's discussion of Lyotard in his earlier book focuses much more on art and aesthetics and is less quick to condemn the notion of the differend. See Williams, *Lyotard: Towards a Postmodern Philosophy* (Cambridge: Polity, 1998) especially 104–13.

11 Newman contrasts his work with that of the European avant-gardes, including Malevich's, in the following exhibition note:

> I realise that my paintings have no link with, nor any basis in, the art of World War I with its principles of geometry that tie it into the nineteenth century. To reject cubism or purism, whether it is Picasso's or Mondrian's, only to end up with the collage scheme of free-associated forms, whether Miró's or Malevich's, is to be caught in the same geometric trap. Only an art free from any kind of the geometry principles of World War I, only an art of no geometry, can be a new beginning. (Newman, "from The New American Painting' in *Selected Writings and Interviews*, ed. John P. O'Neill [Berkeley: U of California P, 1992] 179)

12 Jean-François Lyotard, "Newman: The Instant" in *The Inhuman: Reflections on Time*, trans. Geoffrey Bennington and Rachel Bowlby (Cambridge: Polity, 1993) 80.

13 Thomas B. Hess, *Barnett Newman* (New York: Museum of Modern Art, 1971) 55.

14 Barnett Newman, "The Sublime is Now" in *Selected Writings and Interviews* 173.

15 Newman, "The Sublime is Now" 171.

16 Newman, "The Sublime is Now" 171.

17 Newman, "The Sublime is Now" 172.

18 Newman, "The Sublime is Now" 173.

19 Newman, "The Sublime is Now" 173.

20 Lyotard, "The Sublime and the Avant-Garde" 93.

21 Newman, "Ohio, 1949" in *Selected Writings and Interviews*, ed. John P. O'Neill (Berkeley: U of California P, 1992) 175.

22 Newman, "Ohio, 1949" 175.

23 Lyotard, "Newman: The Instant" 79.

24 Lyotard, "Newman: The Instant" 78–79.

25 Lyotard, "Newman: The Instant" 82.

26 For Burke's description of the possibility of the cessation of happening in the sublime, see Edmund Burke, *A Philosophical Enquiry into the Origins of our Ideas of the Sublime and the Beautiful* (Oxford: Oxford UP, 1990) especially 53–68.

27 Jean-François Lyotard, "Discussions, or Phrasing 'After Auschwitz'" in *The Lyotard Reader*, ed. Andrew Benjamin (Oxford: Blackwell, 1989) 389.

28 Lyotard, "The Sublime and the Avant-Garde" 90.

29 Martin Heidegger, *Being and Time*, trans. John Macquarrie and Edward Robinson (Oxford: Blackwell, 1962) 62.

30 Otto Poggeler, *Martin Heidegger's Path of Thinking*, trans. Daniel Magurshack and Sigmund Barber (New York: Humanity, 1991) 116.

31 Martin Heidegger, *Contributions to Philosophy (from Enowning)*, trans. Parvis Emad and Kenneth Maly (Bloomington and Indianapolis: Indiana UP, 1999) 331.

32 Martin Heidegger, "The Origin of the Work of Art" in *Basic Writings*, trans. and ed. David Farrell Krell (London: Routledge, 1993) 139–212. In the "Addendum" to this essay, Heidegger explicitly links art and *Ereignis* in a way that anticipates some of Lyotard's arguments: "Reflection on what *art* may be is completely and decidedly determined only in regard to the question of *Being*. Art is considered neither an area of cultural achievement nor an appearance of spirit; it belongs to the *propriative event* [*Ereignis*] by way of which the 'meaning of Being' … can alone be defined." (210)

33 This account of the impact of a technological-scientific view of nature is developed most extensively in Martin Heidegger, *The Question Concerning Technology: Heidegger's Critique of the Modern Age* (London: Harper, 1977).

34 Lyotard, "The Sublime and the Avant-Garde" 105.

35 Lyotard, "The Sublime and the Avant-Garde" 106–07.

36 Lyotard, "The Sublime and the Avant-Garde" 102.

37 Barbara Reise, "The Stations of the Cross and the Subjects of the Artist" in exhibition catalogue *The Stations of the Cross: Lema Sabachthani* (New York: Guggenheim Museum, 1966) 58.

38 Barnett Newman, statement from exhibition catalogue, reproduced in *Selected Writings and Interviews*, ed. John P. O'Neill (Berkeley: U of California P, 1992) 188.

39 Lyotard, "Newman: The Instant" 88.

bibliography

Browning, G. *Lyotard and the End of Grand Narratives*. Cardiff: U of Wales P, 2000.

Burke, E. *A Philosophical Enquiry into the Origins of our Ideas of the Sublime and the Beautiful*. Oxford: Oxford UP, 1990.

Hegel, G.W.F. *Aesthetics: Lectures on Fine Art*. 2 vols. Trans. T.M. Knox. Oxford: Clarendon, 1975.

Heidegger, M. *Being and Time*. Trans. John Macquarrie and Edward Robinson. Oxford: Blackwell, 1962.

Heidegger, M. *The Question Concerning Technology: Heidegger's Critique of the Modern Age*. London: Harper, 1977.

Heidegger, M. *Basic Writings*. Ed. and trans. David Farrell Krell. London: Routledge, 1993.

Heidegger, M. *Contributions to Philosophy (from Enowning)*. Trans. Parvis Emad and Kenneth Maly. Bloomington and Indianapolis: Indiana UP, 1999.

Hess, T.B. *Barnett Newman*. New York: Museum of Modern Art, 1971.

Lyotard, J.-F. *The Postmodern Condition: A Report on Knowledge*. Trans. Geoff Bennington and Brian Massumi. Manchester: Manchester UP, 1984.

Lyotard, J.-F. *The Differend: Phrases in Dispute.* Trans. Georges Van Den Abeele, Manchester: Manchester UP, 1988.

Lyotard, J.-F. *The Lyotard Reader.* Ed. Andrew Benjamin. Oxford: Blackwell, 1989.

Lyotard, J.-F. *The Inhuman: Reflections on Time.* Trans. Geoffrey Bennington and Rachel Bowlby. Cambridge: Polity, 1993.

Lyotard, J.-F. *The Assassination of Experience in Painting – Monory.* Ed. Sarah Wilson. Trans. Rachel Bowlby. London: Black Dog, 1998.

Newman, B. *Selected Writings and Interviews.* Ed. John P. O'Neill. Berkeley: U of California P, 1992.

Poggeler, O. *Martin Heidegger's Path of Thinking.* Trans. Daniel Magurshack and Sigmund Barber. New York: Humanity, 1991.

Reise, B. "The Stations of the Cross and the Subjects of the Artist." *The Stations of the Cross: Lema Sabachthani.* New York: Guggenheim Museum, 1966.

Williams, J. *Lyotard: Towards a Postmodern Philosophy.* Cambridge: Polity, 1998.

Williams, J. *Lyotard and the Political.* London: Routledge, 2000.

Simon Malpas
Department of English
Manchester Metropolitan University
Geoffrey Manton Building
Oxford Road
Manchester M15 6LL
UK
E-mail s.malpas@mmu.ac.uk

I have just hastily reread all the preceding; I deplore the gaps. It seems to me that I am still master of the days I have written down, although they are past. But the ones this paper does not mention are as though they have never been.

journal of the theoretical humanities
volume 7   number 1   april 2002

Seven Sisters - Heavy Metal
Dalston Junction - Hymns and Prayers
Hackney Central - Craig David
Shakespeare Walk - Victoria Beckham
Shakespeare Walk - Banghra
Commercial Street - Desmond Dekker
Shakespeare Walk - Craig David

ISSN 0969-725X print/ISSN 1469-2899 online/02/010213-03 © 2002 Lucy Harrison

I'm going back to my home town
I'm going back to stay
I'm going back to my home town today
I'll get myself a rocking chair to rock my cares away
And forget I left the city yesterday

Memories that linger in my heart
Memories that make my heart go cold
But someday we'll leave them all sweetheart
When my blue moon turns to gold again

London Tape no. 8

Londesborough Road, N16

25TH May

2001

Description: Country & Western

kanta kochhar-lindgren

TOWARDS A COMMUNAL BODY OF ART
the exquisite corpse and augusto boal's theatre

Commenting on a 1993 exhibit at the Drawing Center in New York City called the "return of the Cadavre Exquis," curator Ingrid Schaffner describes the *Exquisite Corpse* – a collaborative game elaborated upon by the surrealists – and its offspring as "metaphoric beings" (15), noting that we never know exactly where and under what circumstances the Corpse will turn up. These collectively wrought, spontaneous two-dimensional renditions of fragmented, disconnected, fantastic and diverse body parts, cultural artifacts, abstract doodles spawn multiple manifestations. The Exquisite Corpse, as it oscillates between the human and the non-human, the animate and the inanimate, sparks what Brian Massumi has called the "becoming [that] is in the intensity of the sensation" (25). Becoming, as an opening towards multiple possible futures, unfolds along new perceptual pathways – simultaneously making and marking the shifting boundaries of the body of both individual and the collective. The event of making the Exquisite Corpse and its variants also charts a series of uneven narratives about the production of communal bodies of art – a concern of vital importance to the socially transformative work of the surrealists, Brazilian theatre director Augusto Boal, and, indirectly, Félix Guattari's theory of *chaosmosis*.[1]

The Exquisite Corpse first came about in 1925 when three members of the surrealist group – Marcel Duhamel, Jacques Prévert, and Yves Tanguy – were experimenting with word combinations, an activity that grew out of their interest in parlor and children's games as well as the wordplay of the Dadaists. The first verbal sentence to emerge was "the Exquisite Corpse will drink the new wine." From there the concept of Exquisite Corpse, as a game for spontaneously forming verbal sentences, grew to include a visual version. The visual version of the game entails using a piece of paper that is folded an agreed upon number of times – usually three. Each player draws the respective body sections as he or she desires on the paper, then continues a bit of the lines over onto the next section so that the subsequent participant has a beginning point for the next part of the drawing. Once each panel has been completed, the paper is unfolded in order to display a fantastical being. In locating the site of research in the "parlor," André Breton and other surrealists strove to narrow the gap between the making of art and the everyday – based on the belief that fostering new aesthetic practices based on collective action could lead to new political strategies and social change.[2]

communal body

The resurgence of interest in the Exquisite Corpse in the last decade gives us reason to theorize in more contemporary terms about an artistic phenomenon that at first glance seems bound to its original historical context. New manifestations of the Exquisite Corpse including "Hedwig and the Angry Inch's" song the *Exquisite Corpse*, the film *Exquiste Corpse: A Surrealist Film in Eleven Parts* by Dean Naday and Pierre Naday, Donald Lipski's *Exquiste Corpse* sculptures, and web-based compositions of the Exquisite Corpse, all signal a recurring interest in the surrealist game, in particular chance operations, the body and its many distortions, and collectively wrought artistic constructions. In addition to such readily identified resurrections of the Exquisite Corpse, it is also important to note its power not only as a game, but also as a paradigmatic practice that can be used as a frame for understanding other artistic productions and the relationship of numerous participants to multiple mobile, fragmented, and heterogeneous bodies.

The model of the Exquisite Corpse for artistic practice manifests itself, for example, with particular insistence in the work of Brazilian director Augusto Boal. Boal's *Theatre of the Oppressed*, a community-based political theatre practice inspired by Paolo Freire's *Pedagogy of the Oppressed*, emerged as a result of his work as a director and producer of the Arena Theatre in São Paolo (1956–71) and began to take shape when he toured among the workers and peasants in north Brazil in the late 1960s. Boal's work encompasses a variety of performance techniques and methods such as Image Theatre, the Invisible Theatre, and the Forum Theatre for the non-traditional performer. These theatrical "games" stress the ways in which the mobility of the body is crucial to the building of new cultural stories, and they provide ways to engender community dialogue about unresolved social issues and the exploration of a variety of alternative responses. Boal's work, first conceived of as a "rehearsal for revolution," has more recently been addressed as a "rehearsal for healing" (Schutzman 138) as it moved from working primarily with disenfranchised communities to a variety of workshop settings. Nevertheless, Boal's work continues to emphasize the investigation of new social models as well as to narrow the gap between artistic practice and the everyday.[3]

Although the Exquisite Corpse is two-dimensional and Boal's work is three-dimensional, both practices focus on the rendering, manipulation, and linking of spontaneously generated images in order to transform images and space, and, subsequently, identity and politics. Three aspects of the Exquisite Corpse – the perceptual dimensions of the process itself, the technique of linking, and the way that the use of fragmentation of partialities activates a mobile body – provide useful reference points for examining how collaboration works in both the "original" Exquisite Corpse and Boal's work. Through an examination of these art practices, as processes of leaving the familiar body and approaching the heterogeneous body, we can better understand how social change can take place at the micro-level through the gestures of multiple moving bodies. This understanding provides the frame for a situational aesthetics that marks what Gregory Ulmer has called "a dramatic, rather than an epistemological, orientation toward knowledge" (49). The "dramatic" orientation brings into view the dynamics of the visual/spatial, the movement of "body and bodies" between parts and wholes, games, performance, and the everyday, and the ways in which non-teleological, non-linear meaning accumulates.

As we examine both of these collaborative artistic practices – the Corpse's and Boal's work – we can see how through developing a situational aesthetics each practice acts as a method of research that leads to what Charles Garoian describes as a "hybrid of ethnography and surrealism that enables the repositioning of the body within the matrices of culture" (33). In this case, ethnography – the gathering of personal and social histories and exchanges – melds with surrealism and has become a methodology for cutting across cultural spaces and linking disparate realities, histories, and subject positions. In such a material practice, the body is simultaneously located individually and collectively in its situational immediacy, and yet it proliferates into multiple hybrid bodies and hybrid spaces. How does either practice put in motion "molecular revolution" (Guattari's term) or set the stage for socio-cultural change?

When knowledge becomes "dramatic," it entails a collaborative aspect. Typically, *collaboration* is taken to mean that in which all the participants contribute equally and with conscious awareness of the process at hand, working together jointly. *Communal* action reflects a unified body of individuals. Breton addresses the nature of collaborative activity in the Exquisite Corpse as "blind composition" (*Conversations* 221); this perspective unsettles an expected association of seeing and doing. "Blind" attests to the conjoining of chance operations and automatism as a type of "blindness," not knowing what is happening. Boal emphasizes the use of dialogue through a variety of interactive techniques in order to create a sense of community and new possibilities. As one form of processual creativity, it unfolds through an engagement with the collective and emphasizes the process of making as what produces the artist(s) and the community of exchange – not the other way around. For our purposes, we will focus on how collaboration is actually constructed in both examples in order to grapple with how these patterns impact "molecular revolutions," the making of new perceptual pathways and the performance of everyday life.

The very act of making various types of Exquisite Corpses, or new organizations of bodies and bits, creates, in simple terms, a collectively based subject – a reordering of self and community that relies on attention to juxtaposition and flux. In *Chaosmosis, An Ethico-Aesthetic Paradigm*, Guattari notes that:

> [I]n studies on new forms of art (like Deleuze's on cinema) we will see, for example, movement-images and time-image constituting the production of subjectivity. We are not in the presence of a passively representative image, but a vector of subjectivation. We are actually confronted by a non-discursive, pathic knowledge, which presents itself as a subjectivity that one actually meets, an absorbent subjectivity given immediately in all its complexity. (25)

Chaosmosis, the practice generated from *chaosmos* (chaos and cosmos), or the becoming-world, positions the "subject as task" (Boundas and Olkowski 6). The notion of *vector of subjectivation* – as the activity of the subject – posits the trajectories of artistic generation and exchange in a dynamically spatial paradigm, rather than in a more static frame of interpretation. We ask not so much what things *mean* but what they are *doing*, and in this field the Exquisite Corpse resonates as multiple subjects-in-fold.

The pastiche of images created in the game and in Boal's work forms a *living* tissue of disparate bits and bodies in which politics and aesthetics are built *into* the process rather than as something added on to a previously established subject. In this sense, the various models of the Exquisite Corpse are anti-Kantian and anti-Romantic, dispensing with the notion of artwork created by the individual genius that forms an enclosed and teleological whole. Kant, in the *Critique of Judgement*, posits *genius* as an inborn ability to convey nature's speaking, but the artist as genius can express his relationship to nature only through the fine arts and remains a figure who operates outside conventional social parameters in order to reanimate culture. The critics are the aristocrats who mediate between the speakers of nature and of art and the receivers of the art.[4]

The Romantics exalted the voice of the imagination as the site of inspiration, yet vested that voice in the individual genius-artist. Romantic aspiration revolved around reconciling the infinite with the here and now, promulgating an almost mystical unity of subject and object, spirit and nature. Novalis writes:

> The world must be romanticized. In this way one rediscovers the original meaning. Romanticizing is nothing but a qualitative raising to a higher power [Potenzierung]. The lower self becomes identified with the better self. Just as we ourselves are such a qualitative exponential series. This operation is still quite an unknown. Insofar as I give the commonplace a higher meaning, the ordinary a mysterious countenance, the known the dignity of the unknown, the finite an appearance of infinity, I romanticize it. (Vol. 2, 545, no. 105)

The Romantics exalt the inner world of imagination and the outer world of nature as ultimate sites of creative contemplation.

Both positions ultimately work by dislocating the aesthetic production of meaning from the body – seeing the aesthetic experience as a sojourn into a realm of the "other" beyond the everyday. In his *Theory of the Avant-Garde*, Peter Bürger writes:

> As regards the difficult question concerning the historical crystallization of art as an institution, it suffices if we observe in this context that this process came to a conclusion about the same time as the struggle of the bourgeoisie for its emancipation. The insights formulated in Kant's and Schiller's aesthetic writings pre-suppose the completed sphere that is detached from the praxis of life. (26)[5]

Surrealism (and there are many surrealisms, just as there are many romanticisms) aimed for the transformation of life through the dissolution of distinction between "dream and reality, poetry and desire, and the individual and the group" (De Mul 94). This experience, however, was not considered transcendent but immanent.

For Boal, "truth" emerges locally in the sociopolitical context; it is produced through interactions and exchanges in collaboration with the community of people. In both the case of the Exquisite Corpse and Boal's theatre, the process of participation is open to all those who are interested, and prior training is not a prerequisite for participating. Thus the notion of the specialists of an academy and exclusive artistic tradition is also subverted. Consequently, the relationship between tradition and innovation, and in these particular cases, the past and the future, has to be reassessed.

The Exquisite Corpse and its variants stake the claim for a creativity that can be generated by using certain inclusive procedures or rules. In moving art away from the Kantian separation of culture into distinct spheres, each practice becomes accessible to anyone who follows the rules of the game; these approaches, as harbingers for the performance of everyday life, create communal spaces for artistic practice.

In the game of the Exquisite Corpse, folding creates new subjectivities, and folding collectively cerates new communal bodies. In Breton's definition of the Exquisite Corpse as a game of folded paper that consists in having a sentence or drawing composed by several persons, each is ignorant of the preceding collaboration. In this definition, the separateness or partial engagement of each player is stressed, and subsequently the approach to this game works by virtue of the accumulation of parts. The sum of the parts creates a whole that is greater than each of its parts. The surprise element in the game leads to the conjunction of the critique of traditional frames of representation as well as the emergence of new realities. Body parts are replaced randomly, and the Exquisite Corpse replaces the "mimetic model of the body by the semiotic model, to produce a hybrid body, or other body" (Adamowicz 80).

But as Hal Foster notes in Breton's ambivalence about the outcome in his response to what the practice of making Exquisite Corpse's effects, he writes:

> In "Le Cadavre exquis, son exaltation," Breton remarks that the effect of exquisite corpse drawings was "to bring anthromorphism to its climax." Is this to imply that the human form is somehow achieved only if it becomes disarranged – that it climaxes only if it comes, is corpsed, or recombined like some machine? (274–75)

For Breton this "anthromorphism" suggests reactivation of the human form, its return – to a threshold of appearance and disappearance. Yet likeness and difference are uneasy partners. The Exquisite Corpse "hovers between contingent matter and significant fragments" (Adamowicz 87), and it fragments, giving rise to the delight of the unexpected. This process is not the *recuperation* of the old form, but a transformation of the old form into something surprisingly different; it is the production of difference that never becomes anything but hybrid.

In the beginning, the page lies quiescently, almost virginal, as if waiting in expectant silence to be marked and folded, waiting for the image(s) to emerge from the purity of the receptive space. The page is emptiness awaiting the imposition of a unique order. Lines appear, the paper is folded, more lines, another fold, and finally, the "bottom" – if we can still talk about directionality and hierarchy with the Exquisite Corpse – of the drawing takes place.

This, of course, is a primary fantasy, the story of *creatio ex nihilo*, where body and vision merge momentarily as the image is drawn across the space of the paper. The paper always already swirls with possibility; it has always already been marked as "page," as "virginal," as "blank," as "waiting." The page belongs to a history – both a past history and a future history – just as it belongs to three bodies: three pairs of eyes, three pairs of hands, and an inexhaustible imagination. The page creates makers as the makers create the page, and the corpse – the work and the body as *corpus* – are hinged together in an asymmetrical appearance of the art event.

In the moments as the corpse emerges, another type of hearing, through what (following Nietzsche, Freud, and Lyotard) I call the "third ear," propels the simultaneous making of the collective space and figure. Hearing occurs through the channels of subterranean pathways; it deals with the understanding of "negative spaces" and amplifies the unconscious as it accumulates through the collective interactions of rhythms of silence and gesture. This type of listening, facing the blank page as co-producers of the Exquisite Corpse, generates a simultaneity of inner seeing, hearing, and the production of meaning. Meaning is not simply translated from the predetermined spaces of the past; it is transmuted, emergent.

Folding provides the mechanism for linking the disparate realities, creating a hybrid body. In the process of helping to make the figure, the fold also dislocates it. Folding simultaneously constructs and deconstructs, connects and disconnects. It gives form as it takes away form, and as such it stands as a metaphor for all acts of artistic (un)making. The fold, which occurs across the space of the page, also takes time, showing identity to be a multiply folded phenomenon in space–time that, to return to Guattari, collaboratively creates subjectivities. The folding unfolds paradox.

The fragment breaks apart, tears space–time asunder, deconstructs the fantasy of wholeness. Foster notes in *Compulsive Beauty* that it is George Bataille who, despite his strained and conflictual relationship with the surrealists, offers insight into the power of the Exquisite Corpse as both "exquisite" and "corpse."[6] In writing about cave drawing and early children's drawings, Bataille notes the tendency toward the deformation of the human figure, which he terms *altération*.

> *Altération* ... signifies both a "partial decomposition analogous to that of cadavers" and a "passage to a perfectly heterogeneous state" related to the sacred and spectral. It is precisely this *alteration* ... read simultaneously as a corpse and a corps *morcelé*, as the body "after subjecthood, absolutely delimited, and as the body "before" subjecthood, given over to its heterogeneous energies. (113)

Morcelé comes from the French word meaning "parts of things or bits of food."[7] From this perspective, Bataille's interest in an "exquisite corpse" emphasizes the ways in which decomposition is linked to a strange form of nourishment. New bodies are composed from old bodies and bits – hovering between life and death, the human and non-human.

Yet there is paradox, for we can write a history of the art of the fragment, whether in writing, the plastic arts, or performance. Perhaps this history intensifies with Romanticism, with its own fragments and its love of ruins artificially situated in the gardens of the rich. And, today, we hear all too often of the collages of postmodernism. As the participants of the "return" of the Exquisite Corpse say: "Here, together, situating ourselves on the very edge of the postmodern gesture, with its revolutionary reliance on the fragment and the part ..." (Caws 40). There are no metanarratives; there are no metaimages: only the folded (dis) articulations of the playfully animated corpse.

In Boal's collaborative approach to performance, the production of a type of Exquisite Corpse moves from the hand to the whole body, from two dimensions, to three and four dimensions. Boal's *Theatre of the Oppressed* provides a venue for the voices of the disenfranchised where alternative strategies, solutions, and realties can be tried on, examined, and rehearsed. The enactment of visual tableaus, formed by linking, lining up, or adding on individual embodied images, creates an experience where the performer not only makes the Exquisite Corpse, but also becomes a part of it. Within this model, the emphasis is on the moving body and how it forms images. Boal explains, asserting the power of the body, "we have, before all else, a body – before we have a name, we inhabit a body" (*Games* 114).

Boal likes to start his workshops by carrying a chair to an empty space, and sitting there, he waits. Eventually all of the workshop members turn attention toward him – in that charged moment they sit there expectantly, receptive in a state of mobility. Audience members make each other as they both spectate and act by completing the performer–audience circuit, doing what Boal calls *spect-act*. Boal's theatre crystallizes through the animation of the empty space – which though full of possibility is brought to life by the collaborative efforts of the performers and audience members – as we construct numerous landscapes of images through the use of the body, in particular its position in space and how we direct our energies through our shifting attentions.

Boal's emphasis on the body can be seen in his creation myth for theatre. He tells "the fable of Xua Xua, the prehuman woman who discovered theatre" (*Games* xxv–xxx) that places theatre's beginning "in the pregnant body of Xua Xua who after giving birth to a son and losing control over this being that was once a part of her discovers theatre" (Auslander 125). New possibility is born from this fantastical being – on the way from the old body to the future body. Manifest in the in-between, theatre becomes the space where as we make theatre it also makes us – in and through the welter of movement-images and time-images that Guattari describes.

Boal explains "the moment when Xua Xua gave up trying to recover her baby and keep him all for herself … emptied part of herself. At that moment she was one and the same time Actor and Spectator. She was Spect-Actor" (*Games* xxx). In this myth both doubling and splitting are operating paradigms. At the moment that Xua Xua doubles she also splits in two, creating what is her and not-her. In this space in-between, the materiality of the moment, the shifting and emergence of new matter (her son), is simultaneously animated and brought into critical awareness. This double focus of seeing and doing connotes a multi-sensorial moment, the harbinger of a type of cross-sensory facility that Boal explores in many of his preparatory exercises. What occurs at the fold of new meaning is also a moment of great attention – physical, visual, and emotional.

For those of us who are metaphorically Xua Xua in our primal fantasy, theatre is birthed on the empty stage in the to-and-fro between the empty stage and the proliferation of embodies images. Through these landscapes of images, often built through exercises exploring non-linearity and a multiplicity of images that are generated spontaneously, the parallelisms of the many bodies next to each other foster a type of "first" dialogue. By foregrounding the performance of Guattari's "nondiscursive, pathic knowledge" (through embodied images), uncharted pathways of listening and speaking unfold through the first dialogue of bodies next to each other.

In Boal's Image Theatre, the emphasis is on the use of images rather than words. In one exercise the joker (who acts as the facilitator) picks a subject and asks the participants who are in a circle to present their image of that subject with their bodies. As first we feel and sense our own relationship to the subject; in the second part we are invited, while maintaining our own positions, to notice what others have embodied. While these images are multiple versions of the "same" subject – just as the construction of the Exquisite Corpse provides extensional variations of the body – we still take in partial views of multiple bodies-in-space. A presentational approach short-circuits the limitations of representation, and it allows for a polysemy of images to resonate across the theatrical space. In another exercise, a participant, working quickly so that visual thinking can be accessed, will illustrate a subject using other people's bodies. In creating a body-to-body exchange, perceptual and spatial differences are inhabited and highlighted in the format of simultaneity. As participants shift from pose to pose, they gain facility in taking on different bodies, different masks – thus producing new "vectors of subjectivation."

These vectors rely on movement – the use of the body in space and time. According to Philip Auslander, "[t]he Boalian body never comes to rest in a neutral state; rather the point is for the spect-actor to be able to move from one [image] mask to another while retaining a critical distance from all masks" (131). In Boal's work, "[the] mechanisms of oppression shape the body, [and] it is through the body and its habits that those mechanisms can be exposed" (Auslander 128). Participants work to "hear" the impress of ideology – the ways in which it exists in tension with, or contradistinction to desire, perceptual and visceral differences as well as personal histories – through their bodies, but they also work to hear beyond it to new bodies and social configurations.

This listening takes on a particular power in Boal's Invisible Theatre in which a group of performers who have practiced a drama beforehand enact a version of the drama in public. The public becomes involved without knowing that they are participating in an Invisible Theatre. In another theatrical form, Boal's Forum Theatre, a drama is a workshop about a particular issue that highlights an oppression. The scene is performed once to present the model of the story, and then is played again as a type of contest in which audience members can yell "stop" and insert themselves into the dramatic storyline in an effort to change the outcome. The original players work to take the story to its original outcome; the new players try to change the outcome. The Forum Theatre is an extraordinarily powerful method for the creation of new stories that relies on the intervening of multiple realities and multiple bodily perspectives. Though operating as the unfolding of multiple variations of a particular narrative, the Theatre works by virtue of the ways this physical/verbal dialogue leaps across spaces between the performers and also between performers and audience members.

It is, in fact, crucial that the audience has the opportunity to participate – to add their voices and perspectives, and as a result Boal has developed numerous strategies for folding their presence into the performance. This expanding site within-ness emerges through the construction of meaning in the moment. Just as with the Exquisite Corpse there are no metanarratives; there are no metaimages: only the folded (dis)connections of the playfully animated corpses.

Schaffner provocatively remarks that "the Exquisite Corpse transgresses against the traditionally masculine construct of modernism and listens for the post-modern feminine ideal" (Après Exquis 70). As we listen across the spaces, gestures, and images of our micro-cultural moments, we pass into and out of the empty space, linking, unlinking, and relinking. We experience what Guattari calls "an open redefinition of the body" (117) in which "[s]omething is absorbed – incorporated, digested – from which new lines of meaning take shape and are drawn out" (96). Boal's theatrical approach, consequently, facilitates a prodigious linking of disparate bits and bodies across multiple realities, voice, and communities. As the performative Exquisite Corpse shifts and mutates, new social realities emerge.

In this "hybrid of ethnography and surrealism," where art making is a communal action that reorders perception and subsequently history, we can witness the shift from the phenomena of the individual genius – as a regulatory premise for creative practice – to the practice of collective art making. Art making is not outside the *socius*, but that which makes and confirms a transforming *socius*. Molecular revolutions occur through attention to absorption of discrete shifts in perceptual realities. In tracking these shifting outlines of self as the sites of multiple bodies and bits, we discern "mobile bodies forming at the crest of waves" (Cannning 93), the patterns of the two-dimensional Exquisite Corpse melds with its many variations in three dimensions. We can follow the emerging outlines of new social forms in both practices: that of the Exquisite Corpse and that of Boal's theatrical techniques. We swerve toward and away from the space of theatre and everyday life where "[a]n evaluation of performance and the quotidian takes as its object the neglected and undocumented, reviewing the unwritten theatre in a local network of work and recreation" (Reade 2). As we link and unlink realities and collide with pieces and bodies, we are always already fragmented, yet replete with potentiality. We are our own Exquisite Corpses.

Whirling vertiginously toward and away from the exigencies of form and communality, we

communal body

listen across bodies and spaces and are thrust into the space of paradox toward the "excess of energy that obscures containment" (Schaffner 47). As we think we make the social body of the Exquisite Corpse, we are startled – it is the Exquisite Corpse that is making us.

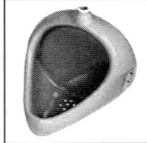

notes

1 This paper was first delivered at the Re-thinking the Avant-garde Conference at Notre Dame University, Notre Dame, IN, April 2000. My thanks to the astute comments of my two anonymous readers as well as for the feedback from Gray Kochhar-Lindgren, Petra Kuppers, and John Moore.

2 For more on surrealist politics, see, for example, *Surrealist Politics* by Helena Lewis.

3 Both Breton and Boal have positioned themselves in relationship to Marxism. An analysis of this issue is outside the scope of this project. For more on Breton and the communists, see Breton's writings, "Political Position of Surrealism" in *Manifestoes of Surrealism*. Also see Franklin Rosemont's "Introduction" to Breton's *What is Surrealism?* or Mary Ann Caws' "Introduction" to Breton's *Free Rein*. On Boal's relationship to Marxism, see in his own writing, *The Theatre of the Oppressed*. For other commentary, see *Playing Boal: Theatre, Therapy and Activism*, eds. Mady Schutzman and Jan Cohen-Cruz, and Carmel O'Sullivan's article, "Boal and the Shifting Sands: the Un-political Master Swimmer."

4 In his *Critique of Judgement*, Kant focuses on laying out a topography for knowledge in which he tries, as John Moore puts it, to "domesticate aesthetics."

5 While Bürger focuses on the affinity of Kant and Schiller in delineating the category of aesthetics, it cannot be seen as a strict one. Schiller asserts the rights of imagination against Kant, who tries to link imagination with reason.

6 Bataille's entire project can be viewed in terms of its effort to work out the paradigm of the "exquisite corpse." Though such an investigation is beyond the scope of this paper, it is important to note Bataille's involvement in the Acéphale, a secret society in existence from 1929 to 1935.

The figure of the Acephal, a headless body of man, displays Bataille's commitment to overturning the classical notion of the body (Leonardo). In his introduction to *Encyclopedia Acephalica*, Alastair Brotchie writes: "The *Acephal* is headless, not only a man escaping his thoughts, but a headless organization, one abjuring hierarchy. Bataille criticized the Surrealists as hierarchical, and hierarchy is the hallmark of fascist organization" (12). Following the line of thought implied where the drawing of the corpse begins, Breton's Exquisite Corpse emerges at the head; nevertheless, as Adamowicz and others have noted, the Exquisite Corpse does break up the classical body. More recent drawings shown at the Drawing Center in 1991 further critique the need even to stay within the frame of the human body; one drawing, for example, replaces the head portion with an image of a locomotive.

7 I am indebted to John Moore for his insight on *morcelé* and its implications for Bataille's work.

bibliography

Adamowicz, Elza. *Surrealist Collage in Text and Image: Dissecting the Exquisite Corpse*. Cambridge: Cambridge UP, 1998.

Auslander, Philip. "Boal, Brecht, Blau: The Body." *Playing Boal: Theatre, Therapy, Activism*. Ed. Mady Schutzman and Jan Cohen-Cruz. London: Routledge, 1994.

Bataille, Georges (ed.). *Encyclopaedia Acephalica: Comprising the Critical Dictionary and Related Texts. And the Encyclopaedia Da Costa*. Ed. Robert Lebel and Isabelle Waldberg. Assembled and introduced by Alastair Brotchie. Trans. Iain White. London: Atlas, 1995.

Boal, Augusto. *Theatre of the Oppressed*. Trans. Charles McBride. New York: Theatre Communications Group, 1985.

Boal, Augusto. *Games for Actors and Non-Actors*. Trans. Adrian Jackson. New York: Routledge, 1992.

Boundas, Constanin and Dorothea Olkowski. "Editors' Introduction." *Gilles Deleuze and the Theater of Philosophy*. Ed. Constantin Boundas and Dorothea Olkowski. New York: Routledge, 1994.

Breton, André. *Manifestoes of Surrealism*. Trans. Richard Seaver and Helen Lane. Ann Arbor: U of Michigan P, 1972.

Breton, André. *What is Surrealism? Selected Readings*. Ed. Franklin Rosemont. New York: Pathfinder, 1978.

Breton, André. *Conversations: The Autobiography of Surrealism*. Trans. Mark Polizotti. New York: Marlowe, 1995.

Breton, André. *Free Rein=LA Cle Des Champs*. Trans. Michael Parmentier and Jacqueline D'Amboise. Omaha: U of Nebraska P, 1996.

Bürger, Peter. *The Theory of the Avant-Garde*. Trans. Michael Shaw. Minneapolis: U of Minnesota P, 1984.

Canning, Peter. "The Crack of Time and the Ideal Game." *Gilles and the Theater of Philosophy*. Ed. Constantin Boundas and Dorothea Olkowski. New York: Routledge, 1994.

De Mul, Jos. *Romantic Desire in (Post) Modern Art and Philosophy (SUNY Series in Post Modern Culture)*. Trans. Alan Reeve. Albany: SUNY P, 1999.

Foster, Hal. *Compulsive Beauty*. Cambridge: MIT P, 1993.

Garoian, Charles. *The Performance of Pedagogy*. New York: Routledge, 1998.

Guattari, Félix. *Chaosmosis: An Ethico-Aesthetic Paradigm*. Trans. Paul Bains and Julian Prefanis. Bloomington: Indiana UP, 1995.

Hegarty, Paul. *Georges Bataille: Core Cultural Theorist*. Thousand Oaks: Sage, 2000.

Jean, Marcel (ed.). *The Autobiography of Surrealism*. New York: Viking, 1980.

Kant, Immanuel. *Critique of Judgement*. Trans. J.C. Meredith. Oxford: Oxford UP, 1997.

Lewis, Helena. *Politics of Surrealism*. New York: Paragon, 1988.

Massumi, Brian. *Deleuze, Guattari and the Philosophy of Expression (Involutionary Afterword)*. Available <www.anu.edu.au/HRC/first_and_last/works/crclintro.htm>. July 2001.

Novalis. *Schriften*. Ed. Richard and Paul Kluckhorn. Stuttgart: Kohlhammer, 1998.

O'Sullivan, Carmel. "Boal and the Shifting Sands: The Un-political Master Swimmer." *New Theatre Quarterly* (Aug. 2000).

Philbin, Ann. *The Return of Cadavre Exquis*. New York: Drawing Center, 1994.

Reade, Alan. *Theatre and Everyday Life: An Ethics of Performance*. London: Routledge, 1993.

Schaffner, Ingrid. "Aprés Exquis." *The Return of Cadavre Exquis*. New York: Drawing Center, 1994.

Schaffner, Ingrid. "In Advance of 'the Return of the Cadavre Exquis.'" *The Return of Cadavre Exquis*. New York: Drawing Center, 1994.

Schutzman, Mady. "Brechtian Shamanism: The Political Therapy of Augusto Boal." *Playing Boal: Theatre, Therapy, Activism*. Ed. Mady Schutzman and Jan Cohen-Cruz. London and New York: Routledge, 1994.

Schutzman, Mady and Jan Cohen-Cruz (eds.). *Playing Boal: Theatre, Therapy, Activism*. London and New York: Routledge, 1994.

Ulmer, Gregory. "Applied Grammatology: Post (E-pedagogy from Jacques Derrida to Joseph Beuys." *Writing and Reading Differently: Deconstruction and the Teaching of Composition and Literature*. Baltimore: Johns Hopkins UP, 1985.

Kanta Kochhar-Lindgren
Theatre Department
Central Michigan University
Mt. Pleasant, MI 48858
USA
E-mail: kantakl@aol.com

He does not fear to eat fruit or cheese over an open book, or carelessly to carry a cup to and from his mouth; and because he has no wallet at hand he drops into books the fragments that are left. Continually chattering, he is never weary of disputing with his companions, and while he alleges a crowd of senseless arguments, he wets the book lying half open in his lap with sputtering showers. Aye, and then hastily folding his arms he leans forward on the book, and by a brief spell of study invites a prolonged nap; and then, by way of mending the wrinkles, he folds back the margin of the leaves, to the no small injury of the book.

PLAIES-IMAGES II
Nicole Jolicœur

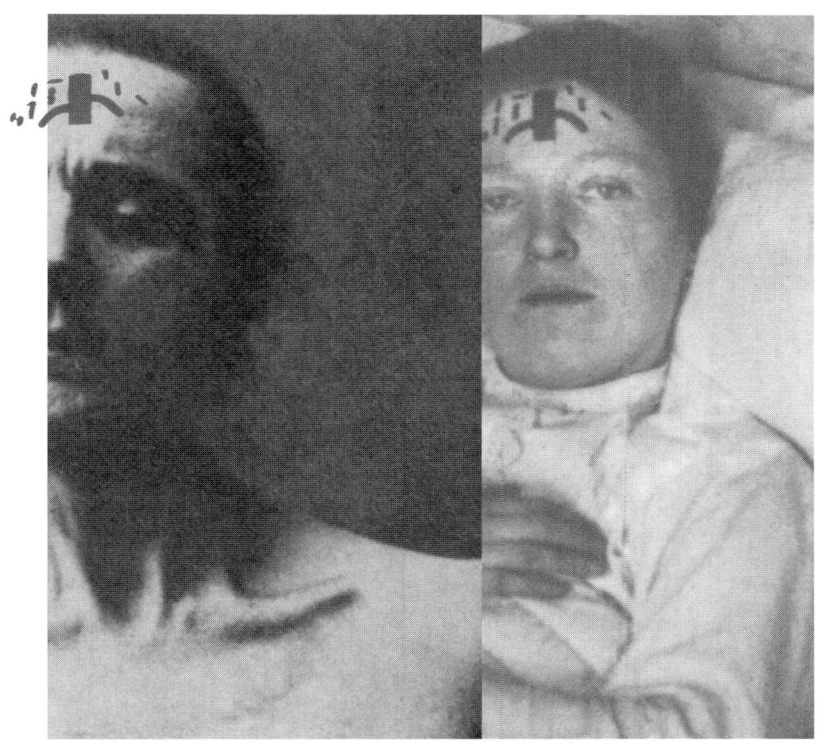

journal of the theoretical humanities
volume 7 number 1 april 2002

lewis johnson

VARIATIONS ON THE WORK OF ART
sound, space and some compositions by mutlu çerkez

There have been at least two Beethovens, we may infer from Barthes's essay "Musica Practica," one born in the nineteenth century and another whom Barthes would have been in the process of introducing to us. The first would be the subject of a biographical construction which has heroised the composer, "the first *free* man of music," reading the oeuvre as a "movement," in some apparently ideal composition, from one "manner" to another, unfolding the truth of the artist's search to deliver a "totally legible message" – in short, Beethoven as "complete hero"; the second, turning around the included–excluded trace of corporeality of the first, reopening the oeuvre to a consideration of its status as modern – as something "with an intelligibility somehow perceptible to the senses," something neither simply to be played – the "Musica Practica" of Barthes's title – nor simply to be heard. "Something *inaudible* in Beethoven's music" led Barthes to remark something which removes us from a consideration of music as the to-be-heard as well as dislocating our sense of that for which, as performance, the work calls. It is this problematisation of performance, what Barthes terms a "utopia" of the stage – "no dream, no image-repertoire, in a word no 'soul'" – which Beethoven's music leads us to sense, and which, remarking the trace of the inaudible without giving it a destiny of manifestation (destiny requiring its signs), would be protected in the neologism of the following:

> this Beethoven is exemplarily the one of the *Diabelli Variations*. The operation which permits us to grasp this Beethoven (and the category he inaugurates) can no longer be execution or hearing, but reading.[1]

For Barthes, then, music may be "read." Not that "we must sit down with a Beethoven score," but that "we must assume with regard to this music the state, or better the activity, of a performer."

It has perhaps become difficult either simply to accept or to reject the use of the term "reading" with regard to what may be seen, and it would perhaps be timely to re-argue the uses of the term in such a context. Not everything to be viewed would presumably call for a reading if Barthes's strictures concerning music are to be followed. We would only become the performers of something to be seen if we were drawn not simply to redraw it or remake it – not for it to become the occasion of an inception of some career of emulation – but to find ourselves searching for some space within which some work, which we nevertheless could see, was

ISSN 0969-725X print/ISSN 1469-2899 online/02/010231-20 © 2002 Taylor & Francis Ltd and the Editors of *Angelaki*
DOI: 10.1080/09697250220142146

neither evident to us as such, in its meanings and effects, and could at least not yet, if ever, simply become the work we felt, and thought, it to be. The straits of some intelligible sensible. A visible which calls up something of the invisible, which is yet not this simple negative, but which, in being seen, is, for all that, not to be reduced to the same.

The modes of this work, of this engagement in a production of that which does not confirm existing modes of seeing and looking, may be responsive to different axioms from those which Barthes puts into play in his account of the second Beethoven. In particular, so far as what is yet to be seen and may have to be understood as to be looked at — to rehearse the phenomenological limits of the visible work — is concerned, we would presumably have to reflect with some care on the notion of the utopian. Arts of space would never simply be without space, neither something which was not distributed spatially nor, for someone, at some time, somewhere. The utopian would be of the body, as I read Barthes — a structure, actively constituted (and thus not belonging to any work by virtue of its figurative representation of the utopian, irrespective, that is, of our desire), of the ecstatic. From somewhere, now, here, as if nowhere.

What follows might be termed a variation on Barthes's argument concerning the body and the work of art, a variation on a theme of variations if his contention concerning the modern work is to be credited. It might seem that work by Mutlu Çerkez signals, in its apparent preoccupation with the musical, that Barthes's argument concerning reading and the utopian may have something to do essentially with music. If that work by Çerkez has various musics for its themes, then would it not be the musical, perhaps the rhythmic, which escaped the "image-repertoire" or the stage? The work of the modern work would thus be a sort of dissolution of its topics, in a paradoxical operative suspension of the transcendentality of rhythm. However, something else seems to me to be in play in Çerkez's work, something concerning the status of the remark about art and/or the arts which mimes a beginning of reflection on these, and thus bears on questions of ends, and which escapes from the already known themes of any variations on what a work may do or be. Variations without themes — variations on works of art irreducible to themes; or to particular arts, knowable as such in their generic belonging and stability.

For Barthes, the *Diabelli Variations* are exemplary of the work of Beethoven as modern. But if no work is merely an example of and for such exemplification, and may not thus by definition correspond to its thinkability, for Barthes there is yet the exemplification of that, the effective destruction of the idealisation of the body, as actor of role, support of mind or thought, as vehicle of soul. Such a body would nevertheless have to sustain a memory if what a work provoked by way of a sense of what was to be thought of what was sensed, which exceeded the thinkable, was not to go without trace. But what if the beginning of the break which Barthes senses in Beethoven's *Diabelli Variations* may not be delimited as such? Who is to say that, if it had not exactly been made before, it had not already been rehearsed in other works — but what is a break which may be rehearsed if not more and less than a break? What if what Barthes had been drawn to write was the very problematic of variation in commentary of any sense of the radically new or innovative? Or, indeed, a sense of the variation of the body which exceeded its known themes, genera, species or any other such mode of remark, not excluding the way the body as utopic may be understood to go beyond a sense of being situated, being or having a site?

The stakes of this enquiry into what I would term, of Çerkez's work, discomposure, may be stated with reference to another Beethoven. From the essay "The Origin of the Work of Art," by Martin Heidegger, comes a third Beethoven, a figure of some neglect, a neglect neither alleviated for long nor finally prevented when Heidegger notes that "Beethoven's quartets lie in the storerooms of the publishing houses like potatoes in a cellar." Music is mentioned in the following paragraph, in the introductory section of the essay concerned with characterising, against "the much-vaunted aesthetic experience," the "thingliness" of works of art and it is clear enough that Heidegger has been preparing for this argument with the remark about the quartets. Yet what succeeds hardly answers to what may be thought by way of thingliness. Heidegger pulls his argument together, against a threat of some dispersal, the very dispersal which Barthes's paradoxical utopic reading would remark. Protection against this dispersal is provided at the cost of a splitting and doubling of the thingliness of the musical work as score and as sonority:

> There is something stony in a work of architecture, wooden in a carving, coloured in a painting, spoken in a linguistic work, sonorous in a musical composition. The thingly element is so irremovably present in the art work that we are compelled rather to say conversely that the architectural work is in stone, the carving is in wood, the painting in colour, the linguistic work in speech, the musical composition in sound. "Obviously", it will be replied. No doubt. But what is this self-evident thingly element in the work of art?2

Heidegger summons an interlocutor as if to distract from two crucial issues, I think. One, Derridean: the of-the-voice character of the "linguistic work" (just before the earlier sentence about Beethoven's quartets, we have been invited to recall that "During the First World War Hölderlin's *Hymns* were packed in the soldier's knapsack together with cleaning gear" – my emphases) accompanying the specific putting-aside of the thingliness of the printed text – effectively leaving room for a denegation of writing; and, second, the role played by this splitting in protecting against the problematisation of performance in Barthes's sense so far as music, or any other art may be concerned – a protection against the acknowledgement of the division in the reception of sonorities, between what is instrumentalised and what may be doing the instrumentalising.3

It is thus – to cut a long story short, and to forego any more detailed account of Heidegger's essay – that Heidegger protects his argument against an involvement in the musical which Barthes characterises. And it is crucial, I believe, for that argument: if, for Heidegger, it is a painting by Vincent Van Gogh which exposes that the world of the peasant woman or man depends on an unthought of the reliability of equipment, and that this may be more than and/or other than emblematic of an epochal determination of subjectivity; then, this exclusion of a problematic of the musical – a splitting of the argument over "thingliness" refusing the division in the working of the conceptuality of that term, a refusal which apparently doubles Heidegger's position on the truth of the untruth of the work of art comprising an economy of the possibilities of "refusal" and "dissembling"4 – insists on a certain visibility, beyond and apart from the audible, suggesting why certain certainties are preferred concerning the exemplary use of visual art per se. Were there any such thing. It is not my purpose here to problematise Heidegger's selection of Van Gogh as example so far as an essentialising concentration on structuring of the to-be-seen and understood as such may be remarked.5 Other than I have already done so.

I shall not be following Heidegger in other ways either, I trust. Derrida asserts the "strong necessity of Heidegger's questioning" in "The Origin of the Work of Art," "even if it repeats here, in the worst as well as the best sense of the word, the traditional philosophy of art." The deconstruction of necessity itself, pursued by Derrida in "Restitutions of the truth in pointing," opening it to a necessity of a chance of chance – and thereby relativising necessity as "strong" or otherwise – would desediment the terms of the hold of the philosophical and tradition. Any such hold, necessitating such a repetition, would be opened to a putting into play of the work of the work which seemed to occasion such a repetition. As Derrida's polyvocal text suggests, to follow any order of questioning given by Heidegger's text would neither be able to protect that order of questions from something other than a question prompted by that which was, as art, in question nor to forestall the generation of a question which did not rely on the same as something other than a work.6 Any a priori determination of what may be questioned and what may become the occasion for something other than questioning would be to put the risk involved in understanding into a sort of trap concerning guarantees. And to protect a certain formalisation of the problematisation of reliance, reliability and symbolicity, so far as the thinking of art is concerned.

Those musical works which call for a reading, a sort of division in their being heard and even as being attended or attended to as performed or performable, seem at work in Heidegger's mention of music. That thingliness of the work of Beethoven would effectively be a sort of quasi-projection, dependent on a disavowal – perhaps the term for a particular mixed-up-ness of refusal and dissembling – of the appeal of music – not not Beethoven's, for Heidegger (his essay mentions no other) – and the answer given (though music would not be a question, precisely according to this responsiveness), which admitted an interruption of the determination of any epochal subjectivity which had not also problematised the relation to notation. The score as thing? Sonority as (more like) the thing? The workliness of the work of art, at least the musical work, may not have been posed *as a question*. In what follows, I may manage to suggest why – why, perhaps, the works of Beethoven solicited such a sense of what may lie hidden within the work which was not not of the earth – in the specific senses which Heidegger's analyses give this term, of something which cannot not appear to refuse or dissemble, but which may not be understood as such – and yet, still, not not of the work too. In the cellar of what would be an architectural work, the quartets of Beethoven resound with an unasked question of what would be being listened to if we were to hear what could be heard.

Perhaps it has been the role of the work of Mutlu Çerkez to assist me in distributing these questions in relation to the above reflections on music, having viewed and reflected on what I shall term – partly for convenience, partly in order to remark that relatedness to music and to the musical mentioned above and partly to recall the particular place of viewing – his compositions, shown, staged, put on view at the Istanbul Biennial, at the Beşiktas Cultural Centre, in the early autumn of 1999. Attributed to him, in wall labels and in the catalogue text provided at the entrance to the exhibition space,[7] I do not quite know that the composition of these compositions, of the elements of that which had been put on display, was his. Perhaps a curator, of this large and varied show of work, had had Çerkez's work hung: perhaps following instructions, more or less detailed, as to the positions of the images and things, from the artist himself; perhaps varying those instructions; perhaps acting as if not varying them. Or perhaps the artist had hung them, and it was only the particularities of the space, its position in the exhibition centre, its size, and colour, or texture, which had been decided on by the curator, who perhaps could not have allocated Çerkez any more space, nor easily have gone against the grain of apparently providing a sort of open cubicle, rectangular in its ideality, open on one of its sides (the shorter, perhaps to maximise hanging space) the walls of which had been painted white and lit, more or less evenly from above, within which operative space Çerkez's work had been put on show.

I do not know which individuals decided on the situation of viewing, or hung the work: or, as I might say, composed the compositions in that composition of compositions. I want to call this exhibition of things and images attributed to Mutlu Çerkez a composition (rather than, say, an installation), for the reasons mentioned above, and according to a sense that they may be something other than reason at stake in my capacity so to name it, or in my relative incapacity to name it otherwise. Is it, I wonder, just a coincidence – but the work also encourages me to ask what a coincidence would be – that the word composition names something both in the musical and the visual? Is it that there is some problematic of composition which exceeds any particular art, something which guides us to some question or questions essential to art, visual, musical or literary? A literary composition would be, like a musical one, something which at least delayed, if not suspended, its being assigned some reliable generic nomination. All literary and musical works would be compositions, perhaps in lieu of remarking this non-belonging – which tends also to suggest that such compositions may not quite make it as works; may not quite justify this nomination. But are all visual works compositions? Does a visual work have to be composed – rather than just have to have been composed – to be called a composition, have to have some value of being composed or of composing its viewer, in order to be referred to as a composition?

Yve-Alain Bois has argued that, little as they may have shared, both Duchamp and Mondrian knew that composition could not be disposed of so far as what may be known as visual art is concerned. One the composer of the image, the other of things beyond the image? My interest in Çerkez's work is provoked in part because this opposition is not confirmed by him (any more than it would be by a careful examination of the works of Mondrian or Duchamp), suggesting that the effects of acts of composition and thus of particular compositions spill over beyond themselves, in particular beyond even composing effects of compositions. Is this why the name arrives, that of Çerkez, Duchamp or Mondrian, to allow us to remark on or believe we may catch what falls outside the opposition of the organised and the unorganised?

Questions of naming and attribution recur in Çerkez's more or less composed composition of compositions. Titles may be included in what may be termed the elements of this work. Titles which begin *untitled:* ... , with a small "u"; uniformly and included, indeed, in some of the images, the colons followed by various dates. Inscribed in the work, they would perhaps occupy the space of an authorising legend. Perhaps not a myth – although maybe this is again something other than a coincidence of naming; for while these legends – in the sense of a caption inside the frame – would not be legendary – they should rather be informative, reliable and, indeed, they are, within the work, accompanied by the artist's name, printed before and alongside them, separated only by a punctuating stop-mark (not quite a full stop, these: not being preceded by a sentence or, indeed, even a phrase). Yet these legends are also contenders for the legendary in the sense of apparently occasioning, if not indeed belonging to, some story neither mythical nor obviously historical. For the dates which follow the *untitled:* works are yet to come. To enumerate these dates, there is 10 June 2018; there is 11 June 2018; then – but this is only a convenience of my narrative and narrating,

to vary and yet to give order – there are 16 June and 17 June of the same year. A leap, in a non-leap year. Four days not mentioned. But then, another jump, to 26 June 2018 (Fig. 1). Could there be a legendary of the future? Would it function in some essentially different way to a legendary of the past?

Perhaps there is a sort of common milieu offered here, of a sort of error over something which seems like an evidence. The legendary of the past – to pass for something which was other than myth – would have to proffer something up as if in evidence. In so doing, it may not be distinguishable from myth, functioning as a credible or reliable narrative of the past. But the legendary perhaps differs from the mythic in so far as there is something to be remarked as the excessive, an invitation to believe, the desire so to do being invoked and, as it were, circumscribed if not cancelled. To offer up these dates, as parts of the images, bearing titles of which those same dates – there is this correspondence, apparently inviting us to trace if also to retrace what we may be relying on here – are part both invokes a notion of a work of visual art and, in including that legend, along with something of the legendary, suggests a sort of erasure or cancellation, be it only partial, a part erasure, of that visual work. If, that is, a visual work were one which could be seen.

Elsewhere, in the composition to which I am referring, without having sought exhaustively to describe it (in naming it as such, with that remarked upon coincidence with music, it is as if I imitate the work I intend, nevertheless, to endeavour to describe), there is an element which less complexly bears a title beginning *untitled:* and this and two others which conclude with dates of days which, according to the calendar as I rely on it, have not yet occurred. A painting of a figure wearing a black dress, a figure of a woman wearing dark red lipstick, perhaps some pale face powder, perhaps some on her rather thin upper torso. But, titled *R.N.: 24 April 2029* (Fig. 2) and perhaps "super-titled" (to multiply the apparent coincidences of naming) *make-up design studies for an unwritten opera*, any such confident nominations slide. The dramatic contrasts of the shortish hair of the figure,

variations

Fig. 1. *untitled: 26 June 2018*

Fig. 2. *R.N.: 24 April 2029*

Fig. 3. *untitled: 14 July 2030*

whitish grey crossed with a darkish brown, along with the whitish face, the dark red lipstick, all are recrossed by the possibility of their making-up a figure to resemble a woman. The name is apparently withheld. Why this painting of this figure of a woman, there, as part of this composition? There, in the sense of apparently represented in this painting hanging there as part of the larger composition of elements – and I say apparently to do no more perhaps than to signal the possibility that there is no internal limit which is not in part at least to be taken up from beyond the frame which would segregate the representational truth of the image from its truth or excess of truth as there, as presentation, of a figure whose identity, whilst remarked from beyond the frame, may also be there to be varied: is she to be considered as someone who might play a character in the "unwritten opera" for which Çerkez has apparently also designed an overture curtain and for which he has provided stage furniture in the form of a Marshall stack, amplifier on top of loudspeakers (Fig. 3)?

If not, then what? She might be a sort of performer, but also a muse or a patron. Or some combination of these. A performer–muse; a muse–patron. Someone playing different roles at different times, in the project projected by this composition but which is also, and almost before it looks as if there might be a projecting of a project here, qualified by its dating as to come. The project which has been projected to be projected? Has it been projected?

Çerkez's work opens up here, in its structure and structuring of themes, to sustain the sense that projects of art have to get going by means of a certain artlessness of art, an artlessness which may be understood to be supplemented by a sense of what art might be and become if it worked like something which we can imagine works as art. Not without its problems, though, such a working of art is also, from within this work, qualified, as it must be, for there to be some sense that something here might work in a way which could be a way in which art, and not just techné, worked. Which would be, apparently, that it wouldn't just work.

Thus, projected as if from the beginning is a staging of an opera unwritten (Fig. 4). Would this still be (enough like an opera to be) an opera? We may not know. If only for the obvious reason, that it may not take place. But Çerkez's composition asks of us that we imagine what the taking place of an unwritten opera would be like. Could it be like an opera? By means of this projection of the staging of something like an opera, this rather project-like quasi-project introduces us to a sense of a role which seems important – following Barthes – if we are to grasp what is at stake in the problems of understanding things as works of art. A role divided perhaps between composer and conductor, between actor and director, between singer and actor, or between musician and dramatist; but, nonetheless, something which we are given to assume as a role, by virtue of being addressable as a body. As a productive/receptive performer of the same, which only operates as such by being performable but, yet, as soon as it has done so, has given itself away in a certain, limited but nevertheless irreducible plurality of modes. Not a role to play, but a play which exceeds any playing of a role which provides the milieu for any separation of actor from part or performer from piece.

The questions "what is art?" or "what is a work of art?" would always come along afterwards as if to enable separation, reassembling what may have been seen or heard or otherwise sensed as a work apart from such a milieu. Çerkez's work suggests that, in moving from

Fig. 4. *untitled: 15 January 2028*

something which might be a work to such questions, we may find that some comparison has already apparently been insinuated or insinuated itself, in the process of detachment from the work as a work. The provocation of the unwritten opera would be to remark the art which might become evident here in our reception, or reading, of a dance, a play, or our imaginary opera to come. What seems to come along as we take our pleasure or pains in whatever it might be that we have taken as something of a piece? A question of the work of this art done or in process, complete or incomplete as art, which nevertheless is something which is not – to reaffirm some of Heidegger's questions (following Derrida's problematisation of the localisability of issues of detachment from and by means of the work) if not the order of their asking – just a thing, and not just a worked upon or produced thing.

In question, then, is the very time of things being perceived and ideated as what could support such a questioning concerning their identity as art. It would thus be no mere accident that the musical came along here, music as a non-present sense of presence, apparently to mediate the questions of art and work which I have mentioned. Yet if the necessary was exposed to its own misprision as such, and there is no pure model here for the questions which seem to comprise aesthetic questioning (no pure model as a work; or work as model), then we may begin to reprise differently the milieu, or milieux, of the problematics of the comparative in the aesthetics of art, or the art of aesthetics.

More directly, the model of music may be questioned for the role it plays in articulating the milieu(x) of comparison between arts and works both for its apparently exemplary temporariness, as non-present coming and going, and for its closeness to, all but inseparable closeness with, its instruments – as something being done with something else, which has already blurred this boundary and set in motion a certain thought of comparison.

For Çerkez's work, with opera and with rock, assists us to and fro along the paths of comparison so that we may note that music is not one answer to a question of the sonic, and music itself cannot be adequately thought as what addresses us as sound any more than visual art may be adequately thought as what addresses us to be seen. Indeed, and not as a matter of uncovering what thought would excavate here, we may note that what is not to be seen of what may be seen, crossing the production of objects with the production of a subject, has already been given us, in part, as the heard. Though, in principle, and crossing in turn the necessary with the contingent, and memory with desire, as some part which may not be limited as such.

Such a position contends with two significant traditions of criticism, which are tributary to each other. The one argues that the arts are addressed to the senses; the other – apparently superfluously – that the arts should address themselves to the senses to which they address themselves.[8] To discover, however, the necessity in this second, apparently redundant argument is to uncross the necessary and the contingent in this account of sensing and of production which, in mixing up its "is" and its "ought," misses the possibilities of thinking given as and by the arts, as well, perhaps, as the impossibilities of thinking given by the same. For the necessity would be that there is and has been no necessity to the effect that the senses are (what are) addressed by what we call art. And that reflection on what may be called and thought of as art is haunted from the outset by a question of what is at work in what may be felt to have addressed us as a work of art.

Jean-Luc Nancy, at an important point in a recent essay, apparently answers this question, without quite posing it, by averting to an "irreducible material difference." Outlining a "scenario" in "three acts" – "Kant, Schelling, Hegel" – Nancy provides a provocative sketch of a history of the thought of the plurality of the arts, but it is one which remains in a sort of complicity with a rationalising account of plurality, one which appears to stage the thought of art as a thought of the failure to think, and as the necessary captivation before the same. Be it as the Kantian sublime, or the Schellingian representation of the absolute or the Hegelian absolute in exteriority, Nancy produces a sort of theatrical staging of the thought of art in which these several denouements are offered by a fundament of a double axiomatic of the thought of art: "The plurality of the arts is as essentially irreducible as the unity of art is absolute."9 This thought of irreducibility of the arts as a plurality is perhaps conserved by him, in the move to think that "irreducible material difference" mentioned above, a sublime of exteriorisation which would repeat and protect the thought of art as a human project. For it is as project, and project as protection, that thought apparently gets going here. Thought as the thought of all which is not quite thought, the model of which would be the apparent fact of expression, for Kant, or the activity of the same, for Hegel, which provides him, in his *Aesthetics*, with the principle of the exposition of the history of the arts as an exteriorisation.10

Significantly, this difficulty appears to be echoed in much of the work – on the sociology of art and of production, for example – which has succeeded Hegel, as Nancy appears to understand, exactly in taking the turn towards the "material" as what is given, in and by the arts, as irreducible – the material understood as generative and plural. But the difficulty returns, if this time at an apparently higher level: out there, somewhere, lies that which has been appropriated as ground, even if only as the ground of "difference." The work of art is understood thereby through the model of the protection and production of this ground of difference. Be it pre-comprehended as such, or apparently sort of post-comprehended, what is called and may be thought of as a work operates as model.

Perhaps this difficulty operates as a sort of occasion for work. Art for a gallery about a projected opera, or – to take up the strand of Çerkez's show which concerned itself with what might be thought of as a sort of opposite of the operatic, recorded bootleg, the low-cultural, apparently alternative and spectacular rock gig – about a series of singular performances – whichever: as it seems to me, following the links and breaks between the modes of showing and composing deployed in this "composition" as best I can, and remembering a certain sense of discomposure accompanying the beginnings of this, in the exhibition in Istanbul in the autumn of 1999, Çerkez has side-stepped that proposed as

johnson

solutions by Nancy to witness the difficulties of thinking that there might be something like art, be it absolute or otherwise, and something like the arts, however irreducibly plural, as what might be called art.

Perhaps this display of work seemed to some only imperiously to raise a sort of muffling curtain, as if that could stand in for what might be heard as the discourse on these questions of art and of the arts. And I might think this were the case, if there were not good enough reason, in the very reversal of any hyperbole of the curtain, veil or barrier which *untitled: 15 January 2028* (Fig. 4) enacts, by being the display of a certain failure of art as art which does not just reach out for its justification as a homage to music, but which, in thematising design, as in the legend, painted white against a black ground (the painting of which is shown, process suspended, with a figure, apparently the artist looking up, pathetically perhaps, but also perhaps defiantly, in a photograph in the catalogue text), "a design for the overture curtain of an unwritten opera," draws us apparently towards an impossible stage. The text, painted in white figures against a black ground, appears to exist as descriptum. What else would it be doing there? Two by two, the words spread out across a vertical axis, disposed in their standard reserves of space which defines the non-proportional use of a typeface. Oddly, then, it is precisely the apparent ordinariness of the ordering of the letters that encourages a viewing and reading of them which would allow them to evaporate – as if to reveal more of the black curtain behind them – in an ether of descriptive designation: as if to say, or show, that there is here a curtain, albeit one in a preliminary state, one we may identify as if with safety with the model, standard standard of design itself.

This curtain, there as if before the very beginning of a work, is not an overture curtain. A curtain of another curtain, in the place of a safety curtain, in front of the overture curtain proper? The overture, the gathered disposition of the themes of an opera, as Michel Leiris suggests it,11 may itself be accompanied by the lifting of a protective curtain to reveal the stage design proper: which itself, according to the logics of

variations

Çerkez's work, would have a curtaining function, framing the action, if not including another curtain per se. The design shown, if it were quite something which could be shown, would thus obscure the design to come. As if what were on show here was the work of an apprentice designer, only let loose on the preliminary and adjunct elements of work for the design of a production.

The fiction of rivalry here serves as a sort of feint towards, and a move away from, the topic of a topic, however. By which I mean that what opens here, in the showing of the curtain, which is not a showing, and is in part instead an obscuring, not a design, but the apparent proclamation of a design – indeed, which is also not a curtain, for it is not to be removed, not to reveal another work apparently, though this would be its subsidiary function – is a figuring of a sort of space of a work, which is not occupied, not by a work and not by a plan, a mode or a topic of a work, but which is traversed, crossed and recrossed, by the odd indicator of the comparative of one art with another, one mode of communicating with another, one loss of the same with another, and, at another moment, another loss of loss in a sort of apparent coincidence of the work with its announcement, or its advertisement (a term to be understood here outside of any generic stabilisation as any particular genre of images or objects), as well – apparently – as with any sort of discourse on the work which would conceptualise or, rather, be the possibility of a discourse about it. As itself or as art.

The referring to design, which Çerkez's work involves us in, leaves us either with a sense that this work is a sort of site of apprenticeship to the artistic as such, as in the case of the stagy version of something which mentions the operatic, or something which fakes and disguises the appropriation of the artistic, as in the covers or cover-like images for the recordings of musical performances by Led Zeppelin. As such, it is not clear that, according to Çerkez's composition, from its detailed structures of referring to its particular overall disposition, that art is betrayed or salvaged by design, not excluding the design of exhibitions. The nature of the space to which the curtain refers us both indicates and mentions a particular theatrical space. But it is one which is not yet and perhaps would not be ready to supervene on the space of its showing, as given to be imagined, negotiated and noted, in its reserving of a space which may only be reconstructed.

It is this space which, in borrowing from music, performance and musical theatre, which remains, for me, the especially crucial stake of this work. For what might we say about the spaces mentioned and indicated here? Perhaps just that they are those spaces where the issue of the becoming generic of certain activities may be retried, both after the event – given any particular diversity of the arts in effect and known, in some degree, as such – and again in the light of some unknown becoming of particular practices. Not yet a particular, however, a chance is given to sense the matrix out of which would emerge any such possibility of activity. In effect, therefore, the work of this composition offers itself to us as an as yet uncompleted process of a discovery of a plurality which may not be fulfilled – not of possibilities, given or pre-given, but of what we may do; how we may work, perform, disaggregate our possibilities or reaggregate them.

To conclude this critical exercise, therefore, which would not be, as an exercise, some simply regularly undertaken reworking of the body, according to some pre-given model or thought of health, I shall return to a possible modelling of the play between music and art, between the conceptuality and corporeality of such a comparison, as Çerkez's show suggests it. A sort of double modelling, which would traverse the very possibility of a modelling of the double.

The lookalike Led Zeppelin LP covers give us this much, taking up the ambiguities of the portrait entitled *R.N.: 20 April 2029*, to press them to a limit. For this lookalikeness cannot be told apart from that which would be, for the collector of album covers, if not of the LP recordings themselves, the thing itself. Without exhaustive archival work, and without recourse to supplementary discourses of verification of the evidential as such, I would say that that which bears the title *Killing Floor* in the catalogue (and did so in one of the several wall labels on the occasion of the exhibition of the work in Istanbul when I saw it) looks like an example of the cover for a recording which could, according to the traditional protocols of the deciphering of LP covers, be what could pass as an authentic recording by Led Zeppelin called *Killing Floor* (Fig. 5). Without the legend *untitled:* ... of this or that date to come, the thing-in-a-frame looked enough like an example of an album cover as could have been obtained by the artist – who is represented examining LPs in a record shop in a photograph included in the catalogue (Fig. 6) – to pass as such. The surface of the object/image framed, and reproduced in the catalogue, appears to have been worn away, the red of the ground of the cover design disappearing to reveal, inconveniently enough for the propriety of the terms figure and ground quite to apply without question or doubling, a white ground of the ground. Not just support, it is also what of the image reveals that, however frank, clear, simple or honest, or whatever, the design or any element thereof may be said to be, that which is produced goes not without the possibility of supporting traces other than those that would belong to the design as such.

The erosion of the surface of the LP cover proffers a sort of subcultural patina. But it is also, as erosion and as part of what is gallery art, a subculture of patina itself: an erosion of accretion as erosion. As such, it empties the concept

Fig. 6. Photograph of artist

of patina of its reassuring function in discourses of authentication, reminding us of an exposure to wear and tear as damage and as loss. Moreover, with this wear and tear not being directly attributable to any over-attentive or negligent user of the works – the *Killing Floor* cover eroded in an arc as a record inside would have eroded it – we are also at odds with the classic framing of the visual arts as arts of the unique object guaranteed as such, as Gérard Genette has it, following Nelson Goodman, as an "autographic" rather than "allographic" art. Such a distinction is sustained apparently to distinguish between literary and visual objects, which are not quite – as Genette is well aware – protected in their discreteness by the quantitative, enumerative judgements implied in the opposition between the unique and the multiple.[12]

It would hardly exhaust Çerkez's work, I think, to continue to point it towards the problematics of the identification or evaluation of the unique or the multiple, as what I have said about the theatrical and impossible space above may be taken to imply. But let us see what Genette's clearer distinction, between the allographic as

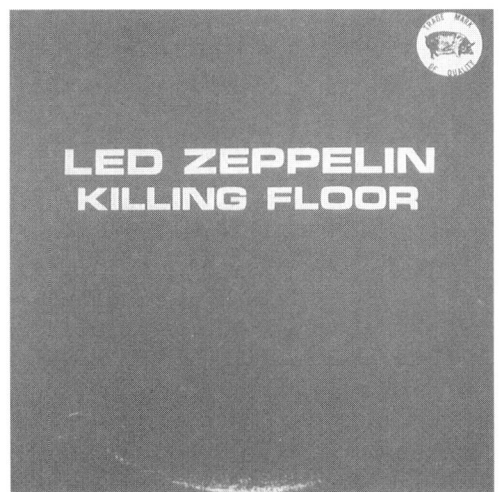

Fig. 5. *Killing Floor*

those arts which result in objects which may, as ideal, be "exhaustively defined by their specific identity (since they do not possess a numerical identity distinct from it), and … autographic (material) objects [which] are essentially defined by their numerical identity, or, as Goodman says, by their 'history of production,'"13 suggests in relation to Çerkez's pirate-like procedures, and their more-or-less excessive variants in the exhibition of what looks like, according to the categories of art criticism, a found object.

In question, here, then would be not only the stakes of a philosophy of art or of the arts, but also the possibility that such an activity or activities may be found or may find themselves to be indistinguishable from their objects – which would, therefore, and according to an essentially philosophical scruple, no longer be distinguishable as its or their objects at all. A philosophical scruple, but one which could not be limited in its causes or its effects to anything pre-comprehended as philosophy or the philosophical.

Lest this sound too much like a rehabilitation of criticism, let it be noted also that this want of the philosophical would also, in principle, include that of criticism, as well as of art or the arts as such. The want would not be essential, and would not therefore be supplied by the constitution of any mode of discourse, or thought of thought. Lest this seem too negative as a series of strictures, let me add that such a seriality would be prescribed to the indications of something like a becoming-practice and a becoming-pragmatic which would be at stake in this; and which, in principle, and apart from a comparative critique and evaluation, would tend to be *indicated* in the comparison of one art with another.

Çerkez's work pirates designs, praying on their repeatability, their allographic character, to follow Genette. But in so doing, in so parasiting designs for recordings, authorised or otherwise, of music which they, as designs, would designate as such, they also indicate an excess of this designation: we can no longer tell, if we ever could, what in the musical is being protected or exposed by these cover-versions of covers, or, indeed, in such of these covers as may be imagined to have been covers which is exclusive of what would have been fetishised, desired as object, as the collectable, repeatable object or event, which was, in its turn, exclusive of its desirability as a spatial phenomenon. Quite simply, and as any collector of recorded music would know, the line between the work and its performance is opened up to an uncontrollable delectation, in which all and any of the passions which music may provoke may not find their moorings in a knowledge of the work. For what is being collected in the collection of recordings? Some having been present at the event itself? So Çerkez's work, concentrating on bootlegs, would suggest.

And yet, what the apparently *echt Killing Floor* cover puts in play, read as document, is that what is being collected here is also the very blurring of the line between the performance as authentic event, belonging to the art of the artists themselves, and the artistic as the very occasion of such a blurring. For, as the catalogue informs us, *Killing Floor* is an eponymously entitled recording, including a version of the song "Killing Floor" by the blues singer-composer Howlin' Wolf (aka Chester Burnett). This version of the song, says the catalogue:

> was recorded by Led Zeppelin
> with reference to the Robert Johnson song
> "Travelling Riverside Blues"
> and released on the album *Led Zeppelin II* as
> "The Lemon Song"
> sometimes credited to Burnett
> sometimes credited to Page, Plant, Jones, Bonham.

Sometimes, it seems, the artists of the recording no longer knew what it was that they were recording: something of their own, perhaps, but something which sometimes seemed as if it would be better credited to another. Çerkez seems not to judge this in a judiciary fashion; and is rather contented, if I am to credit him with the authorship of such notes, with indicating a sort of doubling of authentication of composition here.

For, as it was noted above, the ambiguities of the authorship of the elements of Çerkez's composition, the composition of the compositions, seems to belong also to what has been recorded and packaged and designated by the designs he has found and/or pirated. This remark, in the catalogue, which is also another composition of the elements of the composition, discrete as they seem to be, if thereby, in each of their occurrences, in principle, if not also in fact, innumerable, seems to infect with uncertainty not just the border between one work and its outside, or one work and another, but also, and perhaps more generally, between a work and its inside. To whom or to what – genre, or type of type – might such a work belong?

Hyper-specificity: to find that a work, which is no less a work to be thought than any of the others, may not be thought under the aegis of any one particular art and, indeed, that it seems to trespass, as the specific work that it is, on the modes of apprehension apparently more proper to another art than to the one it more obviously, as an example, belongs. And I am tempted to add … hyper-materiality.

But let this return to the traditions of the philosophy of art and of the arts which Nancy endeavoured to summarise and to criticise that I mentioned above. Such might be the "irreducible material difference" of which he writes, this plurality of the substantial, of the underlying, or of the excess of the concepts of the same. Not present in and as recordings, and thereby corrupting of the possible uniqueness of the work, there is nevertheless a chance that this plurality, that of which there is some irreducibility, will be communicated. To be seen, read, listened to, if not heard. Something which leads us away from the status of the unique, autographic object, if not towards any resolution of these ontological difficulties.

No less unique, the so-called autographic work would be, and from the outset of its having been begun, characteristically exposed to time. It might thus, as in a recent account, be conceived, as a Husserlian "temporal object," as intersecting with a sort of category of "pictorial objects."[14] But this intersection may be more precisely characterised too. The object-work is exposed to erosion, as in the example of the apparently worn "Killing Floor" cover. But as the futural dating of Çerkez's compositions suggests, by anticipating and, as it were, overleaping time as if it were an interval to come, there is also a possibility not of erosion but of accretion: of an addition to the object which a picture, as an ideal in and of itself, would seem to stand against. In the light of this, the use of the name of the artist alongside the date in these titles beginning *untitled:* performs an auto-parasiting of the artist's signature which testifies, indeed, to nothing so much as the want of certainty that any actual signing of a work, of visual art, conceived of as the production of unique, autographic objects, is not at the same time a part of a work the whole of which ought to render such signing superfluous and, as such a superfluity, in effect an obscuring accretion to the work. Çerkez's solution to this difficulty is apparently to offer up his name as a part of a regularised series of figures, regularised, that is, by a selected typeface – by the typeface and by its selection.

At the same time, however, the act – not the choice itself, but the act of inscribing of those of the more or less unclosed series of "untitled:"s dependent on the act of selection – exposes the production of a mark to its machinic repetition, a repetition which is, in turn, a condition of the impossibility of a signature as a single, indivisible, unrepeatable mark.

It is as if whatever comprises Çerkez's work cannot get going without another signature or signature-effect. We might consider the several designers responsible for the album covers of bootleg recordings of performances of the band Led Zeppelin. That of Led Zeppelin, of the four members of the band, or of Howlin' Wolf, who was really Chester Burnett: in which case, the play of signatures opens out to a sort of abyss, between performer and composer. And it is this most importantly which Çerkez's work stresses, in any possible rivalry with the musical, I think, one which has its auratic confirmation in the use of the Marshall amplifier, which tellingly carries a version of the signature-like logo well known from the stages of electrically amplified sound production and projection. Apparently more modest than Marshall himself, the eponymous inventor of the Marshall amplifier, in so far as it sometimes bears a mark which does not, apparently, mimic the handwritten, Çerkez's work nevertheless might also – and according to the same logic of comparison – be understood, from within the discourses of the evaluation of the visual arts, as quite perfectly immodest: his name as if produced by a hand which seems to mimic the geometrical without fault, as when Vasari praises Giotto for being able to produce a circle by hand.15

In the non-milieu of the simulacral, there would be no segregation of the true from the false, including that of the truly or falsely modest or immodest. Perhaps this is why Çerkez's work has attracted the attentions of an author who reiterates Baudrillard's contention — now, apparently, out of date — that "2000 will not take place," and reads this to indicate that there is now, as perhaps never before, no chance of the happening of an event, a condition which Çerkez's work paradoxically confirms, at least in so far as it is not simply the same event as this contention. (If it were, the comparison would not obviously be possible.) Offered up to the archiving forces of the art press, which dates things in a fashion which the author of this piece on Çerkez's work fails to note, and which would presumably be part of the same logic of the production of sameness in so far as that press does this, that work is apparently prepossessed for a treatment of the problem of the sameness of the same by means of a certain thought of the future as the futuristic, as the sameness of that genre.16

Against this, we may note that what enables the production of this sort of sameness, in the case of Çerkez as well as in the genre of such texts as circulate under the generic nomination of science fiction, is what we may think of as the reproductive, the production of the multiple, the text as the apparently non-appearing, and disappearing, support for this fiction of fiction; of what a fiction is, or would be. Returning thereby to the question of the alignment of the multiple and the allographic, we may begin to remark the particular force of Çerkez's compositions — in the various possible senses which this phrase may convey — and their concern with the musical.

Would music — if there were such — not already have resisted the very distinction which Genette repeats, drawing on Goodman, between the auto- and the allographic? Not in the name of the autographic, music would be neither the manuscript score or even, at another threshold, the unique performance, heard or recorded; nor, yet, would it merely be the performability of its scoring, or its mere repeatability as phrase, heard once, as it were, and played "by ear." As this idiom suggests, by comic relief, the process of instrumentalising would have to be considered as immanent to music, to music as an art. This would be as true for anything like song or music of the voice as for any other "type" of music understood as thinkable — not simply or even as recognisable — as a type determined by its instruments. The musician plays a part, perhaps, but not only one which cannot be done without without loss of a sense that music would be music as this risk of loss, between the autographic and the allographic, perhaps the very risk which what we may come to call music would have performed for us.

I shall not say, or insist, that there is nothing to be called music which is not marked by this sense of a risk of a loss of loss. It is not my point, here, either to produce a new treatise on music or to regulate the uses of the term. I cannot, however, quite make the points, about Çerkez's work, I feel drawn to make, without endeavouring to understand something of the frame of reflection on music, be it as sound, composition or the question of the roles of the instrument, even as indicated by that work. Indeed, all of these issues may be understood to be at work in Çerkez's work, in ways which are over-determined by something inescapable, irrespective of the thematisation of the comparison between music and any visible, or visual art. The stakes of such a comparison — neither an analogy nor, even, a homology but, less and more than this, what I have been calling an "indication" — Genette gives us a clue towards, I believe, by rewriting the distinction between the autographic and the allographic as one in which what seems to count, so far as the former is concerned, is one in which what he calls the "history of production" is to be understood at least as part of the mode of apprehension of the work. If it is to be thought of as a work of art.

So I understand him to be arguing. Such a "history" would then, in principle, exceed any already written text; and it would be something like the "mode" of its "writing," its production of some iterability — to follow Derrida — which could not – again in principle – be reduced to any previously existent "mode of production," as a phrase in any discourse pre-comprehended as such – or as such-and-such a discourse.[17] The musical work of art would be that which tended to give rise to this question of history, even if it also tended to seem to supply something in place of an answer.

Thus, it seems to me, Çerkez's work: its compositions, both its apparently discretely framed elements and their combinations, actual, in any given-space, as well as in terms of their place in a project intended before or after any fact of their existence (their effects as "reproduction" or even as "realist," to cite the apparently repelling poles of a classificatory thought of pictures and images, not acting conclusively to confirm one account of the genesis of this project from within the series; and this not just because of the dating), risk losing themselves on the one hand to music and on the other to design. The one insures against the real risk of the other? Really? Is it not that there is no taking of a risk? The rhetoric of the idiom is itself a trace of the performativity of risk, which is itself not to be grasped, taken from some given situation to be spent in another. Risks may be taken. We are not, essentially, risk takers.

The philosophy of action is broached here again, and it might be what I had to "say" in this essay. I mentioned above "something like a becoming-practice and a becoming-pragmatic." This would be neither a philosophy of practice in art, comprehending what has been or prescribing what may be done; nor a pragmatism, a philosophy that one does one's best, or one's worst, with what one may do something with. More a sense of pragma as naming neither merely what had to be done like that nor, indeed, what had to be done, but something which gives us something more like a sense of a model that something may be done at all – the philosophical problems with pragmatism being more of the order of the difficulties of understanding that idealisation is protected from critique, remains pre-critical, than that that it is really worldly or whatever.[18]

This "becoming-practice" and "becoming-pragmatic" would be what draws critical attention. (Perhaps art is not much more than that which draws such attention. And life would then be what was mistaken for the grounds of this sort of contracting.) In preliminary fashion, as if to "cope" with any such stabilisation of a desire to know what is at stake in and as art, comes this possibility of the thematisation of art by art. Such thematisation, however, is also other than a thematisation if the preceding is the case, for no art may be reduced to thematisation. The mode of any such stabilisation of its apprehension as this term might imply would also have not to be just any old mode, not just the same thematisation as any other. Çerkez's work about music may be of the order of rivalry and of homage. There may have been no intention for it to be otherwise.

Yet, irresistibly perhaps, two other strands may be unravelled from what may be reflected on here, two possibilities of a sort of truce apparently between modes of address and modes of apprehension. Uncannily enough, what Çerkez's work shares with music is a sense that neither may be thought of as sound, as what may seem to address us as that which is to be listened to. Çerkez's compositions, in whatever *combinatoire* of exhibition, may draw attention to this as something touched upon with melancholy: whatever this work is, it is not something which addresses us as the to-be-listened-to. Sound may be caught up in it – a line, a colour, may echo for us with recollection of sound, even if we cannot authenticate this memory. Music may be that which, in so far as it does seem to address us as something to be listened to, is constrained to secondarise this melancholy – most musical melancholy would be of the order of the melancholy that something, about a tone, a note or an instrument, may not have been heard. In the prescribed or performed sequence of the musical composition or work, the effects of recurrence or return of motifs, phrases, notes or timbres may be accompanied by an attention that what has come again may not have been heard because it has been listened to in a particular way. A kind of tragedy of the performance of the musical. Perhaps there have been performances which draw attention to the ways in which what may be performed as the to-be-listened-to may have addressed its audience with an impossibility of hearing what addresses – some movement of the body, some aspect of the instrument. Even if these were visible, they would not, as impossibles of some musical event or work, be what addressed us as this not to-be-listened-to – this enregistration of visible marks and figures, or some composition of compositions that may bear the name of Mutlu Çerkez.

What may have seemed like a clue in the term composition becomes enigmatic, no longer a clue.

Neither a melancholy nor a to-be-mourned, this improbable work touches on a problematic of the body, of its otherness, generating a sense, out of these composings with the musical, of awkwardness. Several square images, or framed found or produced objects. Another a portrait, in a classical portrait format. (And there are, in the series, though not shown in the exhibition I visited, landscapes in classical landscape format, if also a landscape, as well as a self-portrait, in portrait format.) The Marshall stack – more rectangular-like things. And the "design for an overture curtain for an unwritten opera" is, of course, rectangular too; although, in being something like a design, if not a design itself, it can vary in its dimensions, perhaps to fill the space of the end wall of an open-on-one-side space. Moving between these framings, and their greater or lesser availability of dimension as such – the frames of the album cover and pirated album cover designs may appear present and in a sort of proportion with what they frame, smaller, less noticeable; but the space framing the curtain distends, moves out of view and out of such estimations. One source of some awkwardness. And as we move from one type of to-be-looked-at thing to another which also has to do with the musical, this awkwardness is as if thematised. As the composition of these perhaps predictably composed things perhaps predictably lacking a certain music in their arrangement together.

Yet whatever they may be thought to lack, they also rejoin the question of the musical as that which hands on a sense of space. Not of the order of the geometrical and its reactive reformations, there is a sense of space which has not belonged somewhere; has perhaps been mysteriously invented, or found, but which does not belong somewhere.

This is what Heidegger seems to me to resist understanding, in his tale of the thingliness of Beethoven quartets, lying around "in the storerooms of the publishing houses like potatoes in a cellar." The figure splits: potatoes like notes, hidden away in the darkness, as if shaken from their staves or stems, rootless, unread and perhaps unreadable roots – as if the musical work might only by chance be an unreadable text; but also, the potato-quartets, lying around in cellars, are reclaimed for built space, a sort of crypt of what may be constructed as a work. The sense of space arising from a musical work is rendered as if in relation to other created spaces, of authorship to which a name may be more or less reliably given. But the potato, though it arises from the earth, and even shows the earth jutting up in it, does not quite respond to the structuring of the untruth of truth, as Heidegger proposes it. The double concealment, of refusal or dissembling, is both resisted and multiplied by the tuber. The potato is neither a rootless body nor a bodiless root; instead, it is a body which exceeds the fall into belonging, via the reliance on the reliability of the equipmental, and falls short of the dream of an erectable, resurrectable body.

This would be the body which music transmits: the body caught up in instrumentalising itself, even via the instrumentalising of things as instruments, is yet that which communicates about more than itself. The very space of this relation, between instrumentalising and the instrumentalised? Except that this would be open to a play of the unisolatable, a space which does not lie between one limit and another; but which allows for a sense of body which moves across limit, as if towards the illimitable. Horizonless, such a sense of space touches on what is given by what may be reassembled as Çerkez's work, the space produced between the mention of design and the veiling of the stage, a space which infects all the other elements of the "unwritten opera" project which thereby partake of this chiasmus of the sense of project. And the pirated or borrowed bootlegs, in citing recordings of what may not, as performances, be recorded as sound, hang around like enigmas of when and where a composition may be said to take shape, as well as take place. In that photograph in the catalogue mentioned above, the artist stands as if sorting through a stack of record sleeves. Looking down, apparently intently, was he wondering what of what is recorded on the record may show in what is to be seen on the sleeve? That something would not be caught in the notation of a piece, something which would make the formal and legal questions of the authorship of music unstabilisable if not irrelevant: perhaps this is the dream of Çerkez's own work – both to give shape to the site of the giving of shape, and to let that space wander, even before the showing of the work, wherever it is shown, is finished and the compositions, variations on the work of art, packed away to be re-composed elsewhere.

All of the above has perhaps run too close to the problematic of the synaesthetic, without mentioning it. The literature is extensive. Characteristically, Baudelaire has been taken as a source, a beginning point for this figure of what art and the arts may provoke. Nancy mentions the "appeal" for a moment of "sensuous unity" and a sense of a response to this from "synesthetic unity or 'correspondences' (Baudelaire, Verlaine, Debussy, among others)." Nancy goes on to note an "obvious" correlation between art as art or "'art' in the singular and of the reference to 'genius' as well as with the postulate of 'total art.'" He then goes on to argue:

> But one quickly realises that perceptive integration and its lived experience would be more correctly located at the opposite extreme from artistic experience and that poetic "correspondences" do not belong to the register of perceptive unity, which has no knowledge of "correspondences" as such and knows only integrated simultaneity.[19]

Nancy cites an informational model of the brain, an organ – although the following position effectively de-negates any difference between brain as organ and as processor – which "puts to work only one per cent of the approximately twenty megabits of sensory information it receives every second." Correspondences may have a place, it seems, in art, but they do not afford an access to artistic experience as such. Rather, they provide the key for understanding non-artistic perception perhaps: the "integration" which purportedly characterises "lived experience" which would be specifically exceeded by a sense of correspondence, a sense that one sense "calls up" another.

Nancy lets go too much in this argumentation, it seems to me. For what is broached, in Baudelaire's "Correspondances," the fourth poem from "Spleen et Ideal" of *Les Fleurs du Mal*, is a sense of a work which may not be stably related either to experience as such or to the type of work it may be understood to be. The one dislocates the other. The borderline status of correspondence as artistic would, then, be precisely to the point, one which would be retraceable in the thematisation of relations between different arts.

The poem "Correspondances" opens with a violently arbitrary identity, which may perhaps be taken to argue for the total work and sustain the arbitrariness of genius, but which may be understood rather to state the problem. "Nature is a temple," one which may be, according to Walter Benjamin's reading, taken to sustain a decadent sense of art – an art which would retraverse the problem of the becoming-ritual of art. For Benjamin, "What Baudelaire meant by *correspondences* may be described as an experience which seeks to establish itself in crisis-proof form."[20] Baudelaire seems to have retraced the becoming art of art, and, apparently in paranoid style, found himself trying to protect against its failure to become such. Benjamin's retracing of the history of art, in emergence from and falling back into ritual, entails a revaluation of beauty. What Benjamin's reading releases, for us, would be the very breach within Baudelaire's poetic argument which re-exposes that violent identity of the opening to a play which escapes the description of "correspondences" by the poem, but which may not fail to provoke the movement towards the same, even if it is not one which may be completed as such. Playing between the title and the main text of the poem, we find that Baudelaire's poem turns into a variation on poetic composition itself, one which is at odds with its philosophical comprehension. Like

variations

Çerkez's compositions, it too plays a game of comparison between arts, between writing and music, an art of colour and even of the making of perfumes:

> The pillars of Nature's temple are alive
> and sometimes yield perplexing messages;
> forests of symbols between us and the shrine
> remark our passage with accustomed eyes.
>
> Like long-held echoes, blending somewhere else
> into one deep and shadowy unison
> as limitless as darkness and as day,
> the sounds, the scents, the colors correspond.
>
> There are odors succulent as young flesh,
> sweet as flutes, and green as any grass,
> while others – rich, corrupt and masterful –
>
> possess the power of such infinite things
> as incense, amber, benjamin and musk,
> to praise the senses' raptures and the mind's.[21]

To write has, for Baudelaire, become to detail the displacement of its models. Trees give out confused speech. Perfumes, colours and sounds fade into each other like echoes. Metaphor may not be controlled by simile, and what seems literal may only be an unstable mixing of the two. Perhaps the sense of smell may be relied on to re-found writing across the abysses of rhetorical modes? Flesh of children tells of this *crise de vers*, with its suggestion of a disturbed patrilineality, a *crise perverse*. Soft as oboes and green as meadows, the object of the comparison waivers, be it odours, flesh or writing. But perhaps we may forget forgetting in the suggestions of the infinite of other fragrances? Perhaps; but for the reminder of the displacement of voice in the singing of these "transports" of spirit and sense.

To finish with this poem would be to have lost the sense of "des sens," the sense of this phrase as the senses *and* the senses as sense. Neither reading may be relied on. Between them, indications of the unreadability of experience – either as Benjamin's "Erfahrung" or "Erlebnis"[22] – and, via the abyssal comparisons of writing, a generation of intelligible sensibles which escapes any single truth of reading.

Variations, in excess of organon.

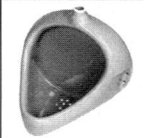

notes

With thanks to Gregg Lambert, Simon Malpas, Zafer Aracagök and Özge Ejder.

Mutlu Çerkez's work is reproduced by kind permission of the Anna Schwartz Gallery, Melbourne, Australia.

1 Roland Barthes, "Musica Practica" in *The Responsibility of Forms: Critical Essays on Music, Art, and Representation*, trans. Richard Howard (Berkeley and Los Angeles: U of California P, 1985) 261–66 (265).

2 Martin Heidegger, "The Origin of the Work of Art" in *Poetry, Language, Thought*, trans. Albert Hofstadter (New York: Harper, 1975) 15–87 (19).

3 See Derrida's account of Heidegger's resistance to the two-handedness of the typewriter as figuring a work of writing in configuring the body in "Geschlecht II: Heidegger's Hand" in *Deconstruction and Philosophy: The Texts of Jacques Derrida*, ed. John Sallis (Chicago: U of Chicago P, 1987) 161–96.

4 Heidegger specifies the modes of the concealments of unconcealment, refusal and dissembling, towards the end of the fourth section of his essay ("The Origin of the Work of Art" 53–54). Their limited interplay, resistant in effect to the unknown of their specific co-operation, is confirmed in his account of the "establishment" of the "Openness of the open." See, in particular, the passage beginning, "The more solitary the work, fixed in the figure, stands on its own and the more cleanly it seems to cut all ties to human beings …" (66). Music would be that which even when written, "fixed" in its figures, could not apparently "stand" on its own and would not "cut" such ties as could not be comprehended in an economy of refusal and dissembling.

5 But cf. Antonin Artaud, "Van Gogh: The Man Suicided by Society" in *Artaud Anthology* (San Francisco: City Lights, 1983) 135–63. As if fulfilling Van Gogh's wish to be a "musician with colours," Artaud, for whom "an exhibit of Van Gogh's paintings is always an historical event, not in the history of painted things but in plain historical history," writes – in the same sentence – of "a Van Gogh painting – brought out into the sunlight, and put directly back into view, / hearing, touch, / smell, / onto the walls of an exhibition hall – finally launched anew into present actuality, reintroduced into circulation" (140).

6 See Jacques Derrida, "Restitutions of the Truth in Pointing [*Pointure*]" in *The Truth in Painting*, trans. Geoffrey Bennington and Ian Macleod (Chicago: Chicago UP, 1987), 255–382 (262–64). Derrida writes of the "fit … clinging tightly but flexibly" of "question-idioms" (264), problematising the relations between the work, language, corporeality and questioning.

7 The book-text Mutlu Çerkez, *a design for the overture curtain/of an unwritten opera/and/stage furniture/props/for an unwritten opera/and/make-up design studies/for an unwritten opera/and variations on album covers/for bootleg recordings of Led Zeppelin* (Melbourne and Istanbul: Anna Schwartz Gallery and 6th International Istanbul Biennial, 1999) (unpaginated) is not simply a reliable document of that exhibition, as the recognition of its antedating that event would signal. There are photographs included in this text which alter and develop meanings and effects of the exhibition and, thus, vary the work in a site whose characteristics have been important in art practice since, say, Dan Graham's *Works for the Pages of Magazines* from 1965 to 1969: on which, and other conceptualist works for bound volume spaces, see Anne Rorimer, "Siting the Page: Exhibiting Works in Publications – Some Examples of Conceptual Art in the USA" in *Rewriting Conceptual Art*, eds. Jon Bird and Michael Newman (London: Reaktion, 1999) 11–26. The contention that "By placing works in magazines, [Graham] substituted the ideational space of the magazine page for that of the enterable exhibition space" (15) supports a notion of the page as a "self-reflexive" space (26), a sort of redemption of an ideal of reflection to be given by art. In the consideration of Çerkez's work which follows, I argue for an aporetic conceptualisation of the sense of site generated by a work of art, in keeping with the problematisation – implied by the use of the page – of relations between work and the subsidiarity of any related materials.

8 By way of example here, we could read Clement Greenberg's account of the "historical tendency" of the modern in art apparently towards the establishment of "its own *difference* from other art practices," as Victor Burgin's "The End of Art Theory" has it, "a culmination of the Enlightenment project of organising knowledge" (in *The End of Art Theory: Criticism and Postmodernity* [London and Basingstoke: Macmillan, 1986] 140–204 [177]): but this is something which, were it ever to have been possible, and something which we could be through with, would not have seemed to require its very isolation and identification in critical work as such. A sort of protection, unbeknown to those in the thrall of a desire for a grounding axiom to the question of the work of art as addressed to any particular sense, knowable as such apart from what may have been sensed, of the impossible.

9 Jean-Luc Nancy, "Why Are There Several Arts and Not Just One? (Conversation on the Plurality of Worlds)" in *The Muses*, trans. Peggy Kamuf (Stanford: Stanford UP, 1996) 1–39 (9).

10 Nancy, "Why Are There Several Arts and Not Just One?" 8–9.

11 See Michel Leiris, "Opera: Music in Action" in *Brisées: Broken Branches*, trans. Lydia Davis (San Francisco: North Point, 1989) 260–66. I am indebted to Leiris's account of opera as "music in action": not, it is argued, any single action nor reducible to any precise analytic of its instruments, but something entailing a view of theatre as a space of "operations" and a production of "a sort of sonorous space" to be characterised by "the striking plurality" of the sources of sounds (264).

12 See Gérard Genette, *The Work of Art: Immanence and Transcendence*, trans. G.M. Gosharian (Ithaca and London: Cornell UP, 1997). Genette's text situates itself carefully in relation to Goodman's *Languages of Art* and pursues what seems a necessary argument against Goodman's nominalism – something is a work of art if it has been or may be called a work of art – by indicating the recurrence, across the incidence of any such acts, of the co-implication of the transcendent and immanent as indicators of the problematics of the ontology of art, which Goodman effectively avoids. The debate concerning Borges' account of the text of Don Quixote, transcribed by Pierre Menard, which Goodman excludes from consideration as a work of art, indicates that the author of *Languages of Art* would not admit a case of a literary work which threatened the categorical assignation of literature to the allographic. Genette's defence of the necessity of considering the claim of a rewritten version of Cervantes' text as a work is perhaps at odds with a limited version of what may, from within the literary, provoke a sense of the immanence of the work, but which may not be divided into an innumerable plurality. On the "inexhaustible story of Pierre Menard," see Genette, *The Work of Art* 246.

13 Genette, *The Work of Art* 22.

14 See George Collins, "Incidence of Instant and Flux on Temporal and Pictorial Objects," *Tekhnema: Journal of Philosophy and Technology* 4 (1998): 26–61: borrowing the definition of temporal objects from Husserl – "objects that are not only unities in time but that also contain temporal extension in themselves" (52) – insisting, apparently quite correctly, that neither painting nor photography can be a temporal object, "though [their] aim is" (54).

15 Giorgio Vasari, *Lives of the Artists: A Selection*, trans. G. Bull (Harmondsworth: Penguin, 1965) 64–65. Vasari relates how Giotto's drawing, with a brush dipped in red ink, of "such a perfect circle," designed to impress the Pope as to the artist's superiority over others for a commission, relied on a mimicry of a compass, Giotto "closing his arm to his side ... so as to make a compass of it." Vasari also notes the circulation of the saying "You are more simple than Giotto's O" or "tondo" in Tuscany ("the Tuscan word meaning both a perfect circle and also a slow-witted simpleton" [65]), analysing its significance as concerning a judgement of the scepticism of the messenger asked to carry the drawing to the Pope. The value of sustaining a discourse particular to the visual arts – the "O" or "o," letter and syllable, referring us to the same – goes unremarked by Vasari, whose authorship would mimic the claim on the theological which Giotto's persuasive gesture would have obtained.

16 Rex Butler, "Mutlu Çerkez: The Year 2025 Will Not Take Place," *Art/text* 64 (1999): 58–63 (58). Butler tries to argue for a post-modern and post-historical practice, remaining in the thrall of the apparent paradox that the "happening" of 2000 "is always about to happen," in so far as that which is expected of an event may not just occur. The dream of an event "entirely unexpected" (62) hands the futural back to the rule of art and to the evidentiality of the date. The conclusion of the piece, however, notes the "real 'border problems' *Notes* and *More Notes for an Unwritten Opera* raise" concerning "painting, opera, sculpture, photography, rock music, installation" (63).

17 See Jacques Derrida, "Signature Event Context" in *Margins of Philosophy*, trans. Alan Bass (Brighton: Harvester, 1982) 301–30, in which "iterability," condition of possibility of communication as condition of its impossibility, at once repetition and alterity, sameness and difference, is linked to the impossibility of the "'pure' performative": loss of origin – of sense, of meaning – traversed by a necessary plurality of determination of the mark as mark and, thus, of contexts.

18 This argument may be contrasted with that of Thierry De Duve in "Art and Psychoanalysis, Again," the first chapter of *Pictorial Nominalism: On Marcel Duchamp's Passage from Painting to the Readymade* (Minneapolis: U of Minnesota P, 1991): trying to resist either a psychoanalytic or Marxist account of the emergence of new work as symptom or sign, De Duve promotes a sense of the "fact" of the new ("Artworks are facts already interpreted and ceaselessly reinterpreted by their specific history" [7]), in excess of existent modes of valuation, insisting thereby on a certain separation of reception from work. The role of work as becoming-model suggests that the split between fact and interpretation, complicit with positivism, need not be repeated; and the modernism of the value of art as its suspension of modes of evaluation, rather than a sense of the generativity of the same, need not recur.

19 Jean-Luc Nancy, "Why Are There Several Arts and Not Just One?" 12.

20 Walter Benjamin, *Charles Baudelaire: A Lyric Poet in the Era of High Capitalism*, trans. Harry Zohn (London: Verso, 1997) 140.

21 Charles Baudelaire, *The Complete Verse*, ed. and trans. F. Scarfe (London: Anvil, 1986) 61.

22 For this critical distinction see the conclusion of Benjamin's essay "On Some Motifs from Baudelaire" in *Charles Baudelaire* 154.

Lewis Johnson
Faculty of Arts and Social Sciences
Sabancı University
Orhanlı, 81474 Tuzla
Istanbul
Turkey
E-mail: ljohnson@sabanciuniv.edu

They say it is good to make children start work at a tender age, that it makes them better practitioners. I am not a very convincing example of this, because I, for all my good will, have never been anything but a very mediocre worker. Be that as it may, I did pick up the habit, or better, the love of work, which is certainly something.

Although I have lived more on dreams than realities, I fear illusions. I destroy them by analysing them, given that age has calmed my passions. But I have enough left to satisfy the optimism that colours my disappointments and sustains me.

notes on the contributors

gary banham (issue editor)

is the Research Fellow in Transcendental Philosophy at Manchester Metropolitan University. He is the author of *Kant and the Ends of Aesthetics* and co-editor (with Charlie Blake) of *Evil Spirits: Nihilism and the Fate of Modernity*. He is the editor of a special issue of *Tekhnema: Journal of Philosophy and Technology* on technics, teleology and critique, and general editor of the new series being published by Palgrave, Renewing Philosophy. He is currently in the process of completing a book on Kant's practical philosophy.

david bate

is currently Course Leader of the MA in Photographic Studies at the University of Westminster. Recent exhibitions and publications include *Zero Culture*, Danielle Arnaud Gallery, and *Taking in the Air*, Five Years, London. He is the author of *Photography and Surrealism: Sexuality, Colonialism and Social Dissent* (I.B. Tauris, forthcoming).
David Bate, Communication, Design and Media, University of Westminster, Harrow Campus, Watford Road, Northwick Park, Harrow HA1 3TP, UK.

john x. berger

lives in London and Brittany. He has shown regularly, if infrequently, in solo or group exhibitions, and has written from time to time for various journals. He edited *Incunabula of British Photographic Literature 1839–1879* and co-edited *Other Than Itself*. "Ride" is adapted for presentation here from its occasional Internet version.
John X. Berger, La Touche, 22 330 St Gilles-du-Mené, France. E-mail: jfxtberger@hotmail.com

ricardo bloch

was born in Mexico City of French parents. Raised on nineteenth-century bourgeois and colonial mentalities, he escaped to the USA to pursue a career as a molecular biologist. He presently lives in Paris where he makes artists' books.
Ricardo Bloch, 25 rue des Dames, 75017 Paris, France. E-mail: ricardo@assouline.fr

pavel büchler

is Research Professor in Art and Design at Manchester Metropolitan University. The first part of the reproduced work "How to Make It Go Away" appeared in the Austrian daily *Der Standard* in March 2001 as a contribution to *The Mission of Art* organised by Catherine Pichler and the Museum in Progress.
Pavel Büchler, 1 Moon Grove, Rusholme, Manchester M14 5HE, UK.

howard caygill

is Professor of Cultural History at Goldsmiths College, University of London, and the author of *Art of Judgement*, *A Kant Dictionary*, *Walter Benjamin: The Colour of Experience* and *Levinas and the Political*.

stephen cornell

lives and works in London. He has been researching and working with snapshots and domestic photography for a number of years, both directly as "found material" and also as a starting point for further work. He is currently working on a digital project for Gallerie VU.
Stephen Cornell, 47 Bowring Green, South Oxhey, Herts WD19 6UP, UK. E-mail: stephen.cornell@virgin.net

jim drobnick
is a critic and curator living in Montreal. He teaches at Concordia University and is Assistant Editor of *Parachute*. He is the co-editor of *Living Display* (U of Chicago P, forthcoming) and editor of *Aural Cultures* (YYZ Books, forthcoming). He is currently writing a book on the historical and contemporary uses of the non-visual senses by visual and performing artists.

maria fusco
was born in Belfast in 1972 and lives and works in London. An artist and writer, she has recently exhibited at W139 Gallery, Amsterdam, *Cast by Inertia/The Dorsal Fin* (2000) and published *Something Wonderful is Going to Happen*, funded by the Irish Arts Council.
Maria Fusco, 33 Kenton Road, London E9, UK. E-mail: maria@bookworks.org.uk

lucy harrison
lives in London. Her work uses details of social situations and examines what happens within public, and less public, spaces in the city, often using found or borrowed texts.
Lucy Harrison, 107 Shakespeare Walk, Stoke Newington, London N16 8TB, UK. E-mail: lucyh.harrison@virgin.net

joanna hodge
is Professor of Philosophy and Director for Research at Manchester Metropolitan University. She is currently chair of the Society for European Philosophy. Her most recent book, *Heidegger and Ethics* (Routledge, 1995), traced out the ethical horizon within which Heidegger's enquiries take place. She is currently working on a study of the rethinking of temporality to be found suspended between Derrida's texts and the writing to which he responds. For this the writings of Kant and of Husserl turn out to be quite as important as those of Heidegger.

gill houghton
is an artist who lives and works in London. She has exhibited in the UK and also in Europe. She has recently contributed work on film and photography to *Revisioning Duras*, on Marguerite Duras, published by Liverpool UP. She is currently a Ph.D. student in the Visual Arts Department of Goldsmiths College. *Time and Again* comprises photographs from a series that is concerned with how we see time now.
Gill Houghton, 48 The Keep, Blackheath, London SE3 0AF, UK.

lewis johnson
teaches history and theory of Western European art at Sabancı University, Istanbul. He has published on the work of contemporary artists in books, catalogues and journals. Recent work concerns topics in sound and vision. He is the author of *Prospects, Thresholds, Interiors* (Cambridge UP, 1994).

nicole jolicoeur
lives and works in Montréal, Québec, Canada. Since 1980 she has developed her practice through a revisiting of nineteenth-century medical archives (J.M. Charcot, P. Janet et al.) and images from other related sources (M. Mead and G. Bateson). In her installations and bookworks she has used drawing, sculpture, video, photography, and text. Her work is represented in institutional collections in Canada and in France. She has taught in L'École des arts visuels et médiatiques at UQÀM (Université du Québec à Montréal) since 1990.
Nicole Jolicoeur, 5247 Garnier, Montréal QC H2J 3TJ, Canada. E-mail: jolicoeur.nicole@uquam.ca

dalia judovitz

is Professor of French at Emory University in Atlanta. She is the author of *Subjectivity and Representation in Descartes: The Origins of Modernity* (Cambridge UP, 1988), *Unpacking Duchamp: Art in Transit* (U of California P, 1995), *The Culture of the Body: Genealogies of Modernity* (U of Michigan P, 2001) and co-editor of *Dialectic and Narrative* (SUNY P, 1993).

sharon kivland (curator)

is an artist, writer, and occasional curator. She leads a fractured life between London and France. Reader in Fine Art in the School of Cultural Studies, Sheffield Hallam University, she is also a Research Associate of the Centre for Freudian Analysis and Research, London, for which she has organised a series of exhibitions since 1997. She has exhibited widely in Europe and North America, and her work takes up the propositions of psychoanalysis. Publications include *A Case of Hysteria* (London: Book Works, 1999) and *Memoirs*, a modest collection produced in response to St Edward's Hospital near Stoke-on-Trent, as part of *Making History*, a countywide visual arts project. Filigrane Editions, France, will publish a book on her recent work *Le bonheur des femmes* in 2002, a work that began in the perfume departments of the *grands magasins* of Paris, where she retreated after walking the streets in pursuit of both Marx and Freud.

Sharon Kivland, Brizard, 22490 Plouer-sur-Rance, France. E-mail: sharonkivland@wanadoo.fr

kanta kochhar-lindgren

a performance artist and scholar, teaches at Central Michigan University in the Theatre Department. She has written about performance and disability, South Asian diasporic performance, and creativity studies. She is currently co-editing two anthologies, one on the aesthetics of disability and the other on the exquisite corpse. She is also directing a series of community arts projects involving women and their stories about the land.

nayan kulkarni

the smell of stale urine distracted me from the moist grip of his free hand. I looked to the nurse. He kicked the table and smiled (Ross-on-Wye Community Hospital, autumn 1999).

Nayan Kulkarni, 119 Woodbridge Way, Lewisham, London SE13 6PW, UK.

simon malpas

is Lecturer in English at Manchester Metropolitan University. His *Postmodern Debates* was published by Palgrave in 2001, and he has written a range of articles on Romanticism, aesthetics and critical theory. He is currently completing a book on Lyotard for Routledge, and is also writing *The Postmodern* for its New Critical Idiom series.

anne ramsden

is a multidisciplinary visual artist who lives in Montréal. She teaches in L'École des arts visuels et médiatiques at the Université du Québec à Montréal. For more information about her work see <www.eavm.uqam.ca>. Thanks to Laurier Lacroix for his explanation of anastylosis.

Anne Ramsden, 6837 rue Boyer, Montréal, Québec H2S 2J6, Canada. E-mail: ramsden.anne@uqam.ca

cheryl sourkes

is a Canadian artist. She writes and curates for pocket money. In the mid-1990s she fused with her computer. This situation motivated her investigation of Artificial Life. More recently, the reversal of foreground and background shifted her focus to Artificial Worlds. Virtual Cities is her current spawn.

Cheryl Sourkes, 45 Havelock Street, Toronto, Ontario M6H 3B3, Canada. E-mail: cherylvs@total.net

henry staten

is Professor of English and Comparative Literature and Adjunct Professor of Philosophy at the University of Washington. He is the author of *Wittgenstein and Derrida* (1984), *Nietzsche's Voice* (1990), and *Eros in Mourning: Homer to Lacan* (1995). He is currently at work on a new theory of agency that arises at the intersection of Nietzschean will to power and poststructuralist "social constructionism," with the title "The Social Form of Will to Power."

james thornhill

lives and works in Glasgow, Scotland.

James Thornhill, 3/1 110 Garthland Drive, Glasgow G31 2SG, UK. E-mail: thrnhll@hotmail.com

philip vernau

is optimistic and enthusiastic about his future. He tends to be impatient at times and ignores certain details. He is not afraid of making choices and simply bypasses them in his desire to press onwards. He is more concerned with immediate concerns, logical ability and self-esteem. Philip is currently studying on the Fine Art MA course at the Royal Academy of Art in London. He has exhibited in London, Sheffield and Vancouver, and has recently created the web-based artwork *Alphabetic Portraits* at <www.philvernau.co.uk>.

Philip Vernau, c/o 35 Fletchamstead Highway, Coventry CV4 7AW, UK. E-mail: philvernau@yahoo.com

isabelle wallace

is an Assistant Professor in the Department of Fine Arts at the University of New Orleans. She has published an article on the subject of Michael Fried's art criticism and is currently preparing a manuscript on the subject of contemporary advertising and cloning. Her dissertation, "Signification and the Subject: The Art of Jasper Johns," is being revised for publication.

michele white

is an Assistant Professor of Emerging Media in the Department of Telecommunications at Bowling Green State University. She has been a National Endowment for the Humanities Fellow at the Institute for Advanced Study and a visiting faculty member at the University of California, Santa Cruz, and Emerson College. Her Internet-studies articles include: "Cabinet of Curiosities: Finding the Viewer in a Virtual Museum," *Convergence: The Journal of Research into New Media Technologies* (Autumn 1997), "Visual Pleasure in Textual Places: Gazing in Multi-User Object-Oriented Worlds," *Information, Communication, and Society* 2 (1999), and "Where is the Louvre?," *Space and Culture* 4.5 (2000).

robert j. yanal

is Professor of Philosophy at Wayne State University. Publications include *Basic Logic* (1988), *Institutions of Art* (1994), *Paradoxes of Emotion and Fiction* (1999), and "Rebecca's Deceivers," *Philosophy and Literature* 24 (2000). He is completing a book on epistemological issues in Hitchcock's films.

ANGELAKI
journal of the theoretical humanities

BEST NEW JOURNAL
Council of Editors of
Learned Journals 1996 Awards

Modern Language Association Convention, Washington, D.C.

Transcript of the presentation

This year's Best New Journal is *Angelaki*.

One judge called *Angelaki* "A strong and surprising publication that is interested in a wide range of cultural studies issues from harder-theory perspectives," while another praised its "speaking-to-the-moment stance." *Angelaki*'s "position papers" and "substantial essays, addressing current concerns in cultural theory" zero in on "interesting and problematical topics and fields," with results that are "resourceful," "rigorous," and "lively."

Another judge remarked on *Angelaki*'s physical strengths: "The covers and small format are attractive, and the two-column layout is readable, the paper good." The following remark, however, sums things up best: "I put *Angelaki* at the top because I find it refreshingly alive, buzzing with critical energy."

Angelaki 36A Norham Rd
Oxford OX2 6SQ UK

E-mail: editorial@angelaki.demon.co.uk
http://www.tandf.co.uk/journals/routledge/0969725x.html

back issues

vol. 1, no. 1
the uses of theory

Publication: September 1993. Pages: 144.
ISBN: 1 899567 00 3

Editors: Pelagia Goulimari
Oxford
and Gerard Greenway
Oxford

vol. 1, no. 2
narratives of forgery

Publication: April 1994. Pages: 176.

Editor: Nick Groom
University of Exeter

vol. 1, no. 3
reconsidering the political

Publication: January 1995. Pages: 200.
ISBN: 1 899567 02 X

Editors: David Howarth
University of Essex
and Aletta J. Norval
University of Essex

vol. 2, no. 1
home and family

Publication: November 1995. Pages: 208.
ISBN: 1 899567 03 8

Editor: Sarah Wood
Oxford

vol. 2, no. 2
authorizing culture

Publication: March 1996. Pages: 168.
ISBN: 1 899567 04 6

Editors: Gary Hall
University of Middlesex
and Simon Wortham
University of Portsmouth

vol. 2, no. 3
intellectuals and global culture

Publication: July 1997. Pages: 232.
ISBN: 1 899567 05 4

Editors: Charlie Blake
    University College Northampton
and Linnie Blake
    The Manchester Metropolitan University

vol. 3, no. 1
impurity, authenticity and humanity

Publication: April 1998. Pages: 203.
ISBN: 0 902879 06 5

Editor: Mozaffar Qizilbash
    University of East Anglia

vol. 3, no. 2
the love of music

Publication: October 1998. Pages: 201.
ISBN: 0 902879 11 1

Editors: Timothy S. Murphy
    University of Oklahoma
Roy Sellars
    National University of Singapore
Robert Smith
    West Hollywood

vol. 3, no. 3
general issue 1998

Publication: December 1998. Pages: 207.
ISBN: 0 902879 16 2

Editor: Pelagia Goulimari
    Oxford

vol. 4, no. 1
judging the law

Publication: May 1999. Pages: 222.
ISBN: 0 902879 21 9

Editor: Barry Stocker
    Yeditepe University

Contents
Editorial Introduction, *Barry Stocker*. **Section I: The Law of Philosophy**:- Francis Bacon's "Verulamium": The Common-Law Template of the Modern in English Science and Culture, *Harvey Wheeler*. Kierkegaard's Absolute Decision: Dialectic of Ethical Law in *Fear and Trembling*, *Barry Stocker*. Aporia and Phantasm: Modern Law, the Tragic and Time, *Richard Beardsworth*. Lacan and the Law, *Martin Murray*. **Section II: Limits of Justice**:- Capitalism, Justice and the Law, *Iain MacKenzie*. Utilitarian Conscience and Legal Fictions in Bentham, *Dieter Paul Polloczek*. Human Rights at the End of History, *Costas Douzinas*. Judging Without Law: Obligation, Justice and the Individual Particular, *Monika Kilian*. **Section III: Tragedy and Art**:- Naming the Abyss: Aeschylus, the Law, and the Future of Democracy, *Gray Kochhar-Lindgren*. Vengeance Is His: Justice in the *Oresteia*, *George Newtown*. The Poor Law – Büchner, *Diane Morgan*. **Section IV: Case Studies**:- Judging the Voices of Judicial Law, *Glenda Conway*. Critical Hermeneutics and American Legal Interpretation: A Search for the Meaning of *New York Times v. Sullivan*, *David S. Allen*. Pregnant Reproduction and the State: Between Bodily Performance and Legal Performativity, *Heather Schuster*. Doing the "Right" Thing: Queer Censorship and the "Force of Law" in Canada, *David R. Jarraway*. Habeas Corpus, *pictures throughout by Sharon Kivland*.

vol. 4, no. 2
machinic modulations
new cultural theory & technopolitics

Publication: November 1999. Pages: 209.
ISBN: 0 902879 26 X

Editor: John Armitage
  University of Northumbria at Newcastle

Contents

Editorial Introduction, *John Armitage*. **Section I: New Cultural Theory**:- All That is Solid Melts into Airwaves, *McKenzie Wark*. Situationist Strategies and Mutant Technologies, *Alastair Bonnett*. Theory, Technology and Cultural Power: An Interview with Manuel Castells, *Joanne Roberts*. Crash Theory: The Ubiquity of the Fetish at the End of Time, *Roy Boyne*. A Virtual Theory of Global Politics, Mimetic War, and the Spectral State, *James Der Derian*. Dissecting the Data Body: An Interview with Arthur and Marilouise Kroker, *John Armitage*. Bathos of Technology and Politics in Fourth Order Simulacra, *Mike Gane*. The Information Bomb: A Conversation, *Paul Virilio and Friedrich Kittler*. Data Crash: Apocalypse and Global Economic Crisis, *Michael A. Weinstein*. Stories from the Research Labs, *Louise K. Wilson*. **Section II: Technopolitics**:- Globalisation from Below? Toward a Radical Democratic Technopolitics, *Douglas Kellner*. Ontological Anarchy, The Temporary Autonomous Zone, and The Politics of Cyberculture: A Critique of Hakim Bey, *John Armitage*. Whither the Virtual: Slavoj Zizek and Cyberfeminism, *Verena Andermatt Conley*. Theory of State: Deleuze, Guattari, and Virilio on the State, Technology and Speed, *Patrick Crogan*. The Female UNIX, *Mark Dery*. Touch, Digital Communication and the Ticklish, *Cathryn Vasseleu*. Against Virtual Community: For a Politics of Distance, *Kevin Robins*. Conducting Technologies: Virilio's and Latour's Philosophies of the Present State, *T. Hugh Crawford*. Getting "The Real Facts": Contemporary Cultural Theory and Avant-Garde Technocultural Practices, *Nicholas Zurbrugg*. Practical Anarchy: An Interview with Critical Art Ensemble, *Mark Little*.

vol. 4, no. 3
general issue 1999

Publication: April 2000. Pages: 200.
ISBN: 0 902879 31 6

Editor: Pelagia Goulimari
  Oxford

Contents

Sounding Desire: On Tricky, *Simon Citchley*. The Experience of Deconstruction, *Peggy Kamuf*. The Eclipse of Coincidence: Lacan, Merleau-Ponty and Schelling, *Peter Dews*. Bodies of Experience and Bodies of Thought: Freud and Kant on Excessively Intense Ideas, *Stuart Dalton*. Bernard-Marie Koltès and Relations of Interest, *Peter Hallward*. Money, Gift and Sacrifice: Thirteen Short Episodes in the Pricing of Thought, *Philip Goodchild*. Figures in (De)Composition: The Genesis of the Paradoxical Self in Paul Auster's *Moon Palace* (A Fuzzy Grammar of Subjectivity), *Salah el Moncef*. Levinas in the Realm of the Senses: Transcendence and Intelligibility, *Stella Sandford*. Ultimate Trope: Towards a Postcolonial Tropology, *Christopher Kelen*. **Angelaki Dossier: Glissement** (edited by Gerard Greenway):- Pipedreams: Magritte and Beckett, *Mary Bryden and Walter Redfern*. Glozing, *Robert Smith*. The Beautiful Does Not Get Elected Like Miss World, *Diane Elam*. Speed Factory #1–14, *John Kinsella and McKenzie Wark*. Slippery Threads (An Amplified Concert Critique), *Christof Migone*. Duchamp's "Mechanistic Sculptures": Art, Nudes and the Game of Chess, *Gary Banham*. The Slide in the Sign: Lacan's Glissement and the Registers of Meaning, *Kirsten Campbell*. The Thing from Inner Space, *Slavoj Zizek*. Purple Phosphene, *Brian Massumi*. The Calling: "Can I Tell You Something Personal?," *Jane Adan*. "Glisser dans le vide": Blanchot, Thomas L'Obscur and the Space of Literature, *Garin Dowd*. Capiton, *Sharon Kivland*.

vol. 5, no. 1
poets on the verge

Publication: April 2000. Pages: 212.
ISBN: 0 902879 36 7

Editors: Anthony Mellors
    Richmond
  and Robert Smith
    London

Contents
Editorial Introduction: Poets on the Verge, *Anthony Mellors and Robert Smith*. Call for Papers: Poets on the Verge, *Anthony Mellors and Robert Smith*. Taking the Side of Poetry: An Open Letter to the Guest Editors of *Angelaki*, *Gilbert Adair*. I is Reading, *Anthony Mellors*. The Two Poetries, *Ken Edwards*. Five Poems, *Clark Coolidge*. Hoax Poetry in America, *Margaret Soltan*. Four Poems, *Bruce Andrews*. Simple Words and Complex Politics: Language and Identity in Giuseppe Ungaretti and Joan Brossa, *John London*. News of the Wold, *Adrian Clarke*. Deferred Action: Irish Neo-Avant-Garde Poetry, *Alex Davis*. Extract from *The Clump*, *Peter Larkin*. "The Bachelor in His Mediocrity": Late Modernism and the Minor Literature of Weldon Kees, *Nicholas Spencer*. Knowing the Land where Neon Blooms: Ian Hamilton Finlay's 1999 Installation in Erfurt, *Harry Gilonis*. Three Poems, *Frances Presley*. "Connect-I-Cut": George Oppen's *Discrete Series* and a Parenthesis by Jacques Derrida, *Garin V. Dowd*. Irrigation, *John Wilkinson*. Anonymous Poetry, *Peter Middleton*. Allele, *Michael Haslam*. A Child in Question, *Vicky Lebeau*. Trial / Peace, *Maurice Scully*. The Word Folly: Samuel Beckett's "Comment dire" ("What is the Word"), *Shane Weller*. Mallarmé: Serenity and Violence, *Malcolm Bowie*. From *100 Sonnets*, *Robert Smith*. The Memory of Modern Life (Baudelaire), *Cynthia Chase*. Two Poems, *Charles Tomlinson*.

vol. 5, no. 2
rhizomatics, genealogy, deconstruction

Publication: August 2000. Pages: 239.
ISBN: 0 902879 41 3

Editor: Constantin V. Boundas
    Trent University

Contents
Editorial Introduction, *Constantin V. Boundas*. The Folds of Friendship: Derrida–Deleuze–Foucault, *Charles J. Stivale*. Deleuze and Derrida, by way of Blanchot: An Interview, *Zsuzsa Baross*. Spirit of Philosophy: Derrida and Deleuze, *Philip Goodchild*. A Nearly Total Affinity: The Deleuzian Virtual Image versus the Derridean Trace, *Len Lawlor*. Death and Temporality in Deleuze and Derrida, *Bruce Baugh*. Infinite Subjective Representation and the Perversion of Death, *Eugene W. Holland*. The Limits of Individuation, or How to Distinguish Deleuze and Foucault, *Peter Hallward*. Foucault and Derrida: The History of a Debate on History, *Antonio Campillo*. The Rhizomatic Genealogy of Deconstruction: Some Features of "the French," *Andrew Wernick*. Nietzsche, Foucault, Deleuze, and the Subject of Radical Democracy, *Alan D. Schrift*. On Tendencies and Signs: Major and Minor Deconstruction, *Constantin V. Boundas*. The Subject of Literature between Derrida and Deleuze: Law or Life?, *Gregg Lambert*. Eluding Derrida: Artaud and the Imperceptibility of Life for Thought, *Dorothea E. Olkowski*. The Thought of the Outside, The Outside of Thought, *Peter Pál Pelbart*. The Mask of Death: Foucault, Derrida, the Human Sciences and Literature, *Tilottama Rajan*. Philosophy as a Spiritual Exercise in Foucault and Deleuze, *Todd May*.

vol. 5, no. 3
general issue 2000

Publication: December 2000. Pages: 160.
ISBN: 0 902879 46 4

Editor: Pelagia Goulimari
Oxford

Contents

Editorial Introduction, *Pelagia Goulimari*. Hostipitality, *Jacques Derrida*. From Animal Life to City Life, *Simon Glendinning*. The Body in the Thought of Kenneth Burke: A Reading of "The Philosophy of Literary Form," *Kumiko Yoshioka*. Born with the Dead: Blanchot's Mourning, *Lars Iyer*. Having to Exist, *Andrew Benjamin*. The Idea of Genesis in Kant's Aesthetics, *Gilles Deleuze*. Bad Timing: The Subject as a Work of Time, *Agata Bielik-Robson*. Didion's *Democracy*: "Dated in a Deconstructing Universe," *Stephen Jarvis*. Math Anxiety, *Aden Evens*. What's Lacking in the Lack: A Comment on the Virtual, *Nathan Widder*. **Debate:** From Proto-Reality to the Act: A Reply to Peter Dews, *Slavoj Žižek*.

vol. 6, no. 1
subaltern affect

Publication: April 2001. Pages: 206.
ISBN: 0415 27109 6

Editors: Jon Beasley-Murray
University of Manchester
and Alberto Moreiras
Duke University

Contents

Editorial Introduction: Subalternity and Affect, *Jon Beasley-Murray and Alberto Moreiras*. Separation and the Politics of Theory, *Alberto Moreiras*. Subject Scenes, Symbolic Exclusion, and Subalternity, *Brian Carr*. Making an Example of Spivak, *David Huddart*. The Sovereign Individual, "Subalternity," and Becoming-Other, *Kenneth Surin*. Feeling, the Subaltern, and the Organic Intellectual, *Brett Levinson*. Managing Ecstasy: A Subaltern Performative of Resistance, *Samir Dayal*. Reflections on the Origin: Transculturation and Tragedy in *Pedro Páramo*, *Patrick Dove*. Tribalism, Globalism, and Eskimo Television in Leslie Marmon Silko's *Almanac of the Dead*, *Eva Cherniavsky*. Hear Say Yes in Piglia: *La ciudad ausente*, Posthegemony, and the "Fin-negans" of Historicity, *Gareth Williams*. Porno-Revolution: *El fiord* and the Eva-Peronist State, *John Kraniauskas*. Trashing Whiteness: *Pulp Fiction*, *Se7en*, *Strange Days*, and Articulating Affect, *Paul Gormley*. East of the Sun and West of the Moon: The Balkans and Cultural Studies, *Arthur Redding*. Anti-Fascism as Child's Play: The Political Line in *The Laurels of Lake Constance*, *Jon Beasley-Murray*.

vol. 6, no. 2
gift, theft, apology

Publication: August 2001. Pages: 206.
ISBN: 0415 27110 X

Editor: Constantin V. Boundas
Trent University

Contents
Editorial Introduction: Gift, Theft, Apology, *Constantin V. Boundas*. The I–You Relationship in the Works of Emmanuel Levinas, *Léonard Rosmarin*. Philosophy of the Gift: Jacques Derrida, Martin Heidegger, *Charles Champetier*. The Double Inconceivability of the Pure Gift, *Alain Caillé*. The Time(s) of the Gift, *John O'Neill*. The Midwinter Sacrifice: A Sequel to "Can Morality Be Christian?," *John Milbank*. Problems in the Phenomenology of the Gift, *Simon Jarvis*. Bataille and Baudrillard: From a General Economy to the Transparency of Evil, *Leslie Anne Boldt-Irons*. Bataille/Wilde: An Economic and Aesthetic Genealogy of the Gift, *Richard Dellamora*. Exchange, Gift, and Theft, *Constantin V. Boundas*. Logics of the Gift in Cixous and Nietzsche: Can We Still Be Generous?, *Alan D. Schrift*. Bearing Witness to Cultural Difference, With Apology to Levinas, *Rosalyn Diprose*. Working Towards Reciprocity: Critical Reflections on Seyla Benhabib and Iris Young, *Elaine Stavro*. Noli Me Tangere: For Jacques Derrida, *Zsuzsa Baross*. The Return to, the Return of, Peoples of Long Ago and Far Away, *Alphonso Lingis*. Woman: Gift or Curse?, *Shadia B. Drury*. The Gift of the Ordinary, *Charles E. Scott*

vol. 6, no. 3
general issue 2001

Publication: December 2001. Pages: 238.
ISBN: 0415 27111 8

Editor: Pelagia Goulimari
Oxford

Contents
Editorial Introduction, *Pelagia Goulimari*. Never Before, Always Already: Notes on Agamben and the Category of Relation, *Alexander García Düttmann*. Photography and the Exposure of Community: Sharing Nan Goldin and Jean-Luc Nancy, *Louis Kaplan*. Cave Paintings and Wall Writings: Blanchot's Signature, *Lars Iyer*. To Follow a Snail: Experimental Empiricism and the Ethic of Minor Literature, *Peter Trnka*. Placing the Void: Badiou on Spinoza, *Sam Gillespie*. In the Space of the Cursor: An Introduction to John Kinsella's "A New Lyricism," *Philip Mead*. A New Lyricism: Some Early Thoughts on Linguistic Disobedience, *John Kinsella*. Foucault's Evasive Maneuvers: Nietzsche, Interpretation, Critique, *Samuel A. Chambers*. The Aesthetics of Affect: Thinking Art Beyond Representation, *Simon O'Sullivan*. Judgment is Not an Exit: Toward an Affective Criticism of Violence with *American Psycho*, *Marco Abel*. The Comedy of Philosophy: Bataille, Hegel and Derrida, *Lisa Trahair*. Humanism after Auschwitz: Reflections on Jean Améry's *Freitod*, *Andrew McCann*. Human Rights, Humanism and Desire, *Costas Douzinas*. **Debate:** Just Hoaxing: A Reply to Margaret Soltan's "Hoax Poetry in America," *Bill Freind*. The Bicameral Mind: Response to Bill Freind's "Just Hoaxing," *Margaret Soltan*